The ARVN and the Fight
for South Vietnam

ALSO BY NGHIA M. VO
AND FROM MCFARLAND

*Legends of Vietnam: An Analysis
and Retelling of 88 Tales* (2012)

Saigon: A History (2011)

*The Viet Kieu in America: Personal Accounts
of Postwar Immigrants from Vietnam* (2009)

*The Vietnamese Boat People,
1954 and 1975–1992* (2006)

*The Bamboo Gulag: Political Imprisonment
in Communist Vietnam* (2004)

The ARVN and the Fight for South Vietnam

Nghia M. Vo

McFarland & Company, Inc., Publishers
Jefferson, North Carolina

LIBRARY OF CONGRESS CATALOGUING-IN-PUBLICATION DATA

Names: Vo, Nghia M., 1947– author.
Title: The ARVN and the fight for South Vietnam / Nghia M. Vo.
Other titles: Army of the Republic of Vietnam and the fight for South Vietnam
Description: Jefferson, North Carolina: McFarland & Company, Inc.,
Publishers, 2021 | Includes bibliographical references and index.
Identifiers: LCCN 2021037350 | ISBN 9781476685854 (paperback : acid free paper) ∞
ISBN 9781476643199 (ebook)
Subjects: LCSH: Vietnam (Republic). Quân lực—History. | Vietnam War,
1961–1975—Campaigns—Chronology. | Vietnam (Republic)—History,
Military. | BISAC: HISTORY / Military / Vietnam War
Classification: LCC DS558.6.V5 V6 2021 | DDC 959.704/34095977—dc23
LC record available at https://lccn.loc.gov/2021037350

BRITISH LIBRARY CATALOGUING DATA ARE AVAILABLE

ISBN (print) 978-1-4766-8585-4
ISBN (ebook) 978-1-4766-4319-9

© 2021 Nghia M. Vo. All rights reserved

*No part of this book may be reproduced or transmitted in any form
or by any means, electronic or mechanical, including photocopying
or recording, or by any information storage and retrieval system,
without permission in writing from the publisher.*

On the cover: U.S. trained drill instructor with new Vietnamese recruits.
August 11, 1964; an Army of the Republic of Vietnam Ranger and
a CH-46D helicopter from Marine Medium Helicopter Squadron 263
during Operation Durham Peak (Defense Department Photographs,
National Archives); *background* © 2021 Shutterstock

Printed in the United States of America

*McFarland & Company, Inc., Publishers
Box 611, Jefferson, North Carolina 28640
www.mcfarlandpub.com*

To the more than
350,000 ARVN soldiers and
58,000 U.S. soldiers who died
defending the freedom of South Vietnam.

Table of Contents

Introduction: The Life and Death of the ARVN	1
1. From the National Army to the ARVN	9
2. 1963: The Ấp Bắc Battle	28
3. 1964: The Bình Giã Battle	36
4. 1965: Sông Bé, Đồng Xoài, Ba Giã, Thuận Man, Plei Me	40
5. 1966: The South Vietnamese Economy	52
6. 1967: The Year of Decision	61
7. 1968: The Tết Offensive, Saigon, Huế, the Huế Massacre	68
8. 1969: Vietnamization, Hamburger Hill	93
9. 1970–71: Cambodian and Laotian Incursions	105
10. 1972: Quảng Trị–Kontum–An Lộc–Charlie	119
11. 1973: Nguyễn Văn Thiệu's Four Wars	148
12. 1974: The Paracel Islands, Thượng Đức, Phước Long	161
13. 1975: Ban Mê Thuột, the Fall of I Corps, Phan Rang, Xuân Lộc	175
14. Self Sacrifice, Reeducation Camps, Postwar Killings	189
15. Identity	216
Epilogue	227
Glossary	233
Appendix I—List of Vietnamese Reeducation Camps	235
Chapter Notes	237
Bibliography	255
Index	259

Introduction

The Life and Death of the ARVN

The Vietnam War has been compared to a hunt for one of the biggest and most dangerous game in Asia, the Tiger. "Tigers are furtive and silent; their ranges are immense and, to the untrained eye, trackless.... It is nearly pointless to stalk tigers.... They, instead, must be waited upon. It calls for baiting, careful preparation and, most of all, superhuman patience for that one fleeting shot.... To hunt the tiger requires a different mindset, a mindset the French had to learn and relearn."[1]

The French author Jean Larteguy once explained how the French and the North Vietnamese communists waged war in the 1950s. "It's difficult to explain exactly, but it's rather like bridge as compared to belote.[2] When we make war, we play belote with thirty-two cards in the pack. But their game is bridge and they have fifty-two cards: twenty more than we do. Those twenty cards short will always prevent us from getting the better of them. They've got nothing to do with traditional warfare, they're marked with the sign of politics, propaganda, faith, agrarian reform...."[3]

Having been unable to change the war game to their benefit, the French to their despair lost at the Điện Biên Phủ Battle and were forced to get out of their colonial Vietnam. They left North Vietnam in 1954—after the partition of Vietnam—but departed from South Vietnam two years later in 1956.[4]

The Americans came and tried to build a non-communist frontier land against the expanding communist red wave. By 1964 General William Westmoreland—the "best" U.S. general according to President Johnson—was made commander of U.S and Allied Forces in Vietnam. A year later in 1965, he "Americanized" the war by relegating the ARVN (Army of the Republic of Vietnam) to support the pacification process while letting U.S. troops deal with enemy main force elements. He decided early on to "take over the war effort, get the job done promptly, then hand it back to the South Vietnamese and depart in glory."[5]

Among the various military options, he favored a war of attrition against the communists by attempting to drain them of manpower and supplies through the use of United States' edge in artillery and air power, both in tactical confrontations and in relentless strategic bombings of North Vietnam.[6] Although the battles were tactical victories, holding the terrain gained this way proved to be difficult, if not unsuccessful. Three years later (1968), his experimentation came to an end as he was reassigned as Army Chief of Staff, U.S. military forces in Vietnam and replaced by General Creighton Abrams.

This was followed by the "Vietnamization" of the war: a rapid withdrawal of U.S.

forces out of Vietnam and their replacement by the ARVN. If the U.S. involvement was rapid and massive, its withdrawal was also fast and unpredictable. The "active" U.S. military involvement in the Vietnam War thus lasted only three years (1965–1968) or at most seven years if the 1969–1972 drawdown was included. This amounted to at most 33 percent of the 21-year war (1954–1975).[7]

Although taken aback by the withdrawal, the South Vietnamese not only were grateful to the U.S. for their involvement, they were also indebted to them for their help in lives and money during that difficult period. But the Americans have a way of jumping in quickly and getting out as fast as possible while sucking up all the oxygen and leaving nothing else to others. Out of a 33 percent active involvement, all the reports and literature about the war were about the U.S. minimizing the effort of the ARVN, which was criticized for not "pulling its weight" or being "content to let the Americans do the fighting and dying."[8]

The ARVN mainly referred to the army within the RVNAF (Republic of Vietnam Armed Forces), which also consisted of an air force, a navy, marines, rangers, regional and popular forces, although the two terms are used interchangeably. It was one of the most maligned—if not one of the most misunderstood—armies in modern history. U.S. Secretary of Defense Robert McNamara stated that the ARVN was "weak in dedication, direction and discipline."[9] George Carver of the Central Intelligence Agency's Vietnamese affairs staff concluded in July 1966 that the ARVN was "not pulling its weight."[10] Frances Fitzgerald added that the ARVN was never more than a collection of individuals.[11]

All these preliminary statements were made over a short period of time in the late 1960s with no further follow-up from that time onward. This corresponded to the time when the U.S. planned their withdrawal after the 1968 Tết Offensive; but the ARVN had rapidly moved forward to plug up the holes left by the departing Americans. Although there was some truth to the above statements before 1968, they no longer rang true after that date since the ARVN was taking over most if not all the war effort. It was, therefore, surprising to see some writers repeating the same accusations five decades later without any explanation or supporting documentation.

> To most American soldiers, the local forces were known as Arvin, and the name was not applied kindly. It suggested a caricature: a small Asian man in an oversize American helmet and uniform, inadequately trained, ignorant of basic infantry tactics, equipped with Korean War vintage weapons, incompetent, reluctant to fight, and all too often given to thievery and desertion.... All too often, the officers who led them were incompetent and corrupt.[12]

This statement could be seen as a distortion or incomplete report of facts that is unworthy from someone searching for truth. After 1968, the ARVN had markedly improved. No one knew about the bravery of the ARVN and the South Vietnamese in general who fought from the beginning until the end of the war through victories and defeat even after the departure of their allies. There was no reporting about these ARVN officers who spent part of their adult life in reeducation camps after they lost a war in which they bravely fought for their freedom. Hastings once wrote,

> The world never heard of the Ranger lieutenant commanding an encircled position, who called in an air strike on his own red smoke grenade, killing him along with half his platoon,

but saving the rest of his company. There were no headlines for a twelve year old boy who led to safety a pilot of a US Air Force F-101 that crashed in a VC controlled area, although helicopters were sent to extract the child's family from their village before communist vengeance struck them. A PF soldier named Nguyen Van Moi of Duc Lang in Chuong Thien received two bravery awards which seemed exceptionally well-deserved, because he was seventy years old.[13]

The 1968 Tết Offensive turned out to be the wakeup call for the ARVN that was caught off guard by the multiplicity and viciousness of the communist attacks. All of them were repulsed within a few days, except in Huế, which was held by the enemy for three weeks, following which a gruesome discovery was unearthed. More than 3,000 civilians were found killed—execution à la communist style—with hands tied in their backs and bullet holes in their skulls. The Việt Cộng infrastructure, which was almost completely wiped out during this offensive, had to be replaced by NVA troops.

Then came 1970, when the ARVN with minimal support from U.S. troops moved into Cambodia to engage against NVA troops that were hiding across the border under the protection of the "neutral" Sihanouk government. In late 1970, the ARVN launched another attack into "neutral" Laos against NVA forces that came down through the Hồ Chí Minh Trail. However, it was neither a well-prepared nor well-led attack that fizzled under the direction of President Thiệu, who proved to be a better politician than commander-in-chief.

In 1972, the PAVN initiated a three pronged multi-divisional attack against three different targets: An Lộc, Kontum, and Quảng Trị. The ARVN held An Lộc and Kontum against the aggressive NVA attacks that were supported by heavy artillery and T-54 tanks. Generals Lê Văn Hưng and Lý Tòng Bá defeated them in An Lộc and Kontum respectively. The city of Quảng Trị, however, fell under the PAVN assault and General Hoàng Xuân Lãm was replaced by General Ngô Quang Trưởng, who engineered the retaking of Quảng Trị. Well led this time, the ARVN defeated the battle-seasoned PAVN troops with the assistance of a few U.S. advisers.

In 1975 President Thiệu made another tactical error by pulling his troops out of the highlands, which led to the collapse of the II Corps. He then pulled the Marines and paratroopers out of I Corps, causing it also to collapse. Local people who remembered well the killings of Huế citizens by the communists during the 1968 Offensive were the first to flee areas where the communists would be arriving. Then General Lê Minh Đảo and his understrength 18th ARVN Division held on against the enemy at the magnificent battle of Xuân Lộc. Without further reinforcement, the 18th Division had to withdraw.

Over the years, the RVNAF had matured by fighting against its enemies and itself. Led by a new crop of young, aggressive generals who came out of obscurity—Ngô Quang Trưởng, Lê Văn Hưng, Lý Tòng Bá, Lê Minh Đảo, etc....—the ARVN went from one victory to another until the U.S. cut its funding, causing the million-man army to crash.

Only a few books have dealt with the "social history" part of the ARVN.[14] They offer a glimpse into the lives of ARVN enlisted men as well as their perceptions about the war and fall of Saigon. But no one has looked at the war strategy, the major battles waged by the ARVN and the "story of men and maneuvers" during the Vietnam War. This study proposes to fill up that large gap.

Three tropes were used to define the ARVN: apathy, incompetence, and corruption.[15] In postwar representations for some Americans, the RVNAF does not exist outside its role as subordinate and scapegoat to the Americans. To the charge that they were apathetic about fighting communists, the Vietnamese émigrés argued that the South Vietnamese government did not spend enough effort on educating their citizens on the evils of communism. It was only after their confinement in the reeducation camp that many noticed their errors and realized they should have fought more vigorously.[16] The government also "forbade us to do much political training because they did not want an army of nationalists. That would have placed their own precarious political careers in constant jeopardy."[17]

The apathy also stems not from lack of desire to fight or lack of patriotism, but from the desire of having a normal civilian life and a future outside the military.[18] As to the suggestion that they were less competent than communist fighters, the émigrés argued that the communists were indoctrinated to behave like "machines"; they were victimized by their own government, chained to antiaircraft machines and guns and forced to die and sacrifice their lives. This was how the communist government treated its people as opposed to the Republic of South Vietnam.[19] Finally, as to corruption that was mentioned as one of the causes of the downfall of the RVN, the émigrés responded that corruption, linked to skyrocketing inflation and inadequate pay, did exist in the army. Consumer prices in South Vietnam rose 900 percent between 1964 and 1972. The cost of rice rose an unbelievable 1,400 percent.[20]

Soldiers who barely made ends meet had to choose between two humiliating options: asking for financial support from their families or stealing from the government. Corruption was a common feature in all countries involved in wars, although it did not cause their collapse. Besides, corruption is much worse in the present communist government than at the time of the ARVN probably on a scale of $1 for ARVN compared to $1,000 for the communist government.[21] In sum, the ARVN fought bravely and for the duration even after the U.S. left. What was missing was a balanced and aggressive leadership[22] along with continued U.S. military support.

Following the collapse of Saigon, ARVN officers and government officials were sent to reeducation camps to do hard labor. Civilians were driven to the new economic zones (NEZ), the civilian equivalent of reeducation camps, while Hanoi wiped out the last vestiges of Saigon and the ARVN. There was no case we know of, of brothers sending brothers from the same country to concentration camps, except under the communist regime. Forty-five years after the war one can make a few assumptions. First, the communist Revolution has failed in Vietnam as elsewhere because it did not liberate anyone, but rather enslaved the Vietnam populace against its will. "Looking into actual consequences of the Vietnam conflict..., the [communist] war to unify the country under their rule has been nonsense."[23] Second, Hồ Chí Minh and his communists were no saviors for they killed millions of people in this tragic war in order to take control of the whole country and spread communism. Third, there may be no reconciliation possible between communists and non-communists in Vietnam with the way the former treated the latter.

As to the war, Hastings noted that "The Vietnamese wounded don't cry or moan or complain. They suffer silently and patiently. I've never seen anything like that. It tears your heartstrings to see them—and to watch them silently die."[24]

> The ARVN died in 1975
>   It died but not of a full death.
> It was too big to die in one time in one bloc;
>   In the end, it died in pieces and parts, here and there.
> It died in the highlands, then in Huế, Đà Nẵng, Xuân Lộc.
>   The communists did not let it die gracefully;
>   they razed ARVN cemeteries, defaced the headstones,
>   and even barbed wired the Biên Hòa National Cemetery,[25]
>   the sacrilegious act of which "stood as a symbol of national shame."[26]
>
> The ARVN died in the reeducation camps, in the camps of North Vietnam,
>   In the highlands of central Vietnam,
>   at Vĩnh Phú, Bú Đốp, Katum, Lao Kai, Ba Vi etc....
>   It died in the depth of oceans,
>   in the bellies of fish, big or small.
>   It died in the reception camps of Pulao Bidong, Palawan, Galang,
>   all these strange names and places and
> among strangers who never knew them.
>   Then it finally died in the lands of freedom
>   of the world: USA, Europe. Australia, etc....
>   It died everywhere, in pieces and bits,
> for it represents humanity,
>   and the FREEDOM of the world.

In the solitude and despair of the terrifying and punishing concentration camps, where they did hard manual work and were starved and mistreated, many vegetated from three to 17 years. They courageously suffered from the humiliation of defeat, the negative racial stereotyping, and the indignities of the concentration camps and therefore, after their release and whenever financially stable,[27] they emigrated abroad. Unrepentant once in the lands of freedom that offered them refuge, healing, and citizenship, they vowed never to bow to the communist dictatorship and doctrine that killed people right and left, deprived its survivors of their freedom, and condemned them to a life of misery and poverty.

> Despite all its flaws, the ARVN was a "well-organized entity with recognized laws and regulations, a system of discipline, an independent spirit, and an ideal to serve. Although defeated, they contributed a lot to national science and technology, education, culture, music, arts, and sports—besides fighting the war.... I am certain that I served on the right side in the nationalist/communist conflict in Vietnam," claimed one ARVN officer and survivor of the camps.[28]

This book is a chronological study of all the major battles waged by the ARVN from 1963 to its demise in 1975. It is composed of 16 chapters.

This introduction briefly details the chronology of the war and the newly-minted ARVN.

Chapter 1: *From the National Army to the ARVN* details the circumstances of the formation of the National Army under the French to that of its successor, the ARVN under the Americans. The works of three men responsible for the building of the ARVN from the Vietnamese side—Bảo Đại, Ngô Đình Diệm, and Nguyễn Văn Thiệu—are described.

Chapter 2: *1963: The Ấp Bắc Battle* discusses the different views about the Ấp Bắc Battle, an insignificant battle that propelled the ARVN into the news and the forefront of the war against the communists.

Chapter 3: *1964: The Bình Gĩa Battle.* Profiting from the political instability that followed the overthrow and the murder of President Diệm, the VC launched for the first time a division-size attack against the Bình Gĩa hamlet where they experimented with new techniques (lure and ambush) and used new armaments (AK-47, grenade launchers) and NVA troops against the ARVN that was supported by air cavalry.

Chapter 4: *1965: Sông Bé, Bà Giã, Đồng Xoài, Thuận Man, Plei Mei.* The VC and PAVN multiplied its attacks throughout South Vietnam and experimented with new measures designed to neutralize the power of the air cavalry. These attacks forced the U.S. to introduce troops into Vietnam.

Chapter 5: *1966: South Vietnamese Economy.* With the war in full bloom and all young males drafted into the army, the South Vietnamese agrarian society (rice and rubber) fell into a downward spiral, rescued only by U.S. aid and money spent by U.S. soldiers.

Chapter 6: *1967: The Year of Decision.* The election of ARVN General Nguyễn Văn Thiệu stabilized the four years of political disarray in South Vietnam. General Westmoreland launched the massive search and destroy *Cedar Falls* and *Junction City* Operations against the VC with minimal results for they ran away refusing engagement. They laid low preparing for their next year attack.

Chapter 7: *1968: Tết Offensive: Saigon, Huế, the Huế Massacre.* The communists launched an all-out attack on over 100 targets: towns, cities, camps, and provincial capitals of South Vietnam in violation of the *Tết* truce (*Tết Offensive*). All attacks were vigorously repulsed by ARVN soldiers. Only the city of Huế was held for three weeks. The battles of Saigon and Huế were described in detail as well as the massacre in Huế where 3,000 civilians were executed in the communist style. Civilians, however, stuck with the government and the ARVN.

Chapter 8: *1969: Vietnamization, Hamburger Hill.* President Johnson decided to pull U.S. troops out of Vietnam forcing the understrength ARVN to expand and fill the gaps left by the departing U.S. troops. An ARVN battalion was asked to participate in the U.S. assault against Ấp Bia or Hamburger Hill; details of the operation is described.

Chapter 9: *1970–71: Cambodian Excursion (1970)—Lâm Sơn 719 (1971).* As part of the Vietnamization process, for the first time the ARVN launched divisional attacks against NVA forces and weapon and ammunition depots in Cambodia and Laos to disrupt the flow of communist troops and armaments into South Vietnam. While the first operation was successful and raised the fighting spirit of ARVN troops, the second was mired in difficulties because poor leadership and lack of preparation.

Chapter 10: 1972: *Quảng Trị-Kontum-An Lộc-Charlie.* In 1972, with the Americans gone, the communists launched a multidivisional, three-pronged attack (*Eastern Offensive*) against the cities of An Lộc, Kontum, and Quảng Trị. The ARVN under the leadership of Generals Lê Văn Hưng and Lý Tòng Bá successfully defended An Lộc and Kontum against communist forces. But Quảng Trị fell and General Ngô Quang Trưởng taking over the leadership of the I Corps successfully recovered the lost city of Quảng Trị.

Chapter 11: *1973: Nguyễn Văn Thiệu's Four Wars.* In 1967, ARVN General Nguyễn Văn Thiệu won the presidency of South Vietnam, bringing needed stability after four years of political turmoil and uncertainty in Saigon. He went on to win the *1968 Tết Offensive* and the *1972 Eastern Offensive* against the communists. But he failed in his last war against Kissinger and the U.S. Congress, which cut off all military aid to South Vietnam.

Chapter 12: *1974: The Paracel Island Battle; Thượng Đức; Phước Long.* Deprived of U.S. aid, the ARVN waged a *poor man's war* against the communists who were still fully supported by the Soviets and Chinese. For the ARVN, this was the beginning of a lopsided war against the communists with the battles of Thượng Đức and Phước Long. U.S. Congress would no longer lift any finger to assist South Vietnam.

Chapter 13: *1975: Ban Mê Thuột, Fall of I Corps, Phan Rang-Xuân Lộc.* The communists launched a third invasion against South Vietnam. Following the fall of Ban Mê Thuột, Thiệu decided to pull his troops out of the highlands turning it into a disastrous retreat. By pulling the Marines and the Airborne out of I Corps, Thiệu caused its collapse. The ARVN took a last and magnificent stand at Xuân Lộc, but General Lê Minh Đảo's understrength troops were overwhelmed by the communists. Saigon fell after a 21-war effort.

Chapter 14: *Self Sacrifice, Reeducation camps, Postwar Killings.* A red curtain fell over South Vietnam after the war. Five generals and scores of others killed themselves instead of surrendering to the enemy. ARVN officers and troops were sent to reeducation camps where some vegetated for up to 17 years. Civilians were sent to new economic zones. Thousands were killed extra-judicially at random, in reeducation camps or at sea by drowning. Millions of people tried to escape by boat and more than two million people arrived on new freedom shores.

Chapter 15: *Identity.* The Vietnam War was a fight over the nature of the Vietnamese society. By turning it into a killing field, the North Vietnamese implied that North and South Vietnamese were different in terms of belief and aspiration.

Chapter 16: *Epilogue.* The ARVN is dead, although it has done its job. It left behind a yellow flag for the Vietnamese to unify the overseas émigrés who will continue to fight for the basic rights of all Vietnamese.

The ARVN has brought pride and recognition to its servicemen despite its final collapse. Through its enormous contribution in the war effort to preserve the freedom of South Vietnam and to highlight the bravery of its soldiers and officers who fought the war until the end despite U.S. withdrawal, it has unified the community of three million overseas Vietnamese under the yellow flag, which has been in existence since 1802.[29] The flag with its three red stripes has become the proud symbol of freedom for the aging ARVN fighters and by extension the overseas Vietnamese community. For forty-five years after the war, it has been recognized by many U.S. states and countries in the world as the Vietnamese-American FREEDOM and HERITAGE flag.[30]

1

From the National Army to the ARVN

World War II significantly altered the political alignment and social structure around the world. By the end of the war, the influence of great European powers began to wane and this led to the decolonization of Asia and Africa. In the confusing and chaotic aftermath of the war, the various local political and religious factions and groups in French Indochina (Vietnam, Cambodia, and Laos) on one side looked for power and/or state independence while France on the other end struggled to hold them back in the French Union.

The First Vietnam War: 1945–1954[1]

In Indochina during these years, the French decided to wage war on two fronts: one in Tonkin (North Vietnam) and the other in Cochinchina (South Vietnam) against the Việt Minh, a preceding name of the communists. Since the French did not have enough forces in Tonkin to deal with pacification, their strategy there was to "strike at the head" of their enemy in order to defeat them. The war was a conventional one with troops, armored cars, artillery, cannons, and aircraft. It lasted nine years and ended in 1954 right after the fall of Điện Biên Phủ.

The war in the South, on the other hand, took a more restrained approach because most of the resources—men and materiel—on both sides, had been diverted or kept north to be used in a very active northern war. Therefore, it was focused on the politically and economically vital cities eschewing the large-scale mobile operations, except for the defense of the already pacified zone. Because of its late start, the war in the South would continue for two decades longer than its North counterpart.[2]

The Việt Minh—short for Việt Nam Độc Lập Đồng Minh Hội (League for the Independence of Vietnam)—had their own problems: they tried to hide their communist origin in order to compete against local non-communist organizations, which also fought for independence. The Việt Minh organization soon lapsed into inactivity and was replaced in 1941 by the Indochinese Communist Party (ICP) and later by the Vietnamese Communist Party (VCP).

The non-communist parties were many and included the Tân Việt based in Annam (formed in 1926); the Thanh Niên Cao Vọng (the Hopes of Youth) group formed by Nguyễn An Ninh of Cochinchina; and the Việt Nam Quốc Dân Đảng (Vietnamese Nationalist Party or VNQDD) formed in December 1927.[3] Later came the groups under Bảo Đại and Ngô Đình Diệm, and the Constitutionalist Party founded by the wealthy Cochinchinese landowner Nguyễn Văn Thịnh. One has to include the Đại Việt founded in 1939 by Trương Tú Anh and Nguyễn Tường Tâm, the Cao Đài and Hòa Hảo.[4]

Westerners often thought that Vietnam as a country was formed at the same time as a bloc. It was not. That difference explains why North and South Vietnam are different for a number of reasons: geography, formation, age, governance and, not least, the people who lived in these regions. While North Vietnam dated back to the first millennium or earlier, the South was a newly conquered territory that existed as a true entity only in the first part of the 19th century. One could say, there always has been a two-Vietnam country in the heart of each Vietnamese: an ancient Vietnam and a new modern Vietnam formed at the expense of the Cham and Khmer nations.

While people in the North are fairly homogeneous (90 percent Kinh ethnic group),[5] the South was a mixture of Kinh, Khmers, Chinese, Chams, and natives. The Chams are Hinduized people who lived in central Vietnam from present-day Đà Nẵng to Vũng Tàu. Their civilization flourished from the 6th century CE to the 13th century. The Khmers, officially of the Angkor Empire, the precursor of the Cambodian state, were a Hindu-Buddhist empire that peaked in the 11th to 13th century. It once stretched over Thailand, Cambodia, and Vietnam.[6]

The South, more recently formed although it was at least five centuries old, could be considered as a graft onto the ancient and original North Vietnam. The real and divisive fracture came in 1602 when Lord Nguyễn Hoàng—a warlord at the northern court—tired of squabbling with the northern Trịnh and Lê clans decided to move to Thanh Hóa Province to rule over what would later become South Vietnam. On his deathbed in 1613, he described his land as a place of opportunity with "mountains full of riches and oceans teeming with fish."[7] He thus became the founder of the southern Nguyễn dynasty with Emperor Bảo Đại as the last ruler.

Beginning with the 15th century, the Vietnamese slowly moved southwards in search of new lands and to distance themselves from their huge and threatening neighbor, China. The process, called *nam tiến* (southern expansion), lasted from the 15th to the 19th centuries during which they followed the coastline southwards. In the process they displaced the Chams, who lived in present-day central Vietnam, and then the native Khmers of the Mekong Delta. They conquered and transformed a small fishing village into the city of Saigon in 1689 and spread all the way to the Gulf of Siam (Thailand). That migration did not occur overnight but very slowly over a period of almost four centuries.

The south was then sparsely inhabited and was the land of plenty and freedom in contrast to hardscrabble northern rigidity.[8] It was also a frontier area, a still undeveloped land despite being under the control of the Nguyễn for more than half a century (1802–1862) prior to the arrival of the French in 1859.

Confucianism,[9] which strongly anchored the people's life in Tonkin and Annam (central Vietnam), held little sway in Cochinchina (South Vietnam).[10] While the northern Confucian society was rigidly divided into four groups: scholars, peasants, artisans and traders, the southern society was much simpler and differentiated only workers (farmers, merchants, etc.) and non-workers (bureaucrats, entertainers, etc.).

While Buddhism was highly formalized and structured in the north, frugal and austere forms of Theravada Buddhism flourished in the South, mixed with Confucian ideas and Taoist principles.[11] This left a lot of room for three main politico-religious sects or organizations to proliferate and predominate: the Hòa Hảo, the Cao Đài, and the Bình Xuyên in colonial Vietnam. They appeared to be anti-modern, feudal and anachronistic in outlook.[12] But that was the way it was: a combination of old and new like Vietnam itself. It may have something to do with the combination of Confucianism and Buddhism, two ancient religions that have lasted until today. But it reflects the wide diversity of the southern society that includes the Vietnamese (Kinh), the Chams, the Chinese, and the Khmers.

The Hòa Hảo were predominant in the western part of Cochinchina (miền Tây). Founded by the sickly Huỳnh Phú Sổ in 1939, this millenarian religion followed an older branch of the Theravada Buddhism called Bửu Sơn Kỳ Hương (Strange Flagrance from the Precious Mountain). Claiming himself as a messenger of the Jade Buddha, Sổ was a formidable faith healer who extolled frugality and hard work and decried capitalism and communism as foreign influences. The group once had a military component consisting of several "brigades" (battalions) of men. At the start of the First Vietnam War, they were the second most powerful politico-religious group in the South as their followers were one million-men strong.

The Cao Đài or "Third Manifestation of God in the East" was and is a syncretic religion native to the Mekong Delta. It mixed Eastern mysticism and Western metaphysics and followed the hierarchy of the Catholic Church but was prone to intense factionalism. It aimed to achieve spiritual elevation in order to escape the endless cycle of reincarnation. It has a pantheon of spirits: Descartes, Joan of Arc, Louis Pasteur, Shakespeare, Sun Yat Sen, Mencius, etc.

The Bình Xuyên was a criminal enterprise that monopolized all manner of vice around Saigon. It was a gang with a firm code of honor fused in a blood oath. It is vaguely related to the Chinese heaven and Earth societies. Cochinchina was thus a confused and confusing place especially for outsiders.[13]

The 1954 Geneva Accords

Following the Indochina cease-fire agreement (Geneva Accords) of 20 July 1954, Vietnam was divided through the 17th parallel into communist North Vietnam led by Hồ Chí Minh and the Republic of South Vietnam (RVN) headed by Prime Minister and later President Ngô Đình Diệm. The armistice did not

> mean peace in any real sense of the term. The armistice left two rival governments in Vietnam, each claiming to represent the entire country.... South of the 17th parallel, the population accepted the results of Geneva with stoic resignation; in Saigon, flags were flown at half-staff. North of the 17th parallel, a vast exodus got underway from the 'non-liberated' areas, while the [communist] party solidified its control everywhere.[14]

In North Vietnam, the communists competed for power with non-communist nationalist parties, like the Việt Nam Quốc Dân Đảng (VNQDD) and Đại Việt among others.[15] The VNQDD or Vietnamese Nationalist Party or Việt Quốc was a nationalist and moderate socialist political party that sought independence from French colonial rule in the early 1920s in Vietnam. It modeled itself on the Republic of China's Kuomintang. The Đại Việt or Nationalist Party of Greater Vietnam was a nationalist and anti-communist political party active in Vietnam in the 20th century. These non-communist parties were gradually pushed aside and eliminated by the communists who remained the dominant party in the north. In particular, non-communist politicians Nguyễn Văn Sâm and Dr. Trương Đình Tri were assassinated 24 hours apart for saying in public that Hồ's government was a communist government that followed a partisan and totalitarian policy.[16]

In South Vietnam, the South Vietnamese and their non-communist leaders were led by Prince Bảo Đại, the former Emperor of Vietnam who met with 24 nationalist leaders on 8 September 1945 before meeting with the French at Hà Long Bay on 7 December 1947 about the independence of the State of Vietnam.[17]

The Vietnamese National Army (VNA) was created on 23 May 1948, which was later celebrated as Armed Forces Day by decree of former Emperor Bảo Đại. The latter, who had abdicated a few years earlier, had remained in power as head of state until Ngô Đình Diệm became the president of the Republic of Vietnam.

Once the independence of the State of Vietnam was ratified by the French National Assembly, Bảo Đại celebrated the birth of the State of Vietnam on 14 June 1949 at the Saigon City Hall. Following the speeches, the raising of the yellow flag with three red stripes, and a 21-gun salute, Bảo Đại addressed the nation as head of state followed by a review of troops. The guard of honor, which was entirely Vietnamese, included units of Cao Đài, Hòa Hảo, Bình Xuyên, and Catholic local defense forces.[18] This was a great day for South Vietnam, which finally had an army of its own.

The Initial Vietnamese National Army: 1949–1955

In mid–1949, 41,500 Vietnamese troops actively participated in military operations in Vietnam with the French forces.[19] That group constituted the nucleus of the Vietnamese National Army, which rose to 30 battalions by the end of 1950 and to 51 in 1951.[20] The result was due in large extent to the work of Bảo Đại who felt it would take eight years to replace the French.[21]

The State of Vietnam raised four divisions in 1951, which were placed under the command of Bảo Đại and the ministry of national defense. Bảo Đại in turn would delegate command of military operations to the French commander in Indochina.

The first American foray into the Vietnamese military buildup began on 1 May 1950 when President Harry S. Truman approved a $10 million grant for urgently needed military assistance items for Indochina. The latter was part of the French colonial empire and included the associated states of Laos, Cambodia, and Vietnam. From 1950 to 1954, the United States contributed about $1.1 billion directly to France for the prosecution of the war against communism in this region.[22]

It was not until July 1951 when the Bảo Đại's government decreed mass mobilization that everything began moving forward. Young Vietnamese had another option to fight for their country: join Bảo Đại's army instead of the Việt Minh; win independence by non-violent means instead of fighting a class struggle.

At the time of the 1954 armistice, the Vietnamese armed forces numbered about 205,000 men and consisted primarily of infantry units under French officers and non-commissioned officer cadres. These units were reorganized into four standard field divisions of 8,100 men each and six light divisions of 5,800 men each and a number of territorial regiments.

The war cost the French Expeditionary Corps (FEC) 59,745 dead and missing. The Vietnamese National Army had lost 58,877 dead and missing. But the main casualties had been the civilians, some 400,000 in all, of which 100,000 to 150,000 had been assassinated by the Việt Minh.[23] Thus, by 1954 South Vietnam, a small country of around 12 million people, had lost—in the first Vietnam War (1945–1954) alone—almost the same number of troops the U.S. would lose in the second Vietnam War. They were the first unsung heroes of that small army, which would lose more than 300,000 men during the second Vietnam War.[24]

From July 1954 to January 1956—when the French left Vietnam—the Vietnamese National Army (VNA), which was part of the French Expeditionary Corps, was trained by the TRIM, a Joint Franco-American Training Relations and Instructions Mission. The VNA was organized into small units and lacked trained leaders, equipment, and adequate logistical capabilities at all levels. The Americans took over after the French advisers withdrew on 28 April 1956.[25]

The plan for a Vietnamese national army depended on obtaining financing from the United States, which had already provided aid to the French (the $1.1 billion to halt the expansion of communism included some $746 million worth of Army materiel delivered directly to the French Expeditionary Corps in Indochina). This was followed by an agreement in December 1954 between France, the State of Vietnam, and the U.S. to supply aid through the Military Assistance Program (MAP).[26]

Ngô Đình Diệm: 1955–1963

On 19 June 1954, Bảo Đại, who resided in France, named Diệm as his prime minister. This position was unusually difficult as suggested by the number of ministers who assumed that position but had failed before Diệm took office. In a country the size of California, there were three politico-religious sects and five armies: the FEC (French Expeditionary Force), troops from the Cao Đài, Hòa Hảo, Bình Xuyên, and the communists.

Diệm commanded a claim to loyalty from the nationalists, but he had few supporters besides his own family as a result of having been out of public view for a few decades. His naysayers were legion and many thought that he was too rigid, too unworldly to be an effective leader. However, according to one communist defector, Diệm ranked as "the only nationalist the communists were worried about."[27]

The sects, fearing the loss of freedom and autonomy they had enjoyed in the past, jockeyed for new positions and gradually became opposed to Diệm. The Bình Xuyên in April 1954 bought for themselves the control of the Saigon-Cholon police and Sureté by paying Bảo Đại 40 million piasters. Lê Văn Viễn (Bẩy Viễn) became a military counselor, Lại Văn Sáng director of the Securité, and his brother Lại Hữu Tài was nominated director of the Saigon-Cholon police.[28] General Ely, the commander of the French Expeditionary Corps (FEC) prevented Diệm from using the Vietnamese National Army against the Bình Xuyên. He also voiced objections to General Collins, the U.S. president's special envoy to Vietnam, about Diệm's plans to remove Sáng forcibly.[29]

Bẩy Viễn, in response, began arming his 5,000 Bình Xuyên followers and fortifying strongholds in Saigon-Cholon. To meet Viễn's open challenge, Diệm brought into the capital three Nùng minority battalions from Tonkin as well as two battalions of paratroopers under the command of Lt. Col. Đỗ Cao Trí.

Tensions rose when troops began positioning themselves within the city. In some cases, VNA troops and Bình Xuyên thugs bivouacked in fortified encampments on opposite sidewalks of boulevards and streets. On 27 March 1955, Diệm ordered the paratroopers to occupy the police headquarters on Boulevard Gallieni, which had been fortified by the Bình Xuyên. General Carpentier of the FEC promised Lt. Col. Trí 200 million francs if he would ignore the order. The latter responded he had lost contact with his battalion commanders.[30] Bẩy Viễn ordered an assault on VNA headquarters by more than 200 troops. For three hours the VNA and Bình Xuyên clashed inside Saigon. The hostilities were inconclusive, although innocent bystanders were killed.[31]

The French then imposed a cease-fire which put a stop to Diệm's advance. General Collins who listened to Ely, urged Diệm not to resume the attack and decided that Diệm had to go. On 7 April he also sent a telegram to this effect to the State Department, which luckily was met with skepticism in Washington, DC.[32] Collins thus engaged in plotting in collusion with the French, as Diệm did not know what was afoot.

On 28 April, a truckload of VNA soldiers received fire when it passed a building held by the Bình Xuyên on Boulevard Gallieni. The army moved four battalions of paratroopers and an armored unit against other Bình Xuyên installations around the city. The Bình Xuyên fired four mortar shells against the palace grounds. During the exchange of gunfire, a large area of shacks close to the Bình Xuyên headquarters caught on fire leaving 20,000 people homeless and filling the bright sky with dark smoke. As Trí's paratroopers moved forwards, the resistance collapsed and the Bình Xuyên retreated from Cholon.[33]

Bảo Đại summoned Diệm to Cannes with the obvious intention of dismissing him. But he could not fool the latter who replied that he was needed in Saigon. Bảo Đại sent General Nguyễn Văn Vỹ to take control of the VNA and to carry off a coup against Diệm. However, the presence of colonels Minh and Đôn and General Lê Văn Ty was sufficient to induce Vỹ to flee to Dalat.[34] During the next few days, the ARVN pursued the Bình Xuyên outside Saigon and drove them into the marshes of Rừng Sát where they were annihilated. Through this battle, Diệm achieved the unification of the government and the armed forces. Bảo Đại's National Army became Diệm's ARVN.

Diệm had found the decisive commander he needed in Colonel Trí of the paratroopers. Colonel Dương Văn Minh, however, proved to be indecisive when it came to combat. The main assistance Dương Văn Minh and Trần Văn Đôn gave to Diệm was their appearance at the palace on 1 May and their message to Bảo Đại that they would only follow a regime "chosen by the people." Nevertheless, Diệm promoted Minh to the rank of full colonel and Đôn to that of brigadier general after they renounced their French citizenship.[35] On 26 October 1955, by winning the presidency of the First Republic, Ngô Đình Diệm ushered in the era of the Army of the Republic of South Vietnam (ARVN).[36] Military assistance from then on was directly provided to the government of Vietnam instead of through France.

[Diệm] held his own ideas about the best way for South Vietnam to move ahead, conceptions that proved to be deeply flawed but that were nevertheless forward looking and, in their own way, thoroughly modern.... He did articulate a vision of a modern Vietnam, but his government encountered enormous problems attempting to translate his ideas into practice.[37]

American officials, who supported him, worried about his "obstinacy, self-righteousness, and lack of experience." He was not a politician or someone who was willing to compromise in order to get a better deal later on. Although Diệm's failings were legion and manifest, the "U.S.-Vietnamese relationship was neither a colonial one nor an alliance of equals, yet the Americans frequently behaved in a manner more akin to the former than the latter." Policy makers imagined the Vietnamese to be innately incapable and badly in need of U.S. tutelage.[38]

Diệm at the suggestion of Generals Nguyễn Văn Vỹ and Trần Văn Đôn wanted to create an army with light infantry battalions to deal with the communist insurgency, which Saigon saw as its primary problems. These mobile units, equipped with howitzers, would conduct local anti-guerrilla and civic operations. They would be close to the people from whom they got their recruits and motivated by strong personal ties to an area to protect local villages.[39]

The Americans, however, thought differently. Experience in Korea taught them that guerrilla attacks in South Vietnam were just the precursors of more potent cross-border communist attacks, for a revolution could not be instigated or successful without the support of an external sponsoring power.[40] Therefore, cross border attacks should be dealt with more seriously than any local insurgency attack. Then South Vietnam should possess a conventional army with big units to defend its territories. Were Diệm to refuse the offer, he would not receive any U.S. military aid for American advisers would be ineffective in a non–U.S. Army model[41] and small units would be structurally incompatible with large U.S. divisions.[42] There would also be no infusion of dollars into the local economy, thus no modernization of Vietnam.

Diệm deeply agonized over that decision for the rest of his presidency.[43] He was well aware that accepting the U.S. offer meant accepting U.S. strategy as well as U.S. troop involvement sooner or later, which would lead to a loss of sovereignty—a huge loss in the mind of a mandarin trained official like Diệm. The decision was painful and difficult. But in the end, he signed off and paid dearly with his life.

The implications were many. From that time onward, the conduct of the war was dictated by American strategy. General Trần Văn Đôn once asked Chief of General Staff General Cao Văn Viên about his military strategy. The latter responded, "As long as the conduct of the war remains an American responsibility, we have no doctrine of our own."[44] That statement would forever cast the ARVN in an inferior military role in the defense of South Vietnam.

In order to build up this huge army to face the communist invasion, the ARVN would need more and more recruits all the time. By the 1970s, the ARVN grew to more than 1.1 million men out of a country of 16 million people—one of the largest armies in the world—with one out of six South Vietnamese males serving in the active military and the full mobilization of all males from 16 to 50 years old.[45] Just for comparison in order to see the scope of South Vietnam's contribution to the fighting: had such mobilization started in the U.S. in 1972, with a population of 200 million people, the U.S. would have 13.7 million of recruits under arms.

To get ready for the war, the ARVN leadership should have prepared the whole country for the needed sacrifice besides the pain, suffering and hardship inflicted on their families. There was minimal ideological training to mitigate or reward the sacrifice. Most of the suffering fell on the peasants because South Vietnam was at that time a labor-intensive agrarian society. Sending ten young able bodies to the army meant taking ten farmers away from the fields. Production in general, and in each household in particular, would suffer. Although the South Vietnamese army was a rural army, because of lack of ideological training by mid–1966, it was no longer a people's army, a far cry from its early years.[46]

The Americans wanted Diệm to establish order, but also to gradually move into a liberal direction. For them these two elements were intertwined. But for Diệm who presided over a war-torn country that just walked out of a hundred-year colonial rule, that had not known freedom for almost a century and whose aspirations were boundless, the boundaries between freedom and oppression were closely linked. Any minor infringement to the former could easily be felt as oppression by the people and lead to revolt and violence.

Having to walk a fine line between the concept and its application, Diệm had to be extremely cautious. He moved slowly, taking time to make up his mind, and proved to be a notoriously "uncooperative" U.S. ally. Decisions were difficult and as a leader of a country that had recently gained its democratic voice, he had his own pride and that of his country. "Far from playing the part of a grateful supplicant, the Ngos deeply resented their dependence on the United States and their treatment at Washington's hands."[47]

The Americans needed the Ngos to hold the line in Southeast Asia but viewed their client with a jaundiced eye; for their part, the Ngos regarded the United States as an indispensable but far from ideal patron.

ARVN: 1955–1964

The building of the Vietnamese National Army and of its successor, the Army of the Republic of Vietnam (ARVN) did not follow a linear upward curve, but rather a curvilinear trajectory with ups and downs depending on the political stability of the Republic of Vietnam, the vision of its leaders, the assistance of the French and U.S. governments, and the opposition of its enemies (the Việt Minh, the politico-religious sects).

Eager to leave Vietnam for North Africa, where they faced a deteriorating situation that required increasing quantities of personnel and equipment to deal with, the French salvaged the best equipment for their own use. They dumped mountains of equipment upon the Vietnamese; most of it "was improperly packed, indiscriminately piled, often placed in outside storage, and controlled by inadequate or meaningless inventory records." Overall, the quality and quantity of the equipment were inadequate.[48]

The earliest MAP (Military Assistance Program) proposed a force of 150,000 starting on 1 July 1956. From 1957 to 1959, the ARVN was further restructured under MAAGV—Military Assistance Advisory Group, Vietnam—guidance to meet the threat of external attack. More than 200 tables of organizations and equipment and tables of distribution were developed in the search for the proper organization. By September 1959, the ARVN had been reorganized into seven standard divisions of 10,450 men each and three Army Corps headquarters. The I Corps was located at Đà Nẵng, the II Corps at Pleiku, and the III Corps at Saigon.

The training program began in 1958 and consisted of a six-phase cycle of 32 weeks leading to advanced unit training and concluding with field maneuvers at regimental level, followed by an annual training cycle of 52 weeks within each corps area.

The Americans, on one hand, planned to equip the ARVN to deal with a conventional invading force. But this conventional military force, which was not properly organized, equipped, or trained to contest the guerrilla forces, was contrary to the wishes of Diệm, who saw the war as a low grade guerrilla affair.

By 1960, it was apparent that the ARVN had problems dealing with the insurgency, which had transformed the countryside into a battlefield of unconventional warfare. Besides providing MAAGV advisers all the way down to infantry regiment level, the U.S. began training indigenous "Ranger" companies for counter-guerrilla warfare.

Although progress had been noted during training, deficiencies were encountered that were due to a lack of knowledge of techniques in combined arms operations and other joint operations. Officers at all levels lacked the experience and military schooling needed to qualify them for their positions. There was a shortage of officers and enlisted specialists for the technical services as well as a shortage of trained instructors.[49]

In August 1960, the U.S. Departments of Defense and State, being not happy with the progress of the training and direction of the war, approved the JCS outline plan for counterinsurgency operations in Vietnam and Laos. The plan raised the support of the ARVN to 170,000 men along with a Civil Guard force of 68,000.

By 1962, the ARVN strength grew to 219,000. The Civil Guard expanded to 77,000 and the Self Defense Corps to 99,500. A new paramilitary force, the Civilian Irregular Defense Group (CIDG) was established and by the end of 1962 totaled 15,000.

The Ranger units were created by President Diệm, against U.S. advice, by taking the fourth company out of each infantry regiment and re-designating it. The ARVN at that time had three corps headquarters, seven infantry divisions, one airborne brigade, the 9,000 Ranger force, three Marine battalions, a token Air Force and Navy, all with a total of 137,000 men.[50] The Civil Guard and Self-Defense Corps were largely untrained and not considered part of the ARVN until 1964. In mid–1961, the ARVN Joint General Staff authorized MAAGV advisers to accompany Vietnamese battalions and company-sized units in combat with the understanding that they would only observe and advise. On 8 February 1962 a U.S. Military Assistance Command, Vietnam (USMACV) was established and Lieutenant General Paul Harkins (who was promoted to general) was named commander (COUSMACV). The latter was responsible for all U.S. military policy, operations, and assistance to Vietnam.

By 1962, regular force strength grew to 219,000, exceeding the 200,000 authorized level. The Civil Guard expanded to 77,000, the Self-Defense Corps to 99,500. A new paramilitary force, the Civilian Irregular Defense Group (CIDG), was established and by the end of 1962 totaled about 15,000. Separate Army, Navy, Air Force, and Special Forces commands were established.

The Civilian Irregular Defense Group (CIDG) program began in February 1961 to win over and train ethnic Montagnards into an anti–Việt Cộng, irregular, paramilitary group. The CIDG had, among other missions, that of collecting intelligence in the highlands of central Vietnam and in Laos. The program had also a civic action aspect, such as providing treatment, medicines, seeds, clothing, and other social welfare goods to win over the ethnic groups. After the U.S. Army took over the military aspect of the CIDG program, the medical phase of the civic action evolved into the Special Forces Village Defense Medical program. By October 1963, this group consisted of 16,084 strike force members, 40,765 hamlet militiamen, 4,912 mountain scouts, and 3,256 border surveillance personnel.[51]

By mid–1963, a peak armed strength of 575,000 was noted and the million-man mark was reached in 1971–72 (see table 1 below).

On 20 June 1964, General William Westmoreland became commander, U.S. Military Assistance Command, Vietnam. The following year, he pushed the ARVN aside, believing "that only American soldiers could properly defend South Vietnam."[52] And three years later, he returned to Washington, D.C., to become the Army Chief of Staff while the ARVN took on new responsibilities of defending its territories. It was apparent that the Vietnamese armed forces levels were still too low to satisfy South Vietnam's security without sacrificing their own training and reorganization.

"Poor training or its complete absence was a continual handicap for all South Vietnam armed forces units."[53] Many units were formed and filled out with hastily drafted personnel with no formal training who were expected to learn by doing. Training time had been cut back from 12 to nine weeks for certain units, to accommodate a larger number of new recruits in 1964. Units scheduled for training did not show up because of operational requirements. This lack of training worsened the combat readiness of the units.

ARVN and PAVN Soldiers

There were major geographic, social, political differences between the North and South Vietnamese people and the way they approached the war. Seeking to build the Great Society and secure his own place in American history, President Lyndon Johnson was unhappy with anything that diverted his attention and resources from his programs. He could not ignore Vietnam, but was unwilling to pay the necessary price to win decisively there.[54] He, therefore, opted for half-baked measures to avoid military defeat while hoping for a possibility of success.

Hanoi's goal was to unify the country under communist rule.[55] In 2019—44 years after the war ended—anyone in Vietnam who dares to protest against the communist regime is severely beaten and jailed. What happened next in communist jails is unknown: some did not survive their jail terms. Such was the recent case of a man who was found to possess some yellow "material" in his house. He was suspected of preparing to make a huge South Vietnamese yellow-red flag, although no red material was found in his house. Nonetheless, he was jailed while awaiting for court appearance. A few days later, he was found dead in his cell with his throat slashed. Investigation continued as people were puzzled as to how a prisoner could have his throat slashed while in detention.[56]

The communist government exists to prolong the rule of the communist regime, not to promote the well-being or freedom of the citizens. This was why the South Vietnamese in 1955 chose to live under the Bảo Đại/Ngô Đình Diệm—led government rather than the communist regime. During the war, citizens fled with their feet toward the ARVN side because they spontaneously knew who eventually would protect them. The people in Quảng Trị in 1972 and 1975 ran away from the communists toward the ARVN side to the point of overwhelming South Vietnam's capability to defend them.

"Having to defeat and occupy the South to win, it assumed the strategic offensive. Possessing the initiative, Hanoi chose when, where and how to attack and controlled the duration and intensity of any fighting."[57] Since this was a planned and premeditated conquest, Hanoi should bear all the consequences of the crimes it had committed, all the terror it had imposed on the people of Vietnam, north and south. Merle Pribbenow, the translator of the *Official History of the People's Army of Vietnam: 1945–1975*, after analyzing all the data from communist publications,[58] came up with at least 980,000 North Vietnamese troops being sent by Hanoi to the South during the war years.

Besides, Hanoi played Moscow off against Beijing, as these countries needed to maintain their claims to leadership of the "anti-imperialist" struggle by giving Hanoi the help it sought. Saigon, a relatively open society, did not contemplate conquering or subjugating the north. Its leaders were not unified and therefore did not have a common goal in mind and did not engage in tightly coordinated political and military struggle. What strengthened the spine of northerners was the communist dialectic of spreading communism. Democracies did not use any propaganda or ideology while fighting for freedom around the world. One cannot blame the South Vietnamese for not being as aggressive as the North Vietnamese. It was just inherent to democratic states to be aloof about fighting for democracies around the world.[59]

The life of the PAVN soldier was difficult. Bảo Ninh wrote that, for that autumn in the highlands, orders came for food rations to be sharply reduced. "Hungry, suffering successive bouts of malaria, the troops became anemic and their bodies broke out in ulcers, showing through worn and torn clothing. They looked like lepers, not heroic forward scouts."[60] In the summer, PAVN troops smoked *rosa canina*, which blossomed in the rain and grew in any area carrying the scent of death. "Its perfume vapor permeated our sleep, fueling erotic, obsessional dreams, and when we awoke the perfume had evaporated but we were left with a feeling of smoldering passion, both painful and ecstatic." Some dried the *canina*, slicing the flowers and roots, then mixing them with tobacco as a smoke.[61]

The average ARVN soldier was young—19 to 24 years old—with little more than a rural education. He was small, but usually an experienced combat veteran, for in Vietnam soldiers sign up for the duration of the war. Properly led, he developed a fighting spirit under the most difficult combat conditions. He must fight often and in his less hectic hours he was expected to help the rural people build a new life. He must guard long stretches of road and railroad and canals, thousands of bridges, hamlets and government facilities. For this, if he was a private with no dependents, he earned 4,000 piasters in a month (US$30). Men with dependents and elite troops—those wearing the jaunty berets (green for the Marines, red for paratroopers, black for armored troops, maroon for Rangers)—earn more. But the average pay remained low because the government feared the dangerous inflationary impact that raises to more than a million soldiers would have on the nation's strained war economy.[62]

Most ARVN soldiers preferred to live in a free and independent South Vietnam. Although most considered themselves patriots, their government had failed to deliver a powerful message of national sacrifice and a brand of patriotism wrapped in nationalism.[63] They felt the same sense of history as their PAVN adversaries but saw their own "lives connected to a non-communist, anticolonial activist of the early twentieth century."[64] The ARVN soldiers did their best under the circumstances: they fought a long and bloody war despite a low pay, dependency on foreign military assistance, poor training, poor armament, and low morale.

"In the struggle for Hue City in the Tet Offensive, it is time finally to give the ARVN its due for what was perhaps its greatest victory ever.... The ARVN forces had actually done the majority of the fighting in the Citadel, their understrength units besting the vaunted NVA and VC in a long and bitter struggle largely without the aid of organic heavy direct-fire weaponry," commented Andrew Wiest.[65]

According to James Willbanks, Vietnam veteran, and former General of the Army George C. Marshall (chair of military history and director of the department of Military History at the U.S. Army Command and General Staff College, Fort Leavenworth, Kansas), the 18th ARVN fought valiantly at Xuân Lộc.[66] General Văn Tiến Dũng, the PAVN officer in charge of the Hồ Chí Minh Campaign, agreed. He was especially impressed by the "stubbornness of the enemy" and by the ARVN's "relentless pursuit" of PAVN soldiers.[67]

Indoctrination

Anticolonialism fueled by nationalism was present ever since the French set foot in Đại Việt—the name of the country in 1858. Trương Định or Trương Công Định was one of the most celebrated of the southern guerrilla chieftains.[68] He set up a "military colony" from which he trained soldiers who later attacked the French forces located at Gò Công in 1862. Then came many revolutionaries, including the two Phan: Phan Bội Châu and Phan Châu Trinh, who were not blood related.

Phan Bội Châu, a neo–Confucian scholar and activist, traveled to Japan and China to seek technical help to fight the French. He symbolized the continuity of resistance, a stubborn unwillingness to be cowed by French forces. In 1906, he sent students to Japan for training in preparation for a future rebellion. He was the role model for future anticolonialists, including the communists.[69]

Phan Châu Trinh, a Confucian scholar advocated educational changes through nonviolent reforms and gradual progress toward independence as a democratic republic with the help of the French. He represented the reformist group. He was averse to violence after witnessing his father's killing by scholar-gentry associates. His biggest achievement was the opening in 1907 of the Đông Kinh Nghĩa Thục or Eastern Capital Non-tuition School where mathematics, economy, hygiene, political history, science, French and Chinese were taught. It was an unprecedented venture for Vietnam never had a public educational system prior to that date. The other revolutionary idea was the inclusion of women, not previously allowed to receive any education, on the teaching staff. Trinh was a reasoned debater and a master of symbolic gesture, although not a profound thinker.[70]

In their own ways, Châu and Trinh managed to change the way the country, especially the youth, was thinking at the time. They emphasized modernization with or without armed rebellion and suggested that everyone had to sacrifice for the good of the country. Demonstrations multiplied in 1908 as demands for modern education, tax cuts, and reduced corvée labor increased. Suspecting dark political motives behind the creation of the Đông Kinh Nghĩa Thục School, the French closed it ten months after issuing a temporary permit and created in its place the University of Hà Nội and a government sponsored school to replace the Đông Kinh Nghĩa Thục School.

Alarmed by the demonstrations during which many leaders were either imprisoned or killed, the French rounded up all the reformists. Châu, still in Japan, was sentenced to death in absentia. Trinh was sentenced to death with commutation to life in prison and sent to Poulo Condor in 1908.[71] He was pardoned in 1911 after intervention of the League of Rights of Man and later sent to exile in France. Châu and Trinh were two nationalist leaders who introduced the Vietnamese to two ways of fighting the French: the activist method spearheaded by Châu would be followed by northerners while Trinh's reformist way would be adopted by the southerners. Activism led to communism in the North while reformism was more compatible to the capitalistic, commerce-oriented south.

The year 1926 marked the end of the old nationalist way of fighting the French. Trinh who returned to Saigon in 1925 passed away the following year because of tuberculosis. On 4 April 1926, tens of thousands people came to laud and mourn the man who gave his life to Vietnam's freedom and to accompany him to his final resting place from Saigon to his gravesite near Tân Sơn Nhứt Airport. Châu, who was caught in Shanghai in 1925 by the French through Hồ Chí Minh's betrayal,[72] was brought back to Hanoi where he was sentenced to death. His sentence was later commuted to house arrest for life in Huế.

The fight passed on to a younger generation that used demonstrations and strikes as tools to ask for political changes. The leaders were Bùi Quang Chiêu and Nguyễn An Ninh in the South and Hồ Chí Minh in the North, although the latter was hiding in China to avoid being caught by the French secret police.

Diệm used a doctrinal import from Europe called "Personalism," which was developed by the Frenchman Emmanuel Mounier in the 1930s. It was considered to be a third way between capitalism and communism. As a conservative, Diệm was afraid of the anarchic freedom of capitalism and the suffocating collectivism of communism. He believed that personalism emphasized spiritual and humanist values, the importance of personal struggle and responsibility and the need to provide people with the material requirements for existence.[73] The plan was to "morally rearm" people in terms of restoring traditional virtues—discipline, responsibility, honesty, and sacrifice—that would help create civic minded citizens dedicated to developing an ethical counter to communism.

The problem was that personalism was difficult to understand and vague and unpractical for daily practice. As it did not catch on with Europeans, it never caught on with the Vietnamese in general. The Ngos genuinely sought to build up a nation, although they intended to keep a firm hand on the tiller as they guided the process. They planned to "build the state from the bottom up by exercising strong leadership from the top down."[74]

Diệm at least had ideas about building up a strong nation to counter the communist threat and to link the soldiers' enormous sacrifice to nation building. But once he was toppled by his generals, indoctrination fell by the wayside. The generals—harshly intellectual people by nature—busy fighting among themselves and busy stabilizing the government, forgot to motivate their soldiers. Of course, there were exceptions. Although the soldiers understood the generals, the disconnection between the two groups remained. However, South Vietnam and the ARVN would have been better served had they been prepared and thanked for their enormous sacrifice.

Lacking a strong and solid ideology to provide a backbone to their struggle, the South Vietnamese and the ARVN were unable to match the dedication and persistence inspired by the communist ideology that "helped Vietnamese communists persevere against great odds."[75] The Vietnamese revolution "was, at heart, a communist revolution, and Vietnamese revolutionaries as a group were internationalists no less than their comrades in the Soviet Union or China."[76]

The Vietnamese communist movement emerged in the late 1920s as an offshoot of Vietnamese nationalism. It was then imagined as an integral part of world revolution. It faithfully copied Soviet and Chinese political institutions and models of economic development—from Stalin's 1936 Constitution to his cult of personality, from land reform to collectivization, and from central planning to the preoccupation with building heavy industry. By the late 1960s, the outpouring of world support made Hanoi leaders imagine themselves being the vanguard of world revolution.[77]

Ideology, however, caused the party to make wrong interpretations of world events. It led to gross miscalculations and grave losses of revolutionary forces during the Tết Offensive. In the post–1975 period, they misread the world situation and create enemies for themselves left and right. Following the Stalinist model led Vietnamese economy to disastrous consequences. The regime by 2020 had lost its legitimacy because the party clung to an outdated doctrine. Each wave of agrarian reform (1953–1956, 1958–1960, and 1976–1978) was followed by a grave economic crisis. When the leadership abandoned central planning and rural cooperatives in the late 1980s, Vietnam was third poorest and one of the most repressive countries in Southeast Asia.[78]

On the other hand, without strong indoctrination, the ARVN continued its fight until the end in 1975—a 21-year war that almost never ended. More than 350,000 ARVN soldiers died during the whole Vietnam War.[79] The RVNAF won significant battles such as the Tết Offensive in 1968, An Lộc, Kontum, and Quảng Trị in 1972. Eleven U.S. Presidential Unit Citations were awarded to South Vietnamese Ranger units in 1972 in recognition of their gallantry in the field at a time when almost all U.S. troops had left Vietnam.[80] Lê Câu, a highly decorated former ARVN colonel, remarked, "As a man who spent twelve years in combat, I can honestly say that we had many brave, diligent, and patriotic soldiers in our armed forces. They fought valiantly and selflessly against the communists year after year. Many sacrificed in silence and gave their lives [for] their country."[81]

South Vietnamese Divisions (1968–1975)

The ARVN consisted of regular and elite forces. Regular forces formed the backbone of the Corps' defense. The ARVN had at its peak eleven divisions that were spread over the four Corps: each Corps had three divisions except for the II Corps that had only two. For the sake of simplicity, the militia or territorial forces (Regional and Popular forces) are not included in this discussion, although they account for almost half of the total forces.

I. Regular Forces

There were four Corps from North to South and from I to IV, with I Corps the closest to the DMZ.

A. I Corps had three divisions:
- 1st Infantry Division—Considered "one of the best South Vietnamese combat units," it was based in Huế; because of its close proximity to the DMZ, it had four regiments instead of the usual three:
    * 1st, 3rd, 51st, and 54th Infantry Regiments.
    * 7th Armored Cavalry Squadron.
    * Engagements: Battle of Huế (1968).
    * Reconquest of Quảng Trị City (1972).

    NOTABLE COMMANDER: **Gen. Ngô Quang Trưởng** as 1st ARVN Division commander held Huế City during the Tết Offensive; as I Corps commander, he recaptured Quảng Trị City in 1972.

- 2nd Infantry Division—Based in Chu Lai, Quảng Tín Province; considered to be a "fairly good" division;
    * 4th, 5th, and 6th Infantry Regiments
    * 4th Armored Cavalry Squadron

- 3rd Infantry Division—Created in October 1971 around one regiment of the 1st ARVN Division (2nd Infantry Reg.); based in Quảng Trị; it collapsed during the Easter Offensive, was reconstituted, and again destroyed at Đà Nẵng in 1975.
    * 2nd, 56th, and 57th Infantry Regiments
    * 20th Armored Cavalry Squadron

    Gen. Nguyễn Duy Hinh, originally an Armored officer, became the last 3rd ARVN Division commander.

B. II Corps had two divisions
- 22nd Infantry Division—based in Kontum; it collapsed in 1972 and was reconstituted and was in Bình Định in 1975; it was the last ARVN unit to surrender.
    * 40th, 41st, 42nd, 47th Regiments
    * 19th Armored Cavalry Squadron

- 23rd Infantry Division—based in Ban Mê Thuột; it went into Cambodia in 1970; defeated three NVA Divisions in Kontum in 1972; but lost the battle of Ban Mê Thuột in 1973.
    * 43rd, 44th, 45th, and 53rd Infantry Regiments
    * 8th Armored Cavalry Squadron

  ENGAGEMENTS: Battle of Kontum (1972), Battle of Ban Mê Thuột (1975)

  NOTABLE COMMANDER: **Gen. Lý Tòng Bá** defeated three NVA Divisions at the battle of Kontum in 1972.

C. III Corps had three divisions

- 5th Infantry Division—Originally created in North Vietnam as the 6th Division or "Nùng" Division (ethnic highlander); renamed the 3rd Field division when it moved to Sông Máu; based in Biên Hòa.
    * 7th, 8th, and 9th Infantry Regiments
    * 1st Armored Cavalry Squadron

  ENGAGEMENTS: Coup in support of President Diệm (1960), Cambodian Incursion (1970), Battle of An Lộc (1972)

  NOTABLE COMMANDERS: **Gen. Nguyễn Văn Thiệu** quashed a coup against President Diệm (1960); he led a successful coup against Diệm (1963) and was made general. **Gen. Lê Văn Hưng** held An Lộc against three NVA divisions. **Gen. Lê Nguyên Vỹ** was the last commander of the 5th ARVN Division. He committed suicide instead of surrendering to the enemy.

- 18th Infantry Division—Created as the 10th Division; renamed as the 18th Division in 1967 ("number ten"—slang for "worst"—is not good for the image); based in Xuân Lộc; became famous for its defense of Xuân Lộc in April 1975 against four NVA divisions; soldiers were known as the "Supermen."
    * 43rd, 48th, and 52nd Infantry regiments
    * 5th Armored Cavalry Squadron

  ENGAGEMENT: Battle of Xuân Lộc

  NOTABLE COMMANDER: **Gen. Lê Minh Đảo** held off four NVA Divisions at Xuân Lộc.

- 25th Infantry Division—created in Quảng Ngãi in 1962, it was moved to southwest of Saigon in 1964; it participated in the Cambodian incursion in 1970 and the western approach of Saigon in 1972 and 1975.
    * 46th, 49th, and 50th Infantry Regiments
    * 10th Armored Cavalry Squadron

  ENGAGEMENT: Cambodian incursion

D. IV Corps was a well-defended corps: none of the provincial capitals was captured by the VC in 1975. The IV Corps Commander Maj. Gen. Nguyễn Khoa Nam and deputy commander Brig. Gen. Lê Văn Hưng did not surrender their IV Corps. They killed themselves instead. The IV Corps had three divisions.

- 7th Infantry Division—Based in Mỹ Tho.
    * 10th, 11th, and 12th Infantry Regiments
    * 6th Armored Cavalry Squadron

  NOTABLE COMMANDER: **General Huỳnh Văn Cao** used the 7th Infantry Division commanded by General Trần Thiện Kiêm to storm into Saigon to save President Diệm in 1960. **Gen. Trần Văn Hai**, last commander of the 7th ARVN Division, committed suicide instead of surrendering.

- 9th Infantry Division—Formed in 1962; based in Cần Tho and served the IV Corps.
    * 14th, 15th, and 16th Infantry Regiments
    * 2nd Armored Cavalry Squadron

- 21st Infantry Division—Based in Chương Thiện and served the IV Corps.
    * 31st, 32nd, and 33rd Infantry Regiments
    * 9th Armored Battalion

  ENGAGEMENT: Battle of Highway 13 (1972)

II. Elite Forces

The Airborne, the Marine, and the Ranger divisions were the reserve forces of South Vietnam.

- Airborne Division—A branch of the Vietnamese National Army, it was created by the French as the Airborne Group in 1955; expanded as a brigade in 1959, then as a division in 1965. It included nine Airborne Battalions and three Airborne Ranger Battalions. It fought in Cambodia in 1970 and Laos in 1971. It was used as brigade groups in 1975, the 1st at Xuân Lộc, the second at Phan Rang, and the third at Nha Trang. A fourth brigade was added in 1974.
- Marine Division (Thủy Quân Lục Chiến)—A branch of the Navy created in 1954 with two battalions, expanded to six battalions to form two brigades in 1965, then a division in 1968. A third brigade was added in 1970 and a fourth one in 1975. Had a good reputation as a combat force.
- Rangers (Biệt Động Quân). Eleven U.S. Presidential Unit citations were awarded to Vietnamese Ranger units. On 11 November 1995, American Ranger advisors and their Vietnamese counterparts gathered at Arlington National Cemetery to unveil a living memorial and a bronze plaque to honor their fallen comrades. The plaque reads, "Dedicated to the honor of the Vietnamese Rangers and their American Ranger Advisors whose dedication, valor, and fidelity in the defense of freedom must never be forgotten."[82]
- Special Forces (Lực Lượng Đặc Biệt)

RVNAF Strengths

This is the approximate strength size of the RVNAF during two periods, 1959–60 and 1971–72.

Table 1-1. Republic of Vietnam Armed Forces Strength

Adapted from Collins, James. *The Development and Training of the South Vietnamese Army, 1950–1972*. Department of the Army, Washington DC, 1975: p. 151.

	1959–60	1971–72
Army	136,000	410,000
Air Force	4,600	50,000
Navy	4,300	42,000
Marine Corps	2,000	14,000
Total Regular	146,000	516,000
Regional Forces	49,000	284,000
Popular Forces	48,000	248,000
Total Territorial	97,000	532,000
Grand Total	243,000	1,048,000

Notable Generals

- **Cao Văn Viên**, chairman of the South Vietnamese Joint General Staff.
- **Đỗ Cao Trí**, commander of ARVN's III Corps during 1968–71, known for his fighting prowess, but also his flamboyant lifestyle and allegations of corruption.
- **Đỗ Kế Giai**, last commander of the Ranger forces. Spent 17 years in communist re-education camps for his fervent anti-communist resistance.
- **Lê Minh Đảo**, commander of the 18th Division that fought against PAVN forces at Xuân Lộc in 1975. Spent 17 years in re-education camps.
- **Lê Nguyên Vỹ**, last commander of 5th Division, one of the five generals who committed suicide on April 30, 1975.
- **Lê Văn Hưng**, commander of the 5th Division; defender of An Lộc during the Easter Offensive in 1972, one of the five generals who committed suicide on April 30, 1975.
- **Lý Tòng Bá** defender of Kontum during the 1972 Easter Offensive; last commander of the 25th Division; spent 12 years in reeducation camps.
- **Ngô Quang Trưởng**, I Corps commander renowned for his competence, tactical proficiency, forthrightness, and incorruptibility. Widely regarded by both American and Vietnamese contemporaries as the finest field commander of the ARVN.
- **Nguyễn Khánh**, Head-of-State 1964–65.
- **Nguyễn Ngọc Loan**, Chief of the Republic of Vietnam National Police who fought in Saigon during the 1968 Tết Offensive.
- **Nguyễn Khoa Nam**, last Commander of IV Corps, one of the five generals who committed suicide on April 30, 1975.
- **Nguyễn Đức Thắng**, commander of the 1st, then the 5th ARVN divisions; head of the Ministry of Revolutionary Development (pacification); considered

to be one of the four most honest and capable ARVN generals: Nhất Thắng, Nhì Chinh, Tam Thanh, Tứ Trưởng.
- **Nguyễn Viết Thanh**, commander of the IV Corps (1968–1970); killed in action in Cambodia when his helicopter collided with a U.S. Cobra.
- **Nguyễn Chánh Thi**, "Coup Specialist," Commander of ARVN's I Corps during 1964–66.
- **Nguyễn Văn Thiệu**, President during 1967–71, 1971–75.
- **Phạm Ngọc Sáng**, commander of the 6th Air Division; spent 17 years in re-education camps.
- **Phạm Văn Đồng**, Military Governor of Saigon 1965–1966, suppressed Buddhist movement.
- **Phạm Văn Phú**, last Commander of II Corps, one of the five generals who committed suicide on April 30, 1975.
- **Phan Trọng Chinh**, commander of the 25th Division.
- **Trần Văn Minh**, Ambassador of the Republic of Vietnam to Tunis, Tunisia, 1969–75.
- **Trần Văn Hai**, Last Commander of 7th Division 1974–75, one of the five generals who committed suicide on April 30, 1975.

The following eight ARVN generals were the last ARVN officers released from communist re-education camps after 17 years of imprisonment each. It occurred in two phases:

- Phase 1 (Feb 1992): BG Phạm Ngọc Sáng, Phạm Duy Tất, Mạch Văn Trường.
- Phase 2 (Apr 1992): Gen. Trần Bá Di, Lê Minh Đảo, Đỗ Kế Giai and BG Trần Quang Khôi and Lê Văn Thân.

In conclusion, throughout a very complex military and political history, the ARVN had grown from a few regiments within the French Expeditionary Army to a separate army of more than a million men thanks to the assistance of the United States. However, the quality of its training was marginal at best; it was equipped with World War II vintage armament until 1968; the military institutes got built only in 1968. The ARVN was pushed aside during the critical years of 1964 to 1968. Despite these drawbacks, the ARVN fought well and when Vietnamization began, one could see that the RVNAF was lacking in armored troops, helicopters and airplanes, a strong artillery force, and a well-trained leadership. Had Vietnamization started in the early 1960s, coupled with the direct tutelage of the American forces, it was clear that Allied forces would have won the war easily by 1968.

2

1963

The Ấp Bắc Battle

Ấp Bắc was a battle among the hundreds of battles, large and small waged between the Việt Cộng insurgents (VC) and the South Vietnamese forces in the 1960s. Its impact on the overall Vietnam War was minimal at most, although it was a tactical failure from the U.S. and South Vietnamese, a failure of coordination between these two forces and the various units involved in the battle. It was the first combined air cavalry–infantry attack mounted by the Armed Forces of the Republic of Vietnam (ARVN), the first battalion-size assault conducted by helicopters, and one of the few combined battles using ARVN forces and militiamen waged in Vietnam. As a result, errors and missed opportunities were unfortunately bound to happen. It is therefore necessary to revisit the battle of Ấp Bắc to have an idea of what had happened that day of 2 January 1963.

The Battle of Ấp Bắc

In late December 1962, U.S. intelligence picked up VC radio signals of a transmitter located in the hamlet of Tân Thới in Định Tường Province, home of the 7th ARVN Division. Tân Thới was located about 1½ kilometers northwest of Ấp Bắc (or the hamlet of Bắc), a small, remote, sparsely inhabited hamlet in an area crisscrossed by flooded rice paddies, deep mud-filled canals and irrigation ditches. Ấp Bắc, 60 kilometers southwest of Saigon, sat close to the Ba Bèo communist controlled area.

A small contingent of 120 VC was thought to protect the transmitter. Details about the surrounding terrain, which turned out to be a nightmare for attackers, were not adequately obtained prior to the attack. To reach Ấp Bắc from the southwest, the 7th Mechanized Company had to cross three canals: Tân Hợi, Nhỏ and Lạn Canals, the latter the worst of the three. A battle plan designed to deal with a much weaker enemy than actually existed was rapidly drawn based on these incomplete information.

Unbeknownst to the U.S. and South Vietnamese forces, the enemy committed both the Mỹ Tho main force 514th Battalion and the COSVN[1] main force 261st Battalion to the battle, in addition to local guerrillas and militia members. Enemy forces had been beefed up to more than 350 combatants while the transmitter had been moved away to another location. Three companies of VC regulars were equipped with medium machine guns and 60 mm mortars.[2] Although they relied on captured arms, an increasing number of firearms came by sea. Disguised fish trawlers from the North delivered 112 tons of arms and ammunitions in 1962, and this would rise to 4,289 tons in 1963–64.[3] The insurgents were definitely gearing up for a big fight and had built strategically placed bunkers and foxholes. Both banks of the Trung Lương (Eel) Canal, which were covered with tall trees and heavy vegetation favored the defense.[4] All these factors and the way the VC fought suggested that they had the intention to lure government forces into a battle in which they held tremendous advantages.[5]

On 29 December, the 7th ARVN division was assigned to destroy the transmitter. The D-date for the operation, code named "Đức Thắng 1" (Victory 1), was scheduled for either January 1 or 2 with the expectation that a victory would be a sweet present for President Diệm, whose birthday fell on January 3. Since it was senseless to schedule troop movements at 0400 hours on January 1, or just four hours after the New Year celebration, the D-date was moved to 0630 on January 2.

The VC in Ấp Tân Thới and Ấp Bắc were well aware of ARVN preparations as they witnessed the arrival of fifty truckloads of ammunition in Mỹ Tho. With additional information provided by Phạm Xuân Ẩn, a well-connected journalist and undercover VC agent in Saigon, the VC knew of the attack plan and positioned themselves along the tree-lined creek on the western side of Ấp Tân Thới and Ấp Bắc where the brunt of the ARVN attack would be carried out.[6]

The ARVN preparations for the attack began at 0400 hours on January 2, 1963, as trucks and boat engines were heard around the usually quiet hamlets of Tân Thới and Bắc, forcing the VC to take their positions and the population to escape in the nearby swamps.

The plan called for a simultaneous attack by a battalion of the 7th ARVN division from the North and by two Civil Guard battalions[7] from the South. This would be combined with a cavalry attack from the southwest. The 4th Troop/2nd APC Regiment, formerly the 7th Mechanized Company (M-113), had been temporarily placed under the control of the Định Tường sector headquarters. Since its formation in April 1962, the company had achieved many victories over the communists in the Mekong Delta. The last one was on 25 September 1962 when nine of the 7th Mechanized Company's M113s killed 150 VC and captured 38 prisoners in the Kiến Phong Province.[8]

Thirty U.S. CH-21 Shawnee helicopters, or "Flying Bananas" due to their curved shape, were supposed to ferry the 1st Battalion/ARVN 11th Infantry Regiment to the northern end of Tân Thới by 0700 hours, although only 10 helicopters showed up because the rest had been diverted to another battlefield in the Tây Ninh Province the same day.[9] Troops were therefore delivered piecemeal forcing this unit to hold its attack past the scheduled time. The fog, which was dense that morning, caused an additional two-hour delay in troop delivery with the last unit arriving close to 1000 hours. Five UH-1 helicopter gunships, which provided protection for the CH-21 helicopters, were under order not to fire first unless fired upon.

Due to the delayed northern attack, the two Civil Guard (CG) battalions under the command of Định Tường provincial chief Major Lâm Quang Thơ moved into positions by 0635 hours, slogged through flooded rice paddies in two parallel columns and attacked the enemy by themselves from the South. Artillery support was not effective because the lush vegetation prevented the precise location of enemy positions. Vietcong forces ambushed the first battalion (Task Force A) when the Civil

Guardsmen arrived within 100 feet of their positions killing the company commander and wounding the Task Force commander. For the next two hours, two attacks that were launched against VC lines were thrown back with high casualties. The attack bogged down as Thơ failed to send the second Task Force to support the first one. He called for reinforcements from the 7th Infantry division. One of his lieutenants had asked Thơ's permission to attack the eastern side of the battlefield, but was turned down on several occasions throughout the day.

North of Tân Thới, the 11th Regiment infantrymen did not fare better. For the next five hours following the landing of the first unit, three assaults had been launched against the defensive line without success. Colonel Bùi Đình Đạm, the brand new 7th ARVN Infantry commander decided to insert additional troops either to the western or eastern sides of Ấp Bắc. He asked his U.S. adviser, Lieutenant Colonel J.P. Vann, who was circling over the battlefield, to look for a possible landing zone. The dense vegetation along the tree line prevented Vann from detecting the well camouflaged enemy soldiers, causing him to make a fatal error in judgment that led to a cascade of unfortunate results.

As Col. Vann was making low passes over the southwestern battlefield area on his L-19 observation aircraft, the VC decided to hold their fire and let him fly over the area without any problem. Thinking the area was safe, Vann claimed he told the command pilot of the ten CH-21 helicopters to drop the reserve companies within 300 meters of the Ấp Bắc western tree lines in order to minimize the effectiveness of the VC .30 caliber machine guns.[10] As command relationships between the various U.S. units were not well established during that period, American crews tended to disregard the advisor's suggestions, especially those of Vann, who was perceived as domineering. U.S. pilots apparently landed their helicopters within 200 meters west of Ấp Bắc where they were hit by VC machine guns and small arm fire.[11]

After dropping its load of soldiers, one CH-21 was too severely damaged to get off the ground. The infantry aboard the helicopter escaped without injury. A second CH-21 came to the rescue, but was immobilized as it touched the muddy ground. One of the Hueys returned to pick up the two grounded crews when its rotor was hit by enemy gunfire. The aircraft flipped over and crashed. A third CH-21 sustained heavy damage and was forced to land on the rice fields a short distance from the previous two. Many exposed ARVN soldiers became "shooting ducks" for the VC.[12] Because of poor coordination in the ARVN and U.S. chains of command and inability for commanders to grasp the rapid succession of events on the battlefield, they became confused, concerned, and then overly excited about the situation.

Witnessing the first two helicopters being shot down, J.P. Vann immediately called Captain James Scanlon, adviser to the 7th Mechanized Company/2nd Armored Cavalry Regiment, to ask him to move the M-113s to Ấp Bắc right away in order to rescue the trapped South Vietnamese, the Americans and the helicopters. The company was at that time about two kilometers west of the hamlet and had not crossed the Lạn Canal yet. Scanlon relayed the message to Captain Lý Tòng Bá (he became a general in the 1970s), the commander of the company, one of the most aggressive ARVN officers; Bá retorted that he would not take orders from the Americans. Scanlon continued to badger Bá to move forward and finally handed him the radio transceiver for a direct conversation with Vann: "Bá! If you do not get your vehicles across the canal, I will tell Four-Star General Lê Văn Tỵ to throw you in jail."

Even though he was angry, Bá wondered how Vann could make such a statement about the 7th Company, which no one had ever criticized before. He told Vann, "Lieutenant Colonel Vann! I wish you would land here so that you could see with your own eyes the difficult situation we face and the things I and my men are doing. If not, and if for some reason I am sent to prison, that will be my honor as a soldier."[13]

This was how Captain Bá later described the situation,

> This terrible stream had no bank. It was like a bone in the throat that my M-113 "iron buffaloes" just could not swallow.... I suggested to the Advisory Team and to the Operation Headquarters that they should order the nearest friendly unit to march on foot to the helicopter crash site ... we could not get a vehicle across because the canal was simply a bottomless pool of mud. Because they did not understand this particular factor, the American advisors misunderstood my actions. They thought I was irresponsible, that I did not want to fight....[14]

While the exchange of words was going on, artillery pummeled VC defensive lines, although it was again ineffective in the presence of dense vegetation. Vann flying at low altitude in his reconnaissance plane directed the strikes. For such a daring feat, he later received the Distinguished Flying Cross.[15] Out of fear of being blamed for the battlefield incidents, Vann shifted the blame to the 7th Mechanized Company by accusing it of having moved too slowly. As for Captain Scanlon, the adviser assigned to the M-113 company, according to Bá, he did not understand the situation and did not report to Vann the difficult terrain encountered by the company. When the latter began engaging the enemy and three crewmen of the command vehicle became wounded, Scanlon threw open the rear doors of the command vehicle, ran away to escape and did not return to the company until the next morning, 3 January 1963.[16]

The South Vietnamese M-113s had no problem crossing streams and rivers in the past, but the 10-ton M-113 had difficulty crossing the Ba Kỳ Canal (Lạn Canal for the locals) with its bottomless muddy flow. Crews and infantry had to cut brush and trees to fill the canal until it was shallow enough for the M-113s to cross.[17] Attempts to obtain proper authorization to advance caused further delay. Because of a lack of uniform command, Bá had to clear orders with his immediate supervisor, Major Thơ and then the 7th Infantry division commander, Colonel Đạm.

A fourth CH-21 attempted to rescue the downed helicopter crews, although it too was hit by VC ground fire, forcing it to land in the mud. Overall, five U.S. helicopters were downed or destroyed over a short period in this one-day battle.

By 1330 hours, Bá's M-113s had crossed the Lạn Canal and headed toward the enemy's defensive line in a single file as the Americans had taught the Vietnamese. The many impressive victories of the M-113s in the past had sowed fear into the hearts of the VC, who called them the "green dragons." The VC did not plan to face them that day either; however, they had the choice of fighting back by holding on to their positions or retreating in broad daylight through muddy and open fields, which meant certain death. Having neutralized the northern and southern attacks, VC Colonel Hải Hoàng decided to put up a fight and concentrate his troops on the incoming green dragons. The South Vietnamese gun crews who were exposed from the waist up in their gun turrets became easy targets for snipers; at that time, the metallic shields that would protect the gunners had not been installed yet. This was a major defect in the design of the American vehicles, which would be corrected only later.

Overall 14 expert Vietnamese crewmen were killed by enemy fire by the end of the day.[18]

Bá in the meantime was knocked unconscious by the gun handlebar for at least fifteen minutes inside his carrier. When he recovered from his concussion, his unit continued to launch an attack on the holed up VC who in turn tossed grenades at the carriers. An M-113 equipped with a flamethrower was sent to within 100 meters of the VC formation. When the device was fired, the flame died at only 30 meters because the crew had mixed an incorrect amount of jelly agent with the gasoline.[19] The intense fighting continued until Bá's M-113s conquered the target, Ấp Bắc at 1630 hours.[20]

Vann then flew to Tân Hiệp to ask General Cao—who at that time decided to take over the command of the operation—to deploy an airborne battalion on the eastern side of Ấp Bắc to trap the VC inside the hamlet. Cao, however, decided to drop his airborne troops on the western side of Ấp Bắc behind the M-113 formation. He argued that he had lost confidence in the abrasive Vann because the latter had made many mistakes, berated his counterparts in front of others, and placed the lives of many South Vietnamese in danger to save a handful of Americans.[21]

Three hundred paratroopers, the elite of the ARVN, scheduled to be dropped at 1600 hours, arrived at the scene only at 1800 hours. To avoid ground fire, the C-123 pilots changed course, and without correction from either the jumpmaster or the lead pilot, the jumping was initiated, causing the paratroopers to land right in front of the entrenched VC who picked them off easily. Some paratroopers got stuck in trees while others landed in the open rice paddies where they became targets for the VC. Despite adversity, the airborne battalion continued their fight until sundown. By the end of the day, 19 had died in action and 33 were wounded.

By 2200 hours, the VC began their escape, taking with them the dead and wounded and heading east toward the Plain of Reeds, which was left unguarded. Their escape was facilitated by darkness as Cao refused to approve the use of flares fearing it could expose the airborne battalion's night defensive positions.[22] Eighty ARVN soldiers were reported killed and 109 wounded. The Americans reported three dead and six wounded. An estimated 100 VC had been killed.

Discussion

1. On 3 January—one day after the battle ended—a team of journalists, including Sheehan, and Halberstam tipped by Phạm Xuân Ẩn, took a cab to Ấp Bắc and toured the hamlet with the American advisors who were still angry at the ARVN commanders for missing an opportunity to score a victory. Vann, who had made major decisions during the battle, gave a distorted version of the events to cover his shortcomings. He blasted the South Vietnamese: "It was a miserable damn performance, just like it always is. These people don't listen. They make the same mistake over and over again in the same way."[23]

He added that the ARVN's inaction had its roots in the defective Diệm government. Halberstam, based on these comments, wrote in the *New York Times*, "The advisers feel that there is too much political interference in the Vietnamese army and that promotion too often depends on political loyalty rather than military ability."[24]

The journalists went on to criticize U.S. policies in Southeast Asia and what they called the "dictatorial" and "erroneous" policies of President Ngô Đình Diệm.[25]

Vann, however, did not mention the following: (1) based on previous similar encounters, the American advisers had expected that the VC would flee upon seeing the M-113s and would not offer stiff resistance; (2) the Americans had landed the ARVN company too close to the VC defensive line based on Vann's faulty assessments; (3) Vann had chosen a most inauspicious area (flooded paddy) on the western aspect of the battlefield to launch an assault on the VC; (4) defective designs led to the death of M-113 machine gunners and stalled the attack; (5) the communists were well prepared and had enormous defensive advantages; and (6) the Vietnamese cavalry had been following procedures learned from the Americans when it attacked Ấp Bắc in small units. Besides, there was no communication and coordination between the different units engaged in the battle; intelligence about enemy units was lacking if not inaccurate; and battle plans were drawn on the rush and did not reflect the geographic difficulties of the terrain and the potential changes in intelligence reports.

Worse, in his after-action report Vann blamed an American pilot for landing too close to the enemy line, causing the helicopter to be shot down. He then told the above reporters a different story: the loss of the helicopters was "virtually inevitable" because the enemy was well-armed, well-trained and was everywhere. A few days later, he told Richard Tregaskis that he himself had made the decision to put the helicopters close to the tree line, the most costly mistake anyone made during the battle.[26]

Vann, although a competent military commander, was also described as abrasive, arrogant, stubborn, and emotional. His tendency toward emotional outbursts and demanding style may have soured his relationship not only with some ARVN officers, but also with U.S. pilots. Vann was a "combination of impatience, arrogance, and boundless courage."[27] Captain Bá later remarked,

> John P. Vann was too enthusiastic and too concerned about the fate of the U.S. personnel and the number of helicopters lost, so he lost his cool and slandered both the Army of South Vietnam and me personally because I was involved in this battle. On several subsequent occasions when he saw me, in Binh Duong Province in 1968 and in II Corps in 1972, Vann apologized to me and asked me to forgive him. That is the truth.[28]

General Huỳnh Văn Cao, commander of the IV Corps, in his autobiography argued that the operation had failed because the 7th Infantry Division's operation plan did not suit the muddy terrain and did not focus its primary effort on the objective.[29]

General Paul D. Harkins, first commander of the Military Assistance Command, Vietnam (MACV), considered the operation a success based on World War II's U.S. military doctrine because the hamlets had been captured by the ARVN. Harkins, an imposing figure, was not considered in the Army to be "an intellectual giant."[30] A purely conventional warrior who had fought under Patton in World War II, he was brought up in the traditional army "can do" spirit of professional optimism, even at the expense of reality.[31] He believed in U.S. firepower and failed to switch his World War II mentality to adapt himself and his staff to an unconventional war, despite Sir Robert Thompson's advice to the contrary. Thompson, a British expert in counterinsurgency in Malaya had suggested that firepower and military solutions would be counterproductive to political problems.[32]

Harkins' optimism by not trying to solve the shortcomings of the ARVN and Civil Guardsmen (CG) troops/system ultimately affected the performance of the South Vietnamese military and the American advisers attached to them.[33] It also led to led to misconceptions in Washington and later policy failure. "Misled by the unsubstantiated assertions of progress on the military front made by Harkins, McNamara and Taylor upon their return to Washington gave a monumental misreading of the Vietnamese situation to the National Security Council on 2 October 1963."[34]

In early 1963 and especially in this battle, the chain of command was not well established, leaving room for many people to jump in and make last minute decisions that adversely affected the outcome of the battle. Major Thơ who commanded the CG and the 2nd Armored Regiment was not under the command authority of Colonel Đạm. As a province chief, he reported directly to the Minister of Defense, a civilian while Colonel Đạm reported to the ARVN Joint General Chief of Staff.

Without a clear chain of command, coordination between the various units, Vietnamese and American was obviously lacking. Lieutenant Colonel Vann thought he was the commander-in-chief of the battlefield while in fact he was only the adviser of the 7th ARVN division. As an adviser, according to a memorandum issued by General Lê Văn Ty, Vann did not have any command or supervisory capacity.[35] Even U.S. pilots would not listen to him because of his abrasive character; besides, this was the first large helicopter assault in the Vietnam War.[36] And of course, these same pilots would not listen to Vietnamese commanders. Captain Lý Tòng Bá who worked under Major Thơ was correct not to obey Vann's orders.

Officials who had command authority included: General Huỳnh Văn Cao, the IV Corps commander; Colonel Daniel Porter, the Corps adviser; Colonel Bùi Đình Đạm, the commander of the 7th Infantry Division, whose units were on the field; Lieutenant Colonel Vann, the division adviser; Major Lâm Quang Thơ who was Định Tường Province chief and commander of the CG forces and the 2nd Armored Regiment.

When General Cao was promoted from commander of the 7th ARVN division to IV Corps commander, he suggested that his Chief of Staff, Colonel Đạm, replace him. Although a good staff officer, Đạm held some reservation about his own ability to command.[37] Halberstam then wrote that one contemporary characterized Đạm as "a nice little man and good staff officer, but [he] did not want responsibility.... [He was] terrified of battle, helicopters, and Cao."[38] No other party had stepped up to concur with that statement. Sheehan then speculated that Đạm was promoted as division commander because of political loyalty and he would not present any threat to Cao.[39] From these innuendos and unconfirmed statements, Sheehan and Halberstam built a case that there was too much political interference in the army and that promotion was based on loyalty rather than ability.[40] To extrapolate what happened at the 7th Infantry division to the whole ARVN was a gross overgeneralization of the facts during this state building period.

President Diệm—who had the unenviable task of building a state in South Vietnam and an army, the ARVN, at the same time from scratch during a time of war—obviously had a big interest in the ARVN 7th Infantry Division, which headquartered in Mỹ Tho, IV Corps, protected the Mekong Delta. Diệm depended on the ARVN for his survival just as the ARVN depended on the government of Vietnam for its existence. It's worth noting that Saigon was berated for relying on a coterie of loyal officers while nothing was said about Hồ, who similarly relied on a group of loyal communists for his survival in the North. Until now, more than 55 years after the end of the war, those who are not members of the Communist Party are excluded from power and official functions, relegated to the fringes, or simply land in jails.

Being close to Saigon (40 miles southwest of Saigon), the 7th division staff thus received close scrutiny from Diệm who needed their support, especially after the 1960 military coup. In early 1962, division commander Colonel Huỳnh Văn Cao had good success in pacifying the area under his control. However, Diệm, a conservative and hands-on man, did not want the army to sustain high casualties. When a VC attack on an ARVN convoy caused some casualties, Cao was called back to Saigon and reprimanded by Diệm. From that time onward, Cao became less productive as a military fighter.[41]

In 1962, Diệm decided to split up the III Corps into two with the former III Corps reduced to covering northeast Saigon and the IV Corps protecting the west and southwest of South Vietnam. Cao who became general and commander of the newly formed IV Corps promoted his Chief of Staff, Colonel Bùi Đình Đạm to commander of the 7th ARVN division.

The U.S. since 1954 had decided to help Vietnam build an army. However, building an army does not simply mean equipping it, but "build[ing] or chang[ing] the society from which it comes in order to meet the demands of fielding a modern military."[42] It means taking peasants, villagers out of their ancestral homes, and plugging them into the military so that their allegiance to their families and villages could be switched to the state. The role of building the army was left to Diệm, who was too busy building the state to worry about building an army at the same time. But Diệm who was neither a military person nor had any military experience, did not have the service of a good and experienced general to lead his army and transform the mentality of the military. The failure of the Diệm's state building ultimately could be traced to the lack of an experienced and strong Army Chief of Staff who was willing and committed to mold the ARVN into a modern army.

What was a small regimental-sized battle among the many battles that were waged yearly in South Vietnam became a major event for the leftist U.S. press, which used it to criticize the U.S. and South Vietnamese governments. It claimed the ARVN was incompetent and not strong enough to stand up against the North Vietnamese Army. It completely ignored the many battles that the 7th Mechanized Company had won against the communists, including the one in September 1962. It failed to report the victory Captain Bá won against the VC a few months later at Ấp Bắc II.

In sum, the battle of Ấp Bắc's overall importance is mixed. Some advisors, the press and the VC called the battle a significant event. General Harkins, Admiral Felt, and Ambassador Nolting, on the other hand thought it was just an ordinary battle.[43] It only became important because Vann and the leftist press felt it that way.

Moyar summarized it best when he wrote,

> The South Vietnamese did not perform well at Ấp Bắc, but neither did they display gross ineptitude or cowardice.... Vann committed the most grievous error of the battle by landing the reserve company too close to the western edge of the Việt Cộng's defensive positions.... Vann succeeded in misleading the American press corps, and hence the world by exaggerating the faults of the South Vietnamese and hiding his own.[44]

3

1964

The Bình Giã Battle

The year 1964 marked a turning point of the war in Vietnam. Following the murder of President Diệm, the generals fought against each other for the control of the military-dominated government. For much of the year, General Nguyễn Khánh spent his efforts in consolidating his political power instead of fighting the insurgents.[1] The fragility of the government was reflected on the battlefield where the military suffered setbacks against the National Liberation Front (NLF). The newly-created VC 9th Division by the end of 1964, launched its first attack against the ARVN at the battle of Bình Giã.

Prelude

In mid–1964, Major Nguyễn Văn Nho was appointed commander of the 4th Marine Battalion and by December, the battalion was transferred to Di An, Biên Hòa Province, to serve as the III Corps rapid deployment force. There, it was ordered to move to the hamlet of Bình Giã in Phước Tuy Province to conduct a counterattack against the VC 272nd Regiment, which had ambushed a South Vietnamese armored group at Bình Ba on the Interprovincial Route 15 linking Phước Tuy and Long Khánh a day earlier. The 4th Marine Battalion was ordered to clear the road up the district headquarters.

The Marine battalion was airlifted early in the morning to a landing zone close to Bình Ba hamlet. Because of logistical problems, only one company could be lifted at a time. It was dusk when the whole battalion marched toward Bình Ba. As it crossed the Bình Giã hamlet, it was warmly greeted by villagers. It continued toward Route 15 before deploying into defensive position for the night. In the morning, it located the ambush area but found no trace of VC. It gathered the bodies of dead soldiers for army trucks to pick them up, then continued its sweep toward Long Thành before finally being driven back to their Di An camp.

Bình Giã Battle (28 December 1964–1 January 1965)

In the early hours of 28 December 1964, the VC 271st Regiment and the 445th Company attacked the Bình Giã strategic hamlet located in Phước Tuy Province (later known as Bà Rịa-Vũng Tàu Province) in the III Corps. They easily overwhelmed the local Popular Force militiamen who sent a bicycle messenger to the Bà Rịa District to ask for help. Bình Giã was a strong anti-communist hamlet composed of Catholic refugees from Thanh Hóa and Nghệ Tĩnh Provinces of North Vietnam who fled South in 1954. The 400 by 1,000 meter hamlet sat astride a gravel road that linked the Bình Ba hamlet and the Quảng Giao Rubber Plantation. The VC regimental commander's troops set up a network of defensive fortifications around the hamlet, with trenches and bunkers protected by landmines and barbed wire.

On 29 December, the Bà Rịa District chief sent elements of the ARVN 33rd and 30th Ranger Battalions to retake Bình Giã. Once the soldiers arrived at the landing zone, they were overwhelmed by the Việt Cộng in a deadly ambush. They initially failed to penetrate the VC defensive lines despite attacking from different directions. The Rangers retreated back to the hamlet with the help of the Bình Giã local civilians who retrieved weapons and ammunition from the dead Rangers and hid wounded government soldiers from VC. The 30th Ranger battalion commander and his American advisor were severely wounded during the attack.[2]

In the morning of 30 December, the 4th South Vietnamese Marine Battalion under III Corps order, moved to Biên Hòa Air Base to be airlifted into the battlefield. Again due to logistical problems, only one company could be airlifted each time. When the 4th Marine battalion was able to link up with the 30th, 33rd and 38th Ranger battalions, the VC had withdrawn to the northeast.

In the evening, the VC returned to Bình Giã and attacked the southeastern perimeter of the hamlet. The villagers sounded the alarm by pounding on drums and gongs. ARVN soldiers repelled the attackers with the help of U.S. Army helicopter gunships flown out of Vũng Tàu Airbase.

A helicopter from the U.S. 68th Assault Helicopter Company while pursuing the VC was shot down in the Quảng Giao rubber plantation about four kilometers away from Bình Giã, killing all four crew members. The 4th Marine battalion was asked to find and retrieve the bodies of the crewmen. An hour after they left Bình Giã, the commander of the 2/4th Marine battalion reported that they had located the wreckage and recovered the bodies of the crewmen.

Unknown to the Marines, the VC 271st Regiment had assembled in the Quảng Giao Plantation. They suddenly attacked the Marine Company, which was forced to pull back and fight its way out with bayonets fixed. The company did not receive artillery support because they were out of firing range of the 105 mm artillery guns based in Phước Tuy and Bà Rịa. The entire 4th Marine Battalion was sent out to confront the enemy. On arrival, they were attacked by enemy fire followed by human wave attacks. They, however, escaped with the support of U.S. aircraft and helicopters whose rocket attacks blunted the enemy attack.

In the morning of 31 December, the 4th Marine Battalion returned to the crash site, located the graves of the Americans and dug up their corpses. At 1500, a single U.S. helicopter arrived at the battlefield to pick up the bodies of the four crewmen, leaving behind the South Vietnamese casualties who had to wait for another helicopter. By 1600, not seeing any helicopter coming back, Major Nguyễn Văn Nho ordered the 4th Marine Battalion to carry their casualties back to the village instead of waiting for an airlift.

As the 4th Marine Battalion walked back to the hamlet, they were attacked by three VC battalions with artillery support. The battalion's commanding and executive officers were immediately killed but air support was not available. Two Marine companies managed to fight their way out of the ambush and back to Bình Giã, but the third was overrun and almost completely wiped out. The fourth company desperately held out on a hilltop against VC artillery barrages and large infantry charges, before slipping out through the enemy positions at dawn. The 4th Marine Battalion of 426 men lost a total of 117 soldiers killed, 71 wounded and 13 missing.

Reinforcements arrived the next morning, but the communist force—estimated at 1,500—had already withdrawn from the battlefield. Peter Kalischer of CBS reported that the village priest had told him of seeing 11 Chinese and one European with the enemy force. One high-ranking officer, possibly a general, from the enemy side was killed with his staff when a bomb hit a regimental headquarters.[3]

Discussion

This was the type of battles that the ARVN units would face more and more in their encounters with the enemy. By 1964 through the Bình Gĩa Battle, the VC were found to be more sophisticated than usual. Besides local insurgents, there were also regular PAVN (People's Army of North Vietnam) soldiers. The enemy was able to strike their opponents with a large number of troops well equipped with new military supplies from North Vietnam. They had artillery and were able to coordinate troop positions and to fight against government troops equipped with armor, artillery, and helicopters. They had moved a long way from the insurgency type of war.

From the South Vietnamese side, the ARVN went into the battle without even knowing the size of enemy troops or their location. Without these crucial bits of information, they just sent in reinforcements piecemeal: first one Ranger battalion, then another battalion, then a third one. After realizing they were dealing with more than a VC Regiment—it turned out to be a division-size force[4]—they sent in an additional Marine battalion. Although this was not enough, the Marine battalion, which was an elite unit, was able to fight back with the help of U.S. Air Force planes in the beginning. The Marine troops, on the other hand, did not bring their own artillery and heavy guns. Without air and artillery support on their evacuation day, they unnecessarily suffered heavy losses.

The battle of Bình Giã reflected the VC's growing military strength and influence, especially in the Mekong Delta region. It was the first time that the VC launched a large-scale, division-size operation while holding their ground and fighting for four days against government troops equipped with armor, artillery and helicopters and aided by U.S. air support. The VC had demonstrated that, when well-supplied with armaments from North Vietnam (AK-47 assault rifle and rocket propelled grenade [RPG] launchers),[5] they had the ability to fight and inflict damage even on the best ARVN units. The latter were still equipped with World War II vintage weapons.

New army schools were established only in 1967, three years later. The National Defense College was established in August 1967 to train top military officers and government civilians for functions involving security. The Vietnamese National Military Academy was converted from a two-year to a four-year institution in 1967 to train regular Army officers.⁶ Besides these schools, the ARVN was still missing highly qualified supervisors and both highly qualified and combat experienced instructors.

The VC had about 100 soldiers officially confirmed killed. In recognition of the 271st Regiment's performance during the Bình Giã campaign, the VC High Command after the war bestowed the title "Bình Giã Regiment" on the unit to honor their achievement. Following the Bình Giã campaign, the Việt Cộng went on to occupy Hoài Đức District and the strategic hamlets of Đất Đỏ, Long Thành and Nhơn Trạch along the inter-provincial Roads No. 2 and 15. They also expanded the Hát Dịch base area, which was located in Bà Rịa and Bình Thuận Provinces, to protect the important sea transportation routes they used to supply Việt Cộng units around the regions of the Mekong River.

With the ARVN leadership tied up in Saigon, the war against the communists was somewhat neglected. This was reflected by the increasing number of battle losses, casualties, and towns and villages captured. The South Vietnamese and their American allies lost a total of about 201 personnel killed in action, 192 wounded and 68 missing. In just four days of fighting, two of South Vietnam's elite Ranger companies were destroyed and several others suffered heavy losses, while the 4th Marine Battalion was rendered ineffective as a fighting force. At that stage of the war, Bình Giã was the worst defeat experienced by the South Vietnamese. Despite their losses, the South Vietnamese Army considered the battle as their victory and erected a monument at the site of the battle to acknowledge the sacrifices of the soldiers who had fallen to retake Bình Giã.

On 30 January 1964, General Nguyễn Khánh mounted a coup against the military junta that ran the country after the overthrow of President Diệm. Although he remained a central figure in the South Vietnamese government, he was unable to control the rest of the junta. Throughout 1964, there was continued infighting and incessant reshuffling of positions in the armed forces as well as in the general administration. There was no consistency in policy at the top and considerable confusion at lower levels of the armed forces and in the provincial administration.⁷

Although there were no major battles in the highlands during the week of 3–10 October 1964, more than 700 incidents were reported per week for the fourth consecutive week causing ARVN forces to feel intense pressure.⁸ Starting in September 1964, Hanoi sent whole PAVN regiments down the HCM trail. The first to make the journey was the 320th (aka 32nd) Regiment.⁹ The "...infiltration route started began in Na Nam Province, North Vietnam, crossed the North Vietnam-Laos border, continued through Laos and terminated in Kontum Province. By the end of January 1965, all elements of the regiment had completed infiltration."

4

1965

Sông Bé, Đồng Xoài, Bà Giã, Thuận Man, Plei Me

In 1965, the communists launched a series of attacks across the country that tested the ARVN mettle. Five battles were worth mentioning during this period, among them the Sông Bé, Đồng Xoài battles in III Corps, the Bà Giã battle in I Corps, and the Thuận Man and Plei Me battles in the II Corps. Although these were small to medium-sized battles—battalion to regiment sized—one could see the overall change in communist strategy and tactics. They used new strategies designed to neutralize the advantages of U.S. and ARVN's forces: air cavalry and accurate artillery bombing (grab them by the belt techniques[1]) while improving their ambush tactics.

During that period, they deftly used nature for cover. In Sông Bé and Đồng Xoài, they used the French rubber plantations as a stepping stone for their attacks and sites for ambushes. In Thuận Man and Plei Me, they hid in the mountains under a double canopy forest. To counterattack them, the U.S. and the ARVN had to denude the forests and mountains though heavy bombing only to find out that the enemy had taken off. The communists' aggressiveness, which improved overall as they began receiving better armament (AK-47 and rocket-propelled grenade launchers) by the end of 1964[2] from the Soviets and later the Chinese, was reflected by the multiplicity of attacks against ARVN units in all Corps.

The PAVN troops, which came down regularly through the Hồ Chí Minh Trail, strengthened the backbone of the VC and allowed them to wage bigger battles in many places.

Combat effectiveness of the ARVN, on the other hand, fell after the downfall of the Diệm government and the instability of the civilian government. The latter was caused by the infighting between the various political groups, the junta members, and the Buddhist revolt. This forced the U.S. to inject additional troops into the battlefields. Sông Bé was the "beginning of large unit offensives designed to annihilate enemy's elite main-force manpower."[3]

The Sông Bé Battle (10–15 May 1965)

At 0145 on 10 May, the VC 761st and 763rd Regiments, consisting of 2,500 infantry troops, attacked Sông Bé, the provincial capital of Phước Long in the III Corps 45 miles north of Saigon from multiple directions using mortar barrages first. They were stopped by ARVN forces and a detachment of U.S. Special Forces. Helicopter gunships arrived at 0345 but could not see the ground because of dense fog and clouds. They just attacked the enemy mortar artillery west of town. Then came F-4 Phantom fighter planes that used cluster bombs to silence the machine guns.

Even though the town was well-defended, most of it had fallen to VC control for at least six hours. At noon the ARVN 36th Ranger Battalion bravely attacked into town and drove off the VC in hand-to-hand combat. They were joined a few hours later by the 34th ARVN Rangers and the entire town returned to ARVN control.[4]

The Đồng Xoài Battle (9–13 June 1965)

Before Phước Long Province became the coveted "must have" province, as early as 1965 the communists had aimed to take over any province or town inside South Vietnam from which they could spread their attacks and revolution against the rest of the country. That province turned out to be Phước Long on the western side of South

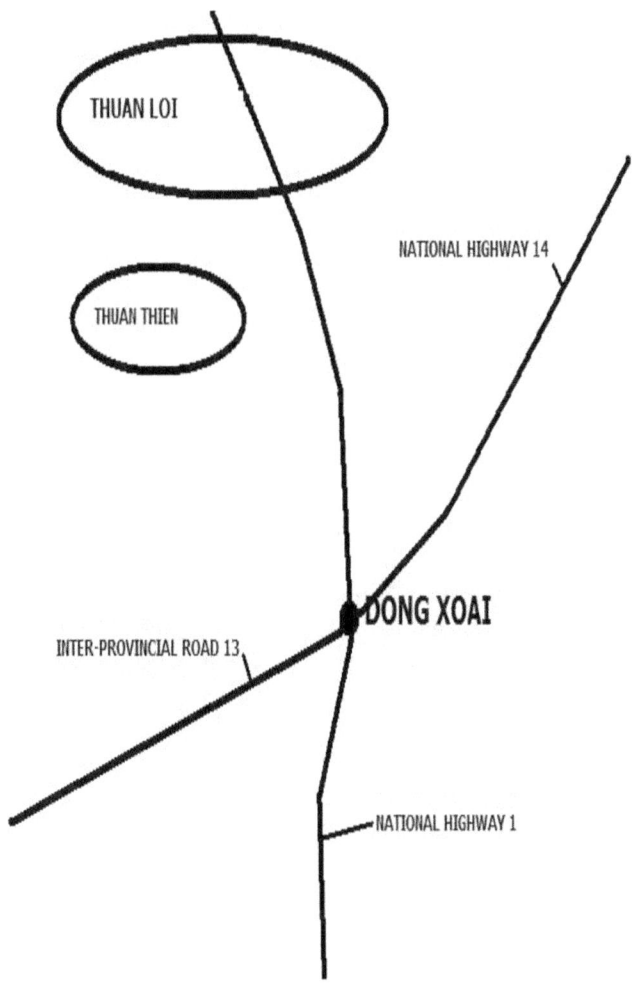

Figure 4-1: Đồng Xoài Battle (Canpark, Wikimedia Commons).

Vietnam close to the Cambodian border. From the end of the Hồ Chí Minh Trail in Cambodia, the VC only needed to cross the Cambodian-Vietnamese border to be inside South Vietnam and about 50 miles from Saigon. The multiple rubber plantations (Thuận Lợi and Thuận Thiên) planted by the Michelin Corporation four miles north of Đồng Xoài provided a safe and ideal hiding ground for the VC forces. In case of retreat, a leap across the border would bring the VC back into the safety of their Cambodian sanctuaries.

The district capital of Phước Long was Đồng Xoài, which sat at the intersection of highways 13, 14, and National Highway 1. The latter bisected the province into two areas in a north-south direction and connected Saigon in the South to Phnom Penh, Cambodia in the North. Highway 13 connected Đồng Xoài with the southwestern provinces of South Vietnam while Highway 14 led to the Central Highlands and II Corps. Minorities in the province included the Cambodians (Khmers), Stieng, and Nùng.

Đồng Xoài was defended by 200 Cambodians of a Civilian Irregular Defense Group (CIDG), 200 local Vietnamese troops (Regular Force/Popular Force: RFPF), six armored cars and two 105 mm howitzers, along with 11 U.S. Special Forces and nine U.S. Seabees. The latter were in town to beef up the construction of defensive fortifications of the camp when the attack occurred.

Battle

On 9 June 1965 at 2245 hours, the VC began their attack by pounding Đồng Xoài with mortar artillery followed by infantry assault led by the VC 272nd Regiment. They suffered heavy casualties while trying to navigate through minefields and barbed wire fences. They then penetrated the Special Forces camp and the district headquarters; these two units were separated by 200 meters of buildings. Despite their numerical superiority, they initially failed to overrun either of these defensive units. They then called in their reserve units and launched new attacks against the district headquarters and the Special Forces camp.

At 0100 hour the following day, they moved their fire support teams closer to the defensive walls of the camp and began collapsing government bunkers and destroying government heavy weapons. At 0200, after using flame throwers to destroy the western side of the Special Forces compound, the VC streamed through the breach and engaged in a brutal hand-to-hand combat with the defenders. At 0230, a VC mortar round scored a direct hit on the compound. The disruption allowed some Americans and Cambodians to retreat to the district headquarters while others ran to the armored car and artillery positions.

At dawn, attack helicopters and jets flew in and strafed areas occupied by VC. One communist report complained of "the savage bombing and strafing attacks" that collapsed bunkers and fortifications and killed "many more of our soldiers."[5] At Biên Hòa Airbase, the flight crews of the 118th Aviation Company were preparing for combat assault at daylight. From Biên Hòa they flew to Phước Vinh, a small town, 18 miles from Đồng Xoài. From Phước Vinh, the first contingent of the ARVN 1st Battalion, 7th Infantry Regiment was airlifted into the battlefield.

Because of the urgency of the situation, there was no time for reconnaissance to find out about the enemy situation. The landing zone was an open field 1.3 miles from

Đồng Xoài and close to Highway 1. The UH-1 helicopters received fire on approach to the LZ, but return suppressive fire was withheld due to the possible presence of friendly troops. Before touchdown, friendly-appearing civilians were waving at the helicopters from the edge of the LZ. As soon as the troops started unloading, the "civilians" jumped into concealed fox holes and got ready to engage the new arrivals. When helicopters became airborne as they were low on fuel, the "civilians" revealed to be VC fired indiscriminately at the incoming troops. It was later learned that the 1st battalion ceased to be a fighting unit twenty minutes after landing into the deadly trap.[6]

When the 118th helicopters loaded with the remaining elements of the 1st battalion, 7th infantry regiment departed from Phước Vinh, two organic armed helicopters conducted a reconnaissance around the airstrip at the Thanh Lợi Plantation. Up until then, the VC had never used a plantation as the staging ground for an ambush. As no evidence of enemy troops was noted, the first helicopter prepared for landing. A herd of cattle suddenly appeared on the landing strip and the lead helicopter decided to land the troops short of the intended area. This move eventually saved a lot of lives. As soon as the skids of the first helicopter hit the ground, the VC exploded a claymore mine planted at the original landing area. Bullets and mortar rounds exploded around the troops. Fire was coming out everywhere from rooftops, windows of houses in the plantation, and from bunkers and foxholes. "Scores of the brave little Vietnamese soldiers were falling in front of the eyes of the helicopter crews as they watched them leap from the aircraft and fall as enemy bullets slammed into their bodies."[7] One helicopter was hit by a mortar round, exploded, and rolled on its side. The entire crew was killed. All the other helicopters took off safely. The 118th Aviation Company commander immediately ordered the remaining elements with troops aboard back to the staging area.

The 118th Aviation Company's flight surgeon located at Phước Vinh requested Air Force C-130 air transports to evacuate over 100 wounded ARVN soldiers when a message came in from the Đồng Xoài Special Force compound. It said, "I am using my last battery for my radio and there is no more ammunition; we are all wounded, some of the more serious wounded are holding grenades with safety pins already pulled. The VC are attacking in human waves. The last wave has been defeated but we are expecting the next wave now."

The enemy had sent in its second regiment to take over the town. The commander of the 118th stood up and said, "I'm going in." Five other officers followed him as well as enlisted crew members. Three helicopters took off for Đồng Xoài to evacuate the wounded in the compound.

But this time, they changed their approach, arrived from the South and landed on the soccer field close to the Special Forces compound. Supported by a swarm of fixed wing aircraft and attack helicopters that created a "wall of bullets, bombs, napalm, and rockets," the three helicopters landed and quickly evacuated nine wounded Americans and eight Vietnamese who were rescued from Đồng Xoài that afternoon. These were the last survivors of Đồng Xoài's original defenders. The group returned to Phước Vinh without any problem. The element of surprise and the courage of the group members had helped make the rescue possible.

In the afternoon of 10 June 1965, the 52nd Ranger Battalion arrived at Phước Vinh waiting to be airlifted to Đồng Xoài. The 118th Aviation Company was given the task of inserting the battalion into battle. The flight route was the same, although the soccer field was chosen as the LZ. The reaction of the VC was mild because they did not expect another landing in town. The Rangers were shot at furiously when they moved from the LZ to the compound and toward the center of town. The VC not only ran out of ammunition, but were also subjected to air strikes. They therefore could not cause major damage to the Rangers who gradually reoccupied the town. By the end of the day, the town was again under the control of ARVN troops.

On 11 June 1965, the 118th Aviation safely airlifted 100 paratroopers of the ARVN 7th Airborne Battalion into the Đồng Xoài soccer field. Moyar, on the other hand, reported that the paratroopers were dropped north of town, proceeded looking for the remnants of the 1st Battalion 7th Infantry, and later engaged with the enemy[8] Wounded ARVN soldiers were brought to the soccer field then mass evacuated to Phước Vinh for medical treatment and triage. At one time, there were more than 200 wounded waiting for treatment at Phước Vinh triage center.

On 12 June, the company again airlifted the 1st Battalion of the ARVN 48th Regiment. These troops were to reinforce the garrison at Đồng Xoài, which by then stood at 1,000 and, were strong enough to secure the town. Except for isolated sniper fire from trapped enemy soldiers, the main body of the enemy had vanished.

On 13 June, the 118th Aviation flew to Xuân Lộc to pick up the ARVN 43rd Regiment. A hundred soldiers were lifted to an LZ about half a mile from the original assault on the first day of battle. From the LZ, the troops moved through the jungle and rubber plantation to look for the troops of the 1st battalion 7th Infantry Regiment who disappeared after landing. None was found and the team returned to Biên Hòa at 2330 hours.

During the five day battle in and around Đồng Xoài, the ARVN incurred 416 KIA, 174 wounded, and 233 missing. Search parties found several hundred VC bodies around the Special Forces compound and the district headquarter compound and another 126 VC bodies inside these two compounds.

During the period when they held the town, the VC had taken every civilian possession they could find—pots, mattresses, rice, livestock, and clothing—and had used flame throwers to burn down part of the town. One American adviser commented, "The Viet Cong flame throwers in Đồng Xoài did more damage than our napalm ever has. We have hit selected targets but we have never burned down half of a town that contained no enemy forces of any kind."[9]

Resignation of the Civilian Government

As the battle of Đồng Xoài raged on 11 June 1965 and military reserves rapidly were depleted, South Vietnamese President Phan Khắc Sửu and Prime Minister Phan Huy Quát, along with the ruling committee of the generals, sat down to deliberate on the fate of the civilian government. After lengthy and heated exchanges, the generals asked Sửu and Quát to stop bickering in order to strengthen the regime's political and military ineffectiveness. Quát rose and said he would resign and agreed to let the generals plan a new government under military leadership.

The helm was given not to General Thi, who was an ally of Buddhist monk Thích Trí Quang, but to Air Marshal Nguyễn Cao Kỳ who became Prime Minister. General Nguyễn Văn Thiệu assumed the leadership of the military ruling committee. This was the first time that the generals were able to break Trí Quang's stranglehold on the government. Ambassador Taylor was happy with the results, although Kỳ, while being a capable military leader, tended more toward flamboyance and womanizing than rigor and substance. Thiệu on the other hand was regarded as a highly talented military leader who possessed the political skills required in perilous Saigon.[10]

The Bà Giã Battle

On 29 May at 0545, the 271st VC Regiment attacked the village of Phước Lộc, south of Bà Giã and overwhelmed the two platoons of RF defending the village. At 0600 the 1st ARVN Battalion was sent to the rescue.

At 0950, the 1st Battalion/51st Regiment walked through Lộc Thọ Village, where they were ambushed by the VC 90th Regiment. After one hour of engagement, the battalion was destroyed with only 65 ARVN soldiers and three Americans returning to government lines.[11] Meanwhile the VC 83rd Battalion joined the battle.

Gen. Nguyễn Chánh Thi, commander of the I Corps, formed a Task Force composed of the 2nd ARVN Battalion, the 3rd ARVN Marines and the 39th ARVN Rangers. The Marines would advance on route 5 to reach Bà Giã; the Rangers would capture Mount Chop Non, and the 2nd Battalion would capture Mount Ma To. Before the counterattack could take shape, the PAVN unleashed a torrent of artillery fire, isolating the three battalions and forcing them to fight alone. Detached and confused, the 2nd Battalion used the M-113s for cover and retreated toward Bà Giã. The two other battalions did not fare as well. Encircled by the enemy, they grouped in a circle making it easier for the enemy 75 mm howitzers to strike. On the fifth day of battle, the enemy retreated into the countryside. Only American air power had saved three ARVN battalions from annihilation.[12]

On 7 June, Westmoreland sent a long telegram to CINCPAC headquarters for relay to Washington outlining the difficulties in Vietnam: "In pressing their campaign, the Việt Cộng are capable of mounting regimental-size operations in all four ARVN corps areas, and at least battalion-sized attack in virtually all provinces.... ARVN forces on the other hand are already experiencing difficulty in coping with this increased VC capability."[13]

The Thuận Man Battle (27 June–2 July 1965)

In June 1965, the PAVN 95A Regiment attacked the district town of Thuận Man close to the provincial town of Chèo Reo, Phú Bổn Province. Being cut off from Chèo Reo, the RF (Regional Force) troops called for help. This was a classical communist "lure and ambush" type of operation, the goal of which was to attract and destroy elite ARVN forces coming to the rescue of local forces in order to demoralize ARVN forces and ultimately cause their collapse.

The II Corps sent its 1st Airborne Task Force commanded by Lieutenant Colonel Kha to the rescue. It had two airborne battalions (the 1st and 5th) along with the 2nd Battalion of the 40th Regiment. At Chèo Reo, the task force proceeded with care as three communist battalions were reported in the area. Highway 7B was a single-lane dirt road with rough hills on either side. Dense vegetation prevented anything to be seen beyond ten yards. The area was an ideal location for an ambush. While the 1st battalion used the road, the 5th battalion covered its left flank while the 2nd battalion the right flank. At dusk, the column settled in defensive position for the night.

The troops moved again at 0740 on 30 June. An hour later, they faced mortars, and fire from recoilless rifle and small arm guns. Facing an obvious ambush, the 2nd battalion disengaged and turned eastward. It soon broke contact with the rest of the battalions and the communist attackers. By 1800 it was back at Chèo Reo, its originating point.

The two remaining airborne battalions fought back hard. They were supported by a Marine artillery battery that was also attacked. The 1st Airborne Battalion commander, however, was able to request air support through an American forward air controller who was accompanying the task force. The enemy was systematically struck with bombs and rockets causing the attack to wither. The two airborne battalions were able to link together by 1430 and with the artillery unit by 1700 hours.

It turned out that elements of the PAVN 95A Regiment, while holding the siege at Thuận Man, also engaged in the ambush. The main unit conducting the ambush was the PAVN 2nd Regiment that had four infantry battalions, an artillery mortar battalion, and a sapper company. Another communist unit, the PAVN 18A (aka 2nd) Regiment was roaming in the vicinity of the area and acted as a reserve unit.

In a rare compliment to the fighting spirit of enemy forces, a communist author wrote about the ARVN Airborne in this campaign, "The enemy troops fought back ferociously and launched many counterattacks…. The battle lasted until nightfall without our being able to finish the enemy off."[14] Although the units of the task force had been reunited and was fighting back, they were low on ammunition and had wounded troops who needed medical care. II Corps sent in helicopters but they failed to land because of antiaircraft fire.

General Vĩnh Lộc, then II Corps commander called the Joint General Staff for help. Acknowledging the strategic importance of the Central Highlands and the presence of the additional PAVN 18A that was located in the vicinity of the engagement, the JGS granted the request. The local Marine Task Force Alpha was immediately flown from Kontum to Chèo Reo while additional reinforcements began arriving from Saigon. In the evening of 2 July, the Marines had linked up with the airborne battalions of the 1st Airborne Task Force without encountering any communist force.

The PAVN 2nd Regiment had ceased any serious attack by nightfall on 30 June. Helicopters were able to take out the wounded and supply ammunition and food. The battle had cost the ARVN 26 KIA, 12 MIA, and 56 wounded. Four Americans were killed and four wounded. U.S. advisers reported 122 communist KIA and three captured. There might have been more than 300 killed by air strikes. The PAVN 2nd Regiment had disappeared and was not heard again in 1965.

The Thuận Man RF troops were allowed to stage a break out since they were still confined in the town. Aircraft began pounding communist forces in the evening of 1 July and the beleaguered garrison escaped at first light on 2 July. The RF troops linked up with the Buon Brieng CIDG troops who were waiting for them. The breakout was successful.

The Plei Me Battle (August–October 1965)

This battle in western Pleiku Province was part of a communist master plan to disrupt ARVN and U.S. forces in Kontum and Pleiku provinces as well as parts of Bình Định and Phú Bổn provinces. The attack on this Special Forces camp in Plei Me was the first stage of this large campaign.

On the communist side, General Chu Huy Mẫn in June 1965 commanded two regiments: 320 (32nd) and 325A in the Central Highlands. By August, he had only the 32nd Regiment left; the 325A had been reassigned to another region. Two more regiments, the 33rd and 66th, were moving down the trail and would be available in September. Each of these PAVN regiments had an authorized strength of 2,200 men with the usual three battalions of 550 men each. There were provincial and regional forces attached to each of them.[15]

Plei Me was a Special Force CIDG camp located about 45 km southwest of Pleiku and 12 km east of the Cambodian border. Nearby is the Chu Pong massif where the PAVN had a base area close to the village of Anta that lay adjacent to Ia Drang Valley. Anta was two km east from the Cambodian border. Plei Me was located 21 km west of Highway 14, the north-south route that bisected the Central Highlands. The looped one-lane dirt road that connected the camp to Highway 14 at two places was called Provincial Route 5. Being isolated in the southwest corner of the Central Highlands, if the camp were attacked, reinforcements would have to come through that dirt road, thus susceptible to ambushes. The Plei Me camp was unique for its triangular shape with 24 bunkers altogether. It had a garrison of 12 U.S. and 14 Vietnamese Special Forces personnel and 415 CIDG soldiers. The camp was already crowded as it housed not only the soldiers but also their wives and children.

The communist well-known "lure and ambush" method would be used again. The 33rd Regiment would attack Plei Me, while the more experienced 32nd Regiment that had been in the highlands since December 1964 would ambush the ARVN forces.

Battle

Although there was some firefight between the PAVN units and the CIDG patrols on the evening of 19 October 1965, the real attack began at 0030 on 20 October from the north and northwest. This was followed by attacks from all directions half an hour later. By 0110 hours, the PAVN were within the defensive wire barriers to the south, east and north but were repulsed. Flares were shot from helicopters around 0215 and air strikes with A-1E Skyraiders began by 0410 at the latest.

Reinforcements were requested by American and Vietnamese Special Forces, each through their own channel. II Corps commander Vĩnh Lộc would later send an armored task force by road to relieve Plei Me. In the meantime, two Vietnamese Airborne Ranger companies (about 150 officers and men) commanded by Major Thụt, along with 15 U.S. Special Forces personnel from Project Delta commanded by Major Charles Beckwith, were sent as reinforcement. They landed at an LZ five kilometers north of Plei Mei at 1030 on 21 October. The group got lost through the dense forest and took 23 hours to make the 5 km to the camp. An Airborne Ranger lieutenant and a civilian newsman were killed and four soldiers were wounded.

Major Beckwith was an exceptionally zealous, tough and determined officer with a fierce temper. In Plei Me, he experienced continuing friction with his predecessor, Captain Harold H. Moore, and eventually had to become "physical" with him.[16] Moore later participated in the LZ XRay Battle, which he depicted in the acclaimed book *We Were Soldiers Once ... and Young*. Harris noted many discrepancies between Beckwith's after-action reports and his memoirs, which were published two decades after the event.[17]

Beckwith decided to send the two Airborne Ranger companies and one CIDG company (not his Project Delta personnel) to clear a hill 400 meters north of the camp in broad daylight between 1300 and 1400 on 22 October. The PAVN soldiers who were ready in bunkers and foxholes offered fierce resistance. The Rangers and CIDG who had problems with a North Vietnamese machine gun tried to silence it. During the attack, they ran past the machine gun without seeing it and got hit in the flank and rear. Although they turned around to deal with it, they were unsuccessful. They were pinned down for several hours before being able to return to the camp at 1840. Thirteen Rangers and CIDG were killed, along with a Vietnamese Special Forces lieutenant and Captain Pusser, U.S. adviser to the Airborne Rangers. Another 26 were wounded.[18]

The following morning at 0900 on 23 October, Beckwith sent one platoon of CIDG and one platoon of Airborne Rangers to try to knock out two machine gun positions. The attack was supported by mortar and machine gun fire from the camp. As the force got into position for the attack, a VC came out of his hole and ran the CIDG-Ranger force out of the area. The force withdrew.

On Monday 25 October at 0930, he sent a commando type squad along with two Americans with flame throwers to attack for the third time the machine gun positions. The flamethrowers reportedly malfunctioned and proved ineffective. The operation met stiff resistance and was forced back into the camp.

This was the last attack Beckwith ordered while at Plei Me. The siege would end later that day following the arrival of the Vietnamese relief task force. The repeated failure of these ill-conceived and unnecessary ventures may well have contributed to Beckwith's ugly mood. In an interview given to TV journalist John Laurence at the end of the siege, Beckwith "strongly implied that Americans had done all the real fighting in defense of Plei Me. The Vietnamese ... were dismissed as cowardly, incompetent or both." He, however, "did not enumerate the casualties they had sustained. Nor did he desist from ordering additional daylight attacks, in the absence of armor and artillery support, on an entrenched, alert, numerically superior, extremely determined enemy."[19]

To suggest that the Airborne Rangers who accompanied Major Beckwith to Plei Me were cowardly or incompetent scarcely holds up. On 23 October, Beckwith became concerned about the body of Captain Pusser, the Airborne Ranger's adviser who was killed the same day at the second sortie. He wanted another sortie on Sunday 24 October to retrieve it and asked for volunteers. Major Thụt responded. "The Vietnamese will get his body for you. We want to do this." The commander of the 1st Airborne Ranger Company, to whom the job was assigned, went out and decided to retrieve all the bodies left behind after the first sortie, not just Pusser's. In his after-action report, Beckwith noted that this complex operation that involved organizing fire support and sending out a reconnaissance party and carrying party, was conducted in "a very professional manner."[20] All the bodies were recovered.

Fifteen of Thụt's 135 to 150 Airborne Rangers were killed and 29 wounded during the siege. This was a 10 or 11 percent fatality rate in three or four days—extraordinarily heavy losses given that there were PAVN assaults during that period. The great majority of these deaths occurred during Beckwith's repeated daylight attacks on a well prepared enemy in carefully concealed, mutually supporting bunkers, machine gun nests, and foxholes—attacks that Beckwith should never have ordered.[21]

U.S. airstrikes around Plei Me continued during that time. In over ten days beginning on 20 October, "in 696 day and night sorties, B-57s, A1-Es, F-100s, and F-8s rained 866,300 pounds of GP (general purpose) bombs, 250,380 pounds of frag bombs, 485,880 pounds of napalm, plus rockets, CBU and cannon fire on VC positions as close as 35 meters from the outpost walls." This was "the largest air-supported combat operation so far using almost 600 strikes." The cost was far from negligible. One B-57 bomber was damaged by ground fire and crashed before landing. Another B-57 shot down later that day. Two A-1E strike aircraft crashed on Friday 22 October. Two helicopters also crashed.

In the meantime, the relief task force put together by General Vĩnh Lộc consisted of the 3rd Armored Cavalry Squadron under Lieutenant Colonel Nguyễn Trọng Luật; Armored Personnel Carrier Troop 2/6 (with 15 M-113s) commanded by Captain Du Ngọc Thanh; Tank Troop 3/5 (with 16 M41 Walker Bulldog tanks) commanded by Captain Nguyễn Minh Lâm; one platoon of 222nd Artillery; a platoon of 201st Engineers; and the 21st Ranger Battalion. The designated Armored Task Force (ATF) was placed under Lieutenant Colonel Luật's command. To the ATF would be added later the 22nd Ranger Battalion.

On 20 October, the ATF was ordered to move from Pleiku to Phú Mỹ, the junction of Highway 14 and Provincial Route 5, and to start patrolling up to 5 km to the South. At 1400 on Saturday 23 October, the ATF proceeded down Provincial Route 5 toward Plei Me while helicopters dropped the 22nd Ranger Battalion to an LZ west of Route 5 but adjacent to Plei Me. The ATF's advance on Route 5 was cautious and slow. The APC and tanks of the main force could not exceed the infantry's walking speed. They were supported on the left by the 1st Battalion 42nd Infantry Regiment and on the right by two companies of the 21st Ranger Battalion. The train (the ATF's logistical element carrying fuel and ammunition) protected by one element of the 21st Ranger Battalion followed about 2 km behind the main attack force.

At 1700 hours, the force halted while a pre-planned airstrike took place. After the airstrike was over, the main force but not the train proceeded forward. At 1750, the main force was attacked by the PAVN's 32nd Regiment's 635th Battalion. There was no panic among the ARVN troops. Tanks and APCs opened up with their machine guns. Soldiers joined in with their weapons. American jets struck with cannon fire. The fight continued for two more hours before the PAVN broke it off.

At approximately the same time, the train was attacked. Thunderous explosions were heard as mortars, rocket fire hit fuel and ammunition trucks. Troops were then attacked by enemy forces. American advisers to the 21st Rangers helped troops form a defensive perimeter around the train's vehicles that would continue to hold after dark. They asked for airstrikes that severely hurt the PAVN 344th Battalion.

The fighting of 23–24 October had been costly for both sides. The ARVN side reported 50 killed, 102 wounded, and 19 missing. Two M8 armored cars, two five-ton ammunition trucks, and two gasoline tankers were totally destroyed. Another M8 armored car, two 105 mm guns, and other logistical vehicles were damaged. The next day, Luật had the main force backing up to link with the train and took time to evacuate the wounded and replace the damaged trucks before proceeding forward late on 25 October and arriving at Plei Me at dusk.

The Vietnamese and the CIDG in the camp cheered the arrival of the ATF. But when Luật walked to the gate, he was confronted by Beckwith, who was in an obvious bad mood. Although Beckwith shook hands with Luật, he told Laurence later that he did it with strong reservations. He was deeply upset that Luật did not arrive days earlier "when he was needed." When Luật wanted to take his staff into the camp, Beckwith point blank refused the suggestion. The refusal to allow a superior officer of the host nation to enter a fortification he had just relieved outraged the normally low key Luật. Swearing furiously in Vietnamese, French, and English, he threatened to shoot Beckwith. Some Americans standing with Beckwith released the safety catches off their weapons. At that time, Luật had the good sense to walk away.[22] In terms of military protocol, Beckwith was in the wrong. Not only was he the junior of the two; he was also in the other officer's country.[23]

The siege of Plei Me officially ended on 25 October. The PAVN 32nd Regiment had begun withdrawing from Plei Me on 24 October. The bulk of the 33rd regiment at 2200 of 25 October.

The War in 1965

The major battles the ARVN fought in late 1964 and 1965 (Plei Me, Đồng Xoài, Bình Giã, Ba Gia, etc....) revealed "an ARVN that, while inferior to the enemy in strategic direction and still not freed from the concept of static defense of fixed points, was capable of fighting well when it had to."[24] Its casualties in these battles were eight times those of the Americans.[25] This may have to do with inferior armament and poor strategy. While the communists had moved to the level of divisional attacks, the ARVN still responded with battalion-size counterattacks and got mauled.

The Central Highlands of Vietnam encompass the broader, southern end of the north-south Trường Sơn range or Annamite chain, the mountain range that forms the boundary between Vietnam and its neighboring western countries: Laos and Cambodia. To invade South Vietnam, the communists from North Vietnam had to cross its western border into Laos, then trekked along the western side of the Trường Sơn range into Cambodia. That is why this mountain route was aptly called the Trường Sơn Tây or western Trường Sơn Route or more famously the Hồ Chí Minh (HCM) Trail. From there, infiltration routes turn eastward to South Vietnam leading to Khe Sanh (I Corps), Kontum (II Corps), and Phước Long (III Corps).

The central highland area is mountainous with triple canopy vegetation and dense primeval rainforests. In between are plateaus where the main towns are located. From north to south stand Kontum (550 m), Pleiku (800 m), and Ban Mê Thuột (535 m), linked together by the famous highway 14.

During the First Indochina War (1946–1954) the Việt Minh maintained a north-south communication route using this system of trails and paths. The HCM trail was a jungle road that in the beginning allowed bicycles to transport arms and equipment from North Vietnam to South Vietnam. In 1959, it was enlarged by the 559th Transportation Group under the direction of Colonel (later General) Võ Bầm.

At the height of the war, about 100,000 workers kept the trail open throughout the year. By the end of the war, it was a busy system of interconnecting roads that allowed trucks to ride side by side.

The war could be subdivided into three phases. From the 1950s to mid–1965, the communists first waged a pure insurgency (phase I) or guerrilla war that stressed political *đấu tranh* (struggle) combined with military action. From 1965 to 1968, the war moved to a combination of insurgency and conventional war (phase 2). After the 1968 Tết offensive, the war entered the phase 3 fully conventional war.[26]

The year 1965 was a border-war year during which the communists sent more troops, ammunitions, and materiel down the trail into South Vietnam. As a consequence, the number of battles and their intensity increased as the communists slowly tried to "control" more territories and expanded their range throughout the country, starting in the highland region and the borderland across from Cambodia and Laos.

Sông Bé, Đồng Xoài, Bà Giã, Thuận Man, Plei Me ... all these names sounded strange even to the ears of the local South Vietnamese. They are the boondocks, the remote rural areas of South Vietnam that few Vietnamese ventured into. Not too many people knew these places. But from 1965 onward, these names became commonplace because singers inserted them into their war songs. As more people sang the songs, they became the lore of the Vietnam War.

5

1966

The South Vietnamese Economy

The tragic removal of President Ngô Đình Diệm on November 1, 1963,[1] plunged South Vietnam into more than four years of political instability, military inefficiency, and economic difficulties. Due to political instability and the dismantling by the military junta of Diệm's strategic hamlets,[2] governmental and social structures, the resulting chaotic and social void that ensued further worsened the weak political system in South Vietnam. From 1963 to 1968, South Vietnam endured ten changes of government or one every six months. Not only did the government change, civilian instability caused by the Buddhist Struggle Movement[3] was frequent enough to disrupt schools, markets, and daily civilian life and to severely affect the military conduct of the war.

No matter how dysfunctional the politico-military situation in South Vietnam might be, that of North Vietnam was no better. One had to consider what the revolution had brought to that part of the country: "summary justice with people's tribunals and exemplary public executions, denunciation of one's neighbors, conscription, forced labor, and hours of tiresome political meetings at which the American aggressors and their puppets were denounced."[4]

Since economy plays an important role in nation building, it is important to understand South Vietnam's economy in the mid–1960s, when the U.S. roughly had more than 200,000 troops on the ground.

Economy of a Country at War

South Vietnam was mainly an agricultural country with relatively few minor industries. Because of insecurity problems in the countryside, the productivity of two main products—rice and rubber—decreased in 1964. Exports as a result decreased to VN $1,696 million in 1964 compared to VN $2,685 million in 1963.[5] From 1965 onward, due to the presence of U.S. troops, the total money in circulation and in short-term deposits increased by VN $5 billion from VN $24,781 million 1963 to $30,329 million in 1964.

As security decreased, farmers and their workers slowly and gradually shied away from working in unsafe areas while new job creation was almost absent. As a consequence, the price index rose 5 percent in 1964[6] and gradually increased with time. The other problem was the rapid influx of American soldiers who with their liberal spending literally drove upward the costs of living toward the end of 1965. The increase escalated as the war got worse. U.S. troops in Vietnam rapidly increased from 60,000 to 200,000 in 1965 to 500,000 in 1967.

Table 5-1. South Vietnam's Gross National Product and Budget Revenue Projections 1960–1967 (VN$ millions)

Adapted: Hallinan, Timothy (1969). *Economic prospects of the Republic of Vietnam.* www.rand.org/pubs/papers/2008/P4225.pdf p. 11.

	1960		1967	
	Amount	% GNP	Amount	% GNP
Direct	831	1.0	2,857	0.8
Indirect	3,190	3.9	4,799	1.4
Excise	1,435	1.7	6,254	1.8
Registration	729	0.9	2,989	0.8
Total Internal Taxes	6,184	7.5	16,898	4.8
Customs	1,991	2.4	13,731	3.9
Total taxes	8,175	9.9	30,629	8.7
Foreign aid	4,481	5.5	21,577	6.1
Other revenues	1,577	1.4	13,085	3.7
Total	13,833	16.8	65,292	18.5
Gross National Product (billion)	82	100.0	352	100.0

Table 5-2. Exports and Export Projections 1960–1978 (US $ Millions)

Adapted: Hallinan, Timothy (1969). *Economic prospects of the Republic of Vietnam.* www.rand.org/pubs/papers/2008/P4225.pdf p. 14.

			1978	
	1960	1967	Low	High
Rice	37	0	40	90
Rubber	48	20	40	60
Fish products	*	*	10	40
Other agriculture	5	4	20	80
Subtotals	80	24	110	270
Industrials	4	1	50	170
Totals	84	25	160	440

Table 5-3. Per Capita Incomes, Per Capita Imports, and Per Capita Imports Per US $1.00 Dollar of Per Capita Income: Selected Countries of East Asia (1966–67) (U.S. Dollars)

Source: *AID Economic Data Book East Asia.* Agency for International Development, Washington, D.C., December 1968; United Nations, *Year Book of International Trade Statistics 1966.* New York 1968, Table A, p 18. Imports are all CIF. Reproduced by Hallinan, www.rand.org/pubs/papers/2008/P4225.pdf. p. 16.

	Per capita Income	Per capita Import	Per capita import per US $1.00 p/c Income
Indonesia	100	5.42	0.05
Korea	139	33.44	0.24
Japan	1074	116.83	0.11
Philippines	175	27.61	0.16
Taiwan	247	54.48	0.22
Thailand	141	27.65	0.19
So. Vietnam	126	41.82	0.33

Table 5-3 shows that compared to other Southeast Asian countries, in the mid–1960s South Vietnam used a third of its income in imports compared to 5 to 24 percent for neighboring countries that luckily were at peace.

Table 5-4. Trade Balances: Korea and Vietnam 1953–1967 (in millions of U.S. dollars)

Source: Hallinan (1969): www.rand.org/pubs/papers/2008/P4225.pdf p. 18.

	Korea			South Vietnam		
Year	Import	Export	I/E	Import	Export	I/E
1953	345.4	39.6	8.7	288.5	61.9	4.7
1954	243.3	24.2	10.1	267.0	50.6	5.3
1955	341.4	18.0	19.0	263.2	69.0	3.8
1956	386.1	24.6	15.7	217.7	45.1	4.8
1957	442.2	22.3	19.9	288.7	80.5	3.6
1958	378.2	16.5	22.9	232.1	55.2	4.2
1959	303.8	19.8	15.3	224.6	75.1	3.0
1960	343.5	32.8	10.5	240.3	84.5	2.8
1961	316.1	40.9	7.7	255.1	69.8	3.7
1962	421.8	54.8	7.7	264.5	56.6	4.7
1963	560.3	86.8	6.5	286.2	76.7	3.7
1964	400.4	119.1	3.4	297.8	48.4	6.2
1965	463.6	175.1	2.6	357.3	35.4	10.1
1966	716.4	250.3	2.9	564.9	24.8	22.8
1967	996.2	320.2	3.1	691.9	16.6	42.2

Table 5-4 shows that by 1965 with American troops landing in Vietnam (8 March 1965), the import-export ratio for South Vietnam rose to 10:1 and kept climbing to 42:1 in 1967. Prior to 1965, the annual ratio ranged from 3:1 to 6:1. For Korea, whose war ended in 1953, the import/export ratio never rose above 24:1. Sixty percent of Vietnam's budget went to defense, a deplorable statistic for any country, especially a poor one. Neighboring Asian countries that were at peace during that period spent only 14 to 25 percent of their budget for defense.[7]

The Commercial Import Program (CIP) and the Industrial Development Project (IDP), highly touted features of American aid in times of peace, fell short of their goals in a country at war. Although the CIP provided much needed consumer goods and curtailed inflation, it went out of control. Local profiteers inundated South Vietnam with American-financed wares. Not only consumer necessities were available and affordable, luxury items such as water skis, hi-fi sets, automobiles, and air conditioners gradually became prevalent.[8]

Besides, most of the imports stayed in Saigon, giving it a falsely prosperous air, while leaving the countryside untouched. This maldistribution just aggravated the divide between city dwellers and peasants, those who could afford to live in cities and those who remained in the countryside, and favored the VC who lurked in the vast countryside close to the villagers. In the countryside, middlemen price-gouged U.S. fertilizers, farm tools, milk, plastic goods and textiles.

The CIP also undercut other AID program objectives. Intended as a "quick fix" to stimulate South Vietnamese economy, it gradually made South Vietnam more dependent on American-financed goods and gave the South Vietnamese little inducement to invest in local production of consumer goods and building local industrial complexes.[9]

American advisers and critics in the beginning remained cloistered in the cities rarely working in the countryside. This allowed the Vietnamese to apply an old adage to the Americans, "In the hallways of my nation, strangers who see little remain strangers. They are, verily, tigers in my house."[10] It was in 1962 that American advisers began fanning out into the countryside. Nation building became "pacification" work.

The magnitude of the American presence completely changed the society and even turned it upside down. It created tens of thousands of new occupations for job-hungry Vietnamese, skilled or unskilled. They worked as maids, butlers, cooks, house boys, gardeners, construction workers, stevedores, etc.... They rented rooms, houses, became businessmen, importers, traders. While men were off in the military, women joined the workforce. Of Saigon's labor force of 330,000 close to 250,000 were women. A Mrs. Đà Nẵng owned a villa she rented to Americans, several restaurants and a movie theater, as well as a lavish home of her own. Mrs. Nguyễn Duy Lương owned pharmaceutical laboratories, directed the Nam Bộ Bank, and managed the Park hotel in Saigon, where the U.S. military held briefings.[11]

The abundance of dollars and goods raised the living standards of the middle and working class residents. Ordinary households owned a radio, and one in ten a television. In 1967, the Saigonese possessed 100,000 motorbikes, 25,000 motor scooters and motorcycles, 25,000 trucks and 7,000 automobiles.

Saigon's boom town atmosphere attracted thousands and thousands of rural Vietnamese. The city's population rose from 800,000 in 1957 to 3 million in 1970.

By 1972, a survey revealed that only 25 percent of the Vietnamese questioned "were native of the city they lived in." The rest were either migrants or refugees of the war. Huge shantytowns encircled the city's prosperous center. Half of Saigon's three million dwellers lived in squalor, crunched into hovels slapped together from sheets of tin, cardboard, and mud. Authorities were able to complete 2,000 new public housing units a year, far below the 10,000 to 15,000 houses needed to stay even with the population increase. Sewage and other sanitation facilities hardly existed for Saigon's huge "fringe population." Disease was rampant. During the war, Saigon had the highest incidence of small pox, cholera, bubonic plague, and typhoid of any major city in the world. In 1965, only a dozen antiquated French garbage trucks operated around the city. They dumped most of their refuse at sites within the metropolitan area. Saigon had only 6,000 hospital beds and there was just one doctor for every 8,000 residents.[12]

The dangerous distortion of the economy created a distortion of traditional Vietnamese moral values. A policeman made only U.S. $25 a month, versus an American employed construction worker up to $300. A civil servant with twenty years of experience earned $85 a month while a young bar girl or prostitute could take in ten times as much. The crass materialism of the American dollar fostered anger among many Vietnamese. They abhorred the endemic corruption in the cities—crime, black marketeering, drugs, and graft. A Vietnamese stewardess said, "I don't want the Việt Cộng to take away my freedom. But I can't help hating the Americans for the way they are corrupting my country."[13]

As to the people living in the countryside, they suffered not only from the insecurity, but also from the horrors of the war.

> The barbarity of VC terror, the seeming indifference of the enemy to the lives of their own countrymen had a profound effect on the Americans who came to fight in Vietnam. The cruelty of the VC toward the peasants reinforced the mistaken belief that life was cheap in the countryside. At the same time the inability of the peasants to defend themselves contributed to the contempt with which some GIs regarded them. Their refusal to risk their lives and those of their families by informing on the VC helped nurture the idea that they were themselves the enemy. The strategy of terror employed by the communists raised the level of savagery with which the war was fought....[14]

Anti-Inflationary Measures

The government of South Vietnam (GVN) had to take serious anti-inflationary measures whose main purpose was to absorb the excess liquidity. The latter generated by the massive and rapid insertion of American GIs on the South Vietnamese soil threatened to disrupt the native society through inflation. That was one of the factors that President Ngô Đình Diệm was afraid of and for which he was pushed aside. Raising taxes was not a wise political solution at that time because the government needed the support of its people. Measures taken included:

1. ISSUANCE OF PUBLIC BONDS. In the beginning, bonds were issued to absorb excess funds of business firms and private banks in order to encourage saving and investments while providing the government with a source of financing.

The National Bank could then expand or restrict the credit market by modifying the interest rate and conditions applied to such credit operations as mortgage or discount. However, in 1964, credits to the private sector did not increase despite the rapid increase in bank deposits. As a result, bank liquidity was rather excessive.

2. COMBATING THE SMUGGLING OF BANK NOTES. The old South Vietnamese $500 bills were easy to counterfeit and large amounts of these notes were hoarded on the international market by unscrupulous businessmen. The banknotes were taken out of the country illegally and the total of dealings in Hong Kong amounted to millions per week. Saigon ended up withdrawing VN $5,599,000 bank notes.

   Apart from this measure, the government tried to get more U.S. economic aid, especially commercial aid. It also tried to reduce advances from the National Bank to the Treasury, to increase budget revenues by reforming the taxation system, and to reduce unnecessary budget expenditures.

3. INCREASE EXPORT INCENTIVES. Exporters could earn VN $100 for each dollar consisting of the official rate of VN $35 plus 5/7 allowance of VN $25 and the new supplementary allowance of VN $40. They were also granted 25 percent of their foreign exchange earnings to import such things as beverages, fresh and dried fruits and dairy products. Results were limited, however, because exports of the two main products, rice and rubber, had been declining since 1964 due to insecurity in the countryside.

Measures Issued in 1965 and 1966

By mid–1965, the war had escalated at an alarming rate, which required increased expenditures to control it, far exceeding budget revenues. The National Bank had to provide more advances to cover the deficit. Money in circulation increased from 13 percent in 1962 to 79 percent in 1965, causing the consumer price index to increase and leading to a new phase of severe inflationary crisis. New steps had to be taken.

1. Readjustment of the exchange rate

The strong purchasing power of the 200,000 foreign troops affected the demand for commodities and services and caused a substantial loss for the national foreign exchange reserves when they used U.S. dollars instead of Vietnamese piasters to pay for their expenses.

Decree-Law 10/65 dated 8 August 1965 established a special fund at the National Bank for control of the selling and buying of foreign exchange. Sellers to the fund received a special allowance while buyers had to pay a special surtax of VN $44.50 for each dollar bought or sold.

According to a signed agreement between the U.S. and South Vietnam, from 31 August 1965 onward, all U.S. personnel, civilian and military would be paid in military payment certificates (MPC or red dollar bill) instead of the U.S. currency (green dollar bill). From that date U.S. personnel were not allowed to bring green dollar bills into South Vietnam.[15] Since the National Bank had to spend VN $118 for one U.S. dollar but could get only VN $60 for it, it was not profitable to buy the currency. It also decided not to keep excessive foreign exchange reserves but would use them to increase imports.

2. Anti-inflation measures related to the import program

Imports amounted to U.S. $400 million in 1965 and U.S. $600 million in 1966, of which U.S. $400 million were financed by Washington and U.S. $200 million by Saigon. Because of the abundant foreign exchange available, an increase of U.S. $200 million in imports would increase budget revenues from import duties and the Counterpart Fund.

To improve the efficiency of the import program, old and complicated procedures had to be abolished. This could only be done with the approval of U.S. authorities since two-thirds of the imports were financed by the U.S. This in turn raised another issue. In order to receive all the imported merchandise and since Vietnamese ports were either antiquated or had badly deteriorated with time, establishing new ports in Vũng Tàu and Cam Ranh and constructing more floating bridges and storage facilities were needed. All these measures contributed to the expansion of the import program, which however led South Vietnam into an ever increasing reliance on foreign aid.

3. The immediate working plan

Since the classic method of freezing excess money supply would not work in this case, emergency measures had to be taken. Imports were increased from U.S $550 million to U.S. $660 million to absorb 70 percent of the excess money in circulation. An import fund was established in January 1966 and the main ports had to be expanded to meet the increasing demand of imports. On the other hand, new taxes (excise tax, gasoline tax, land tax, and registration tax) were implemented. National defense bonds and national lottery tickets also increased budget receipts. Taxes on custom duties and luxury goods were also increased.

4. The devaluation of the Vietnamese piaster

Since 1955, there had been a considerable difference between the actual value of the piaster and its official value. It was realized that in 1966, the average exchange rate was even higher than that of the free market. The devaluation of the piaster was bound to occur as an inevitable consequence of a protracted and costly war. Inflation was tolerable as long as depreciation of the piaster was gradual and the upward movement of prices was kept under control. However, from 1963 to 1965 the money supply rose rapidly, reaching VN $51.5 billion in January 1966 compared to VN $36.3 billion in July 1965.[16] While prices increased moderately in 1965, they rose at an alarming rate in 1966.

The people lost their confidence in the piaster and began spending money recklessly or buying gold as a protection or investment against inflation. Most of the gold was brought in illegally from Laos since the amount of gold that could be officially imported was low. The amount of gold brought in from Laos rose from U.S. $2.4 million in September 1965 to U.S. $3.3 million in January 1966 and U.S. $4.4 million in April 1966. Despite this influx, the gold price shot up from VN $7,900 per tael in September 1965 to VN $12,400 per tael in May 1966.[17] Gold had become for commoners a valuable asset for protection against the declining purchasing power of the piaster. The gold rush indicated a dangerous inflationary threat, which required drastic enforcement of governmental measures before it was too late.

The International Monetary Fund (IMF) dispatched a delegation to Vietnam to assess its economic situation. The report suggested that inflation in the second semester of 1966 amounting to VN $16 billion would not have been lower than that of the previous semester had the previous measures been strictly applied. Two solutions were suggested: either open a new foreign exchange market or modify the foreign exchange rate. The second solution appeared to have a sound basis for the national economy since the multi-rate system had caused many objections. For example, while a Vietnamese peasant could get only VN $60 for each dollar in rice export, a foreign soldier got VN $118 for each dollar spent. A single rate was needed to stop such a discrimination.[18]

A modification of the exchange rate would have dramatic economic and psychological effects on commoners, who not only had to endure the physical and economic consequences of the war, but also see their earnings and savings volatilize rapidly. Prices would be expected to rise for three or four months before the effects of the measures would become evident. Then prices would stabilize.

5. Economic measures of June 18, 1966

On June 18, 1966, the Saigon government announced a series of measures aimed at stabilizing the economy: increasing salaries for civil servants and military personnel, selling gold to jewelers, establishing a new exchange rate for the piaster, and abolishing limitations in industry and commerce. To show its concern for individuals most likely to be hit hard by the inflation and usually its staunchest supporters, the government raised the salaries of civil servants and military personnel:

- 30 percent on total salary for those whose pay was less than VN $5,000 per month,
- 25 percent on total salary for those earning from VN $5,000 to $10,000 per month,
- 20 percent on total salary for those earning more than VN $10,000 per month.

The decision was effective retrospectively from June 1, 1966.

A gold fund was established at the National Bank for the purpose of fixing the quotas of gold to be sold, establishing the gold price, and determining intermediary commissions. Designated banks were authorized to buy gold from the National Bank to sell it to licensed jewelers. A new exchange rate for the piaster was set at U.S. $1/VN $80 effective from June 18, 1966. The new exchange rate was applied to all exchange dealings throughout South Vietnam. Allowance to the import of equipment was set at 20 percent of the value of the equipment. Outstanding students abroad were granted an allowance of VN $38 per each dollar transferred. New import licenses were to be granted to anyone who fulfilled the stipulated requirements.[19]

Anti-Inflationary Effects

The economic measures overall had an impact on the inflationary gap, the change in money supply, and the stabilization of prices. The inflationary gap was wide in 1966. Without monetary reform, the inflationary gap would reach VN $36.6 billion. With monetary reform it would be reduced to VN $19.5 billion. This assessment, however, was overly optimistic because excess liquidity could not be solved completely and military expenditures were unlikely to be reduced.

The large reserves of foreign exchange accumulated by South Vietnam caused Washington to level off its commercial aid (the CIP: Commodity Import Program), which was used to make up for budget deficit and to control inflation. While Saigon's foreign exchange reserves rose from U.S. $238.8 million in June 1966 to U.S. $315.9 million in December 1966, the CIP decreased from U.S. $103,839 million in the second quarter of 1966 to U.S. $38,524 million in the fourth quarter. Moreover, according to the foreign exchange policy, the rate of U.S. $1/VN $118 was applied when purchasing dollars, while the lower of U.S. $1/VN $60 was applied for selling them. Therefore, the national budget had to absorb losses from these imbalances. From 1968, the budget deficit rose rapidly, inflation was heavy, and prices continued to escalate.

The 18 June 1966 economic stabilization program caused prices to go up. Increasing salaries and wages in the public and then in the private sectors raised production costs. The tax measures and the piaster devaluation had undesirable effects on the prices of imported commodities, raw materials and equipment. Because the government was not able to control the increase in money supply, the problem of inflation was far from being definitely solved.[20]

Political instability and military insecurity, which plagued South Vietnam from 1963 to 1967, presented serious deterrents to development. Agricultural production and industrial production were both deeply affected while foreign trade deficits soared. The South Vietnamese stabilization program could not increase production and keep price levels stable, although it did bring inflation under control. South Vietnam thus waged two wars in 1966: besides fighting the war against the NVA/VC, which progressively got worse, the GVN continued to fight inflation that threatened to cripple the economy and make hardship worse for the common people.

6

1967

The Year of Decision

The year 1967 was the "best and the worst year" for Washington and Hanoi, which both decided to escalate the war while South Vietnam ushered in the Second Republic four years after the fall of the Diệm regime. The year turned out to be the "D" Year (D for Decision) for both Washington and Hanoi for any decision they made could affect the outcome of the war. Westmoreland felt he was ready to launch the defining phase of his war of attrition against the communists. He had all the troops he needed and the political situation in South Vietnam was the best it could be after four years of instability.

It was the year when northern communist leaders—Hồ Chí Minh, Võ Nguyên Giáp, and Phạm Văn Đồng—realized they could lose the war militarily in South and North Vietnam if they did not do anything drastic. But neither Washington nor Hanoi would recognize that the United States would lose the political and psychological war at home.

Saigon and the Second Republic

After four years of political unrest and infighting between the military junta and the Thích Trí Quang–led Buddhist Struggle Movement, and following approval by the Constituent Assembly, the 1967 South Vietnamese Constitution was approved by the Congress of the Armed Forces then by General Thiệu on 1 April 1967. It called for a civilian government with an Executive branch led by a president, a vice-president, and a prime minister; a bicameral Legislature; and a Supreme Court. This was followed by the election of the president and members of both Houses.

There were 17 tickets competing for the presidency. General Nguyễn Văn Thiệu and Air Marshal Nguyễn Cao Kỳ competed on separate tickets. But the military junta did not want to split up the votes between Thiệu and Kỳ and forced them to remain on the same ticket. Nguyễn Văn Thiệu was elected President of the Second Republic[1] on 5 September with 34.8 percent of the 4,868,281 votes. The Vice-President was Nguyễn Cao Kỳ. The generals did not win in large cities, but in areas controlled by the VC, like the High Plateaus and the delta and central Vietnam, which was the stronghold of the Buddhist opposition.

The election of the 60-member Senate also took place on 5 September at the same time as the presidential election. There were 48 tickets of 10 candidates each.

The large number of candidates caused confusion among the electors. Many voters were confronted with a choice of 6 out of 48 unfamiliar Senate tickets. One paper commented that

> the vagaries of the electoral system have produced an almost crazily unrepresentative body of 60 Senators. Almost half of them are Catholics, a good one third are northerners, that is, exiles who abandoned North Vietnam after the 1954 Geneva Agreement.... By contrast there will be no spokesmen for the more militant wing of the Buddhist Church in the Senate nor, equally important, were any politicians who represented the self-consciously native southerners elected....[2]

Some U.S. Congressmen who were invited to visit South Vietnam and assess the fairness of the election reported that they had been as free and fair as circumstances permitted. Some foreign commentators remained skeptical, pointing out that the U.S. observers had only spent a few days in Vietnam and that none of them spoke Vietnamese. The elections of the House of Representatives took place on 22 October with 132 seats contested by 1,140 candidates. The long list of candidates made it difficult for voters to decide whom to support.

The election of a civilian president, the Senate and the House of Representatives ushered in the Second Republic and put a hold on four years of semi-anarchy that resulted from the ouster of the Diệm regime. This was, by far, one of the biggest achievements of the military rule in South Vietnam.

On the frontline, it was only in April 1967 that some ARVN units received the M-16 rifle. "For much of the war, the South Vietnamese were consistently outgunned with predictable results in battlefields outcomes and morale." They were armed with castoff equipment of World War II vintage, such as the M-1 rifle and the carbine. On the other hand, their opponents received the famous AK-47 assault rifle back in 1964.[3] Some progress was made to insure that ARVN soldiers were fed and housed properly and that their families were cared for. In May 1967, the new deputy commander, Gen. Creighton W. Abrams, was given the responsibility to improve the RVNAF.

Washington and the War

The NVA-VC had 280,000 men including main forces, regional forces, administrative forces, irregulars and political cadres. Of these 50,000 were PAVN forces. The combined U.S., South Vietnamese, and Free World Forces (Australia, New Zealand, South Korea, etc.) totaled 1,173,000 men.[4] Westmoreland in 1967 decided to unleash this massive force against the NVA-VC inside Vietnam with the goal of supporting the pacification of the countryside. He targeted the major enemy bases in the "Iron Triangle" and the "War Zone C" northwest of Saigon and the "War Zone D" northeast of the capital. The enemy used them as supply centers, hospitals, headquarters, training centers, rest areas, etc. From these bases, the enemy would move supplies to forward bases from where they would attack allied forces. Destroying the enemy's main bases would shut down their attacking power and drive the PAVN forces there away from the local VC forces, whom the big units supported.

On 8 January 1967 Westmoreland launched a three-division operation dubbed Cedar Falls into the Iron Triangle. It was a typical "hammer and anvil" operation with

U.S. forces playing the hammer part and attacking from the North and the East. The ARVN 5th Division, the Vietnamese Navy, and the U.S. 25th Infantry Division and 199th Light Infantry Brigade formed the anvil part. Except for small unit actions, no major battles ensued. The enemy slipped away into the dense and widespread South Vietnamese jungle. Combined friendly losses were less than 100 killed and a few hundred wounded with 750 VC killed. Cedar Falls was a public opinion disaster because it forced the evacuation of roughly 6,000 Bến Súc residents to refugee camps and the destruction of their village. It became a rallying point for the anti-war movement.[5] Ten days later, the base area was "literally crawling with what appeared to be Viet Cong." The U.S. only found small arms caches, depots, and enough rice to feed a division for a year.[6]

This was followed on 22 February by another multi-division operation against the War Zone C, close to the Cambodian border and nicknamed Junction City. Three major battles were fought during this period. Enemy battle losses included 2,728 killed and 34 captured. American losses included 282 killed and 1,576 wounded. Although forced to relocate temporarily to safe havens in Cambodia, COSVN[7] had not been captured. Enemy activity in War Zone C had been disrupted, but operation Junction City was not a turning point in the war.[8]

Pacification in Vietnam during the same period sputtered. Westmoreland was committed to big operations like Cedar Falls and Junction City, not to clearing and holding small hamlets and villages around Saigon. The latter part was relegated to ARVN commanders who taking their cue from their U.S. counterparts, wanted to wage "big unit" wars instead of the tedious, unglamorous pacification operations. Pacification got a boost on 9 May 1967 when it was assigned to a civilian, Ambassador Robert W. Komer, deputy commander of MACV.[9]

Komer had tremendous energy and a razor sharp mind coupled with a determination to get the pacification job done. His idea was that pacification had to be assigned to the Vietnamese while the Americans furnished the resources and support. For much of 1967, little progress was made. The 6,500 CORDS (Civil Operations and Revolutionary Development Support) people[10] had to be welded together and assigned to train and work with the Popular Forces (PF) and Regional Forces (RF). The latter were Vietnamese forces that were spread all over South Vietnam in small districts, villages, and hamlets. Komer also initiated the Hamlet Evaluation System, which was designed to evaluate the progress of the pacification effort. Eliminating the VC infrastructure required a massive and sophisticated intelligence effort that required unity of command.[11] Komer left the program in November 1968, more than a year after he began re-organizing it.

General Nguyễn Đức Thắng, head of the Ministry of Revolutionary Development and then commander of Corps IV from 1965 to 1968, was the Vietnamese counterpart of Komer. A clean and well respected general, he unluckily was sidelined by Thiệu because of his connections to Kỳ.[12] Komer on his departure was replaced by Ambassador William F. Colby who changed the CORDS name to Civil Operations and *Rural* Development Support to stress the need for civilian involvement in the pacification effort. Colby expedited the training and equipping of the RF and PF by distributing 500,000 weapons to the countryside. CORDS was one of the most successful programs of the war.[13]

During 1966, communist battle deaths averaged 5,000 men a month. During the first six months of 1967, their losses (casualties, POW's, defectors and non-battle casualties) soared to 15,000 men a month. Since the VC could recruit 3,500 men per month and NVA infiltration ran about 7,000 men a month, they were short of 4,500 men monthly. As a result, they could not wage any major battle in the South and the VC had lost control of 500,000 to 1,000,000 Vietnamese in the last half of 1966 and the first two months of 1967.[14]

On 18 March, General Westmoreland asked for an additional 200,000 troops. The request stunned President Johnson, Secretary McNamara and his deputies. According to the General, troops would be used to go into Laos and cut the Hồ Chí Minh Trail. Had he received what he asked for, might the overall situation have changed? At that time, the indirect cost of the Rolling Thunder operation had exceeded its purely destructive effects. Hanoi had to divert 500,000 to 600,000 civilians to buff up air defense or to repair bomb damage. The people in North Vietnam began to experience shortages of food, clothing and medicine. In 1967, the U.S. Navy began mining internal waterways and coastal estuaries, adding difficulties for Hanoi. Discussions in the U.S. were entertained about using "iron bombs" against the dikes along the Red River. Dikes had been built through centuries, allowing the Red River to flow in a man-made canal above the surface of the surrounding countryside. Had the dikes been breached, farmlands around Hanoi and surrounding villages would be flooded, including Hanoi itself, under 11 feet of water.[15]

All these actions would over a period of time severely cripple Hanoi's ability to fight. Although one single action did not matter, the sum of all these actions taken together might finally bear effect. Westmoreland had finally seen a "light at the end of the tunnel." The question was why did it take him that long to realize it and to act? The crucial time was then. Johnson and McNamara, however, had different opinions. Johnson was always afraid that enlarging the war would force the Soviets and Chinese to jump into the war.

The Joint Chiefs came out swinging. They approved the 200,000 men requested by Westmoreland. They suggested that the Reserves be mobilized and that the war could be extended to Laos, Cambodia, and possibly North Vietnam. They also suggested mining Hanoi's ports. In sum, they wanted to "win the war," although that decision may have been a little bit late.

McNamara and his allies were horrified by the suggestions. They suggested holding the troops to 470,000 men and restricting Rolling Thunder to the southern part of North Vietnam. They then de-escalated the war by decreasing U.S. objectives in Vietnam as set forth by the NSAM 288. Instead of promoting an "independent non-communist South Vietnam" or "defeating the Viet Cong," they suggested that "the people in South Vietnam should determine their own future" and that "the commitment ceases if the country ceases to help itself." In general, the civilians who thought the war was lost recommended a compromise solution in South Vietnam. The Joint Chiefs threatened to resign en masse if McNamara's decisions were approved.

Johnson agonized, fumed, and waffled. He advised McNamara to compromise with the JCS and to let the Stennis hearings settle the bombing issue. McNamara on his trip to Vietnam settled the troop strength issue with Westmoreland and Abrams by increasing it by 45,000 men to a total of 525,000. In August 1967, the hawkish subcommittee of the Senate Armed Service Committee led by Senator Stennis criticized the restraints the civilians placed on the bombing strategy and censured the civilians for overriding the advice of the JCS. McNamara lost the fight and with it the president's confidence.[16]

By September 1967, the Americans had slowly turned against the war: they decided that the war was not making any progress. President Johnson's popularity dropped to 40 percent, a new low for his term in office. The total casualties (killed, wounded, missing) rose from 2,500 in 1965, to 33,000 in 1966 and 80,000 in 1967. Draft calls increased and the Americans were hit in their pocketbook. In September, Johnson called for a 6 percent surtax which Congress approved. The anti-war movement began to take shape. Johnson then failed, or was unable, to explain to the American people about the need to wage war in Vietnam. Polls showed that half of the Americans interviewed did not know why the Americans were in Vietnam. By refusing to sell the war to the Americans, he surrendered to the anti-war protestors. The declining support for the war limited the president's choice of strategies. If the people barely accepted the war in Vietnam, they would not accept an expansion of the war into Laos, Cambodia, or North Vietnam.[17]

In this critical year, Johnson wavered and could not make up his mind. Westmoreland in later years criticized Johnson's conduct of the war: "Johnson ... hoped the war would go away ... but his key decisions were destined to drag the war out indefinitely.... We should choose our leaders carefully, broad gauged statesmen, not slaves to the public opinion polls."[18]

As for Westmoreland, by failing to win the war with more than one million men under his leadership (although half of them were not under his direct command), he had lost it. McNamara in Saigon on 11 July 1967 commented, "We have over a million men here under arms and there are many, many opportunities open to us to increase the effective use of these men, and we will set our minds and hearts to doing that."[19] By finally realizing that he had this many troops under his command, it was too late for Westmoreland to turn back the tide.

Hanoi and the War

Gen. Nguyễn Chí Thanh, who was charged with executing the *Tổng Công Kích-Tổng Khởi Nghĩa* plan (or TCK-TKN or General Offensive–General Uprising) died on or about 4 July 1967. He was replaced by Gen. Văn Tiến Dũng. Lê Duẩn, the real mastermind behind the TCK-TKN made sure his plan moved forward by putting pressure and jailing his opponents.[20] He based his concept on three assumptions. First, ARVN soldiers lacked motivation and would defect or desert when struck a hard blow. Second, since the people did not support the Government of Vietnam (GVN), they would switch their support to the NLF. Third, the people and the ARVN, having despised the Americans, would turn against them.

He thought about a three-pronged offensive, military and political, that would span over many months. In phase I (September–December 1967), attacks would be focused on the bases at the periphery of South Vietnam in an attempt to draw U.S. forces out of the populated areas to the borders of the country. In phase II, there would be a countrywide military assault on South Vietnamese cities, ARVN units, U.S. headquarters, communication centers and airbases. In phase III, the people would rebel against the Thiệu-Kỳ government and topple it. In sum, the goal was to bring about a decisive victory and end the war.[21]

Although bold and imaginative, Duẩn's plan had serious deficiencies. First, it violated the principles of simplicity and mass. It required a lot of coordination, which the communists did not have with their primitive signal coordination. In fact, communication did break down. Duẩn also spread his forces too thin to have any impact. Had he concentrated his forces against fewer targets, he would have achieved better results. Second, he failed to understand the concept of U.S. mobility. In 1967, the U.S. could move troops to the periphery to foil attacks and bring them back into the interior to counter any attack there. Third, Duẩn failed to make any provision in case of failure. Having no withdrawal routes would cost the communists dearly during the Offensive. Fourth, he based his plan on wrong assumptions. The ARVN in general fought "with more courage and effectiveness than it had ever done before or would do again."[22] The people did not join the NLF; they did not turn against the Thiệu government or the Americans.

By mid–September the communists began their TCK-TKN by attacking border-site camps like Cồn Thiên, Dak To and Sông Bé. Cồn Thiên was an outpost in I Corps about two miles south of the DMZ and manned by a U.S. Marine battalion. Rising at 520 feet above the flat countryside, it allowed excellent observation over one of the enemy's principal supply routes into South Vietnam. The Marine battalion was attacked by elements of the 324B NVA Division. When the attack failed, the NVA began an intense artillery bombardment on the outpost. The U.S. responded with their own artillery augmented by air strikes. The siege was broken by 31 October following 790 B-52 sorties.[23]

Dak To was the site of a Special Forces camp in the II Corps along the Laotian and Cambodian borders. This is a rugged mountainous area with peaks rising to 6,000 feet. The camp was attacked on 3 November by elements of the NVA 1st Division and 40th Artillery Regiment. Gen. Abrams ordered a spoiling attack by the U.S. 4th Infantry Division reinforced by the 173rd Airborne Brigade and six ARVN battalions. The 3rd Battalion, 12th Infantry drove the 32nd NVA Regiment off Hill 1338 south of Dak To. Similarly, after a four-day battle the ARVN 3rd and 9th Airborne Battalions drove the NVA 24th Regiment from Hill 1416 to the northeast. Another hill was taken away from the NVA on 20 November and the enemy broke contact and pulled back into their sanctuaries in Laos. Enemy losses were put at 1,644 killed at a cost of 289 U.S. and 73 ARVN killed.[24] The border battles were North Vietnamese failures. Having lured U.S. troops to the periphery, Duẩn and Giáp failed to hold them there for a long time.

Conclusion

The Decision Year for both Washington and Hanoi was 1967. Westmoreland tried to hammer the NVA/VC forces in early 1967 in the Iron Triangle and the War Zone C, but the enemy managed to escape into the jungle. Although he had squandered three years through illusive "search and destroy" operations, he had his troops ready.

Hanoi then began its TCK-TKN offensive by waging the border war. Although

Westmoreland slammed them down, he was unprepared to deal with the full-blown offensive, which would come in early 1968.

Saigon got its civilian government elected and worked on its pacification program. The ARVN was ready to take an active part in the program. Victory was at hand, but Johnson, who did not want to "finish" the war, let the anti-war movement wreak havoc on his war initiative, which later led to the fall of South Vietnam. Westmoreland later concluded, "Our erstwhile honorable country betrayed and deserted the Republic of Vietnam after it had enticed it to our bosom. It was a shabby performance by America, a blemish on our history and a possible blight on our future."[25] History might have turned out differently had Johnson and Westmoreland acted forcefully in 1967.

7

1968

*The Tết Offensive, Saigon,
Huế, the Huế Massacre*

The first U.S. Marines came ashore in South Vietnam in March 1965. And by the end of January 1968, they had been in country for almost three years, during which they had helped the South Vietnamese restore law and order and kill 81,000 VC and PAVN troops in 1967. There were about 220,000 VC and PAVN troops remaining in the country in early 1968 and General Westmoreland felt confident about seeing the "light at the end of the tunnel."

The communists, on the other hand, did not see it that way and were about to launch massive attacks throughout the rest of the county. Hanoi's General Võ Nguyên Giáp borrowed the concept of "General Offensive" (Tổng Công Kích or TCK) from the Chinese communist doctrine. After the offensive would come the general uprising (Tổng Khởi Nghĩa or TKN) during which the people of the South would rise and rally to the communist cause to bring the downfall of the government of South Vietnam and to drive the Americans away.

The success of the TCK-TKN was based on three assumptions: that the ARVN would not fight and would collapse on initial impact; that the people of the South would rise and rebel against their own government; and that the will of the American people would crack under the traumatic shock action.

Although the Vietnamese and Americans knew attacks were coming, they did not know the timing or the intensity. "The U.S. intelligence system, in spite of its technological prowess, has simply failed to fully predict the objectives, the scope, and timing of the enemy offensive."[1]

The build-up started in the fall of 1967 when PAVN and VC attacks along the border were designed to attract U.S. forces to the periphery, leaving the ARVN alone to protect towns and cities across South Vietnam. To confuse and deceive the Americans, Giáp staged a series of bloody but pointless battles in the border regions. On 29 October, the 273rd VC Regiment attacked the district capital of Lộc Ninh, in the "Fishhook" region northwest of Saigon. On 23 November, the PAVN 4th Regiment launched a major attack on Dak To.[2] Giáp brought 20,000 to 40,000 troops to surround and attack Khe Sanh, a military base in the mountainous western part of I Corps close to the Laotian border. To confront him, Westmoreland sent 6,000 Marines to guard the base and hinder NVA infiltration across the Demilitarized Zone. The ARVN sent in a battalion of Rangers to guard the east end of the runway.

Khe Sanh and the nearby Special Forces camp at Làng Vei were important observation posts for monitoring NVA movement on the Hồ Chí Minh Trail across the Laotian border. To lose it would be like the French losing Điện Biên Phủ to the Việt Minh.[3] Therefore, Khe Sanh became such an important battleground that President Johnson had a miniature model of the battlefield installed in the White House Situation Room and told his staff that he did not want "any damn Dinbinphoo."[4]

The communists also used the 1967 Christmas cease-fire to reach their objectives. In the months and weeks before the Tết attack, thousands of soldiers walked many hundreds of miles to get to their assembly points. They walked along the Hồ Chí Minh Trail, passing through Laos and Cambodia before crossing into South Vietnam. They moved during night time, avoiding congested areas, following guides in single file, and stopping in camps hidden in dense jungle areas. On arrival, they dug trenches and bunkers readying for battle.

In the I Corps, their targets were Quảng Trị, Huế, Đà Nẵng, Chu Lai. In II Corps, in the highlands, they would attack Kontum, Pleiku, and Ban Mê Thuột and in the coastal area Nha Trang, Tuy Hòa, Qui Nhơn, Phan Thiết. North of Saigon, there would be Tây Ninh, Biên Hòa, Xuân Lộc, and Phước Long. In Saigon itself, their targets would be the Presidential Palace, the American Embassy, the control and communication centers, Tân Sơn Nhứt Air base and Chợ Lớn. By 31 January 1968 Giáp had 35 PAVN battalions and two VC divisions in and around Saigon.[5]

Since Tết is the most important festival and public holiday in Vietnam—it is a combination of New Year's Day (the first day of the first month of the lunar year), Christmas, and Thanksgiving—most Vietnamese took off from one to three days, although many took a whole week off. The communists had negotiated a truce with the GVN—a three-day cease-fire during Tết. Military units therefore sent half of their staff and soldiers home for the holidays.

Although many Vietnamese and Americans disputed intelligence reports of imminent attacks, Lieutenant General Frederik Weyand, commander of the II Field Forces, was the only one who accepted them at face value. On 10 January 1968, he convinced General Westmoreland to reinforce the area around Saigon and over the next three weeks, 13 U.S. battalions reinforced the ARVN troops inside the Saigon circle. It was a move that would change the course of the imminent battle.[6]

On 29 January, Hanoi officials ordered their front headquarters to delay the attack for 24 hours after realizing that Hanoi's calendar was one day ahead of the South Vietnamese calendar. Many VC units in I Corps and part of II Corps either did not receive the instructions or went ahead with the attacks anyway. These premature attacks on the early hours of 30 January in the northern part of South Vietnam alerted U.S. intelligence, causing Westmoreland to place all garrisons in full alert for 31 January.[7] Overall, the communists launched their attacks on 27 of South Vietnam's 44 provincial capitals, five of six autonomous cities, 58 of 245 district towns, and a host of smaller targets. Their biggest targets were Saigon and Huế, which will be discussed below.

The Battle for Saigon

The VC launched 35 battalions against Saigon on the early hours of 31 January 1968 with one attack coming from the northern end and the other from the southwestern side of the city. The sappers and local forces, in particular, were to attack the Presidential Independence Palace, the National Radio Station, the U.S. Embassy and various other places. Profiting from the overall relaxed vigilance due to the New Year celebration and the noises of firecrackers that the South Vietnamese used on that occasion, the VC C-10 Sapper Battalions came out of their hiding places, fanned out across town and began their attacks.

1. The Presidential Palace

Vũ Minh Nghĩa, 21 years old, the only female in a 15-member platoon, sneaked into the city the night before the offensive with orders to attack an army command post in Saigon's district 5. But at the final meeting with her leader, their target was changed to the Independence Palace, a well-defended institution in the center of the city. Her team was discovered just short of the palace gate. They managed to get to the grounds of the palace at 0130 but were overwhelmed by the defenders who chased them to one of the villas across the street. Eight members of the team were killed and the rest captured. She was imprisoned for six years at the Côn Đảo Prison.[8]

Another platoon attacked the ARVN's Joint General Staff (JGS) compound thirty minutes later but failed to gain entry through gate 5. Reinforced with elements of the 1st and 2nd local VC battalions, they broke through the gate on the second trial and gained control of one of the buildings. At 0400, a truckload of American MPs from the 716 MP Battalion was racing to respond to a trouble call from an American officers' billet near the JGS. The MPs were ambushed in an alley by a VC company on its way to the same JGS compound. The fight in the alley lasted 12 hours. Sixteen MPs were killed and 21 were wounded. In the meantime, other VC forces tried to get into the JGS compound but were evicted by a group of ARVN paratroopers.

A platoon targeted the National Radio Station that was located a few blocks from the Embassy. They brought with them pre-recorded tapes announcing the uprising of the people in Saigon as well as the fall of the government. The station had been reinforced by a platoon of paratroopers who on that night were sleeping on the station roof. The sappers took position on an adjacent building where they could fire down on the ARVN soldiers. After killing all the paratroopers, they stormed the station. The night crew at the transmission site 14 kilometers away shut down the radio link on a prearranged signal preventing the VC from airing the tapes.

The ARVN depot complex at Gò Vấp on the northern end of Saigon was the primary target of the 101st VC Regiment. The plan was to capture ARVN tanks from the Phù Đổng Armored Headquarters and howitzers from the Cổ Loa Artillery Headquarters. The purpose was to use the tanks for the attack on Tân Sơn Nhứt Airbase, one kilometer away. Both attacks were successful. At Phù Đổng, the VC realized that the tanks had been moved somewhere else. At Cổ Loa, they were able to capture 12 105 mm howitzers; but the weapons had been disabled at the last minute by the withdrawing ARVN troops who removed the firing locks. Both headquarters were retaken by the 4th ARVN Marine troops a few hours later.

Throughout the night, most of the Saigonese were tired and sound asleep after enjoying the midnight Tết festivities; had they been awakened by the unusual sounds, they probably lulled themselves into believing that these were only the crackle of firecrackers, unless they lived close to the fighting areas. It was probably at dawn that the persistent detonations and shooting and military planes in the air made them realize that something unusual was going on. Many still refused to believe that the communists would violate the sanctity of Tết.

President Nguyễn Văn Thiệu was not in his palace anyway. He was celebrating Tết like his fellow citizens with his in-laws in Mỹ Tho, 75 kilometers south of the city. Vice-President Nguyễn Cao Kỳ temporarily took control of the situation. General William Westmoreland was asleep in his villa on Trần Quý Cấp Street when attacks began all around his neighborhood. Four blocks away, the security team ushered Ambassador Ellsworth Bunker to his basement in his pajamas before taking him away to a safe house.[9] General Cao Văn Viên, Chairman of ARVN Joint General Staff, and General Phillip Davidson, the chief MACV intelligence officer, were also cut off from their quarters until late morning of the day of the attack. So were, ironically, 200 colonels from the MACV J2 staff who attended a pool party at one of the billets only hours before the attack started.[10]

2. The U.S. Embassy

At 0200 on 31 January 1968 at a greasy car repair shop at 59 Phan Thanh Giản Street, 15 VC sappers loaded into a small Peugeot truck, a taxicab, and an embassy car to get a ride to their objective, the U.S. Embassy.[11] Two days earlier, huge baskets, supposedly containing tomatoes and bamboo containers of rice, had arrived at the home next door to the repair shop, which belonged to a female VC veteran. They, however, contained AK-47s, B-40 rocket-propelled grenade launchers, and satchel charges necessary for the group to complete their work that night. Right after midnight, they were for the first time briefed about their mission: attack the U.S. Embassy.

The convoy headed to Mạc Đĩnh Chi Street where they encountered at the first checkpoint four civilian policemen who paid scant attention to them.[12] The tree shaded Embassy compound was situated at the intersection of Mạc Đĩnh Chi Street and Thống Nhứt Boulevard. Around 0215 they turned onto Thống Nhứt Boulevard,[13] and opened fire on the MP (military police) guards who withdrew into the compound and locked the steel gate. The guards transmitted "Signal 300" over the MP radio net to alert everyone that the Embassy was under attack.

The vehicles stopped at the corner of the street; the sappers climbed out and hurriedly unloaded RPGs and satchel charges. A moment later, a loud explosion which tore up the night blew a huge hole in the eight-foot tall Embassy wall. The VC platoon leader and his assistant were immediately killed as they rushed through the opening. One of the MPs shouted into his radio, "They're coming in! They're coming in! Help me. Help me," as more sappers came through the hole. The two MPs were killed in an exchange of fire. The sappers spread around, blew up the chancery doors with a B-40 rocket but for some reason never entered the building. They exchanged fire inside the compound with the MPs who responded to the alarm call. Having lost their leaders, the sappers took up defensive positions rather than continuing their attacks on the chancery. The MSG (military security guard), outgunned and outnumbered, decided to wait for daylight and additional reinforcement to displace the invaders. Any attack in the darkness could only increase casualties.[14] It was also realized that only MPs at the embassy carried M-16 rifles; the MSG did not.[15]

At 0500, a helicopter carrying airborne troops tried to land on the chancery roof but was driven away by heavy fire from the sappers on the ground. A decision was made to wait until dawn to do another air insertion. At 0800, Army helicopters landed 36 armed paratroopers of the 101st Airborne on the roof. They cleared the building from top down looking for possible infiltrators. On the ground, MPs from the 716th stormed the front gate looking for sappers. At 0915, the U.S. declared the Embassy grounds secure. Scattered about the grounds were the bodies of 12 of the original 15 sappers; the three remaining were taken prisoner and ended up in the Côn Đảo jail. Two armed Embassy drivers turned out to be double agents. Five Americans were dead, including four Army soldiers. Westmoreland maintained in a press conference in the evening of 31 January 1968 that the attacks on cities were a diversion for the main attack that was still to come at Khe Sanh.[16]

3. Tân Sơn Nhứt Airport

At 0320 on 31 January 1968, three VC battalions (the D16, the 267th, and a battalion from the 271st VC Regiment) stormed the western side of the airbase, which paralleled the north-south Highway 1 and faced the open rice paddies and small villages of the outskirts of Saigon. That side also housed the command of MACV. Attacks were also launched against the north and east gates. The cadres in these units were southerners, but due to casualties, half of the soldiers were fillers from the North Vietnamese Army. The 2nd Independent Battalion and the bulk of the 271st Regiment were responsible for taking the JGS HQ and for the secondary attacks on Tân Sơn Nhứt Airport (TSNA). The attack force numbered 2,665 VC and NVA.

Satchel charges and Bangalore torpedoes were utilized by a VC sapper team that simply pulled up on Highway 1 in a civilian taxicab. The explosives blew holes in the fence through which the enemy forces poured through the 051 Gate and onto the runway.[17] The situation was almost inconceivable. Tân Sơn Nhứt, so large as to appear invulnerable, was the command center of the entire allied war effort in South Vietnam. General William Westmoreland, commander, U.S. Military Assistance Command Vietnam (COMUSMACV), and General William Momyer, commander of the 7th U.S. Air Force, were both headquartered at Tân Sơn Nhứt as was the Vietnamese Air Force (VNAF). Pentagon East, as the MACV HQ building was nicknamed, was a massive, two-story, concrete and steel structure with air conditioned office space for four thousand officers and enlisted staff. It occupied almost three acres on the east side of the base and came under mortar and automatic weapons fire during Tết.[18]

Ten USAF generals headquartered at Tân Sơn Nhứt lived in modular units resembling mobile homes, surrounded by a high cyclone fence. They ducked into the bunker in their small compound when the siren alarm rang. They were unarmed except that a captain serving as an aide to one of the generals had a .38 caliber pistol.[19] The base was defended by the 377th Security Police Squadron, two platoons of MACV headquarters' guard force, the ARVN 52nd Regional Force Battalion, and Vice President Nguyễn Cao Kỳ's bodyguard. The only reserves consisted of two companies of the ARVN 8th Airborne Battalion, men who had been sitting in the Tân Sơn Nhứt terminal waiting for air transport north where they were needed as reinforcement troops. By 0415, those reserves had been committed and soon attackers and defenders were fighting hand to hand on the western side of the runway.[20]

Lieutenant Colonel Lưu Kim Cương, commander of the 33d VNAF Air Wing led a composite group of staff officers, air police, ARVN service troops, and National Police into a position southwest of the TSNSA. A call for help went out to the 25th U.S. Infantry Division at Củ Chi, about 30 kilometers northwest of Saigon. The 3rd Squadron, 4th Cavalry had been alerted for a possible relief mission at Tân Sơn Nhứt Airport. The squadron commander, Lt. Col. Glen Otis, was soon ordered to commit his troop C. As the armored cavalry troop raced down Highway 1 in the dark, Otis guided them from his command and control helicopter. By 0600, the armored troop crashed into the rear of the enemy, which received them with rocket propelled grenades. One third of the armored column was destroyed but the VC attack was badly disrupted. Troop C received reinforcement from an armored platoon that was left guarding the Hóc Môn Bridge. Ammunition was brought in by air and wounded were evacuated.

Armored Troop B was called from its alert position 45 kilometers away. Otis positioned the new arrivals across the enemy's northern flank, putting it in a right angle between two U.S. armored columns. More gunships and artillery pounded the enemy. By 1000, the VC attack folded and mopping up continued into the night.[21] All enemy resistance was eliminated by about 1630. The 377th SPS had four KIA and 11 wounded in action (WIA) while TF 35 had two KIA and an unrecorded number of WIA. The ARVN lost 29 dead and with the VNAF approximately 15 wounded. Troop B had three KIA and 17 WIA and Troop C 3–4th Cavalry, twelve KIA and 48 WIA.[22]

One of the villagers told U.S. troops that the NVA had come into the village near the airport early that night and killed everyone they could find to keep them from spreading the alarm. The survivors could not understand the vicious attacks by the NVA. One Vietnamese family was found lying face down in a row by size—husband, wife, then oldest to youngest child—all of them executed with a shot to the back of the head.[23]

4. Chợ Lớn District

The 5th and 6th VC Local Forces Battalions were assigned to hold the Chinese section of Chợ Lớn, on the southwest corner of the Saigon. The Racetrack of Phú Thọ was the hub of key streets in the area and by holding it, the VC prevented it from being used as a landing zone. The fighting in the area would last for days and weeks as Chợ Lớn was a residential and commercial center, therefore very populous. Houses were built close together and the narrow streets favored street to street as well as house to house fighting. A month long reign of terror had begun in Chợ Lớn.

Company A, 3rd battalion, 7th Infantry and the 199th reconnaissance troop arrived in Chợ Lớn at 0800 on 31 January 1968. Communist troops fired an RPG at the lead APC killing the platoon leader. They then fired at the whole column. The infantry dismounted and the fighting continued house to house. By 1300, Company A had pushed the enemy to about two blocks to the racetrack. The VC then withdrew to prepared positions behind concrete at the track. Company A began the attack on the track but was turned back. They tried again at 1630 with the help of helicopter gunships. This time, they succeeded, but the VC withdrew to the residential area. Companies B and C of the 3rd of the 7th were brought to the racetrack by helicopters.

The next morning, the troops at the racetrack were reinforced by two mechanized Companies (B and C) of the 9th Division's 2nd Battalion, 60th Infantry, and the 33rd ARVN Ranger Battalion. By 3 February, the ARVN had five Ranger, five Marine and five Airborne battalions inside Chợ Lớn. The Americans had committed seven Infantry, one MP, and six Artillery battalions. Chợ Lớn was finally cleared on 7 March. A few weeks later, Colonel Trần Văn Đắc, the chief VC political officer for Saigon, defected. The Tết Offensive in the Saigon area was over.

Conclusion

Militarily, it was a tactical disaster for the communists. By the end of March, they had not controlled any city. More than 58,000 PAVN and VC had died in the process, compared to 4,000 U.S. and 5,000 ARVN deaths. By attacking everywhere, Giáp had shown no strength anywhere. He achieved great surprise, but was unable to exploit it. The assaults were launched piecemeal; they were repulsed piecemeal. Giáp had been wrong on two key assumptions. The people of the South did not rally to the communist cause. There was no uprising even in Huế. As a matter of fact, the people felt closer to and sought help from the government. The ARVN did not fold. It did buckle in a few places. But by and large, it fought fairly well.

The Việt Cộng were the big loser. The entire guerrilla structure had been destroyed. From that point, the war was entirely run by the North. The enemy were on the ropes: it was time to finish them off. Westmoreland and JCS Chairman Wheeler put together a plan requesting 206,000 additional troops to exploit the enemy's debacle. The Johnson administration leaked the plan to the press. The story broke on 10 March 1968. While the U.S. and the ARVN basked in their biggest and most important military success throughout the Vietnam War, the troop request was thought to cover up a massive defeat and the American public concluded it had been lied to. President Johnson tersely announced he would not seek reelection. As the American military historian Brig. Gen. S.L.A. Marshall summed up later, the 1968 Tết Offensive was "a potential major victory turned into a disastrous retreat through mistaken estimates, loss of nerve, bad advice, failure in leadership, and a tidal wave of defeatism!"[24]

What happened in South Vietnam's capital happened throughout the country. The people did not rise up. The ARVN did not collapse. During Tết, the communists not only executed government officials and officers but murdered their families as well. It was fight or die. And the ARVN fought.[25] The VC came back a few months later for what was called a mini-Tết—a repeat of the Tết Offensive in a smaller scale. They were again repulsed. On 5 May 1968, four Australian journalists and an English colleague unarmed riding a mini-moke were shot at by VC in Cholon. A VC officer pulled out a pistol and pumped bullets into two wounded men despite another survivor was shouting "báo chí" (press). The survivor ran away into a crowd of people and escaped unharmed.[26]

The Battle for Huế

Huế—a city of 140,000 people, the third largest in South Vietnam—sat on a bend of the Hương (Perfume) River about seven kilometers southwest of the South China Sea. The river divided the city into two sections. On the northern bank sat the

Citadel, a six square-kilometers fortress built in the first two decades of the 19th century. Stone walls up to eight meters high and several meters thick encircled the city as did a moat filled with water. Eleven gates pierced the massive city walls. A shallow canal coursed through the city with a pair of culverts connecting the inner canal to the outer ones. During the war, these culverts were blocked by barbed wire. South of the river lay the newer section of town, a bustling residential and business community—also called the Triangle—that contained the university, the province headquarters and its jail, the main hospital, and the treasury.

Despite its size and importance, the city had few defenders within its limits. On the eve of Tết, fewer than a thousand troops were on active duty. The rest were on leave celebrating the lunar New Year. The headquarters of the 1st ARVN Division was in Mang Cá compound, a mini-fortress in the northern section of the Citadel. Apart from the headquarters staff, the only combat units were the 36-man Reconnaissance Platoon and the elite Hắc Báo (Black Panther) Company. Two kilometers south of the Hương River and west of Highway 1 was the Tam Thái military camp, home of the ARVN 7th Cavalry with its M-41 light tanks. The Americans had 200 troops in the city along with 100 U.S. Army advisers headquartered at the MACV compound a block and a half south of the Hương River.

Preparations

The ARVN's best army unit, the 1st Infantry Division, was assigned to defend the I Corps. Its 2nd Regiment was positioned near Highway 1 just below the Demilitarized Zone (DMZ); its 1st regiment around the city of Quảng Trị, and its 3rd Regiment around Huế City. Nearby were the ARVN 7th Armored Cavalry and two battalions of the 1st Airborne Task Force, part of the strategic reserve of the South Vietnamese Army. Paramilitary forces included 41 Regional Forces companies and 244 Popular Forces platoons with a total authorized strength of 8,500 troops, armed mostly with M1 carbines, light machine guns and 60 mm mortars.

The U.S. had the 3rd Marine Division in Quảng Trị Province and the 1st Marine Division in southern I Corps, both under the authority of the III Marine Amphibious Force. The latter had control over the U.S. Army 108th Artillery Group, which included one battalion of 105 mm howitzers and two battalions of 175 mm guns.

A communist corps-level headquarters known as the B4 or Trị Thừa Thiên Front, hidden deep in Base Area 114 about 30 kilometers southwest of Huế, commanded communist forces in Thừa Thiên Province and the lower half of Quảng Trị Province. The upper half of that province was under the control of the B5 Front with headquarters in southern North Vietnam near the DMZ. These two commands had 30,000 regular troops and 20,000 guerrillas.

In preparation for the Tết attack, the communists had shifted several regiments from Quảng Trị Province to the vicinity of Huế. Among the new arrivals was the 7th Battalion of the 29th Regiment, 325C PAVN Division, a unit that had laid siege at Khe Sanh. Also new to the area was the 5th PAVN Regiment, a three-battalion unit that normally operated near Quảng Trị City. The communists had also created a special logistical and administrative zone known as the Huế City Front to manage the upcoming battle. The latter included officials of the Trị Thiên Huế Front, local party members, and military officers from the units involved in the attack.[27] The multidirectional attacks on Huế came from a northern wing and southern wing, with the southern wing arriving 48 hours ahead of the northern one because it had a longer distance to travel and more difficult terrain to cross.

On 29 January, the main body of the southern wing—the 804th Battalion, the 1st Sapper Battalion, the 815th and 818th Battalions of the 5th Regiment, the southern wing command group, and supporting units—descended from their mountain staging area 20 kilometers south of Huế and headed to the Tà Trạch River ten kilometers south of the city. They planned to take the ferry to cross the river but were spotted by an allied aircraft. Artillery shelling rained on the formation until the following morning. But no ground forces were sent to investigate the situation.

In the early hours of 30 January, due to a discrepancy of calendars, communists in southern I Corps and II Corps attacked their targets prematurely, giving other areas hints about the attack. President Thiệu cancelled the Tết cease-fire at 0945 on 30 January and ordered all troops on leave to return to their units. But General Trưởng had trouble reaching out to troops who were vacationing with their families and it would be days before all reported for duty. He sent out three platoons of Hắc Báo from his limited resources on hand to guard the provincial headquarters, the power station and the jail. The rest were used to improve security at all the gates, at the Tây Lộc Airfield, and at the Mang Cá compound.

Captain Jim Coolican, the Hắc Báo's adviser, returned to Huế in the afternoon with the Hắc Báo, following a month of fighting in the northwest. On the road south, he sensed something was off. There was less traffic north of the city than usual. The children who usually lined the streets when they passed through the villages were nowhere to be seen.[28]

Although the infiltrating sappers—who masqueraded as peasants or in some cases dressed as women—did not trigger a public alarm, Maj. Robert Annenberg from the 149th Military Intelligence Group, who arrived in the city on the eve of Tết, also sensed something abnormal. The festivities were subdued and for some reason shops, which usually were full of customers, closed early. The streets were strangely deserted and no one was celebrating as usual with decorations, flowers, and fruit trays. The silence in the city was unnerving.[29]

That evening, the northern wing of the enemy attack force moved toward Huế from the western base camps. The 806th Battalion, one company of the 800th Battalion, and a sapper platoon of 40 men, all from the 6th Regiment, quietly occupied a forward staging area in a graveyard two kilometers northwest of the Citadel. Other enemy units arrived at their planned positions.

The invading force was split into two units: one for the North and the other for the South. The northern one would take care of the Citadel while the southern would do the same in the Triangle. Their combined strength was four PAVN regiments (Eight, Nine, Five, Six) and eight VC battalions along with local militia. Each of these 24 battalions (each regiment had four battalions) had support companies for scouting, communications, special operations, artillery and crew-served weapons.

The northern force was led by Major Nguyễn Thu, a veteran PAVN officer. He commanded the PAVN 8th and 9th Regiments, four VC battalions. The southern force was led by Major Thân Trọng Một who commanded the PAVN 5th and 6th Regiments and four VC battalions.[30]

Shortly before midnight, a reconnaissance team hiding in the bushes on the north bank of the Hương River saw a long column of PAVN soldiers emerge from the darkness. The team stayed out of sight as the 800th, 802nd, and 12th Sapper Battalion headed west toward the city. The patrol commander reported what he had seen. General Trưởng dispatched a light observation airplane from the Tây Lộc Airfield to look for the enemy force. Flying through overcast skies, the aircraft returned two hours later, its pilot having seen nothing out of the ordinary.

Ngô Quang Trưởng

Trưởng was the archetype of the ARVN officer who fought in many of the major battles of the Vietnam War, from 1954 until 1975 when the RVNAF was dissolved. He was a man of action, a reformer, a builder (he rebuilt the ARVN 1st Division after the loss of Quảng Trị in 1972) and a strategist. He was considered one of the most honest and capable generals of the South Vietnamese Army during the long war in Southeast Asia. General Bruce Palmer described him as a "tough, seasoned, fighting leader probably the best field commander in South Vietnam."[31] General Creighton Abrams thought General Trưởng was capable of commanding an American division.[32]

Born in 1929 to a wealthy family in the Mekong Delta province of Kiến Hòa (presently Bến Tre), he was educated at the College of Mỹ Tho and attended the reserve officer school at Thủ Đức, Saigon. Commissioned in 1954, he immediately went into the airborne at the Command and Staff School in Dalat and was assigned on graduation as commander of the 1st Company, 5th Airborne Battalion. General Cao Văn Viên called Trưởng, "one of the best commanders at every echelon the Airborne Division ever had."[33]

He saw action in a 1955 operation to eliminate the Bình Xuyên river pirates who competed with President Ngô Đình Diệm for the control of Saigon and the surrounding area. For his role, he was awarded a battlefield promotion to first lieutenant. In 1964, promoted to major and appointed commander of the 5th Airborne Battalion, he led a heliborne assault into the Đỗ Xá Secret Zone in Minh Long District, Quảng Ngãi Province.

In 1965, Trưởng led a heliborne assault into the Hắc Dịch Secret Zone in the Ông Trịnh Mountain in Phước Tuy (Bà Rịa) Province, for which he received a battlefield promotion to lieutenant colonel. After the Hắc Dịch Battle, he was assigned as chief of staff of the Airborne Brigade and then became chief of staff of the Airborne Division in late 1965.

In 1966, when violent civil disorders broke out in central Vietnam, he was appointed acting commander of the 1st Infantry Division in Huế. Being a Buddhist, he was uncomfortable leading a unit charged with controlling Buddhist demonstrations protesting military control of the government. He carried his duty with professionalism and his appointment became permanent. Trưởng quickly molded the division, which had a poor reputation prior to his arrival, into one of the best in the ARVN. Lieutenant General Robert E. Cushman, commander of the III Marine Amphibious Force in I Corps Tactical Zone, felt that the ARVN 1st Division was "equal to any American unit."

In 1967, after his units attacked and destroyed a large number of guerrilla forces of the Lương Cơ—Đồng Xuyên—Mỹ Xã Front in Hương Trà District, Thừa Thiên Province, Trưởng was promoted to brigadier general. During the 1968 Tết Offensive, while the enemy was all around him and took over the Citadel, they were never able to run over his Mang Cá command post. With a calm and charismatic demeanor, he repulsed the attackers and was able to chase them out of the Citadel with the help of the Marines. After three weeks of constant fighting, he regained control of Huế and was promoted to the rank of major general. In August 1970, he was assigned to command IV Corps headquartered in Cần Thơ and promoted to lieutenant general in June 1971. He established a system of outposts along the Cambodian border to prevent infiltration of communist troops and supplies into the area.

In March 1972, the communists launched their Easter Offensive attacking Quảng Trị, Kontum, and An Lộc. Three divisions from B5 Front attacked the South Vietnamese northern firebases, which were evacuated. Quảng Trị fell on 1 May 1972. President Thiệu relieved I Corps commander Gen. Hoàng Xuân Lãm and replaced him with General Trưởng who arrived in Đà Nẵng on 3 May. The latter broadcast an order for all deserters to be shot on sight if they did not return to their units within 24 hours. He vowed to hold Huế and to turn back the communists. "He possessed a single-minded devotion to duty, fierce loyalty to his subordinates, and indefatigable energy, all qualities badly needed if the South Vietnamese were to hold the line in I Corps."[34]

He initiated a program to refit and retrain the battered units. By mid–May he launched a counteroffensive with three divisions. The process was slow and deliberate, but Trưởng's forces routed six NVA divisions to retake Quảng Trị on 16 September. Trưởng had turned the disastrous situation in I Corps by the sheer force of his personal leadership.

In 1975, Trưởng faced his greatest challenge. After the ARVN defenses in the Central Highlands collapsed in the face of a new North Vietnamese offensive, President Thiệu ordered Trưởng to defend Huế to the death. As the general set about to strengthen the city's defenses, Trưởng was told to abandon Huế. As he prepared to execute the last order, it was countermanded at the last minute and he was ordered to hold Huế at all costs.

Confusion reigned. The withdrawal from Huế became a disaster as people in crowded cars, buses, and other transportation means competed with troops to get out of Huế under enemy shelling. The situation in Đà Nẵng just was as bad. Trưởng tried to direct an evacuation by sea. That attempt also failed as panicked civilians and soldiers tried to escape to the South by any means possible. Đà Nẵng fell to the communists on 30 March 1975. Trưởng and his staff "swam through the surf to the rescuing fleet of South Vietnamese boats of every description. This fine soldier who was brokenhearted over the loss of practically all of his beloved 1st ARVN division, deserved a better fate."[35]

Despite the outcome of the war in I Corps and the subsequent collapse of South Vietnam, Trưởng's reputation survived intact. General Schwarzkopf called General Trưởng, "the most brilliant tactical commander I have ever known. Simply by visualizing the terrain and drawing on his experience fighting the enemy for fifteen years, Trưởng showed an uncanny ability to predict what they were going to do."

Skinny, short, stooped and hollow chested, he was the opposite of Westmoreland's model of a general. Trưởng walked with a slow shuffling gait. He had a broad, rugged face. A Salem cigarette usually dangled from his lower lip…. But he was one of the few ARVN top commanders fully respected by the Americans. Unlike many who led from the rear, who owed their position to family connections and demonstrated limited military skill, who appointed relatives to key staff positions and who enjoyed perquisites and amenities—homes, cars, offices—that became grander with their rank, Trưởng led his men from the front and seemed both shrewd and incorruptible. He lived like a soldier, sharing the conditions of his men, and had egalitarian manners that appealed to the leadership style of the American officers who worked with him.[36]

The Attack: 31 January–February 1

There were signs in the air. Westmoreland urged Thiệu to cancel the Tết leave and the president relented. But his staff never bother to broadcast the order. Trưởng's new order came too late, for most of the men had left the city to return home. Lieutenant Trần Ngọc "Harry" Huệ, the Hắc Báo commander could only gather a handful of his 200 men. He dispatched those who remained to satisfy the general's new order and had his driver drop him at his home in the southwest sector of the Citadel.

Northwest of the city, Terry Egan, an Australian Army adviser working with an ARVN recon platoon, was startled to observe PAVN regulars in crisp new uniforms moving in a single file toward the city. There were too many of them to attack. He lowered his head but continued to observe and counted two full battalions. He radioed the information to Mang Cá and General Trưởng ordered a spotter plane. But the fog hid everything and after two hours of looking around, the pilot called back to report that he did not see anything unusual.

In the meantime, sappers crept up to the barbed wire fencing around the Tam Thái base close to the Triangle, lifted it up and crawled under with care taken not to disturb the guards. Once inside the base, they approached the tanks, which were parked in neat rows. They placed two packs of dynamite under each—one wedged under the metal tread and the other under the diesel engine. The explosives were armed with primers that could be detonated remotely. Then the sappers crawled back outside the fencing.[37]

At 0333 following a prearranged signal, VC sappers inside the old city cut the telephone lines leading into Trưởng's headquarters. Four sappers dressed in ARVN uniforms[38] approached the sentries on the inside of the closed Chánh Tây Gate on the southwestern side of the citadel and killed them before they sounded the alarm. They then blew the door open to let the 800th Battalion and scores of other sappers enter the citadel. The group rushed toward the airfield through the deserted streets of Huế. The 802nd Battalion and a heavy weapons company took turns to cross the gate. The 806th Battalion, which had positioned itself inside a cemetery along Highway 1 near the western corner of the citadel sent a group of soldiers to capture the An Hòa Bridge. A team of 30 sappers climbed the northwestern wall and overpowered the guards standing watch at the An Hòa and Hậu Gates. They opened the doors of the gates, letting an infantry company to get in. This new group of NVA soldiers headed directly to Mang Cá to try to take over the headquarters.

At 0340, elements of the 164th PAVN Artillery Regiment fired a barrage of 122 mm rockets into the southern half of the city from the western hills. These six-foot tall rockets armed with a 14-pound warhead were powerful but inaccurate; they were designed to spread terror rather than destroy strong points. This was the first time they had been used in Thừa Thiên Province.

Outside the citadel, the 416th Battalion, PAVN 5th Regiment, along with a local force company and a recoilless rifle company, descended on the hamlets of Quê Chủ[39] and La Chủ,[40] which were surrounded by a large island of trees four kilometers west of the city. The leader of La Chủ turned out to be a VC agent who used U.S. seed money to build a huge bunker serving as a bomb shelter for the villagers. The communists used the building as their defense headquarters, which they reinforced with spider holes, trenches, and camouflaged fighting positions. Civilian laborers were used to move supplies from the hills to La Chủ.

At 0400, the 800th Battalion attacked the small Tây Lộc Airfield in the center of the old city. This position was defended by 50 men from the Hắc Báo Company and some ordnance troops. The ARVN used a stockpile of M72 antitank rockets to prevent the 800th Battalion from overrunning the runway. Meanwhile, the 802nd Battalion marched past the northern edge of the runway to get to the Mang Cá headquarters. They got lost but eventually found their way with directions from local inhabitants. They charged into the compound through the outer fence and the barbed wire. The defenders fought back from bunkers and makeshift positions.

There were fights at each of the gates, although the biggest one was at Hữu Gate. The 40-man assault company originally planned to enter the Citadel through a water main outside Mang Cá, which had been blocked by a thicket of barbed wire. They made their way around the western wall, down past Chánh Tây Gate to Hữu Gate. Since there was no assault group on the inside, they had to force their way in head on. There was a watch tower with a machine gun covering a narrow bridge over the moat. The bridge had a knee-high wall on either side. The guards were alert because the attacks had kicked off citywide. The first group raced across the bridge but was mowed down. Two-thirds of the men including the leader were killed or badly wounded. The remaining fell back and exchanged fire with the tower guards. Desperate, they crawled across the span hugging the low walls and made it all the way to the closed iron gate under the tower gun. Placing charges against the doors, they blew them open and ran inside. The guards were attacked from front and back and the machine gun was finally silenced by a rocket. Only 14 assault members were alive.[41]

At 0440, the command group of the PAVN 6th Regiment made its entry into the citadel through the captured Hữu Gate on the southeastern wall. They barred the damaged gate and their arrival completed the assault group assigned to take over the citadel.

The attack was bigger than General Trưởng had imagined and bigger than any he had seen before. His reduced forces were outgunned and outnumbered. He realized that his headquarters would fall unless he got reinforcements within a few hours. And once driven away, it would be difficult for the ARVN to get back. He called the Hắc Báo soldiers at the airfield to return to Mang Cá, then instructed all four battalions of the 3rd Regiment around Huế to return to the Citadel. He ordered the two armored units—the 3rd Troop, 7th Cavalry at PK-17 and the tank-equipped 1st Troop, 7th Cavalry at the Tam Thái Camp southeast of the Triangle—to proceed immediately to the 1st Division headquarters. Finally, he contacted the I Corps commander, General Lãm, to let him know about the critical situation in Huế and asked for permission to take control of the 1st Airborne Task Force. His request was approved.

The planted packs of dynamite went off under the tanks at Tam Thái, scattering parts everywhere. The combined blast was so loud it startled Marines miles away in

Phú Bài. Columns of flame erupted against the night sky. Then the support battalion stormed into the base killing the soldier guards.[42] Eleven tanks and several armored carriers had been away from Tam Thái and when called began heading toward Highway 1. After crossing An Cựu Bridge, soldiers from the 1st Sapper Battalion and the 818th Battalion hiding in and around buildings near the road opened fire at close range on the column with rocket propelled grenades, heavy machine guns, and four recoilless rifles. The ambush destroyed several vehicles and sent the 1st Troop, 7th Cavalry into disarray. Several M41 crews abandoned their undamaged tanks when they found themselves stuck between burning hulks. Later, the regimental commander led a few tanks through the roadblock and continued to Huế.

The Hắc Báo soldiers at the Tây Lộc Airfield had better luck. These street-savvy soldiers made their way back to Mang Cá compound through back alleys to avoid bands of PAVN troops who appeared to get lost. Along the way, they picked up additional soldiers who had been resting at home when the attack began. A total of 150 men sneaked into the Mang Cá compound after 0700. The reconnaissance platoon, which made its way back into the city was stuck at the Imperial Palace. Outnumbered and outgunned, they managed to retreat back to the 1st Division compound.

In the depth of the night the city residents were awakened by the explosions and gunfire. At first, they mistook the pops of gunfire for fireworks, but there was no confusion possible. These were different sounds. They then became frightened and shocked by the intensity of the fighting and the discordant power of the explosions, although not as shocked as they would be a few days later. They were startled because no such fighting had occurred in their peaceful Huế before.

Trần Thị Thu Vân, a writer and poet known as Nhã Ca, who flew from Saigon to Huế to attend her father's funeral and had stayed to offer prayers for him at Tết, was sleeping in her family home close to the Tam Thái tank base when she was jolted awake by the tank explosions. She huddled terrified with her brothers, sisters, and extended family in the middle of the room.[43]

Lieutenant Trần Ngọc "Harry" Huệ, the Hắc Báo commander, was awakened by the sounds of gunfire. He was stocky with a broad face and small, wide-set eyes. He was a fierce and extremely competent commander, one whose abilities outstripped his ranks. Huệ rounded up his children, wife and parents and ushered them into the family bunker. He jumped on his father's bicycle and pedaled toward Tây Lộc. He was shocked to see many NVA soldiers marching in the streets of Huế. He was not in his uniform and the NVA soldiers at that time ignored him. He fell behind a group of PAVN soldiers. When he reached Tây Lộc, he made a dash for it. Enemy troops shot at him, but missed. He finally joined his men and led them in their fight. Theirs was the only point of resistance on the west side of the Citadel until they were called back to defend the Mang Cá compound.

Harry Huệ gathered his men, told them about the order of pulling back to defend Mang Cá, and reminded them they were fighting not only for South Vietnam, but also for their families and homes. He told them they were the best of the 1st ARVN Division and if anyone could save the city of Huế, it was them and only them. "Hắc Báo," he shouted. His men cheered and followed.[44]

The southern end of Huế was the less well defended section of the city. It was also known as the Triangle, an area bordered by the Hương (Perfume) River on the west, the Phú Cam Canal on the south and Highway 1 on the east. This was the New City as opposed to the Citadel (Old City). It included important institutions like the Military Assistance Command Vietnam (MACV) compound, the U.S. Consulate, Huế University, the Provincial headquarters, the Treasury, the hospital, the jail, and so on...

The MACV compound was a rectangular enclosure formed by nondescript two or three-story buildings surrounded by fences and barbed wire as well as bunkers and six .30 caliber machine guns. Inside was a large courtyard with a parking lot and a tennis court. Requests for defensive upgrading were in the work when the Tết attack occurred. There were about 130 U.S. Army advisers and a few Marines in the compound that morning. A VC sapper company coming up Highway 1 fired at the compound. The defenders reacted by using an M-60 machine gun that decimated the squad as it tried to reach the gate. The VC fired their rocket-propelled grenades and mortars before attacking the southwest corner. After some back-and-forth firing, the VC moved to other objectives.

Before dawn, the PAVN-VC 804th Battalion arrived at the eastern side of the Triangle and split off in three different directions. One company occupied an intersection on Highway 1 a few blocks from the MACV compound to prevent mechanized forces from entering the Triangle. It also helped sappers seize the treasury building, the post office, and a radio station. The second company seized the An Cựu Bridge while the third company began controlling a smaller bridge over the canal to the west.

A company each from the 815th and 818th Battalions entered the western edge of the Triangle around 0450. The PAVN 818th targeted the Montagnard military school, the Civilian Operations and Rural Development Support (CORDS) center, the Lê Lai transportation camp, the provincial administration complex and jail, and the Thừa Thiên Capitol and administrative building. Other communist troops attacked the railroad station, the police headquarters near the railroad bridge at the western tip of the Triangle. They also seized the Từ Đàm Pagoda to use as the main command post for the southern wing.

Despite their late arrival, the 815th and 818th took control of the Triangle institutions in short time. They captured the CORDS senior advisor with his huge trove of secret documents. There was sporadic resistance here and there. The policemen at the police station offered some resistance before being overwhelmed, as were the Americans who took shelter at the Hoàng Giang Hotel, the people at the South Vietnamese engineer camp, and the Catholic communities that lay just south of the Phú Cam Canal.

When asked for help, the commander of Task Force X-RAY in Phú Bài, Brig. Gen. LaHue sent a reduced company to assist the MACV compound because he did not recognize the extent of the crisis in Huế and his forces were spread thin. Three kilometers south of Huế, the company encountered four Marine M48 tanks whose crews, after coming upon destroyed ARVN tanks on Highway 1 had decided to return to Phú Bài. After further discussion, the tankers made up their mind to join the task force and try to reach the Citadel via the Thượng Tư Gate. They were later joined by a second Marine company and three ARVN M41 tanks from the 1st Troop, 7th Cavalry. After crossing the Tràng Tiền Bridge over the Hương River, they encountered heavy fire from PAVN troops who were well entrenched in positions located on the Citadel wall. Unable to move forward, they pulled back. Golf's company attack was a fiasco. Ten Marines were killed, 56 wounded. On their way back from the bridge, they picked up Dr. Đoàn Văn Bá, an ARVN surgeon who had been hiding and who ran out to flag the company. He was wearing his uniform and red beret. He would provide help later in the busy compound dispensary.[45]

On the northwest side sometimes after 0900, the ARVN 3rd Troop, 7th Cavalry and 7th Airborne Battalion joined up at PK-17 and proceeded down Highway 1 in response to Gen. Trưởng's call. Around noon as they reached the cemetery about 400 meters from the Citadel, the PAVN 806th Battalion who ambushed them, fired on them from well concealed foxholes next to headstones. Two of the 12 M113 armored personnel carriers were destroyed and the convoy was brought to a halt. The paratroopers decided to make a frontal assault against the enemy under the cover of gunfire from the personnel carriers. As the brave attack failed to dislodge the defenders, they called for help. In the afternoon, the 2nd airborne battalion arrived by truck and executed a flanking attack, which also failed to dislodge the PAVN troops. The firing exchange stopped after sunset. Profiting from the darkness, the enemy withdrew into the Citadel.

The weather was not good that February month. The temperature was in the low fifties and never peaked above the sixties. The cloud ceiling dropped to 300 feet. Rain and fog occurred everyday making life and war miserable. Air support under these conditions was extremely difficult, if not dangerous.

On 1 February, the ARVN in the Citadel began the work of retaking the ground they had lost. Supported by armored personnel carriers and the Hắc Báo, the 2nd and 7th Airborne Battalions pushed southwest from the compound all the way to the Tây Lộc Airfield. The enemy had destroyed all the aircraft, although a group of ARVN ordnance continued to hold on to a corner of the facility. Later in the afternoon, the 1st Battalion, 3rd Regiment arrived at the compound by boat. The U.S. brought two companies of the ARVN 4th Battalion, 2nd Regiment based in Đông Hà to the Citadel.

At almost the same time, the Marines at the Huế MACV and at Phú Bài were working on a plan to recapture southern Huế. Order was given to the MACV Marines to clear the enemy from the southern bank of the Hương (Perfume) River. To complete that mission, they had only two depleted companies, four M48 tanks, a U.S. Army truck with a quad .50 caliber gun and two ARVN M41 tanks. Bad weaker meant almost no support from artillery and air strike.

The Marines decided first to clear a few Huế University buildings one block north to increase security at the helicopter landing zone and the Navy landing dock close by. But the enemy was entrenched in their positions and the Marines made no headway. In the afternoon, the seriously wounded were trucked out and Phú Bài and General LaHue finally realized the size of the NVA attack force. He sent an additional company from the 2nd Battalion, 5th Marine as reinforcement.

La Chủ Hamlet: 2–10 February

General Hoàng Xuân Lãm, I Corps commander and General John Cushman when meeting on 1 February in Đà Nẵng decided that the ARVN would clean the Citadel and the Marines would take care of southern Huế. They agreed while fighting the NVA inside the Citadel to limit the damage to the historic Huế as much as possible.

Colonel Campbell, commander of the 3rd Brigade, 1st Cavalry was given the mission to relieve the pressure on the western side of the city from where the PAVN came. The 2nd Battalion, 12th Cavalry under Lt. Col. Sweet was airlifted from Phú Bài to PK-17, an ARVN outpost on the western side of Huế. PK-17 was a circular compound dotted with tin shacks and a few bunkers surrounded by a strand of barbed wire.

On 3 February 1968 the battalion received the order to march toward the city by going south and east instead of following Highway 1, which probably was mined by the enemy. At 0945, the battalion arrived at the hamlet of Liễu Cốc about four kilometers northwest of the city. On seeing the Americans, villagers fled to the hamlet of Quế Chủ two hundred meters away but hidden in dense vegetation. A map showed a third hamlet La Chủ a few hundred meters further away. When Sweet was told to take Quế Chủ, he tried to call for an air strike to soften the target. But the strike was ineffectual because of the bad weather.

The battalion took Quế Chủ shortly thereafter and found an elaborate system of trenches and bunkers. A decision was made to hold the hamlet for the night and take care of the third hamlet the next morning. This was a good decision for the enemy counterattacked shortly thereafter with 82 mm mortars, 75 mm recoilless rifles, and .51 caliber heavy machine guns, weapons associated with a regiment size formation. Later that night the 2nd battalion received supplies via helicopters.

On 4 February, the 2nd battalion was attacked at regular intervals throughout the day. It was decided to move to a small hill several kilometers south of Quế Chủ otherwise they would be overrun by the enemy. After a few forays, it was realized that La Chủ and Quế Chủ were defended by a regiment or more of well-equipped NVA soldiers and that Col. Campbell did not have enough soldiers to dislodge the enemy.

The Fight for the Triangle and the Citadel: 2–10 February

On 2 February, a truck convoy delivered to the MACV a company of the 2nd Battalion, 5th Marine along with two M50 Ontos carriers armed with six 106 mm recoilless rifles capable of blowing apart concrete walls and fortified enemy positions. That night, the NVA 815th Battalion overran the Provincial headquarters and prison. A Vietnamese turncoat pointed out a weak spot in the building's defense allowing the enemy to get inside. The NVA released 2,500 inmates including 350 communists and sympathizers and pressed them into service as manual laborers and stretcher bearers.

On 3 February, Col. Hughes commander of the 1st Marine arrived at the MACV compound to take charge of the battle in the Triangle. The following day, the marines recaptured a few blocks by using M72 antitank weapons, 3.5 inch rocket launchers, 106 mm recoilless rifles, and tear gas. They received "six 106 mm recoilless rifles. They were the same as the six mounted on the Ontos, rifles as big and heavy as cannons—lifting each required several strong men. The 106-mm fired an explosive round that weighted nearly twenty pounds and delivered a ferocious back blast. Small flatbed vehicles called mules were needed to carry them. They were about the size of a golf cart, fast and maneuverable, and just big enough for the 106s."[46] Since the ARVN did not have these 106s, it recovered sections of the city more slowly than the Americans. But the PAVN 815th and 818th Battalions still controlled the western part of the Triangle. The 810th battalion occupied its northern end. The 804th Battalion and the 1st Sapper Battalion controlled Highway 1 on the South side of the Phú Cam Canal.

On 5 February, the Marines secured the hospital building at 1630. The next day, they took over the provincial building and jail, which had served as headquarters of the PAVN 5th Regiment. On 7 February, the sappers destroyed the Nguyễn Hoàng Bridge preventing the Americans to cross into the Citadel. The battle of the Triangle was almost over as the 818th, 815th, and 810th moved to the South side of Phú Cam Canal while the 804th prepared to cross the Hương River by raft and boat to Gia Hội Island.

The ARVN under Gen. Trưởng were expanding southward toward the Tây Lộc Airfield. On 2 February helicopters brought the 4th Battalion, 2nd Regiment and a company of the 1st Battalion, 1st Regiment to the Mang Cá compound. The depleted 2nd and 7th Airborne Battalions recaptured the Tây Lộc Airfield. The ARVN 9th Airborne Battalion arrived at Mang Cá compound. By nightfall, the ARVN had regained control of the northwestern section of the Citadel.

On 3 February, the 1st Airborne Taskforce attacked the neighborhoods west of the airfield. Although the fighting claimed several hundred PAVN lives, the enemy had transformed houses and buildings into a series of defensive lines and interconnected strong points. They also used dug-in positions on the Citadel walls, which gave them a dominant high ground view of the surroundings. The fourth of February

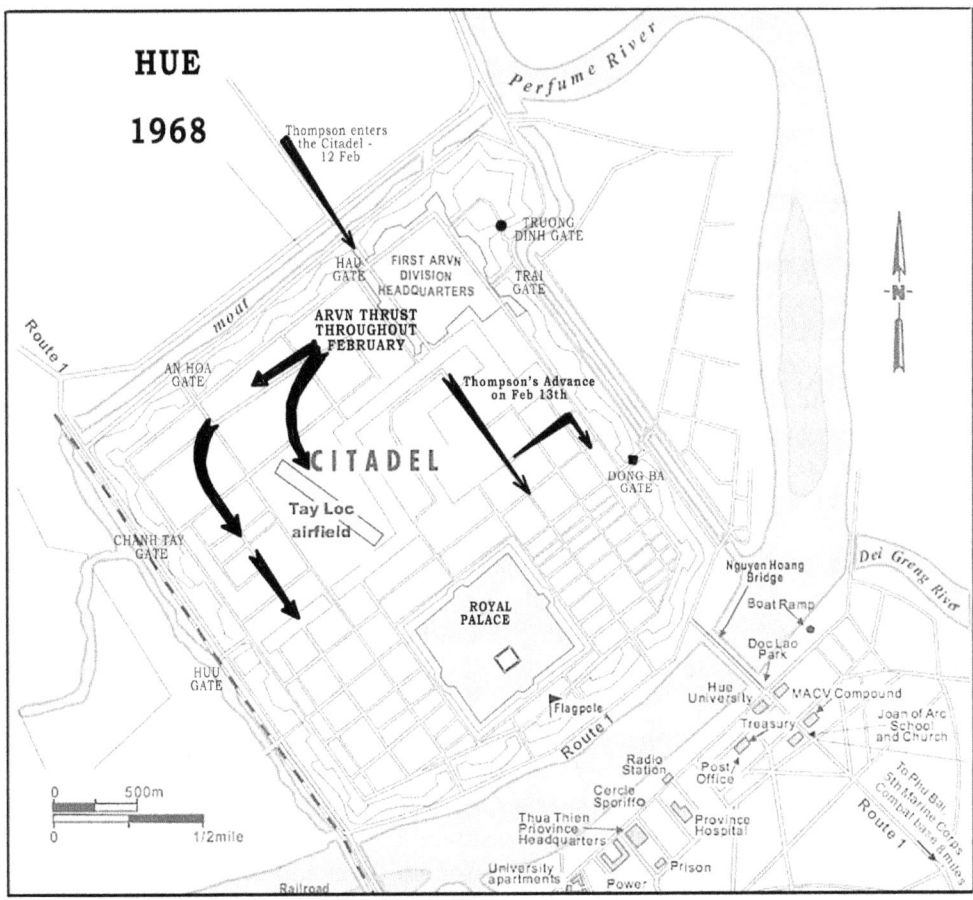

Figure 7-1: Battle for Huế (Ngoc Lung Hoang, *The General Offensive of 1968–69* (Washington, D.C.: U.S. Army Center of Military History, 1981).

was a consolidating day. In the eastern sector, Gen. Trưởng's infantry pushed the enemy back to a line that was roughly halfway across the Citadel. In the northwestern sector, the ARVN had recaptured the An Hòa Gate.

On 5 February, Gen. Trưởng repositioned his forces. He moved the fresh paratroopers from Tây Lộc Airfield to the eastern sector of the Citadel where the enemy was strong. Despite high losses, the PAVN 6th Regiment showed no sign of cracking. The ARVN 4th Battalion/2nd Regiment was moved to the airfield, then toward the southwestern wall. The ARVN 1st Battalion/3rd Regiment headed to the Chân Tây Gate and the western corner of the Citadel. The ARVN 2nd, 3rd, and 4th Battalions, 3rd Regiment were transported by boat to Mang Cá compound.

On 6 February, the 1st Battalion, 3rd Regiment cleared the enemy from the western corner of the Citadel while the 4th Battalion/2nd Regiment pushed the enemy to a few blocks of the southwestern wall. It appeared that the ARVN was on the verge of cutting the 6th Regiment in two, separating the enemy on the eastern sector from those on the southwestern sector. But the enemy received a reinforcement of a battalion or more of the 29th Infantry Regiment from La Chủ. Caught off guard, the 4th Battalion/2nd Regiment fell back to the Tây Lộc Airfield.

On 7 February, U.S. Navy landing craft delivered the 2nd, 3rd, 4th Battalions, 3rd Regiment to Mang Cá. A company from the 1st Regiment and the 2nd troop, 7th Cavalry equipped with 15 M113 armored personnel carriers arrived from Quảng Trị. Gen. Trưởng had his entire regiment, a battalion from the 2nd Regiment, two companies from the 1st Regiment, three paratrooper battalions from the 1st Airborne Task Force, two armored cavalry squadrons, and his elite Hắc Báo Company. Combat had reduced some battalions to half strength. Food and ammunition were running low. The ARVN had few heavy weapons such as mortars and recoilless rifles with which to dislodge the enemy from stone buildings. Progress was bound to be slow unless it received more artillery and air support.

On 8 February, the 2nd, 3rd, and 4th Battalions, 3rd Regiment were sent to seize the southwestern wall. But the PAVN clung stubbornly to a line of buildings at the base of the wall preventing the ARVN from accomplishing their task. Without artillery and heavy weapons, dislodging a well-armed and well-supplied enemy would take a long time.

West of Huế: 11–20 February

On 12 February, after massive artillery bombardment two companies of the U.S. 5th Battalion, 7th Cavalry attacked La Chủ but were repulsed by heavy enemy fire. Campbell decided to hold further attack until the weather improved and he had more troops at his disposal. Then the 2nd Battalion, 501st Infantry was assigned to him. The logistics situation improved by 15 February as the number of daily supply convoys between Đông Hà and Fort Evans increased from one to three. The weather, however, had not improved by 20 February.

On 15 February, General Abrams assumed command of MACV Forward. He met with Vice President Nguyễn Cao Kỳ, General Lãm and General Cushman and the decision was made to take over La Chủ and Quê Chủ. On 19 February Campbell received control of the 1st Battalion, 7th Cavalry, which gave him a total of four battalions he could use against the enemy.

Stalemate in the Citadel: 11–20 February

On 11 February, one day after the ARVN swept the last communist from the neighborhood around Tây Lộc Airfield, U.S. helicopters began bringing the ARVN Marine task force and six 106 mm guns. A reduced company from the 1st Battalion, 5th Marines was airlifted from Phú Bài to Mang Cá compound. The weather turned nasty and it would be two more days before the skies cleared up enough for the airlift to resume. A second company from the 1st Battalion and five Marine tanks traveled by landing craft on the Hương River from the Triangle in southern Huế to Mang Cá. There was fire from the enemy from the riverbank, although no landing craft was hit.[47]

When Major Robert Thompson, commander of the 1st Battalion, 5th Marines met with General Trưởng on 13 February, decision was made for the Marines to take care of the eastern sector and to relieve the 1st Airborne Task Force, which was scheduled to depart for Saigon. On arrival the two Marine units collided with a large PAVN force that had quietly reclaimed several residential blocks formerly under control of the ARVN troopers. Company A sustained 35 casualties in the first few minutes of contact. Thompson moved quickly to stabilize the front line and replaced company A with a reserve company. With the help of two M48 tanks, the Marine companies advanced about three hundred meters before they were stopped by enemy fire coming from an archway tower at the Đông Ba Gate.

On 14 February 155 mm and 8-inch howitzers and 5- and 8-inch naval guns pounded the Đông Ba Gate. A break in the weather allowed U.S. bombers to drop napalm and rockets on the target. Despite the large amount of ordnance dropped, the PAVN soldiers did not abandon it. Although the Marines gained some ground on their flank, they did not make any headway.

In the ARVN sector, the Marine battle group A replaced the ARVN 3rd Regiment, which moved from the southwest to the northwest sector. The Marines moved only 400 meters during the next two days because they did not have the 106 mm recoilless rifles the Americans were using. On 14 February, the enemy in the western corner of the Citadel counterattacked and drove a wedge through the Regiment isolating one of its battalions. It took the 3rd Regiment two days to rescue the unit and clear out enemy pockets.

On 15 February, after a round of artillery, naval gunfire, and air strikes collapsed part of the tower that rose above Đông Ba Gate, the fourth company of Thompson's battalion assaulted the ruined structure with the help of tanks and Ontos carriers. The PAVN units showed no sign of wavering despite the bombardment. When a platoon from Company D won a toehold at the base of the tower, Thompson threw in his reserves and the Americans soon overran the whole structure.

On 16 February. Thompson's battalion made a slow but steady progress toward the southeastern wall. The Marines were under fire from three directions at once: frontally, flanking fire from the tall buildings on Gia Hội Island to the east, and from the walls of the Imperial Palace from the west. They could see the wall a few blocks away but the ground between was a nightmare of crumbled masonry, pockmarked buildings, and craters that gave the enemy excellent defensive positions.

The PAVN troops received new supplies and reinforcements every night. The 6th Battalion, 24th Regiment, 304th Division came from the Khe Sanh area. The 7th

Battalion, 90th Regiment, 324 B Division arrived a few days later after a forced march through the Demilitarized Zone. Even the 803rd Regiment, which stationed on the eastern section of the Demilitarized Zone had been sent down to Huế although the order was later cancelled.

The Final Push: 20–25 February

On the afternoon of 20 February, Major Thompson hatched a plan to break the enemy's last line of defense. He asked for volunteers for a night attack. Although fighting in pitch dark conditions was not ideal in the treacherous ruins of the Citadel, all company leaders agreed. The job was given to Company A, which suffered serious casualties the first day of the attack. The company was well rested and ready to prove itself.

At 0300 on 21 February, three small groups moved into the no man's land, each toward a different building that was vital to enemy's defense. The buildings were found to be undefended because the enemy had pulled back to get some rest at night. When the enemy came back before daylight, they were killed and the 1st Battalion, 5th Marines moved forward to consolidate the gain. By the end of the day, the Marines were about a hundred meters from the southeastern wall.

On that same day, the ARVN 21st and 39th Ranger Battalions arrived by truck convoy in southern Huế. They spent the day clearing the eastern bank of the Hương River to allow allied rivercraft to travel more safely from the coast to the Navy landing dock.

On 21 February, Colonel Campbell launched a three-battalion attack against Quê Chủ and La Chủ: the 5th Battalion, 7th Cavalry from the north; the 1st Battalion, 7th Cavalry and the 2nd Battalion, 501st Infantry from the west. They then used smoke canisters to obscure the enemy's view and 40 mm cannon fire from the M42 Dusters to destroy individual strong points. Once the outer line was breached, they faced a regiment or more of PAVN troops in close range battle. At 1700, the communists abandoned the villages and fled to the Citadel.

On 22 February, the 1st Battalion, 7th Cavalry remained at Quê Chủ and La Chủ to mop up pockets of resistance while the other battalions swept the area all the way to the Citadel.

A few kilometers south of Huế along the South side of the Sáu Canal, a deep waterway that ran toward the Citadel perpendicular to the Hương River were entrenched a few PAVN companies. The latter were armed with mortars, machine guns, recoilless rifles and rocket-propelled grenades. The 2nd Battalion, 501st Infantry positioned about one kilometer north of the Sáu Canal began moving toward that direction. Along the way, as they passed through a hamlet, they were shocked to discover the bodies of 30 civilians apparently murdered by the retreating communists. Many of those slain had been bound and shot while others were dismembered. The 2nd Battalion, 501st Infantry attacked the PAVN troops defending the canal. The attack, which was not successful and as the night came down, was called off.[48]

By 22 February, the PAVN only controlled the Imperial Palace and the southwestern corner of the Citadel. A company of the 3rd Battalion, 5th Marines overran the Thương Tú Gate. This gave the Marines a direct ground connection to southern Huế via a footbridge over the damaged Nguyễn Hoàng Bridge. In the southwestern sector, the PAVN launched a sudden counterattack against the ARVN Marines, which was broken up with a well-timed artillery barrage that killed 150 enemy soldiers. To the east, the ARVN forced their way into the Imperial Palace and began clearing out the snipers who had long resided there. East of the Citadel, the 21st and 39th Ranger Battalions boarded junks to travel to Gia Hội Island where the communist provisional government had been headquartered since the beginning of the offensive. Enemy resistance fell off significantly following the arrival of the rangers. With only the Hữu Gate in the hands of the PAVN, the communist Huế City Front ordered its troops to abandon the Citadel and withdraw to the west.

On 23 February, the 5th Battalion, 7th Cavalry swept the northwestern wall to the An Hòa Bridge, flushing out a number of enemy soldiers who had taken refuge in the tall grasses and weeds. In the northwest, the remainder of the troops moved toward Thôn An, where the PAVN had ambushed the ARVN 7th Airborne on 31 January. The 2nd Battalion, 12th Cavalry and the 2nd Battalion, 501st Infantry resumed their battle with the PAVN on the Sáu Canal. The NVA appeared to have large reserves of ammunition to fight for a long time. The Sáu Canal presented a physical barrier for any attack the Americans might contemplate.

On 24 February, the ARVN recaptured the Ngộ Môn (Southern Gate) and removed the VC flag that had flown over it since the beginning of the battle replacing it with the South Vietnamese flag. The Hắc Báo Company and a battalion from the 3rd Regiment made a final sweep of the Imperial Palace while the ARVN Marine retook most of the southwestern wall. By nightfall only the extreme southwestern corner of the Citadel remained in enemy hands. Another U.S. attack against the Sáu Canal proved to be unsuccessful. Retreating PAVN soldiers who gathered at their last stronghold around the Citadel offered strong resistance to the attack. That night, groups of soldiers were seen marching away from Huế to the North and to the West. Forward observers called in artillery all night long.

Allied forces crushed the last organized enemy forces in the Citadel on 25 February. The 2nd Battalion, 12th Cavalry made another assault on the Sáu Canal only to discover that the enemy had slipped away during the night. They found an abandoned regimental field hospital nearby and many fresh graves near the canal as well as many piles of discarded equipment. On 26 February, President Thiệu flew from Saigon to Huế to congratulate General Trưởng and his men. The sweep around Huế would continue for some time.

Aftermath

The battle for Huế was the longest battle of the Tết Offensive. It cost the U.S. 142 Marines killed and another 1,100 wounded. The ARVN lost 421 men killed and 2,123 wounded. The reported number of enemy killed ranged from 2,500 to 5,000. The U.S. Marines fought heroically under adverse conditions. Two understrength Marine battalions managed to recapture southern Huế by themselves. A third Marine battalion played a large role in the fighting of the Citadel.

The ARVN had performed well during the battle. The Hắc Báo Company, the 3d Regiment of the 1st Infantry Division, and the paratroopers of the 1st Airborne Task Force fought with exceptional skill and valor. Despite having fewer heavy weapons such as recoilless rifles and rocket propelled grenade launchers, they not only held their own but also overcame a sizable force of North Vietnamese PAVN in prolonged close range battles.[49] The mayor of Huế, Lt. Col. Phạm Văn Khoa, who was also the province chief, was found hiding in the rafters of the hospital six days after the offensive began. He was sacked in March 1968 for his poor performance.[50]

The communists had managed to bring two divisions and a complement of heavy weapons including .521 caliber antiaircraft machine guns, 57 mm and 75 mm recoilless rifles and .82 mm mortars to the doorsteps of Huế without being detected. They never seemed to be short of food or ammunitions. However, they were unable to organize a general uprising. They also failed to co-opt Buddhist leaders who had spoken against the government and the war in the past. Only a few civilians offered to help the enemy with food, information or labor. Anti-communist feeling was strong among all segments of the Huế society as a result of the enemy attack and the murderous policy of the revolutionary communist government. By bringing the war to Huế, the communists caused the destruction of at least 75 percent of the houses in Huế. By the end of the battle, about 115,000 of its 140,000 people were left temporarily homeless. Food quickly ran short throughout the city. Four weeks would pass until water service would be restored. More than 2,800 civilians—the real number may be double that number—were systematically executed by the communists. The so-called Huế Massacre will be discussed below.

Nineteen sixty-eight turned out to be the big year for the ARVN, which while unprepared but with U.S. help had defeated the PAVN and VC multidivisional attacks on cities throughout the country. The ARVN had survived; the people had not revolted against the government, but had supported it all along. The VC infrastructure was almost completely wiped out. From then on, the ARVN would fight against the PAVN who filled the void left by the VC.

The Huế Massacre

During the 26-day occupation of Huế (January 31-February 26, 1968), the communists proceeded with the execution of thousands of people, locals as well as foreigners, civilians as well as government officials, priests, teachers, physicians and laborers, adults as well as children, Catholics and Buddhists. Only after the war had ended were mass graves discovered in and around Huế.[51] At least 2,800 people were found executed and thousands more were missing.[52] Victims were found bound, tortured, and sometimes buried alive. Others were clubbed to death. Ben Kiernan called it "the largest atrocity of the war."[53]

Eyewitness Accounts

When the PAVN troops arrived at Huế, they quickly made rounds of the "liberated areas" armed with lists of names and addresses of the Huế citizens. For the communists, the war against civilians was as important as that against enemy forces.

Dr. Horst Gunther Krainick, a German pediatrician from the University of Freiburg, Germany came to Huế in December 1960 to help establish a medical school at the University of Huế. Dr. Krainick and his wife, Elizabeth hoped to return to Germany after the end of the school year and graduation of the small class of senior medical students. As non-combatants and medical workers, they hoped they would be left alone. But they did not know that they were listed—though not by name—as Item 65 of the Right Bank target list.

On the fifth day of the occupation, a well-armed squad wearing red arm bands, neat uniforms and boots arrived in a Jeep and a Volkswagen bus and proceeded to search a building of the university. They came back three hours later and took away Dr. Krainick and his wife, as well as Dr. Raimund Discher and Dr. Alois Altekoester. The four bodies were later found in a shallow grave in a potato field a half a mile away, all victims of the executioner's bullets.[54]

Father Urbain and Father Guy, two French Benedictine priests, lived at the Thiện An Mission in the tall pines in a bluff south of the city. When the fighting began, several thousand local peasants came to the monastery seeking refuge followed by communist troops. Father Urbain's body was found in a common grave with ten other victims near the monumental tomb of the Emperor Đồng Khánh (1883–89). He had been bound hand and foot and buried alive. Father Guy's body was found nearby. He had been shot in the head.[55]

The area occupied for the longest period of time by the communists was Gia Hội, a large triangular section of land east of the walled city of Huế on the northern bank of the Hương River. Besides a popular market place and several commercial streets, it was Huế's residential suburb with rich farmlands. Being devoid of government headquarters or military installations, it did not carry the same strategic importance as the Triangle or the Citadel. Caught undermanned during the Tết Offensive attack, the ARVN had decided to use its available units to fight enemy troops in the Citadel and the Triangle first before taking on the sections in Gia Hội. This decision spared Gia Hội from the extensive physical destruction related to street fighting seen in the Citadel and the Triangle. But it left the communists in total control of the area for more than three weeks. They ripped down all the South Vietnamese flags and called for the flag of the National Liberation Front (NLF) to be flown in its place. Since no one had an NLF flag, permission was given to fly a Buddhist flag in its place.

On the second day civil servants, military personnel and police were called to report to Gia Hội High School. They were told that nothing would happen to those who reported on time and if their attitude was good. People were afraid and most hid in their houses and bunkers. The announcements became tougher as days went by. People were told they would be shot if they were discovered hiding. Informants began making rounds and pointed out to the communists the homes of officials or ARVN officers.[56]

Phạm Văn Tường worked as a janitor at the government information office. He and his family—his wife, eight children, and three nephews—spent much of their time in a bunker on the side of their house. One day, four men in black pajamas came to the door of the bunker. "Mr. Pham, the information office cadre, come out here." He climbed out of the bunker with his five-year-old son, three-year-old daughter, and two of his nephews. There was a burst of gunfire. When the rest of the family came out, they found all five of them dead.[57]

Discovery

Between 1968 and 1969, more than 2,800 bodies were recovered from four major mass graves. A few months after the battle, about 1,200 civilian bodies were recovered from 18 hastily concealed mass graves. A second major group of graves were discovered in the first seven months of 1969.

In September 1969, three VC defectors led the U.S. 101st Airborne Brigade through the royal tombs areas, and through the most rugged country of central Vietnam, to the Đá Mài Creek bed deep in double canopy jungle ten miles south of Huế. There spread out for nearly 100 yards in the ravine were skulls, skeletons and shards of bones of the men of Phủ Cam, washed clean and white by the running brook. The skulls showed they had been shot or brained with blunt instruments. Huế officials later released a list of 428 names. About 100 were ARVN service men, about 100 were students, and the rest were civil servants, village and hamlet officials, government workers and ordinary citizens.[58] In November 1969, a major mass grave was found at Phủ Thư Salt Flats near the village of Lương Viên, 10 miles east of Huế halfway between Huế and Đà Nẵng.

Legacy

There is no word to express the sorrow of the Huế inhabitants when asked about that 1968 tragic event. They just cried and cried. For them, it was their personal "Holocaust." Although their country was at war against the communists, they could not figure out how babies, women, elderly men, foreign workers—all innocent civilians—could be murdered in such a cold-blooded manner. Not only were they murdered, the story was also called propaganda or a "myth."[59] Although the communists continued to deny the accusations, in 1988, or more than 20 years after the war, they admitted that "soldiers may have committed mistakes."[60]

In 1968 the novelist Nhã Ca, born Trần Thị Thu Vân, was returning to her city of birth, Huế, to attend to her father's funeral when she was stuck in the city during this tragic event. Having witnessed the tragedy of the war, she published a book titled *Giải Khăn Khô cho Huế*, which later received a Presidential Award. After 1975, she was jailed by the communist regime for two years for writing the book, which was also banned at that time. Her husband, the poet Trần Dạ Từ, was jailed for 12 years. They later immigrated to Sweden and then the United States. Her book was translated into English as the *Mourning Headband for Huế* by Olga Dror, a former Soviet citizen who was knowledgeable about communist tactics.[61] The PAVN soldier and historian Nguyễn Ngọc admitted to Ken Burns and his group,

> I don't know whether the order to kill them came from the local commanders or higher up. But they killed the people they'd arrested. Some had worked for the South Vietnamese government or for the Americans, but there were people who were wrongly arrested, too, maybe because of some personal grievance and they were all killed. This is a smear against the revolution, a stain on the revolution's record.[62]

8

1969

Vietnamization, Hamburger Hill

In this chapter, two important events in 1969 will be discussed: (1) the Vietnamization strategy; and (2) the battle of Đồng Ấp Bia, or Hamburger Hill. Since the latter was mainly an American battle against the PAVN, and in which the RVNAF was called in to participate in the last phase of the battle, only that late phase of this battle is discussed.

Vietnamization

Although the war was "Vietnamized" from the start, Harry Summers suggested that "the limited war theorists and counterinsurgency gurus so obfuscated the conflict that, to this day, many believe that the Vietnam War was between the United States and North Vietnam, rather than between North Vietnam and South Vietnam."[1]

Vietnamization

On 20 January 1969, Richard Nixon took office with a vague and generalized idea about getting out of the war. Giáp, on the other hand, gave him no breathing room by launching countrywide attacks against South Vietnam (phase IV General Offensive) on 22 February. All the attacks were repulsed without major military or economic gains. The morale of the VC dipped and by 1 July, about 20,000 enemy personnel had defected to the RVNAF.[2]

Washington realized that the war would end in a stalemate and decided to change its policy. Winning had never been a U.S. policy in Vietnam for "military victory is not possible on the strategic defensive."[3] Thus was born Vietnamization, which was the brainchild of Nixon's defense secretary Melvin Laird who saw the war as a "losing proposition" and to whom "Vietnamization offered a way to get the United States, the Republican Party, Richard Nixon, and most importantly Melvin Laird, out of the Vietnamese quagmire. Whether it would work or not was secondary. It was an exit."[4]

Vietnamization became the centerpiece of the American policy in mid–1969. However, there was no overall plan or timetable on the part of the United States. It was a strategy, which would clear the way for United States withdrawal regardless of the South Vietnamese's ability to defend against the PAVN and the VC. The South Vietnamese never used the terminology anyway. Cao Văn Viên, the chairman of the Joint General Staff, wrote, "Why Vietnamization? ... Why make it sound that only United States forces were fighting the Vietnam War? The amount of blood shed by the South Vietnamese was many times greater than that of (the) gallant United States troops."[5]

In the end, in a rush to get out, Vietnamization was done too haphazardly to be successful. Training installations and equipment were grossly inadequate. Training within and by the ARVN units themselves was almost nonexistent. Successful Vietnamization required an almost total restructuring of the South Vietnamese society, government and armed forces,[6] which was never accomplished.

The 1968 Tết Offensive had depleted the ranks of the VC and demoralized them. This gave Thiệu the chance to pursue pacification. By the end of 1969, 90 percent of villages and hamlets of South Vietnam were rated as secure or relatively secure; five million more people lived in government controlled secure areas than in 1967. "The number of VC defectors, both troops and infrastructure, reached 47,000" in 1969 compared to 18,000 in 1968.[7] President Thiệu also took advantage of the nation's survival effort to consolidate his power at the expense of his political rival, Vice-President Kỳ. He fired Kỳ's appointees, reshuffled the cabinet, and reappointed key military commanders then replaced them with his own men.[8]

The South Vietnamese people on the other hand seemed to be patriotic and anti-communist during the Tết offensive. They neither supported the communists nor rebelled against their own government. After the initial bewilderment and terror, they did not panic. They had seen the faces of the enemy, these young peasants' faces full of immaturity and innocence who came to make war on them and their country, to bring destruction to their families. They realized that their ARVN soldiers, the Rangers, the paratroopers, the marines could easily defeat them...

They realized that they too must enroll into the army to support the country's fight against communism and respond to the new mobilization bill. The government had already recalled 65,000 retired servicemen who had fewer than 12 years of service. In all the cities across South Vietnam, people beyond draft age organized themselves into self-defense committees in their neighborhoods, screening people coming in and out or reporting strangers to the police.[9]

During the Tết Offensive, communist forces were equipped with AK-47s and rocket launchers, B-40 or B-41. The superiority of these weapons was recognized immediately by the urban population, even by teenagers. They could differentiate between the sharper, rounder and more uniform AK-41 bursts and the dull crackles of ARVN's Garand and Carbin sounds. The concern caused the JGS to ask for a modernization of RVNAF armament. By May 1968, the first stage of the implementation process began with some troops receiving the M-16 rifles, the M-60 machine guns, the M-79 grenade launchers, and the AN/PRC-35 field radio sets.[10]

Through the same modernization effort, ARVN armor assets jumped to 1,500 vehicles compared to 600 at the time the offensive began. The Airborne Division was upgraded to three artillery battalions instead of a single one to each infantry division. The VNAF saw its helicopter armada increased fourfold to 400 ships, in addition to 60 more jet fighter bombers. An indirect consequence of the offensive was that the rural area was virtually open to enemy penetration and control. ARVN infantry units were extracted from pacification support and redeployed to cities to ensure their defense.

Vietnamization vs. Koreanization

The Vietnam War had some similarity with the Korean War. Both wars were an outgrowth of the Cold War and both North Korea and North Vietnam were supported by the communist bloc, especially China and the Soviet Union. Both wars were fought on the strategic defensive against the spread of communism rather than on the strategic offensive, where the objective was to destroy the enemy's force and occupy his territory. The best possible outcome of a strategic defensive was battlefield stalemate. The latter was reached in Korea in April 1951 although conflict continued for two more years before the 1953 armistice was signed. In Vietnam, the U.S. recognized a stalemate in 1969 and the North Vietnamese realized this after their failed 1972 Easter Offensive.

The Korean Military Advisory Group (KMAG) was formed in 1949. The MACV (Military Assistance Command Vietnam) was formed in 1962 as the successor to MAAG-Vietnam and its predecessor MAAG-Indochina, which dated back to September 1950. When the war began in Korea, the Eight U.S. Army took control of KMAG, which it supervised as one of its several subordinate commands. Things were so bad in the beginning that cynics said KMAG stood for "Kiss My Ass Goodbye." But instead of pushing ROKA to one side, the U.S. continue to train and develop ROKA on the battlefield. When the war ended, ROKA had 16 well trained and equipped battle-hardened divisions.[11]

By comparison, MACV remained in Saigon throughout the duration of the war and no field army headquarters was ever established. During U.S. troop buildup, MACV was occupied with building up the South Vietnamese military. After 1965, its attention was directed entirely to U.S. military operations. The advisory effort and the South Vietnamese Army were shunted aside and rarely operated with U.S. military forces. General Westmoreland wrote in his *Report on the War*:

> I consistently resisted suggestions that a single, combined command could more effectively prosecute the war. I believed that subordinating the Vietnamese forces to U.S. control would stifle the growth of leadership and acceptance of responsibility essential to the development of Vietnamese Armed Forces capable of defending their country.[12]

That was an after-the-fact rationalization of Westmoreland's own decision because he was in Korea during the war and had seen with his own eyes the effect of the supervision of the Eight U.S. Army over ROKA. Why would he want to do it differently with the ARVN? Ultimately, it was that decision which suppressed and killed the education, maturation, and growth of the ARVN—a flawed and fatal decision that in the end prolonged the war and determined its fate.

It was also unfortunate that Saigon, which had no strategy of its own when the Americans were in the country, also failed to develop a real strategy after they left. "It failed to see for itself that to survive without American troops, a comprehensive national plan to mobilize all the resources available ... to take over war responsibilities effectively." However, the Vietnamese leadership became complacent and nearsighted perhaps from ignorance and blind trust.[13] In the aftermath of the Tết

Offensive, the United States gave up the idea of victory in Vietnam. Lieutenant Colonel Bertrand Trainor when he took command of his infantry battalion in 1969 was told by his regimental commander, "We're no longer here to win, we're merely 'campaigning,' so keep the casualties down."[14]

General Westmoreland's War

General William Westmoreland dreamed all his life of being a Greek god. Whether he had achieved it was not known, but he certainly strived to be one. He may not have realized that Greek gods had flaws too, many of them fatal, not only to themselves but also to others.

He was an Eagle Scout at 15, president of the high school senior class, Citadel cadet, First Captain at West Point, battalion commander at 28, full colonel at 30, brigadier at 38, major general—youngest in the Army—at 42. It was an unprecedented meteoric rise that was not strengthened by a limited combat experience. Commissioned in the Artillery branch, he spent many years in this field. During the Korean War, he commanded the 187th Division for 15 months, of which only six were spent in Korea and the remaining nine in Japan.[15]

In Vietnam, he became the COMUSMACV, the commander in chief of MACV and Allied Forces with a strength of more than one million men at one time. But he squandered these forces by using only U.S. forces and by shunning the South Vietnamese to the side. As a World War II warrior, he was stuck in the old-fashioned way of fighting the war and was not imaginative or brave enough to change his strategy in order to deal with a different type of war. Someone else would have been astute and brave enough to put a few divisions around Khe Sanh to interdict and cut off the Hồ Chí Minh Trail and starve off the insurgency war in South Vietnam if fear of China's intervention prevented the U.S. from bringing troops to Laos.

But according to Lieutenant General Charles Simmons, "General Westmoreland was intellectually very shallow and made no effort to study, read or learn. He would just not read *anything* [italics in the original text]. His performance was appalling."[16] At least responsibility for such failure resided more with LBJ than with his field general. "No capable war president," wrote historian Russell Weigley, "would have allowed an officer of such limited capacities as General William C. Westmoreland to head Military Assistance Command, Vietnam, for so long."[17]

The young Westmoreland had developed into an "adult of incredible industry" driving himself to achieve, forever in a rush: "This is the way I operate. Don't talk long to any one person, but talk to as many people as I can." His attitude was one of unbounded ambition, no apparent sense of limitations, doing it by the book, even though he hadn't read the book or studied at any of the Army's great schools.[18]

Westmoreland decided to conduct a war of attrition, using search and destroy tactics, in which the measure of merit was body count. Army Chief of Staff General Harold K. Johnson documented that Westmoreland's approach was not working and could not work because it ignored the real war in South Vietnam's hamlets and villages, where the covert enemy infrastructure worked through coercion and terror. General William DePuy later admitted the futility of the Westmoreland way of war. "We ended up," he said, "with no operational plan that had the slightest chance of ending the war favorably."[19]

Next was the problem of armaments: the AK-47 and the M-16 rifles. The Army had realized that "Their [communist] RPG was better than our LAW. Their AK-47 was better than our M-16."[20] The AK-47 was designed by Russian engineers led by Sgt. Mikhail Kalashnikov. Its reliability derived from having eight big, heavy moving parts assembled so loosely that grit did not trouble them. Chromium plating of the barrel lining, gas chamber, and piston increased its durability. Its simplicity made it the weapon of choice of revolutionaries throughout the world. Its inaccuracy—it tends to shoot left—was unimportant as long as it delivers heavy fire, usually semi-automatic or in short bursts.

Having nothing comparable besides the M-14, the Army turned to Colt's AR-15, which they later renamed M-16. Grievous design flaws became apparent as general issue began. Huge strains on the working parts of a light automatic weapon cause super-energetic detonation and heavy barrel fouling resulting in repeated malfunctions. Through 1966, the weapon corroded fast in tropical conditions. After a round was fired, the empty case often jammed, requiring an extraction, maybe by the soldier plunging a rod down the barrel. There was a chronic shortage of cleaning kits. Of 2,000 early M-16s tested by armorers, 384 malfunctioned.[21]

The Army realized it had a problem in its hands: it was equipping infantrymen with a tool unfit for combat. Its Advance Research Development Agency tried to conceal the M-16's deficiencies, above all from Congress. In February 1967, Marines began receiving the weapons in Vietnam. When users protested about jams, they were blamed on their own sloppiness. Colt's representative in Asia wrote to his employer that the allegations about its product's shortcomings were justified. But the company refused to admit that there was anything wrong with the rifle. The U.S. Army and Marine Corps learned to live with the M-16 rifle and to fight with it. More cleaning equipment was issued. Some of the problems identified in 1966 were solved two years later: a modified version with a new buffer and a chromium plate bore worked better. Yet while the M-16 was a much more sophisticated rifle than the Kalashnikov, it was not as robust.[22]

When improved weaponry became available, U.S. forces got first call on the M-16 rifle, the M-60 machine gun, the M-79 grenade launcher, and better radios. For much of the war, the South Vietnamese were armed with castoff U.S. equipment of World War II vintage, such as the M-1 rifle and the carbine. The NVA and the VC got the most modern weaponry their communist patrons could provide, the famous AK-47 rifle.[23] The recollections of Lieutenant General Đồng Văn Khuyên, South Vietnam's chief logistician, were particularly poignant: "During the enemy Tết Offensive of 1968, the crisp, rattling sounds of AK-47's echoing in Saigon and some other cities seemed to make a mockery of the weaker, single-shots of Garand and carbines fired by stupefied friendly troops."[24]

The NLF and PAVN, on the other hand, began receiving substantial quantities of the Soviet AK-47 in late 1964.[25] The ARVN received the first shipment of M-16 rifles only in 1968 after the Tết Offensive. That made a four year-difference, which on the busy and active battlefields of Vietnam, made a significant difference.

Under Westmoreland, the ARVN were last to receive modern equipment. Priority 1 was U.S. forces in Southeast Asia. Priority 2 was U.S. forces deploying to Southeast Asia. Priority 3 was the training base in United States. Priority 4 was U.S. forces in Korea. Priority 5 was U.S. reserve forces called to active duty. Not until Priority 6 were South Vietnamese forces so much as mentioned, and even then it was to receive materiel dribbled out over time.[26]

Of course, "providing the ARVN with better rifles hardly would have solved the intractable problems of leadership, morale, and military professionalism," as suggested by Daddis.[27] Everyone knew the problems in Vietnam were complex and multifaceted. But anything could help in critical situations: changing one factor to begin with (good M-16 rifles) might cause a cascade of changes that would ultimately affect the overall result. Ambassador Maxwell Taylor succinctly put it: "We never really paid attention to the ARVN army. We didn't give a damn about them."[28]

In 1965 Herbert Schandler noted that, when Westmoreland asked for more U.S. troops he was "recommending a virtual American takeover of the war. There was little or no mention in General Westmoreland's request of South Vietnamese forces, or any program to utilize those forces, or to make them more effective."[29]

General John Galvin expressed a strong opinion on the matter, "Westmoreland firmly believed that any help to the ARVN would be a disadvantage to U.S. forces."[30] General Norman Schwarzkopf wrote;

> The Americanization of the war disturbed me.... I thought we should give them the skills, the confidence, and the equipment they needed, and encourage them to fight. Yet our official position was that we were sending forces to help South Vietnam fight, the truth was that more and more battles were being fought *exclusively* by Americans.[31]

Daddis suggested, "Westmoreland was not a bad general, but rather a good general fighting a bad war."[32] As a World War II conventional warrior, maybe he did not understand the intricacies of the revolutionary war in Vietnam, therefore was not able to deal with them effectively, modify his strategy to mitigate the complexities of the war, and co-op the immense forces he had under him along with the massive power of U.S. armaments and materiel to stop the rogue communist army on its tract. What he lacked was not the will, but the imagination, the ingenuity, and the knowledge to deal with a different type of war. Out of his classic conventional milieu, he seemed to be totally lost.

Besides by not Vietnamizing the ARVN in the beginning and by not equipping it appropriately to fight the war, Westmoreland had "wasted seven valuable years since 1961 by developing the RVNAF in a half-hearted way."[33] After the U.S. decided to abandon South Vietnam, thereby assuring its conquest by the North, Westmoreland was bitter: "Our erstwhile honorable country betrayed and deserted the Republic of South Vietnam after it had enticed it to our bosom. It was a shabby performance by America, a blemish on our history and a possible blight on our future. The handling of the Vietnam affair was a shameful national blunder."[34]

Effects on the RVNAF

In early 1968, as the Republic of Vietnam Armed Forces (RVNAF) began to get bigger, so did its casualties. Under the Vietnamization program, the RVNAF was composed of: the Army of Vietnam (ARVN), the Vietnamese Air Force (VNAF), the Vietnamese Navy (VNN), and the Vietnamese Marine Corps (VNMC). There were additional specialized forces and commands: the Airborne Division, the Regional/Popular Forces, the Special Forces, the Capital Military District, and the Training Command.

South Vietnam was divided into four corps tactical zones (CTZ I to IV) or Military Regions (MR) led by four corps commanders. Each corps commander oversaw two to three of the ten ARVN divisions: the 1st and 2nd (and later the 3rd) to the MRI below the Demilitarized Zone (DMZ); the 22nd and 23rd to the MRII in the Central Highlands; the 5th, 10th (later renamed the 18th), and the 25th to the MRIII; the 7th, 9th, and 21st to the MRIV in the Delta.

A total of 20 ranger battalions were assigned to the corps to serve as corps reserve. The strategic reserve under the direction of the Joint General Staff included the Marine and Airborne divisions. In all, 141 RVNAF maneuver battalions operated throughout South Vietnam in 1968.[35] Besides the regular ground forces were the Regional and Popular Forces (RF/PF) responsible for the protection of hamlets, villages and other important government installations. The RF were organized into companies of 100 men each and the PF into platoons of 40 men each. They were under the control of the sector commander in the province in which they were located.

Thiệu asked not only for an increase in manpower from 800,000 to over one million, but also an increase in armor capability, artillery, airplanes, and air defense units.

The Consolidated RVNAF Improvement and Modernization Plan, or CRIMP, which covered the 1970–72 fiscal years, raised the force to 1.1 million men. The ARVN eventually received 155 mm and 175 mm long range artillery pieces, M-42 and M-55 antiaircraft weapons, M-48 tanks, and a host of other sophisticated equipment and weapons systems. By the beginning of 1972, the South Vietnamese army would increase to 450,000, comprised of 171 infantry battalions, 58 artillery battalions, 22 armored cavalry and tank squadrons, and 60 artillery battalions.[36]

Table 8-1 lists the components and strengths of the RVNAF in 1968, the year when Vietnamization began. At that stage, the RVNAF was composed of 717,214 members.

Table 8-1. Republic of Vietnam Armed Forces, 1968

Source: Nguyen Duy Hinh, *Indochina Monographs: Vietnamization and the Cease-Fire* (Washington, D.C.: U.S. Army Center of Military History, 1980), p. 32.

Organization	Members
Army of the Republic of Vietnam (ARVN)	321,056
Vietnamese Marine Corps (VNMC)	8,271
Vietnamese Air Force (VNAF)	17,198
Vietnamese Navy (VNN)	17,178
Regional Forces (RF)	185,871
Popular Forces (PF)	167,640
Total members	717,214

Table 8-2 lists the casualties (KIA and WIA) of the U.S. and RVNAF from 1960 to 1974. By 1974, RVNAF had suffered 254,256 casualties.[37]

Table 8-2. Military Casualty Comparison

Source: Jeffrey J. Clarke, *Advice and Support: The Final Years* (Washington, D.C., Center of Military History, 1988), 275.

	Killed in Action, US	Killed in Action, RVNAF	Wounded in Action, US	Wounded in Action, RVNAF
1960	—	2,223	—	2,788
1961	11	4,004	2	5,449
1962	31	4,457	41	7,195
1963	78	5,665	218	11,488
1964	147	7,457	522	17,017
1965	1,369	11,242	3,308	23,118
1966	5,008	11,953	16,526	20,975
1967	9,377	12,716	32,370	29,448
1968	14,589	27,915	46,797	70,696
1969	9,414	21,833	32,940	65,276
1970	4,221	23,346	15,211	71,582
1971	1,381	22,738	4,767	60,939
1972	300	39,587	587	109,960
1973	237	27,901	24	131,936
1974	207	31,219	—	155,735
Total	46,370	254,256	153,313	783,602

In table 8-3, Gras[38] has suggested that the South Vietnamese had suffered 58,877 casualties during the French years. To that table, we have also estimated that the RVNAF had suffered another 40,000 casualties (low estimate) in the year 1975 considering the losses in Ban Mê Thuột, during the retreat of the highlands as well as from the fall of I Corps, Đà Nẵng, Nha Trang, and so on. This gives us a total of 353,133 losses for the RVNAF for the whole war (1950–1975). The losses were so minimal from 1955 to 1960 that they were not mentioned anywhere.

Table 8-3. ARVN Casualties During the Vietnam War

Period	Author	KIA/Period
1950–1955	Gras (38)	58,877
1960–1974	Clarke (37)	254,256
1975	Vo (estimate)	40,000
Total		353,133

In table 8-4, the RVNAF casualties are broken down in three phases:

- Build-up phase 1 (1960–1964), during which the RVNAF was supported by MACV (1960–1964): losses accounted for 4,800 people per year.

- Build-up phase 2 (1965–1968), during which the RVNAF was on its own without MACV control (1965–1967), losses rose to 12,000 annually. The ARVN began taking action.
- Vietnamization phase (1969–1975), during which the RVNAF was supported by MACV-DAO. The losses rose to 30,000 per year as the South Vietnamese bore the brunt of the communist attacks.

Table 8-4. ARVN Casualties (Average) from 1960 to 1975

Period	Phase	US Support	Average KIA per year	Total
1960–1964	Built-up 1	MACV	4,800	24,000
1965–1967	Built-up 2	On its own (28)	12,000	36,000
1968–1975	Vietnamization	MACV-DAO	30,000	240,000
1960–1975			18,750	300,000

The rapidly expanding RVNAF, on the other hand, "suffered from a lack of technical competence, weak staff officers, inexperience at planning and executing large-scale combined arms operations, and a number of other serious maladies."[39] Leadership, particularly at the senior levels, lay at the root of all RVNAF weakness. One South Vietnam general wrote, "[U]nless a commander or leader had professional competence, devotion, and moral rectitude, he certainly could not expect his subordinates to be dedicated and aggressive.... There was finally the will and determination to fight, which again depended on motivation and leadership, and without which there was no sense in upgrading mere physical capabilities."[40]

The biggest mistake South Vietnamese leaders made was to view Vietnamization as a way to modernize or expand the RVNAF instead of seeing it as a strategy to survive with greatly reduced American participation. Had Thiệu and the JGS realized that fact, "they would have begun to build a strategy to cope with it. Instead the RVNAF made no adjustments in doctrine, organization, or training to compensate for the departure of American troops and firepower.... Unfortunately, political clairvoyance and wisdom were not the forte of our leadership...."[41]

The Battle of Đông Áp Bia (Hamburger Hill)

When the South Vietnamese had the audacity to do what the Americans asked, to play an important role in battle—an American battle—it had been swept aside and forgotten. Such was the fragile nature of the American ego and national will.[42] Hoping to capitalize on the 1968 gains, the new MACV commander, General Creighton Abrams, told his commanders to maintain "unrelenting pressure" on enemy forces and their base areas, especially in the I Corps, which meant battles in the A Shau Valley that ran at the base of the Annamite Mountain range.

The Đông Ấp Bia Battle

The battle took place from 10 May to 21 May 1969 in the rugged, jungle-shrouded mountains of South Vietnam, 1.2 miles (1.9 km) from the Laotian border. Rising at 937 meters (3,074 ft.) above sea level from the floor of the A Shau Valley, Đông Ấp Bia Mountain is a solitary massif, unconnected to the ridges of the surrounding Annamite range. It is dotted with a series of ridges and fingers, one of the largest extending southeast to a height of 900 meters (3,074 ft.), another reaching south to a 916-meter (3,005 ft.) peak. The entire mountain is a rugged wilderness blanketed in double- and triple-canopy jungle, dense thickets of bamboo, and waist-high elephant grass. Official histories of the engagement refer to it as Hill 937 after the elevation, while the American soldiers dubbed it "Hamburger Hill," suggesting that those who fought on the hill were "chewed up like a hamburger."

During a campaign to destroy the PAVN base areas in the A Shau Valley, the 3/187th of Lt. Col. Honeycutt encountered PAVN soldiers on Hill 937 on 13 May, although they did not know the exact strength of enemy forces. Honeycutt was a protégé of General William Westmoreland, the former commander of U.S. forces in Vietnam. He had been assigned command of the 3/187th in January 1969 and had by replacement of many of its officers given it a personality to match his own aggressiveness.

Although Bravo Company seized Ridge 916 on 15 May, it was not until 19 May that the battalion as a whole was in position to conduct a final assault on Hill 937, primarily because of nearly impenetrable jungle. Steep gradients and dense vegetation provided few natural landing zones (LZs) in the vicinity of the mountain and made helicopter redeployments impractical. The terrain also masked the positions of the PAVN 29th Regiment, making it nearly impossible to suppress antiaircraft fire, while the jungle covered the movement of North Vietnamese units so completely that it created a nonlinear battlefield. The ridges were covered with numerous, well-sited NVA bunkers and constructed with overhead cover to withstand bombardment.[43]

This was a close combat with the two sides exchanging small arms and grenade fire within 20 meters (66 ft.) of one another. An intense thunderstorm on 18 May reduced visibility to zero and ended the fighting. Stuck in three feet of mud, U.S. troops withdrew to safety down the mountain. The 3/187th's losses had been severe, with approximately 320 killed or wounded, including more than sixty percent of the 450 experienced troops who had assaulted into the valley. Colonel Zais, the brigade commander, seriously considered discontinuing the attack but decided otherwise. Both the corps commander and the MACV commander, General Abrams, publicly supported the decision.

Two fresh battalions—the 2/501st Infantry and ARVN 2/3d Infantry—were airlifted into LZs northeast and southeast of the base of the mountain on 19 May. Both battalions immediately moved onto the mountain to positions from which they would attack the following morning. Meanwhile, the 1/506 for the third consecutive day struggled to secure Hill 900.

According to official documents, the 3rd Brigade launched its four-battalion attack at 1000 on 20 May, including two companies of the 3/187 reinforced by Alpha Company 1/506. The attack was preceded by two hours of close air support and ninety minutes of artillery prep fires. The battalions attacked simultaneously, and by

1200, elements of the 3/187 reached the crest, beginning a reduction of bunkers that continued through most of the afternoon. Some PAVN units were able to withdraw into Laos, and Hill 937 was secured by 1700.

Results and Controversies

U.S. losses during the ten-day battle totaled 72 KIA and 372 WIA. To take the position, the 101st Airborne Division eventually committed five infantry battalions and ten batteries of artillery that fired a total of 19,213 rounds. In addition, the U.S. Air Force flew 272 missions and expended more than 500 tons of ordnance. The enemy suffered 630 KIA. After having shed so much blood to take control of Hill 397, the U.S. abandoned it two weeks later on 5 June 1969. PAVN troops were seen returning to the hill some time later. The controversy of the conduct of the Battle of Hamburger Hill led to a reappraisal of U.S. strategy in South Vietnam

The first controversy relates to which unit arrived at the top of Hill 937 first. It was not the 3/187 men who despite their tedious, bloody, and valiant effort arrived first, but the 2/3 ARVN. The South Vietnamese knew that back in 1969 2/3 ARVN under the command of Phạm Văn Định hit the ground to the southeast of Đông Áp Bia on 19 May and would have one of the longer lines of assault at 500 meters below the crest of Hill 397.[44] Through reconnaissance, Định realized that the ARVN's avenue of advance lay across open ground, which afforded the enemy a clear field of fire. He decided not to wait for the proposed assault time and moved his unit in the half-light of 20 May. The PAVN not expecting an attack from the southeast had devoted minimal manpower to the defense of the area. The unit moved quickly up the hill where they encountered a barrage of small-arms fire at the top of the hill. "Around 1000 hours while 3/187 began to batter through heavy enemy resistance, 2/3 reached the crest of Hamburger Hill."[45]

Major Zimmerly, Định's advisor contacted Colonel Conmy who was circling over the hill to let him know that 2/3 ARVN had control of the top of the hill. Conmy told him to "get your people off the hill, because we are going to fire an artillery preparation on top of the Hill." On the ground, although incredulous, Định and his advisers did what they were told. "After Định and their men moved away, the leading elements of 3/187 broke through NVA defenses, moved to the summit of Đông Áp Bia and took their place in history as the victors." An hour and a half later, 2/3 returned to the top of Đông Áp Bia.[46]

Recent research unearthed by Andrew Wiest confirmed that view. Among the pile of documents, there was a one page memo by Colonel William C. Harper, Chief of Command and Control Division, who on 22 May 1969, at the headquarters of the United States Military Assistance Command, reported:

> On 19 May 1969, 2/3 ARVN conducted combat assault on LZ YC324976 and began moving to positions to the southeast side of Hill 937, in preparation for four battalion attack on 20 May 1969. These battalions from the 3rd Airborne Brigade, 101st Division progressed to multi-battalion attack which began 201030H [20 May 1030 hours]. Advance of 2/3 was extremely rapid due to use of high speed trail and light enemy resistance. They were the first to reach the top of Hill 937 and assaulted positions vicinity YC327980. The 3/187 was meeting heavy resistance on their axis of attack. The 2/3 ARVN went to assist by moving N along Hill 937 and relieving the pressure. However, friendly fire from 3/187 prevented 2/3 ARVN from moving close. The 2/3 ARVN then moved on reverse slope of the southeast side of the hill.[47]

This was confirmed by General Abrams who commented:

> They got up to the crest of the hill, as a matter of fact ahead of the artillery preparation that was going in. The resistance was on the west slope—the third of the—3/187. And then they had to back Dinh's battalion off the top of the hill so they could put the artillery in on the reverse slope. So then he—it was an hour and a half later when he got *back* on top of the hill and *met* them. He was there to meet the 3rd of the 187th. So the facts are the first people to the crest was [sic] the ARVN.[48]

The results of Đồng Ấp Bia were simple and chilling. The American people were tired of the war in Vietnam and called for the return of their husbands and sons from the distant battlefields. For the ARVN, it should have been the great year in which the U.S. and ARVN forces took the war into enemy sanctuaries in Laos and North Vietnam. "Instead, it was a year in which the enemy gained the upper hand in the war of wills, in part due to fighting over a desolate and essentially worthless hilltop."[49]

9

1970–71

Cambodian and Laotian Incursions

In 1970, the ARVN made two incursions, one into Cambodia and the other into Laos with different results. In Cambodia, the PAVN forces were surprised by the ARVN attack, which was supported by American troops as well as its logistical support. In Laos, without U.S. advisers on the ground to help call for artillery and air support, the ARVN lost its cohesiveness and fighting power against PAVN forces who knew the battleground well and were well prepared with at least seven divisions against an undersized and poorly led ARVN (three divisions).

Cambodian Incursion

While the Hồ Chí Minh (HCM) Trail supplied the communists' military needs in the northern end of South Vietnam (MRI and II), those in southern South Vietnam (MRIII and IV) arrived through the Cambodian port of Sihanoukville, with the first shipload of weapons arriving in October 1966. From the port, the supplies were trucked to depots west of Phnom Penh, then to regional facilities at Kratie, Svay Rieng, Kampong Cham and Stung Treng before reaching one of the eight communist base areas on the South Vietnamese border.

The distance from Sihanoukville to the Cambodian border base areas (Sihanoukville Trail) was 175 miles compared to 700 miles of the HCM trail from Hải Phòng, North Vietnam, to the same Cambodian border. Until 1970, the Sihanoukville Trail was off limits to American attacks while the HCM Trail was subject to U.S. air strikes through North Vietnam and Laos. In the beginning, the HCM Trail's dirt routes and paths limited resupply efforts to the few months when the roads were dry and rivers passable. Cambodia's asphalt roads from the port to the border, on the other hand, were open even during the monsoon season.

Between October 1966 and July 1969, an arms-bearing ship docked in the port every three months. Sihanouk's relatives profited by letting Hanoi move its supplies to the Vietnamese border. Sihanouk's wife Monique, her mother, and half-brother were also selling protection, weapons, and land rights to the NVA/VC.[1] "The tonnages moving through Sihanoukville were sufficient to meet 100 percent of the requirements of enemy units in the … III and IV Corps, and perhaps two-thirds of the requirements for enemy units in the II Corps area."[2]

The North Vietnamese and Việt Cộng, having secured a swath of land five to ten miles in width along the Cambodian and Laotian borders with South Vietnam, used it as resupply routes and staging areas for attacks inside South Vietnam without fear of reprisal by the United States. Prince Norodom Sihanouk, despite claiming the neutrality of his country, allowed the communists to use this area with kickback to his family and generals. He thought that accommodating North Vietnam's "requests" was safer than risking confrontations with its more aggressive and battle-hardened troops.[3]

There were 14 major North Vietnamese bases inside Cambodia, three neighboring the IV Corps area and seven near the III Corps. "Some were within 35 miles of Saigon."[4]

There were several ways to block the flow of arms, supplies and soldiers across Indochina. The most effective means would be a blockade by either U.S. or ARVN ground troops through Laos and Cambodia, but domestic and international considerations made this impossible. Gen. Bruce Palmer would consider a blockade at the DMZ by an international field force of about seven divisions. The drive into Laos would be undertaken once the DMZ force had been in place.[5] The Laotian and Cambodian governments had the right to refuse Hanoi the use of their lands, but neither government had the strength necessary to enforce such a decision. Allied Special Operations units harassed NVA forces coming down the trail but they lacked both the firepower and the numbers to halt the flow.[6] Airpower remained MACV's only viable military option against the PAVN forces inside Laos and Cambodia. But Hanoi countered the effectiveness of airpower by sending larger numbers of troops than previously down the pipeline.

While some Cambodian generals profited from the communist deal, others were unhappy about the communists' "occupation" of their country. On 18 March 1970, while Sihanouk vacationed in Paris, Cambodian Gen. Lon Nol engineered a bloodless coup and demanded that the communists vacate the area. The latter of course refused. The Cambodian army, which was unable to evict them, asked for U.S. assistance. The war, which engulfed Vietnam, began spreading to neighboring Cambodia. By not enforcing his country's neutrality Sihanouk had finally brought calamity to his kingdom.

On 29 March, the PAVN launched ground attacks against their host and turned westward toward the capital, Phnom Penh. Nixon was following the Cambodian situation closely. The loss of Cambodia would adversely affect Vietnamization and might result in a widening of the war. Options were entertained at that time. The first option was to do nothing. The second option was to attack the sanctuaries with only the South Vietnamese forces. The third was to use whatever forces were necessary, including U.S. forces, to neutralize all the base areas. On 25 March, he ordered the JCS to draft a plan of attack into Cambodia either by U.S. or South Vietnamese forces should communist forces threaten Phnom Penh.

By mid–April, the PAVN forces had surrounded the capital Phnom Penh and the Lon Nol government appeared to be in danger of falling. Nixon's advisers told him that if he withdrew troops, he had to protect South Vietnam's western flank from a potential PAVN invasion from the base areas. On 20 April, he went ahead with his planned withdrawal of 50,000 U.S. additional troops from Vietnam. On 28 April, he made the final decision on Cambodia and gave the green light to Abrams. "We would go for broke, for the big play ... for all the marbles.... A joint ARVN-US Force would go into the Fishhook."[7]

In war, at the strategic level, offensives normally produce victory; Saigon's assumption of the strategic defensive forfeited the initiative to Hanoi. The North had a clear objective—victory—and highly competent leaders fanatically committed to achieving it. The South had leaders to be sure, but they were neither as unified nor as zealous as their counterparts in the North. Saigon's war fighting doctrine, copied from the United States, was inferior to Hanoi's. Called *đấu tranh,* Hanoi's approach emphasized a tightly coordinated political and military struggle.

The South's focus was more of a dream than a reality. Westmoreland, as the senior field commander, concentrated chiefly on the conventional military threat, and by Johnson's orders, only on that within the national boundaries of South Vietnam. His war of attrition, of killing more of the enemy than Hanoi could replace, was doomed to failure against enemy leaders willing to sacrifice as many men as it took to win. In emphasizing the "big battalion" war for the Americans and leaving the political and internal security struggle to the South Vietnamese, Washington and Saigon lacked the cohesive and coherent effort necessary to successfully withstand the North's integral attacks.

Where the North was fighting as a unified whole, the Allies were fighting as a coalition, and one whose members were wildly disparate in strength and true aims.[8]

The Cambodian Attack

The plan includes two attacks: a combined U.S.-ARVN attack into the Fishhook and a solo ARVN attack into the Parrot's Beak. The Fishhook and the Parrot's Beak are Cambodian land indentations into South Vietnam across the border from Tây Ninh in MR III or III Corps.

The combined attack force into the Fishhook numbered over 15,000 (10,000 Americans and over 5,000 Vietnamese). It was designed as a pincer movement to trap elements of the 7th PAVN Division. The U.S. unit included elements of the 1st Cavalry Division, the 25th Infantry Division, and the 11th Armored Cavalry Regiment. The Vietnamese force involved the ARVN 1st Armored Cavalry Regiment (ACR), one armored cavalry squadron each from the 5th and 25th ARVN Divisions, an infantry regiment from the 25th Division, the 4th Ranger group (four ranger battalions), the 3rd Airborne brigade and additional units from both II and III Corps.

The attack into the Parrot's Beak began one day before the Fishhook operation and would involve three ARVN task forces, each composed of three infantry battalions and an armored cavalry squadron. These forces, totaling 8,700 soldiers, would surround Base Areas 706 and 367 in the tip of the Parrot's Beak and then would turn west and north to secure the town of Svay Rieng and to attack Base Area 354.

In a nationally televised speech on 30 April, one day after the ARVN crossed the Cambodian border, Nixon tried to explain the purpose of the incursion into Cambodia. An outcry erupted in response to what appeared like a widening of the war to many Americans.

On April 29, the ARVN launched their operation, called *Toàn Thắng* 42 or Total Victory 42, in division strength into the Parrot's Beak. On 1 May, after preparatory strikes by artillery and tactical air support, the Americans crossed the Cambodian border. They only found light resistance because the enemy had escaped farther into the Cambodian interior. By 3 May, there were 8 Americans killed and 32 wounded. Enemy losses were reported at 476 killed.

The 1st Cavalry Division came upon huge weapon caches and supply dumps, one so extensive they called it "the City." It was a two-square mile complex that included 182 separate stocks of weapons and ammunition, 18 mess halls, a firing range, a chicken and pig farm, and over 400 log-covered bunkers and other shelters containing medical supplies, foodstuffs, and uniforms.[9] Later, another battalion of the 1st Cavalry Division discovered an even larger weapons cache, they called it "Rock Island East." It contained more than 6.5 million rounds of antiaircraft ammunition, a half million rifle rounds, thousands of rockets, several General Motors trucks, and even telephone switchboards.[10]

ARVN in Cambodia

The Cambodian incursion was treated as a test of the Vietnamization program and the concurrent U.S. withdrawal. In 1970, ARVN became increasingly responsible for the security of the country. The ARVN 5th, 18th, and 25th Divisions were active in MRIII that included the ten provinces around Saigon (but excluding the capital itself). U.S. forces included the U.S. First Cavalry Division, which guarded the northern part of MRIII and the U.S. 25th Infantry Division, which was responsible for the western and southern part of MRIII.

Despite years of the U.S. advisory effort, ARVN had serious problems that weakened its overall combativeness. Ambassador Bunker noted to Nixon in late March 1970, "Low pay, poor housing and care for dependents, and corruption in many parts of the officer corps and widespread pilfering by ARVN forces were already part of the picture before the costs of living increases," which started in October 1969.[11]

"A second factor was the relative inexperience of many commanders and staffs. On 2 May 1970, Major General Nguyễn Viết Thanh, the IV Corps commanding general, died in a mid-air collision with an American helicopter above Cambodia; he was 39 and had been on the job since August 1968. His successor, Major General Ngô Quang Trưởng and his III Corps counterpart, Lieutenant General Đỗ Cao Trí, had careers roughly comparable to Thanh's. Though all three were dynamic and tactically aggressive, their promotions had come so quickly that they had been shortchanged in their formal professional military education and staff time at higher levels. In consequence, ARVN generals were on average administratively weaker than their American counterparts...."

The ARVN generals, however, had more combat experience than the Americans. Being the product of wars, they earned their ranks quite rapidly. All three of them were made generals in their late thirties or early forties. Having to fight more often, they had more opportunities to be promoted. They also died earlier as a result of war accidents. Generals Thanh and Trí died early at the ages of 39 and 42 respectively, both in helicopter accidents. In the peaceful U.S., senior U.S. officers had to train, take command of certain units, before being commended for promotion to generals.

In a war torn country like Vietnam, options were limited. An officer either got wounded, killed, or promoted. If an officer did not get wounded, disabled or killed, he would get promoted. As war raged on year after year, those who were lucky and healthy got promoted. The goal was to get out of ambushes and to survive. No amount of bureaucratic or administrative experience would pull an officer out of an ambush or battle. What saved him and his soldiers were his luck and skill to get out of trouble. And that skill cannot be learned by holding administrative positions. That was how these officers earned their promotions.

Over the years, thanks to the U.S. advisory effort, Vietnamese units had delivered solid efforts, especially ARVN infantry, artillery, and RF/PF battalions. However progress was less impressive at higher levels where division and regiment commanders paid little attention to the key functions of command and control, intelligence, logistics, and fire support because they accurately assumed that the Americans would "take care" of the matters.[12]

Toàn Thắng 41

While the IIFFV commanding general, Lt. Gen. Mike Davison, was preparing for the Cambodian incursion, Trí was raiding the Angel's Wing on 14–17 April in Operation Toàn Thắng 41 on the orders of President Thiệu. The ARVN fought against North Vietnamese main force units immediately. After two days, ARVN suffered 30 killed and 70 wounded while claiming 375 PAVN dead.

The main PAVN body escaped into the Cambodian interior. ARVN forces advanced toward Svay Rieng and opened Highway 1 before occupying the lower half of the Parrot's Beak. At Ba Thu, they seized a center for outfitting and retraining NVA and VC units. The complex covered ten square kilometers and included hundreds of houses and bunkers. They received reinforcements from the ARVN 9th division, bringing the total number of ARVN troops in Cambodia to 48,000.

Toàn Thắng 42

On April 29, Lt. Gen. Đỗ Cao Trí, commander of III Corps, was supposed to lead elements of the III and IV Corps across the border into the Parrot's Beak, Cambodia, to destroy communist Base Areas 367 and 706, then drive west toward Phnom Penh to rescue Vietnamese refugees trapped by the Cambodian/NVA fighting. Trí was a dynamic and capable warrior who was well respected by his officers and soldiers. He received the full backing of the U.S. command.[13]

Trí then asked for a 24-hour delay because his astrologer told him the heavens were not auspicious. This was an unusual request from an ARVN commander. Davison "went through the roof" but could not make him budge.[14] Luckily, Washington officials called Abrams, wanting him to postpone the assault for 24 hours while they attended to last minute details.

III Corps crossed into Cambodia on 30 April with two III Corps armored cavalry regiments (ACR), two ACR from the 5th and 25th Divisions, an infantry regiment from the 25th Division and four ranger battalions arranged into three task forces: the 318th, 225th, and 333rd. They overran the Angel's Wing (Base Area 706) and seized the Parrot's Beak (Base Area 367) before pushing west on Highway 1. The ARVN suffered 16 killed and 156 wounded while killing 84 NVA/VC.

Phase II of Toàn Thắng 42 saw the involvement of IV Corps' 9th Infantry Division, which hit the still-resisting NVA/VC forces from the rear. After three days, the total enemy count rose to 1,010 enemy dead and 204 prisoners for 66 ARVN dead and

330 wounded; NVA materiel losses included more than 1,000 individual and 60 crew served weapons and more than 100 tons of ammunition.[15] The assault continued until 19 June although ethnic tensions dominated the news.

Overall, III Corps mauled the 88th PAVN Regiment, 271st PAVN Regiment and weakened the 272nd PAVN Regiment. It boosted the confidence among ARVN and VNAF. ARVN troops performed well during the incursion and VNAF flew more than 1,600 sorties by operation's end.

The operation was a military success. Communist bases areas and training camps in Cambodia were captured along with tons of supplies. The captured weapons were enough to equip at least an entire communist division. The operation prevented the PAVN from overrunning Cambodia and taking over Phnom Penh. The Lon Nol government would last until 1975. It closed Sihanoukville as a PAVN supply port. No communist supply would come through the port and all the supplies would come down the HCM Trail. Because of lack of supplies, it also prevented the PAVN from attacking South Vietnam for another two years.[16] By moving and fighting in Cambodia, ARVN had displayed an aggressive spirit and the ability to conduct mobile operations against a well-trained enemy. Regiments that rarely waged a two-day operation in Vietnam were constantly on the move and faced enemy for six to eight weeks in a row.

Advisers reported a marked increase in the morale of ARVN soldiers who were happy to fight in another country and into the enemy's "home" areas.[17] For the duration of the incursion, they were the attackers, the aggressors rather than those being attacked. That was for them a big change in mentality because they were free to attack at any time and any place of their liking. They did not have to wait to be attacked, to live confined to or feel imprisoned in a bunker or a camp. For a short time, they could soar and roam around.

The incursion caused a backlash in the U.S. Marches and demonstrations were held at colleges across the country including New York, Ohio, Texas, California, Georgia, Wisconsin, and many other states. On 8 May, over 100,000 Americans marched on Washington protesting the war; the government called regular troops to handle the disturbances. In June, Congress rescinded the 1964 Tonkin Gulf Resolution, which administrations had used as authorization for the war.[18]

"Even when he wasn't a general, he always got right into the fight." A newsman who joined in a recent foray was astonished when Trí ordered his helicopter to land virtually in the midst of a skirmish, then ignored vicious communist rocket and machine gun fire, walked to a tank and ordered the reluctant driver to attack; "Go fast, man!" Since he won his first command as a young airborne officer, he had survived three assassination attempts, resulting in his conviction that he is a *baraka*—a French barracks term for one who enjoys immunity from death on the battlefield. For his exploit in Cambodia, *Time* magazine called Lt. Gen. Đỗ Cao Trí the "Patton of Parrot's Beak."[19]

Writing after the war, Brig. Gen. Trần Đình Thọ said that "to operate without U.S. advisers was a source of pride for ARVN tactical commanders.... [T]hey felt more self-assured of their command abilities and, in fact, they all proved that they could manage by themselves."[20] Gen. Dave Palmer called it "a benchmark in the maturing of ARVN."[21]

Not everything, however, went all right for the ARVN. General Trí used mostly elite troops like the armored cavalry, airborne and rangers, rather than the mainstream South Vietnamese troops. He organized task forces under colonels and lieutenant colonels, bypassing the much politicized division commanders and their staff, who played almost no role in the operation.[22] The armored units that participated in the Parrot's Beak were plagued by poor maintenance, gasoline shortage, inadequate spare parts, and faulty communications.[23]

1971 Lâm Sơn 719

During the war, the North Vietnamese had built, maintained, and protected more than 8,000 miles of trails and roads, known as the Hồ Chí Minh Trail, that began in North Vietnam and ended in bases along South Vietnam's 800 mile border with Laos and Cambodia. From these bases or sanctuaries, they only needed to cross the border to wage war in South Vietnam before retreating back in the safety of their Laotian or Cambodian sanctuaries. Between 1966 and 1971, 630,000 troops, 100,000 tons of foodstuffs, 400,000 weapons, and 50,000 tons of ammunition moved from North Vietnam down the trail.[24]

To duplicate the success of the 1970 U.S./GVN successful Cambodian incursion that disrupted North Vietnamese supply lines and destroyed their base areas in the Cambodian borders and to test the effectiveness of "Vietnamization," the Lâm Sơn 719 operation was born.

However, the rugged Laotian territories and the December 1970 Cooper-Church Amendment passed after the Cambodian incursion would prove difficult to manage. The Amendment prevented U.S. forces from going into Laos and U.S. advisers could not accompany ARVN forces to which they were attached. The ARVN had to go by themselves. "The Hồ Chí Minh Trail was in 1971 the *only* means of supplying the entire enemy force in South Vietnam, southern Laos and Cambodia. If the ARVN could cut the trail ... they would deal a devastating blow to all communist operations in South Vietnam.... The North Vietnamese had to oppose Lâm Sơn 719 with every resource they could bring to bear."[25]

The Plan

It was so bold and risky that General Bruce Palmer wrote, "Only a Patton or a MacArthur would have made such a daring move; an Eisenhower or a Bradley would not have attempted it."[26] Scheduled to start on 30 January 1971, it would end 90 days later when the southwest monsoon would end all tactical operations. The torrential spring-summer rains would transform the poorly maintained roads into soggy mud-filled trails that could barely support the weight of troops, tanks, and military hardware.

There were many concepts of a westward attack along Highway 9 long before Operation Lâm Sơn 719, although its original author was not known.[27] Nixon in November 1970 thought about an offensive against the Trail. The JCS authorized Gen. Abrams to discuss with Gen. Cao Văn Viên about planning a cross-border attack on Laos. On 10 December, Abrams was charged with the planning of such an attack. Gen. Haig arrived in Saigon to discuss Abrams' plan. The plan was taken up by the

White House and on 21 December 1970, Nixon approved the Laos operation. Discussion continued about the Cooper-Church Amendment that forbade American troops to cross the border. On 25 January 1971 Kissinger discussed with Admiral Moorer the importance of securing Tchepone and the potential communist resistance to the operation. Moorer tried to convince Nixon that the operation would be successful. Nixon was convinced but Secretary of State Rogers was not. He suggested that Westmoreland once estimated that four divisions would be needed to do the job. Nixon overruled him and the chairman of the JCS gave the official go ahead on 4 February 1971.[28]

The plan was drafted as follows. There was no joint command until 7 January 1971 when authorization was given for joint planning. The overall ground commander in Laos was Lt. Gen. Hoàng Xuân Lãm, commanding general of I Corps. Although a good administrative general, he was not a combat general. His U.S. counterpart, Lt. Gen. James W. Sutherland, commanding general of XXIV Corps, would command and coordinate American support for the operation. Gen. Lucius D. Clay, commander of the 7th Air Force, would command all U.S. Air Force resources supporting the operation.

In phase I or Operation Dewey Canyon II, the U.S. would clear the area to the Vietnam/Laos border and reactivate Khe Sanh as base of the operation. In phase II, ARVN would launch a three-pronged assault from South Vietnam along Highway 9 to Tchepone. The central column consisting of the airborne division reinforced by the 1st Armored Brigade would assault A Luoi, the intersection of Routes 9 and 92 on the way to Tchepone. The 1st Infantry Division minus the 2nd Regiment would advance on a parallel axis south of Highway 9 and establish fire bases on the high ground between A Luoi and Tchepone. A Ranger group would protect the northern flank of the airborne division to prevent the enemy from moving south to impede the main attack along the highway.

Phase III would include the razing of NVA Base Area 604 after taking Tchepone. In phase IV, the ARVN force would swing southward and attack Base Area 611 before returning to South Vietnam. The ARVN force would be supported by U.S. helicopter, air strikes and artillery fire from South Vietnam.

The area was rugged and covered with dense undergrowth; a double canopy jungle, the Xe Pon River, and a sheer escarpment led to a mountainous region south of Highway 9. There were few areas for fire bases or helicopter landing zones. The so-called Highway 9 was a single dirt road so badly damaged by the ravages of the war that it was impassable in many places. It was also susceptible to demolitions and ambushes. The destruction of one tank on this road would stall the whole military column. Low clouds hung over the region and prevented helicopter operation except within corridors and between 1000 and 1500 hours.

Because communist espionage cells were suspected to be present within RVNAF high command, Abrams had ordered that the number of people involved in joint operational planning would be kept to a minimum. The secrecy and hurried way in which the operation was planned could adversely affect the outcome of the operation itself. Preparations and planning being done in a rush would further impact the coordination and cohesiveness of the various units that had not worked together in the past. Although the news embargo was lifted on 4 January, word had leaked out of an impending allied attack into Laos in U.S. and international newspapers. It was realized after the battle that the enemy had long suspected an ARVN offensive into Laos and had been preparing to counter such a move as early as October 1970.

The enemy had roughly 22,000 troops (7,000 combat, 10,000 logistical soldiers manning the *binh trạms* [regimental logistical headquarters], 5,000 communist Pathet Lao) on hand with the ability to bring in 11 or 12 infantry regiments within two weeks for a total of 40,000 troops. They had moved 20 additional antiaircraft battalions with both light (7.6 mm and 12.7 mm machine guns) and medium (23 mm to 100 mm) guns. They also used the medium T-54 tanks that outgunned the ARVN M-41 light tanks.[29] They knew the layout of the land for having been in this region for more than a dozen years.

To fight against the enemy's formidable war machinery, the ARVN committed an understrength 1st Infantry Division (with one regiment left at the DMZ), one understrength airborne division, three ranger battalions, some light armor and a marine brigade as reserve. Not only were these units understrength, they also did not have extensive experience in fighting as divisions at a time when coordination was paramount to the success of a complicated operation. Since they were rushed into this operation to prevent any potential intelligence leak, they were not well prepared to deal with unusual situations in an operation of such magnitude. And they were going into Laos without their military advisers who normally assisted them with calling air and artillery support. Without them, they would have difficulties getting air or artillery support in critical situations. There could be no reinforcement or relief as all the strategic ARVN reserve had been dumped into Lâm Sơn 719. Since there was no room for error, one could feel that President Thiệu was worried and jittery when he sent his troops across the border into Laos.

The Operation

It began on 29 January with U.S. forces repairing Highway 9 within South Vietnam and rehabilitating Khe Sanh. It was dubbed Lâm Sơn 719. Lâm Sơn was the birthplace of the 15th-century Vietnamese hero who expelled the Chinese from Vietnam. The numerals indicate the year 1971 and the Route 9 around which the operation took place. As it rained on 6 February, preparatory air strikes against enemy artillery were cancelled due to bad weather. On 8 February, ARVN forces crossed the Laotian border led by M-41 tanks and M-113 armored personnel carriers. The advance was slowed by dense jungle and huge bomb craters. The heavy rains turned Highway 9 into a quagmire but the airborne division and the armored brigade met at A Luoi, halfway to Tchepone on 10 February as scheduled.

The ARVN built one landing zone after another north of the highway, four of them mutually supporting bases. The 39th Ranger Battalion settled in the Ranger Base North. Light infantry without armor or artillery, they were supposed to hold the enemy until heavier artillery could be brought to bear. The 1st ARVN Infantry troops also built a landing zone on the southern side of the highway and settled in. A total of ten fire bases were thus built on the Laotian soil. Troops who were told to patrol around their bases soon encountered heavy resistance.

Then, unexpectedly, instead of moving forward to Tchepone, the operation froze in place, giving the PAVN the time to bring in additional reinforcements. Many critical days elapsed without any ARVN action. Gen. Abrams, who was furious about the squandered opportunities, talked to Gen. Viên about getting the operation moving again. They finally got together with Gen. Lãm at the I Corps forward command post at Đông Hà and were able to get some action returned on 19 February. It turned out that President Thiệu had told Lãm to be cautious and to cancel the operation once ARVN forces had taken on 3,000 casualties.[30] Lãm, a politically astute but poor soldier,[31] obliged. He knew that the airborne division and the marines were not only the total ARVN reserve, they were also Thiệu's "palace guard." Their destruction would expose Thiệu to dangers from his internal enemies.

In the meantime, the enemy had mobilized its forces. The 308th Division was in action in the northern flank. The PAVN 2nd Division appeared on the west of the ARVN advance and the 304th Division showed up along Highway 9. By the last week of February, the PAVN had four divisions plus tanks and artillery in the area. By early March, the PAVN outnumbered the ARVN by a two-to-one margin.

Rain and dense fog grounded all aircraft. Flying at low altitude made them vulnerable to antiaircraft fire. Resupplying the ARVN became difficult and dangerous. By 20 February, ARVN troops had lost all initiative. Supported by heavy artillery and T-54 and PT-76 tanks, the PAVN forces struck hard and repeatedly against ARVN positions. They surrounded them, cut off their aerial resupply lines with antiaircraft fire, and then pounded them with mortar, rocket, and artillery fire. The ARVN fought back but they were outnumbered. South Vietnamese artillery, being of much shorter range than the PAVN's 122 and 130 mm guns, failed to produce effective counterbattery fire. Close air support was ineffective because bad weather and active antiaircraft artillery. In some cases, close air strikes could not be called because of the absence of U.S. advisers.

On 19 February, 2,000 PAVN troops surrounded the 39th Ranger Battalion at Ranger Base North. Over three days, they pounded the position and pursued the rangers as they attempted to break out. Of the 430 rangers, 178 were killed and 148 were wounded. The 39th was finished as a unit; but it fought hard and inflicted serious damage to the enemy. Reconnaissance photo analysts counted 639 bodies around Ranger Base North. Lt. Col. Molinelli, commander of the 2nd Squadron, 17th Air Cavalry reported, "For three days we were unable to get supplies to them. When they were low on ammunition, they went out and took PAVN rifles and ammunition and fought on. When they decided to move off their hill, they beat their way right through that North Vietnamese Regiment, killing them with their own guns and ammunition."[32]

There were 199 survivors who reached Ranger Base South by nightfall; 107 were still able to fight. Four hundred men, including 100 from the 39th Battalion, held Ranger Base South for another two days before Gen. Lãm declared the position untenable. Many fought courageously until the end, although 17 men did panic and left hanging on to the helicopter skids to escape Laos.

Disappointed by Lãm's performance, President Thiệu turned command of Lâm Sơn 719 over to Gen. Trí, the "Patton" of the Parrot's Peak. The latter, however, died in a helicopter crash and Gen. Lãm retained his post.

At 1100 hours, on 25 February, PAVN artillery fire rained down on FSB 31 while U.S. helicopters scrambled to suppress the source of bombardment. Then antiaircraft fire struck a U.S. F-4 aircraft and forced the pilot to eject. The U.S. forward air controller shifted his attention to the rescue of the downed pilot leaving no air cover for the beleaguered defenders of FSB 31.

Gen. Lãm ordered the nearby armor to relieve the pressure on the firebase. The armor was under the control of Gen. Đống who was equal in rank to Lãm and was unhappy to be subordinated to him. The tanks and APC rumbled northward only to meet a PAVN ambush. The fighting was heavy and despite losing two tanks, Lãm instructed the armor to continue its relief effort. Đống, however, ordered the armor to remain in place 1,800 meters short of its goal. The command breakdown sealed the fate of FSB 31.

By early evening, PAVN armor penetrated the base defenses and the ARVN paratroopers responded with small arms and LAW rockets, which took a fearsome toll on the attackers. However, enemy infantry soon overwhelmed the defenders and the 21st Airborne Battalion Artillery commander sent out a last message for fire directly on his position. A number of paratroopers managed to break out of the encirclement but a total of 135 ARVN soldiers were either captured or killed; they had fought bravely and well, inflicting 250 KIA on the PAVN, which also lost 11 tanks in the bitter fighting.[33]

Between 25 February and 1 March, the relief column consisting of five M-4 tanks, numerous APCs, the 8th Airborne Battalion, and remnant of the 3rd Battalion barely outgunned the PAVN tanks and infantry in three major battles. With the help of U.S. air strikes, the ARVN destroyed 17 PT-76 and six T-54 tanks and killed a reported 1,130 soldiers in the process. The ARVN lost 200 killed and wounded as well as 25 APCs and three of the five M-41 tanks.[34]

On 28 February, Lãm came up with a new plan that was approved by Thiệu. Two battalions of the ARVN 1st Division were airlifted to Tchepone—then a deserted village—on 7 March and the withdrawal began the next day. The airborne and armored forces withdrew along Highway 9 while U.S. helicopters extracted the units on the flanks. The PAVN units concentrated heavy antiaircraft fire on the evacuation helicopters, attacked the fire bases, and ambushed the retreating ARVN troops.

The last ARVN troops crossed back into South Vietnam on 24 March and the operation was officially terminated on 6 April 1971. The statistics were ambiguous. The U.S. XXIV Corps *After Action Report* showed enemy KIA at 19,360 due to B-52's and fighter bomber strikes. U.S. and South Vietnamese casualties totaled 9,065: 1,402 Americans (215 KIA) and 7,683 South Vietnamese (1,764 KIA). The ARVN lost 211 trucks, 87 combat vehicles, 54 tanks, and 96 pieces of artillery. The NVA lost 2,002 trucks, 106 tanks, 13 artillery pieces, 170,346 tons of ammunition. The U.S. lost 108 helicopters destroyed and 618 damaged.[35]

Although the South Vietnamese losses had been severe, the North Vietnamese suffered as badly if not worse, losing by some accounts as much as half of their troop strength committed to the operation.[36] It took them more than a year to replace their losses. "Vietnamization had been tested, had strained but had not cracked, and now had continued room to grow."[37]

A Warrior's Fate

On 5 March Trần Ngọc Huệ's 2/2 along with the 3rd Battalion, 2nd Regiment (3/2) of ARVN 1st Division were airlifted by a combination of 120 helicopters to LZ Hope just north of Tchepone. This was the largest air mobile operation of the Vietnam War. Troops fanned out before moving into Tchepone, the ultimate goal of Lãm

Son 719. There, Huệ was promoted to lieutenant colonel on the spot. For the next three days they searched the area in and around the town before moving south of Highway 9.

By 19 March, cut off by vastly superior enemy forces, Huệ and his men dug in atop Hill 660 and threw out defenses to stem the PAVN attacks. They called for air support, including B-52 air strikes. PAVN units poured forward in the assault. Surrounded and facing death, Huệ requested extraction. U.S. air power that day mounted 1,388 gunship sorties, 270 tactical air strikes, and 11 B-52 missions. Twenty of the 40 helicopters used in the lift were hit and rendered un-flyable; although 3/2 Battalion got out, 2/2 and 4/2 had to remain behind.

The 4/2 Battalion, rejecting PAVN calls to surrender, fought its way out. For two days the battalion kept on the run with the enemy on its heels. Near the Sepone River, the PAVN intercepted the battalion and the resulting firefight lasted most of the day. The battalion commander and most of the officers died in the battle. Thirty survivors escaped again and were picked up the following afternoon by U.S. helicopters. The following day, another 50 stragglers reached safety. In fulfilling its rear-guard mission, the 2/2 Battalion had sacrificed more than three-quarters of its men.[38]

On Hill 660, the remnants of the 2/2 Battalion continued their fight. A mortar shell exploded close by and peppered Huệ with shrapnel. He blacked out but soon regained consciousness. Too wounded to get away, he asked to be left behind as his men attempted a breakout. Sixty ARVN soldiers made it to safety and were picked up by helicopters the following day, all that remained of the once proud 2nd Battalion, 2nd Regiment. Huệ was taken prisoner. Unable to treat Huệ's extensive wounds, the PAVN sent him to North Vietnam via the Hồ Chí Minh trail. His comrades in arms physically carried him from *binh trạm* to *binh trạm* along the trail. They were not allowed inside the *binh trạm*. Unable to eat the meager rations of rice and sugar they offered him, he hovered near death.

The journey was hell as insects and maggots invaded his open wounds and ate the flesh of his fingers. Once he reached North Vietnam, he received treatment but lost several fingers. Shifted to trucks, Huệ and his men reached the town of Vịnh where groups of civilians cursed, spat, and pelted them with rocks. They were paraded through the streets before being herded on trains to Hanoi. He entered Hỏa Lò Prison, the infamous Hanoi Hilton. At age 29, he faced the prospect of life in prison in communist jails.[39]

Huệ spent six months in solitary confinement in Hỏa Lò Prison and was transferred to Sơn Tây as a POW. Attempts by Hanoi to get Huệ to defect to the communist side failed and he was returned to jail. Following the 1973 Peace Treaty, Huệ and his 70 comrades were brought to the Thạch Hản River to be released back to South Vietnam. But at the last minute, they were pulled out of the line and returned to jail because they were told, they were prisoners of the Pathet Lao in Laos and not of the PAVN. Many of the 70 ARVN soldiers later shaved their heads and staged hunger strikes in protest. After the fall of Saigon in 1975, all the ARVN soldiers were sent to reeducation camps and Huệ was lucky to be released after 13 years in communist jails. Post-reeducation life was difficult for Huệ and it was only in 1991 through the help of his former U.S adviser that he was able to immigrate to the U.S. with his family.[40]

Lessons Learned

South Vietnam was a complex, diverse, and multi-party society. When the Thiệu-Kỳ ticket competed for the 1967 presidency, they did it against more than 25 other tickets. Almost everyone had a favored party or group, although not all were active participants in their group. As a reflection of this diversity, the ARVN leadership was also heavily politicized. This diversity, although offering a somewhat wide range of freedom to the people, thrived in a sea of lack of uniformity and cohesiveness. The government of South Vietnam, led by Diệm then Thiệu, had failed to curb the various factions, sects, and religions in order to mold them into a vibrant, aggressive national anti-communist force. Individually, the South Vietnamese might be strong, resourceful, and talented, but they did not have that backbone, that common core, that idealism that held them and bound them together through adversity and pushed them toward the ultimate sacrifice.

Some units fought extremely well; others just caved in and were wiped out. This does not mean they did not fight. They fought through thick and thin; they fought sometimes without reinforcement, re-supply, or reward. Some of them had fought continuously since 1954. No other army in the world had fought longer than these units. In the end, they had no more strength to give. The mettle their nationalism was made of was not strong enough to hold them erect, to keep them fighting. But they would come back and fight again.

General Lãm, the I Corps commander, could not control two of his three principal subordinates: the commanders of the Airborne and Marine divisions, who were also lieutenant generals. The Airborne commander, Lt. Gen. Dư Quốc Đống, although more submissive than the other, did what he pleased. The Marine commander, Lt. Gen. Lê Nguyên Khang, who was more senior in rank than Lãm, boycotted the entire operation and delegated his command authority to a subordinate colonel. Khang made his own decision to abandon FSB Hotel and withdrew his troops from Laos. The dissension affected staff coordination and strategic responses to enemy attacks.[41]

President Thiệu did not intervene on behalf of Lãm because he depended on the Marine and Airborne divisions as his palace guard. He did not want to antagonize them because he needed their support. Lãm, on the other hand, was not without blame. He was a military administrator who had no experience in large unit operations. Gen. Bruce Palmer wrote that Lãm's "reputation as a combat commander was only mediocre, but ... [he] was considered to be a loyal, capable administrator."[42] Being the commander of the I Corps at that time, he was recruited to lead Lâm Sơn 719. Had there been another commander, the results might have been different. The best general for this type of operation would be General Đỗ Cao Trí, the hero of the successful Cambodian operation who was known for his fighting prowess and flamboyant style. Accordingly, plans were made to replace Lãm with Trí. Unfortunately, the latter was killed in a helicopter accident in Cambodia prior to assuming command of the operation.

Thiệu's decision on 12 February to suspend the operation's forward movement not only doomed Lâm Sơn 719, but also put his troops in a vulnerable and dangerous position. Having the offensive edge at that time, he could have moved ahead and completed the proposed operation before turning around to fight against the aroused communists. When the situation got tough, Thiệu in critical situations, had these moments of indecision that ultimately changed history. He would repeat the same mistake in 1975, which led to South Vietnam's final downfall.

In preparation for this incursion—there was no preparation, as a matter of fact—ARVN units had no time devoted to unit preparation, combined tank-infantry training and coordination. The tanks fought alone, the infantry fought alone, and both suffered.[43] There was a lack of a system of accurate and timely reporting. In the case of Lâm Sơn 719, the reporting was deplorable. Reports were slow, inaccurate, and sometimes nonexistent.[44] Since staffs rarely visited the front lines, the operation drifted along without information, intelligence or control. This led to disastrous failings that were indicative of basic deficiencies in training and discipline.

ARVN units had also picked up some bad traits from the Americans. They relied too much on helicopters when it would be easier, safer to travel by foot. When they made contact with the enemy, they sat down and called for air or artillery support instead of maneuvering and attacking. On the ground, the ARVN tactics, developed over nearly a decade of battle against a low-tech threat, proved completely inadequate against an enemy equipped with modern armor, heavy artillery, and sophisticated air defense weapons.[45]

From the ARVN/U.S. planners, there was a careless disregard for the effects of the terrain, weather and road network. There was an underestimation of the enemy forces and their ability to mobilize additional troops. There was a sense of the superiority of one's troops and resources, especially the overestimation of American air power to dominate the battlefield.[46]

One wonders why the experienced, pragmatic, and usually cautious General Creighton Abrams, who had spent four years of 15-hour days among the Vietnamese and the ARVN, not only advocated the operation, but also pushed it on the Vietnamese and his American superiors. He knew the condition, morale, and training of the ARVN units. He knew the terrain and weather in Laos and had intelligence on the enemy. Although he had a good estimation of the odds of winning or losing, he still gave the green light to the operation. Maybe that he thought the PAVN would run away and abandon their bases as in Cedar Falls and Junction City operations? This assumption was wrong for the operations cited above and Lâm Sơn 719 were vastly different. The bases in Laos were critical for future aggressions in South Vietnam a year later in 1972 when the NVA planned to spearhead a three-pronged attack on Quảng Trị, Ban Mê Thuột, and An Lộc. Maybe he just wanted South Vietnam to acquire some experience dealing with the NVA by themselves?[47]

Following Lâm Sơn 719, MACV equipped one South Vietnamese tank battalion with the heavier U.S. M-48; one ARVN artillery battalion received the 175 mm self-propelled guns to combat the Russian 130 mm guns in the hands of the NVA. This upgrading was grossly inadequate and came in reaction to prior modernization in the weapons or tactics of the PAVN. All ARVN battalions should have been given the M-48 tanks and several artillery battalions should have received the lethal 175 mm guns. This was a significant weakness of Vietnamization. The PAVN were always one step ahead of the ARVN in terms of military supply and modern technology.[48]

10

1972

Quảng Trị–Kontum–An Lộc-Charlie

In 1972, the ARVN, having rebounded from the losses during Lâm Sơn 719 campaign, had grown to a million-men strong. It had a new division: the 3rd Infantry Division to be located in the I Corps. In the meantime the U.S. continued its downsizing and by January 1972, it had only 158,000 troops left in Vietnam. The threat of any new invasion by Hanoi was getting more serious. The South Vietnamese and the Americans did not know it yet, but in this *Mùa Hè Đỏ Lửa* or Fiery Red Summer, the North Vietnamese would launch an almost simultaneous, three-pronged attack in South Vietnam against Quảng Trị in the I Corps, Kontum in the II Corps, and An Lộc in the III Corps.

The 1972 summer was hot, red hot as war engulfed three-fourths of the nation. After rebounding from the disastrous 1968 Tết Offensive and after rebuilding its military reserve, Hanoi launched its second Corps-sized attack against South Vietnam in 1972 at a time when the Americans were disengaging.

The Politburo's decision to win the war by military means was reached at the 19th Plenum, which convened in Hanoi in December 1970 and continued into early 1971. It noted that the Cambodian raid had damaged the logistic apparatus supporting the communist cause in the southern half of South Vietnam. Vietnamization was making progress. The pacification program had achieved some gains. On the other hand, U.S. combat troops were leaving. The performance of the RVNAF without U.S. advisers during Lâm Sơn 719 campaign was not great. A resounding military victory would humiliate Nixon and destroy his war policies. Through Resolution #13, the decision was made to launch an attack either in 1972 or 1973.[1]

To prepare for the attack, Lê Duẩn in the spring of 1971 flew to Moscow to request more military assistance in the form of weapons and equipment, including MIG-21 fighter jets, SAM antiaircraft missiles, T-54 medium tanks, 130 mm guns, 160 mm mortars, 57 mm antiaircraft guns, and for the first time, shoulder-fired, heat-seeking SA-7 Strela antiaircraft missiles. In addition, other war supplies such as ammunition, vehicles, and fuels were shipped to North Vietnam in quantities as never before reported during the previous war years.[2]

They then drafted a three-pronged invasion plan of South Vietnam. In the I Corps, the 304th and the 308th divisions plus three separate infantry regiments would cross the DMZ from North Vietnam to attack Quảng Trị and Huế. The 324B Division would attack Huế from the west. In the III Corps, the VC 5th, the NVA 7th, and the VC 9th from Cambodia would take An Lộc, the capital of Bình Long Province, and threaten Saigon. In II Corps, the 2nd and 320th Divisions would seize Kontum and Pleiku from its bases in Laos and cut off South Vietnam in half.

The concept was bold and imaginative. Any attack in any of the three Corps, if successful, would occupy important targets and areas leading to the future conquest of South Vietnam. If all three attacks were successful, Saigon would have fallen and the war would end in 1972.

As weather played a major role in the attacks in these three different regions, the ideal weather nationwide would fall between 1 February and 31 May. During the monsoon months, torrential rains would impede movement making resupply difficult. In the area subjected to the Southwest Monsoon, dry weather occurred from mid–October and the end of May. In the North, which was subjected to the Northeast Monsoon, dry weather was noted from February to September.

As 1972 dawned, both the Americans and the South Vietnamese knew of the impending attack, although their intelligence again failed them. They could neither predict the starting time of the overall invasion nor the direction and weights of the component attacks in each major offensive.

On 30 March 1972, the North Vietnamese committed their total force to launch an attack dubbed the Easter Offensive against South Vietnam in violation of the 1954 Geneva Accords. They employed about 120,000 men divided into 14 divisions and 26 separate regiments—except the 316th regiment, which was located in Laos—and supported by hundreds of tanks and artillery pieces. This aggressive force amounted to some 20 separate divisions (more divisions than George Patton ever commanded in World War II).[3]

The Battle for Quảng Trị (March 1972)

The Fall of Quảng Trị

The five northernmost South Vietnamese provinces below the DMZ formed the I Corps. The jungle-covered mountains extended from Laos to the South China Sea. Between the foothills and the sea lay a narrow strip of farmland, home to the region's population.

In early 1972, the PAVN had three divisions with a total of 11 independent regiments inside or on the border of I Corps. The famous NVA 308th "Iron" Division was on the northern side of the DMZ while the NVA 304th Division stationed over the border in Laos. There were three separate infantry regiments from the B-5 Front, two tank regiments, and five artillery regiments armed with the long-range 130 mm gun with a range of 27 kilometers. The NVA 324B Division was ready to move to the A Shau Valley west of Huế.

The ARVN had three divisions: the ARVN 1st and 3d Divisions in Quảng Trị and Thừa Thiên Provinces and the 2nd Division farther south. To this force were added the ARVN 51st Regiment, the 1st Ranger Group and the 1st Armored Brigade for a combined total of 25,000 troops.

The then I Corps commander was General Hoàng Xuân Lãm. Born in Quảng Trị City in 1928, he attended the national military academy in Dalat in 1950 and in 1953 was sent to France to attend the armored school at Saumur. He was above all a military administrator who proved to be an ineffective, if not incompetent military commander in the ill-fated Lâm Sơn 719 operation into Laos.[4] He was also known to be "the most colorless general in Vietnam. But he has managed, perhaps by being so colorless, to remain in a position of great power over a long period of time [six years as commander of the I Corps]."[5]

The ARVN 3d Division was a brand new unit created in October 1971 as part of the Vietnamization program and for the purpose of filling the gaps left by departing U.S. troops from I Corps. General Abrams agreed with its activation with the understanding that the South Vietnamese would come up with their own equipment. As a result, the division was less well equipped compared to the other ARVN divisions: it had few M-16 rifles and more cast-off armament from other divisions.

The new division was built around the 2d Regiment of the ARVN 1st Division, one of the South Vietnamese most reliable units. The two new 56th and 57th Regiments were made up of reluctant transferees from local militia units, draftees, and even prisoners from military jails. On 20 October, the division was activated although it was at less than one-third strength and sent north near the DMZ. It was commanded by Brigadier General Vũ Văn Giai, former deputy commander of the ARVN 1st Division and one of ARVN best junior officers.

Giai took his job seriously and in late 1971 embarked on a heavy training program to improve the division's combat readiness.[6] He went from base to base surveying the defenses and noting strengths and weaknesses, which were many for a green division and which were discussed with his superior, General Lãm. The latter, however, ignored his requests and made sure any complaints did not reach Saigon.[7]

In late March 1972, Giai decided to rotate two of his regiments to familiarize them with I Corps' defenses. The plan consisted of exchanging the ARVN 56th Regiment from its positions around Firebase Charlie 2 north of the Cam Lộ River with the ARVN 2nd Regiment around Camp Carroll. As a training exercise, it was acceptable; but from a tactical standpoint, nothing would be gained by shuffling forces laterally between bases. The troubling factor was that the exercise was planned for 30 March while intelligence from Saigon suggested an imminent invasion by the enemy on 29 March. Although moving ahead with the exercise in the face of a potential invasion sounded foolhardy, neither Lãm nor Giai cancelled the exercise. To make matters worse, both Giai and his adviser, Colonel Metcalf, planned to take an extended holiday weekend in Saigon leaving the exercise completely unsupervised.[8] On 30 March, the troop exchange went wrong from the beginning due to a shortage of moving trucks, bad weather with low clouds and rain, and disorganization. And at 1100, the attack came with the roar of the shelling. I Corps was unprepared for the attack.

The Bridge of Đông Hà

The main thrust of the attack was through the DMZ and southward along Highway 1. This part of the enemy's offensive was completely unexpected. Analysts at the Defense Intelligence Agency had predicted an invasion through the DMZ although the CIA downplayed that possibility.[9] Even the South Vietnamese were surprised: General Lãm, the I Corps commander, did not expect that the NVA would flagrantly violate the 1954 Geneva Accords by invading across the DMZ.

By 1 April, the entire 3rd division began falling back to the South while the west flank, held by the marine brigades withdrew to the east. Gen. Giai set up a new line of defense on Cửa Việt and Cam Lộ Rivers bending south at Camp Carroll, an old U.S. Marine fire support base. By the next day, all collapsed. The 57th Regiment (3rd division) holding the key sector astride Highway 1 seeing civilians (and their own families) pouring through their lines from the north, panicked and joined the refugees in their flight to the South. Giai tried to stop the rout but could not.

The Vietnamese Marines were a cut above most of the military. The South Vietnamese Marine Corps (VNMC) was established on 1 October 1954 and placed under the control of the Navy. It went through various reorganizations over the next decade. By 1962, it consisted of only a single brigade. In October 1968, a second brigade was added and the Marines were re-designated a division. In June 1970, a third brigade was formed and the division strength rose to 15,000 men. As part of the nation's strategic reserve, they always returned to Saigon, their home base, after participating in an operation anywhere in the country. In February 1971, they moved from Saigon to I Corps to take part in Operation Lâm Sơn 719 into Laos and remained in I Corps from that time. They were placed along the western edge of the so-called Ring of Steel, the South Vietnamese defense line along the DMZ and the Laotian border.[10]

The VNMC 3rd Battalion was ordered to hold the town of Đông Hà, which was located at the junction of the north-south Highway 1 and the east-west national Route 9. It received assistance from the 20th Tank Regiment (20th Tanks), which was made up of 43 M48A3 medium tanks, some of the most modern in the U.S. armor arsenal. As a result of its drawdown of August 1971, the U.S. became aware that it had left behind to the ARVN only three small armored cavalry squadrons, all in the I Corps. It then decided to form the 20th Tank Regiment with a total of 43 tanks, ten fewer than the full-strength regiment because of failure of tank crews to complete the training.

At Đông Hà, naval guns from U.S. destroyers destroyed four PT-76 enemy tanks. A-1 Skyraiders, World War II vintage propeller-driven planes from VNAF, destroyed an additional 11 tanks. The 20th Tank Regiment also managed to take down nine PT-76s and two T-54s.[11]

Other tanks were on the way. On the northern end, a T-54 cautiously began crossing the bridge. On the southern end of the bridge, Marine sergeant Huỳnh Văn Lượm, each hand holding an M72 light anti-tank weapon (LAW)—a single-shot, disposable rocket launcher designed as an infantryman's best defense against armor—tried to stop the tank. As the later moved forward, he lay one LAW besides him, put the other to his shoulder and aimed over the top of the tube. Lượm fired at the tank, but the round went high. The second did not miss. It hit the frontal armor, ricocheted into the turret ring and exploded, jamming the turret. The wounded tank backed off the bridge and the Marines cheered. Captain Ripley, the adviser, called the incident "the bravest single act of heroism I've ever heard of, witnessed, or experienced," and credited Lượm with stopping the momentum of the entire enemy attack.[12]

Various options including a decision to blow up the bridge were discussed among Generals Lãm, Giai, and the U.S. advisers, although no decision was made by noon of 2 April 1972. Five hundred pounds of explosives were hauled to the base of the bridge, although no one had rigged the bridge for demolition. If demolition of the bridge was necessary to temporarily put a hold on the invasion, it would also prevent the ARVN from reconquering the lost territories including Quảng Trị City.[13]

As the South Vietnamese were scared to death about handling the explosives—no one had any expertise in this field—Captain Ripley volunteered to do the job. After spending two hours hauling and setting up the charges on the underside of the bridge, a test showed that the explosives failed to detonate. Then came the order not to blow up the bridge.

While discussions continued as how to handle the situation, the bridge was torn apart by a huge explosion. Some speculated that it was blown apart by "smart" bombs that were detonated by laser beams. Who made the final decision to call the airstrike remained unknown although the credit for the bridge destruction went officially to Captain Ripley who received the Navy Cross, the nation's second highest award for valor.[14] Of course, there were contributions from the Vietnamese Marines who held the ground south of the river, the 20th Tanks that turned the North Vietnamese armor away, and the airstrike that finished off the bridge itself.

The Surrender of Camp Carroll

Having taken the western Firebases Khe Gió, Sarge, and Nui Ba Ho, the communists headed towards Camp Carroll. On 30 March, they bombarded the camp causing fear and chaos among the troops of the ARVN 56th Regiment (3rd division), 1,800 of whom rushed into the safety of the camp. Lieutenant Colonel Phạm Văn Định, the regiment commander tried to reach the various battalion commanders, but few answered over the radio.

Colonel Định was no common soldier. He was a hero of the South Vietnamese Army and the second Hắc Báo commander, but he had mellowed out with the years. Hắc Báo (Black Panther) was the first truly airmobile unit in the ARVN that stood ready to help other units in need in the I Corps.[15] His unit 2/3 ARVN was part of the group that helped recover Huế and raise the South Vietnamese flag above the battered and shell-torn Citadel during the 1968 Tết Offensive. For his role in the fighting, he received a U.S. Bronze Star for valor and the sobriquet of "Young Lion of Huế."[16]

Although the U.S. Marines and the ARVN fought separate battles in Huế—efforts complicated by issues of national and unit pride—both fought well and deserved praise. "The just and warranted attention lavished on the heroic deeds of the leathernecks, though, has in part skewed the overall picture of the fighting in the Citadel, leaving the ARVN's role in the struggle nearly ignored."[17] Major Robert Thompson, commander of the 1/5 Marines, continued the process begun by U.S. journalists of marginalizing the ARVN contributions to the fighting by stating, "The MACV records will reflect that the ARVN, assisted by the 1/5 took the Citadel.... That was strictly public relations hogwash.... The 1st battalion, 5th Marines took the Citadel. The ARVN were spectators."[18] Disdainful of the entire ARVN contribution to the battle, with the exception of the Hắc Báo, Thompson reserved special scorn for the work of 2/3: "2/3 was worthless. And the … commanding officer was a wimp."[19] The grim irony of the situation was not lost upon the ARVN that fought in 1968 with a skill and tenacity that were beyond American expectations. American books barely mentioned ARVN contributions to the fighting.[20]

Even in its greatest victory ever, the ARVN was pushed aside. The U.S. Marines singlehandedly liberated the New City south of the Perfume River and fought an epic battle in the Citadel, losing 147 killed in action.[21] In a much less heralded battle, though, the ARVN had actually done the majority of the fighting in the Citadel, their understrength units besting the vaunted PAVN and VC in a long and bitter struggle largely without the aid of heavy direct-fire weaponry.[22] ARVN forces lost 357 killed in action and inflicted an astounding 2,642 battle deaths on the PAVN and VC forces.[23]

The following year, 1969, the 2/3 ARVN was asked to assist the three battalions from 3rd Airborne Brigade, 101st Division in the final assault of Đông Ấp Bia (the 937 foot–high Hamburger Hill for the Americans). Although the Americans did most of the work, during this final assault the four units moved uphill on different tracts and the 2/3 ARVN managed to get on the top of the hill first (not the U.S. 3/187).[24] But it was asked to step off the crest so that the last NVA defenses could be fired on. Shortly after Định and his men moved away, the 3/187 broke through NVA defenses and moved to the summit. An hour-and-a half later, 2/3 returned to the top of Đông Ấp Bia for a short period before moving southwest to conduct other operations in the Ashau Valley.[25]

During the 1972 Easter Offensive, Định was the commander of the 56th Regiment and of Camp Carroll that had a battery of 175 mm howitzers, one of the biggest field artillery pieces in the world, 22 batteries of 155 mm and 105 mm, plus scores of heavy machine guns. The NVA forces had crossed the DMZ and attacked Khe Gió, Fuller, Núi Ba Ho, and Sarge bases, which successively fell, leaving Camp Carroll isolated and threatened. Food and ammunitions ran low and there was no hope of resupply. During this offensive, Định had already lost five hundred men.

Facing the fight of his life, Định received a call from General Hoàng Xuân Lãm, the I Corps commander who told him that he would not receive any reinforcements. In his mind, his 56th Regiment had been abandoned.[26] On 2 April, heavy NVA artillery resumed, followed by a ground attack that was furiously repulsed. Định called the ARVN 3rd Division and was told that General Vũ Văn Giai, the commander of the ARVN 3rd Division, which included the 56th and 57th Regiments, was devoting his time to the 57th that was under heavy attack by the PAVN at Đông Hà. Định realized that nobody was watching after his regiment any longer.

At 1400, a second PAVN attack struck camp Carroll and the enemy came close to the perimeter wire. As the battle raged, Định received a phone call from the PAVN telling him to surrender, otherwise they all would die. A second offer was made a few moments later. Định gathered his staff—all 13 men—to explain about the situation. They all, except one, decided to surrender.[27] Định told the two advisers about the decision; the latter contacted their superiors and were picked up by a helicopter. An entire battalion of 300 men did not surrender and broke free of the perimeter. Overall, 1,000 soldiers from the 56th ARVN Regiment filtered through enemy lines to Đông Hà and Ái Tử.[28]

Back to Quảng Trị City, during the lull in the fighting from 9 to 22 April, the 3rd Division was reinforced by three ranger groups and the recently reconstituted 1st Armored Brigade. With these reinforcements, Lãm now ordered a counteroffensive over the objections of his field commanders. The counteroffensive went nowhere in the face of the NVA superior strength. Gen. Lãm placed his commanders, especially Gen. Giai under serious operational constraints. Giai had operational constraints over the two regiments in the ARVN 3rd Division, two Marine brigades, four ranger groups, one armor brigade—a total of nine brigades or 33 battalions. That was too much for Giai to handle.[29] Lãm never visited the frontline troops nor personally observed the ARVN 3rd Division. His only contact was over the radio, leaving his subordinates with the impression that their corps commander did not think the situation was serious.³⁰

The enemy resumed its attack on 23 April and tightened the control over Quảng Trị City. On 1 May mass panic and confusion set in among the ARVN troops who abandoned Quảng Trị City. Soldiers and families fled to the South. The PAVN tanks and artillery fired into this mass causing an estimated 20,000 civilian deaths.³¹ Lãm was recalled to Saigon and fired.

Operation Sóng Thần

On 3 May 1971 Gen. Ngô Quang Trưởng, commander of the IV Corps, was made the new I Corps commander. Born in 1929 in Bến Tre, he attended the Thủ Đức Officer Candidate School and the Command and Staff School at Dalat. He joined the 5th Airborne Battalion as a platoon leader in 1954. By 1963, he was a battalion commander. In 1965, he was made chief of staff of the Airborne Division. In the spring of 1966, while seasoned generals could not handle the Buddhist protest in Huế, the 37-year-old lieutenant colonel, a Buddhist, was made acting commander of the ARVN 1st Division. He quickly built it into one of the best ARVN units until August 1970 when he took command of the IV Corps. Gen. Westmoreland said he "would trust him to command an American division."³² Although stooped and paper-thin, he possessed a single-minded devotion to duty, fierce loyalty to his subordinates, and indefatigable energy that helped him achieve his goals.

The ARVN 3rd Division was totally ineffective as a unit and had to be rebuilt. Its 2nd Regiment was almost wiped out. Its 56th Regiment was still retraining and conducted limited operations around Huế. The Marines were still effective and reliable, although the VNMC 147th Brigade would need 1,000 men to return to its fighting shape. The Rangers were in bad shape. The 1st Ranger Group had only 14 percent losses. The 4th Ranger Group lost 500 men and would require one month before the unit could be retrained. The 5th Ranger Group lost 800 men and would take longer to refit and retrain.

Trưởng had the twin duties of defending Huế and retaking Quảng Trị Province. On 3 May, he ordered all troops to return and defend Huế or be shot on sight. As 150,000 people had fled Quảng Trị Province to Huế, they changed the social and moral fabric of the city. Deserters from the ARVN 3rd Division and soldiers from the ranger and 1st Division roamed the streets of Huế like armed gangsters. By 10 May, the rioting died down and officers began to reorganize their troops.

The Marine Division's three brigades and two regiments of the ARVN 1st Division were the only forces the South Vietnamese had north of Huế. Trưởng displayed them in an L shaped line, with the Marines holding Thừa Thiên Province south of the Bo River and the ARVN 1st defending from the Bo River south to Huế. When Thiệu released the 2nd Brigade of the Airborne Division, Trưởng inserted it in the northern front along with the 1st Ranger Group. Later the newly refitted ARVN 3rd Division was moved to south of Đà Nẵng with its new commander, Brigadier General Nguyễn Duy Hinh. A year later, the ARVN 3d Division was rated the best of the South Vietnamese divisions and Hinh was the only division commander promoted to the rank of major general in 1973.³³

On 13 May, Trưởng launched the first attack, code named Sóng Thần or Tidal

Wave 5-72. U.S. helicopters picked up the 3rd and 8th Battalions of the VNMC 369 Brigade for an assault on Hải Lăng. They swept toward Mỹ Chánh to link up with the VNMC 9th Brigade. Caught in the pincers was the NVA 66th regiment.

On 21 May, the enemy launched a three-pronged armor attack against the Mỹ Chánh Line encircling the 3rd and the 9th Battalions. The later withdrew, but with the help of air strikes an ARVN armor cavalry unit pushed the enemy back over the river. The enemy attacked again but were pushed back, leaving behind ten tanks and armored carriers destroyed by TOWs. The enemy suffered 542 killed while the Marines reported light casualties.[34]

On 24 May, a combined amphibious and airlifted assault was launched, code-named Sống Thần 6-72. Artillery, air and naval gunfire struck Red Beach and LZ Columbus to soften enemy resistance. Forty amphibious tractors carrying the VNMC 7th Battalion rushed to the shore. The Marines seized their objective killing 50 NVA. The second part of the operation was an airlifted assault by the VNMC 4th and 6th Battalions to LZ Columbus. They ran into the NVA 18th Regiment the next day. All the three battalions withdrew to Mỹ Chánh Line by 31 May.

While Sống Thần 6-72 was going on, the enemy hit the VNMC 258th Brigade at the Mỹ Chánh Line. The assault by infantry and tanks was poorly conceived and executed, allowing ARVN artillery and air strikes to take a deadly toll. May had been a deadly month for the PAVN as more than 2,900 of their soldiers were killed and 64 armored vehicles were captured or destroyed. They did not gain any ground.[35]

On 8 June, all three Marine brigades committed four battalions to Sống Thần 8-72, an attack across the Tạch Mã River. The Marines killed 230 North Vietnamese and destroyed seven tanks. They stayed north of the river while South Vietnamese engineers built pontoon bridges and brought tanks and artillery to support further attacks.

On 18 June, the three brigades moved again. The VNMC 1st Battalion moved along the beach, while the 5th went along Route 1. In the middle was the VNMC 6th Battalion moving along Route 555. The enemy threw infantry and tanks against the Marines moving in the middle road; but the attacks were poorly coordinated and were broken down. Operation Sống Thần 8-72 ending with the new defensive line was established three miles north of the Mỹ Chánh Line. The enemy lost another 761 soldiers and eight tanks.[36]

Retaking Quảng Trị

On 28 June, Trưởng launched the first Corps-sized assault ever executed by the ARVN in South Vietnam—operation Lâm Sơn 72 with Quảng Trị City as the primary objective. The battle to recapture Quảng Trị turned out to be the longest battle of the war. The task force included the Airborne Division's three brigades and the Marine Division, backed by both units' armor and artillery assets, the 1st Ranger Group and the 7th Armored Cavalry. Around Huế, the ARVN 1st Division would continue to push westward while the 57th Regiment guarded Đà Nẵng.

The Airborne Division's 2nd Brigade led the attack with Col. Trần Quốc Lịch as the brigade commander. It took more than a week for the brigade to cover the 18 miles from the Mỹ Chánh line to the outskirts of Quảng Trị City. For the next two weeks, the 2nd Brigade engaged in urban fighting. The paratroopers fought house-to-house until they were 50 yards from the citadel.

The North Vietnamese defensive lines in the citadel were manned by militia and replacement units. They suffered from constant U.S. air strikes. This was how they described the slaughter: "The new recruits came in at dusk. They were dead by dawn. No one had time to check where they were from, or who was their commander…? No one could count how many lives were lost." Others called the assault a "senseless sacrifice" and referred to Quảng Trị as "Hamburger City."[37] Then as paratroopers crawled forward to attack the citadel, the NVA rained down on them artillery fire and mortars stopping them in their tracks. The PAVN also attacked the airborne troops on the southwest side of Quảng Trị City trying to deflect their attention somewhere else. But the attack turned out to be limited.

Enemy units were also noted to be heading toward Quảng Trị. Hanoi sent two divisions to the rescue: the 325C, Hanoi's only reserve unit left in the North, and the PAVN 312th Division from Laos. Unwilling to wait for reinforcements that might or might not reach Quảng Trị, the North Vietnamese counterattacked on 19 July. A barrage of artillery rounds was followed by tanks and infantry attack. The assault, however, was repulsed by ARVN artillery.

On the east side of Highway 1 and along the coastline, the VNMC 3rd, 5th, 7th, and 8th Battalions encountered stiff resistance from the 304th NVA Division to their advance. Brig. Gen. Bùi Thế Lân, the Marine Division commander, planned a heliborne assault behind enemy lines to relieve pressure on the attacking Marines. On 29 June, the 1st and 4th battalions landed on the coast at two landing sites named Flamingo and Hawk. The attack relieved pressure on the Airborne Division in the South. Gen. Lân then moved one battalion with the help of U.S. helicopters across the Vinh Đình River to the northeast of the city while the two previous battalions attacked from east to west.

Once on the ground, the 1st VNMC Battalion led by Major Nguyễn Đăng Hòa ran into heavy fire from the PAVN 48th Regiment (PAVN 320B Division), which was dug in west of the landing zone. From the west side, the VNMC 7th pushed North Vietnamese defenders from their positions and overran an enemy armored command post.

By 14 July the Marines had cut off the main supply line into Quảng Trị City causing the enemy to slow its attack to conserve supplies and ammunition. For the first time medevac helicopters were able to fly in to evacuate more than 150 casualties sustained since the beginning of the attack. On 22 July, the Marines launched another combined attack against the North Vietnamese north and east of the city. They were able to push the enemy to the north toward Cửa Việt, killing 133 enemy soldiers, destroying five armored vehicles and overrunning a 100-bed hospital.[38] At this point the Airborne Division faltered. Exhausted and depleted from the fighting in the city as well as previous battles near An Lộc and in the Central Highlands, they could not muster the strength to recapture the citadel. They were pulled out to serve as the I Corps' reserve.

On 27 July at 2130 elements of the VNMC 258th Brigade replaced airborne units at the front. Between the Marines and the citadel's walls remained 200 yards of no man's land that had given the paratroopers a tough time. Little changed in August. Defending the city was the PAVN 325th Division with elements of the PAVN 308th and 320th Divisions. The 325th was comparatively fresh while the other two divisions had paid dearly for defending the city for so long. In July, the enemy suffered more than 1,880 dead along with 51 armored vehicles destroyed. The 147th VNMC Brigade held the northern section of the town while the VNMC 258th Brigade's four battalions fought house to house south of the city. On 22 August, the enemy launched another tank and infantry attack that immediately faltered.

On 8 September, Trưởng ordered the 1st Ranger Group to relieve the VNMC 147th Brigade of its blocking positions north of the city. This allowed the Marines to use its two units in an assault against the citadel.

Under a curtain of B-52 strikes and naval gunfire, the amphibious troop ship *Juneau* positioned itself at the mouth of the Cửa Việt River loaded with 400 ARVN Rangers. As the B-52 bombers completed their strikes, the PAVN emerged from the smoke expecting to meet the South Vietnamese. They instead encountered naval gunfire from U.S. destroyers offshore. There was no amphibious landing. That was just another diversion to pull the PAVN off balance.

Profiting from the ruse, the VNMC 258th Brigade attacked from the South while the VNMC 147th Brigade attacked from the north. Progress was slow because of stiff resistance. On the evening of 9 September, a squad of the VNMC 6th Battalion crept into the fortress to look at the enemy's defensive network. There were few enemy troops left inside. This would be the best time to storm the fortress. On 10 September just before midnight, Lt. Col. Đỗ Hữu Tùng launched a night attack against the southeast corner of the citadel. Within hours, the VNMC 6th Battalion had moved in a company to strengthen the position.

To the west, the 1st VNMC Battalion crossed the Thạch Hản River, securing a beachhead close to the western wall. From 11 to 15 September, the VNMC 2nd Battalion fought its way to the river closing the gap between the 1st and 6th battalions. On the north side, the VNMC 3rd and 7th Battalions fought their way through city streets reaching the citadel on 15 September. The PAVN poured a massive artillery fire against the western walls. By 1700 hours, the Marines had control of the citadel.

The fighting continued through the night and the next morning. The enemy put up stiff resistance against the 3rd and 7th battalions from the north, the 6th from the east and the 1st and 2nd from the east. By noon on 16 September, all enemy soldiers were either dead or had surrendered. The Marines climbed the walls and raised the South Vietnamese yellow-red flag over the west gate. Lt. Col. Turley later wrote poetically "Vietnamese Marines, short in stature, / Rich in courage and full of determination, / Stood tall in the eyes of all Marines."[39]

In order to attain that reputation, the South Vietnamese Marines suffered more than 5,000 casualties since June 1972, 3,658 of them during the seven-week battle to recapture the citadel. Almost one out of every four Marines in the entire division was wounded or killed.[40] General Trưởng was the hero of the hour. He had saved Huế and turned the tables on the most successful North Vietnamese offensive of the war. He had denied the enemy the goal of holding a provincial capital.

The Battle for Kontum

The second leg of the three-pronged attack during the *Mùa Hè Đỏ Lửa*, or Fiery Red Summer, fell on Kontum in the II Corps. Although the II Corps area comprised 47 percent of Vietnam's total land area, it was occupied by one fifth of the nation's population. The sparsely populated areas were home to mountains and forests, the "breathing lung," the resource rich territory and the exotic land of South Vietnam.

Although there had been some battalion- and regiment-sized attacks against the ARVN and government of Vietnam in this land-locked region, no corps-sized attack had occurred in the II Corps before 1972. While Washington thought about a war confined within the limits of South Vietnam, the communists expanded it to a regional and international war against the United States. When Washington limited Westmoreland's reaches to South Vietnam's boundaries, Hanoi was building huge camps and safe havens in neutral Laos and Cambodia along the borders with South Vietnam. From these safe havens—untouchable by Washington's orders—they could store ammunitions, military hardware and rest their *bộ đội* (soldiers) before sending them across the border when time came.

The surprise came in 1972 when more than two NVA divisions and scores of T-54 tanks, antiaircraft batteries, and Strela missiles showed up in Kontum.

The U.S. advisory structure in the II Corps, although the same as the other Corps was led by a civilian, John Paul Vann. The latter came to Vietnam in 1962 as a military adviser (lt. col.) and resigned his commission for personal reasons. He returned in 1965 as a State Department official with the Agency for International Development. In 1971 he became the director of the Second Regional Assistance Group (SRAG) in charge of the military advisers with a civilian rank equal to a major general.[41] John Paul Vann was "arrogant, egotistical, and cocky. He could be abrasive, blunt and opinionated. But he was also a hard-driving, hands-on, competitive commander who got results."[42]

His counterpart, Lt. Gen. Ngô Dzu, the II Corps commander, was a meek and malleable officer. According to Brig. Gen. Wear, Vann's deputy, Dzu was "more a politician than soldier and became heavily involved in black market activities, if not drug running.... [He] did not spend much time in Pleiku. He operated mostly out of Nha Trang."[43] This was fine for Vann, who could call all the shots behind the façade of Dzu's command.

The Fall of Tân Cảnh-Dak To II

Kontum was a garrison town of 25,000 people, a trading center, and the northernmost town in the highlands. It was guarded by the regimental base at Tân Cảnh and a number of firebases established on a series of ridgelines, known as Rocket Ridge, parallel to Route 14. About 50 kilometers north of Kontum on Highway 14, there was a district town named Dak To. Five kilometers south of it was an airfield called Dak To I. Adjoining it was a large ARVN base called Tân Cảnh. Four kilometers west of it was another airfield named Dak To II.

The ARVN 22nd Division controlled its 42nd and 47th Infantry Regiments at Tân Cảnh and three Border Ranger Battalions, some armored cavalry and supported by 50 tubes of 105 and 155 mm artillery. The Airborne Division controlled six airborne battalions and one Border Ranger Battalion and was supported by 16 tubes of 105 mm artillery. In Kontum were two ranger battalions and the Kontum Province RF and PF units. The force appeared formidable but it was spread thin over a large area with a limited road network. There was no unity of command. The commanding general commanded his own troops and the Rangers. The Ruff Puffs belonged to the

Kontum Province Chief. The airborne was a reserve force under the control of Saigon and would be sent to the I Corps.

On 3 April as U.S. helicopters flew to Rocket Ridge to try to extract a Chinook crew whose helicopter was shot down a few days earlier, they caught enemy soldiers launching an attack on Rocket Ridge. Helicopters and tactical air strikes drove the enemy out with heavy losses.

The PAVN T-54 was a medium tank that played an important role in the Easter Offensive of 1972 in Quảng Trị, Kontum, and An Lộc. It was so huge that it could send ARVN soldiers fleeing in terror. It was 30 feet long, 11 feet wide and 8 feet high and weighed 35 tons. Powered by a 580 horsepower V-12 engine, it could move as fast as 30 miles an hour—with a great deal of loud clanking, grinding and roaring. The main gun fired a 100 mm shell that could penetrate up to 390 millimeters of armor one kilometer away. There was a 7.62 mm coaxial machine gun beside the main gun and above the turret a .51 caliber (12.7 mm) machine gun that could be fired by the tank commander.[44]

Bến Hét was one of the surveillance camps established by the U.S. in the II Corps to watch over the side trails that brought NVA troops and supplies from the main HCM Trail into the highlands of central Vietnam. Special Forces teams and the Montagnard allies who lived in these camps launched reconnaissance units called Studies and Observation Groups (SOG) in the area.

At Bến Hét ranger camp, hundreds of artillery shells rained down on the huddled soldiers on 7 May. This went on for three days. At dawn on 9 May, they were awoken by unusual noises: yelping dogs, dozens of them. The North Vietnamese had turned them loose to trip mines and booby traps around the perimeter. A few went off and an hour later, the enemy launched an assault led by eight PT-76 tanks. Two PT-76s supported by infantry headed straight toward the main gate. Two rangers popped out of their foxholes and fired off two LAWs, striking both tanks. Other rangers opened fire, killing and scattering the enemy. Half an hour later, the enemy attacked the camp's east perimeter. Five PT-76s led the attack, flattening the defense. Two tanks were knocked out while the three others turned around. The emboldened rangers fired at the enemy entrenched inside the wire. By midafternoon, only a few survivors escaped. Bến Hét held out for the reminder of the offensive.[45]

Attacks on Rocket Ridge continued and on 21 April, ARVN soldiers on FSB Delta were overrun followed by the downfall of FSB 5 and 6 on 23 April. By that date, four of the 19 FSB north and west of Kontum were held by the communists.

Colonel Lê Đức Đạt was made commander of the ARVN 22nd Division in February 1972, after Major General Lê Ngọc Triển retired because of health problems. Đạt set up his forward command post at Tân Cảnh along with the three battalions of his 42nd Regiment. The 43rd Regiment was posted at Dak To II, an airfield five kilometers away. He knew the enemy was somewhere nearby but failed to patrol aggressively and to move toward them.[46]

On 19 April, the 1st Battalion of the 42nd Regiment was cut off and surrounded by two enemy battalions. The isolated troops were not resupplied and ran out of ammunition. Two days later, only 63 men made it back to the regimental compound. Since mid–April, Tân Cảnh received 200–300 rounds a day. On 22 April, a rocket hit a 105 mm howitzer position and more than 900 rounds of artillery in the position exploded.

On 23 April, the enemy fired AT-3 Sagger missiles at ARVN tanks and blew them up. The Division Tactical Operations Center (DTOC) bunker collapsed after being hit by another Sagger missile. Enemy attacks with infantry and tanks continued on Tân Cảnh and Rocky Ridge. Decision was made to replace Colonel Đạt by Colonel Tường, but the latter refused. The battle continued and Spectre gunships worked the area until dawn. Some advisers were extracted at 0800 on 24 April. Dak To II fell some time later.

According to Mr. Vann, part of the collapse of the ARVN 22nd Division was due to "years of very incompetent leadership and the defeatist attitude, particularly of General Triển [MG Lê Ngọc Triển], the former ARVN 22nd Division, who for two-and-a half years had made it one of his major objectives to convince all his subordinates they could not defeat the NVA."[47] After the fall of Tân Cảnh-Dak To II, the ARVN 22nd Division units were reorganized with new battalion and regimental commanders and a new commander, Colonel Phan Đình Niệm. Niệm was a good officer who was promoted to major general and remained in command of the 22nd Division until the end of the war in 1975.[48]

Preparations

After taking Tân Cảnh and Dak To II on 24 April, the NVA took a three-week break before attacking Kontum. It fitted Vann's goal fine as he used the lull to place more responsibility for the defense of Kontum in the hands of Col. Lý Tòng Bá, the commander of the ARVN 23d Division. In January 1972, Vann maneuvered Bá into taking the command of the ARVN 23d Division. But Bá was also his own man. He had an undistinguished career before becoming one of the best commanders of the Army. He was opposed to corruption, which made his rise through the ranks tougher than normal. He was discredited by the Americans when his armor unit was mauled by the VC at the village of Ấp Bắc. After being implicated in a failed coup attempt in September 1964, he was relieved of his armor command and sent to Bình Dương to serve as province chief. Nine years later, he was a division commander.[49] Bá had a reputation for being honest rather than corrupt. His wife came from one of the richest families in Bạc Liêu Province. Bá was related to the wife of General Cao Văn Viên, the Chairman of the Joint Chiefs of Staff. There was also a family relationship between Col. Bá and John Paul Vann. Bá's mother and the mother of Vann's fiancée, Julie, were sisters.[50]

As in Tân Cảnh, there was a lack of unity of command in the defense for Kontum. The only unit that would take orders from Colonel Bá was the 53rd Regiment from his own division. The 2nd Airborne Brigade, the 2nd and 6th Ranger Groups, and the Kontum Province Ruff Puffs having their own command, they would not listen to Bá. On 27 April the 6th Ranger Group commander moved his CP from FSB Lâm Sơn to FSB November while leaving his 34th and 35th Battalions at FSB Lâm Sơn. Gen. Dzu relieved the commander for disobedience.

Gen. Dzu also planned to relieve Bá and replace him with a general because he did not believe that the commanders of other units, also colonels, would listen to another colonel. Vann dissuaded him and suggested replacement of the airborne brigade and the two Ranger groups with the 23rd Division's own 44th and 45th Regiments.

With the arrival of new troops, Bá made some logistics changes. The ARVN 53d Regiment defended the airfield northeast of the city. On the northwest, just a mile north of the Dak Bla River, the ARVN 45th Regiment held the left flank. Center stage went to the ARVN 44th regiment, one of the best infantry regiments in the South Vietnamese Army. It would take the brunt of the enemy attack. Regional and Popular Forces guarded the southern approach along the Dak Bla River.[51]

The Attack

General Dzu, the II Corps commander, suffered from bouts of depression and was replaced on 10 May by Major General Nguyễn Văn Toàn who had served as assistant operations commander in I Corps.

There was a lack of the usual shelling from the enemy before the attack. The attack was planned for 0400 on 14 May. A last minute delay pushed the attack to 0430 hours. The pounding of enemy artillery lasted for an hour before the infantry attack began.

The enemy advanced through three main avenues. The PAVN 48th/320th Regiment plus a company from the 203rd Tank Regiment came down the west side of Route 14. The PAVN 64th/320th Regiment with the second company from the 203d Tank Regiment stormed south along the flatlands west of Route 58. Coming straight out of the North was the PAVN 28th Regiment, an independent unit attached to the B3 Front. The PAVN 141st Regiment part of the PAVN 2nd Division probed the Ruff-Puffs south of the city.[52]

Since the B-52s had not arrived yet, Vann called for the UH-1B mounted with TOW anti-tank rockets. TOW was tube-launched, optically tracked, and wire-guided, a technology designed to steer missiles into tanks no matter where they tried to hide. Attached to the sight mechanism by a thin wire, the missile would fly to the target as long as the sight was locked on by the gunner. Each TOW ship was supported by two Cobra gunships which suppressed antiaircraft gunfire. By the end of the offensive TOWs were credited with 47 kills, 24 of them on tanks (only 10 of which were T-54s). The rest were trucks, artillery and machine gun emplacements, and bunkers; 85 TOWs were fired; only ten were counted as misses.

Artillery deserved the real credit for breaking the PAVN attack. The South Vietnamese artillery commander, a graduate of the U.S. Army artillery school at Fort Sill had prepared his batteries by the book. Asked if he could lay on concentrations of fire along the main avenue of enemy approach, he answered, "Just tell me when and where you wanted it." He later laid down a heavy concentrated artillery barrage on the onrushing armor forcing the supporting infantry to flee or die.

The remaining tanks became easy prey for ARVN soldiers who were armed with the M72 LAW (light anti-tank weapon). Within minutes two tanks had been destroyed, their carcasses burning in the early hours of the morning. Despite heavy artillery and air support, many enemy soldiers managed to close with Kontum's forward defense. Fierce hand-to-hand fighting raged up and down the front line. At 2200 hours another major assault against the ARVN 44th and 53rd Regiments threatened to break through. In the confusion of the night, the two regiments failed to coordinate interlocking fields of fire and a North Vietnamese battalion punched a hole between the two regiments.

Bá and his adviser then designed a plan that was risky for two reasons. The ARVN 44th and 53rd Regiments would fall back to Kontum an hour before the planned B-52 strikes. A maneuver performed at nighttime stands a good chance of failure because communications and orders became mixed. Second, a fall back maneuver risked opening a gap through which the NVA could surge forward. To compensate, Bá would order the ARVN artillery to blanket the area forward of the retreating ARVN units. The plan was approved despite the complex maneuver involved.

At 0300 on 15 May, the order to pull back was given. For an hour, the ARVN artillery guns pounded the area left vacant by the ARVN units, which withdrew in good order to new positions. Then came the bombers that loosed their cargo. The ground trembled under the impact, trees snapped, and rocks flew in the air. When it was over, an eerie calm spread over the killing ground. ARVN soldiers unsteadily stood up. Blood flowed from ears and noses.

On the enemy side, the carnage was obvious. Hundreds of bodies lay scattered, most of them in pieces. Sandals, parts of green uniforms hung from shattered trees. The ground was torn and broken. Howitzers and rocket launchers stay silent, the crew lay dead beside them. Bodies were too many to count. Seven tanks were part of the debris.[53] The first part of the battle had ended. Early events on 14 May seemed to favor the ARVN; by nighttime, the tide had shifted. A bold plan by Bá and Truby, the adviser, well-disciplined artillery fire and movement by ARVN infantry, and a timely B-52 strike had brought temporary victory to the South Vietnamese.

The Counterattack

Colonel Bá shifted his troops, moving the 44th Regiment back into the city and putting it in reserve around Kontum hospital. The 45th Regiment moved up to take the 44th Regiment's place.

On 16 May, three helicopters were damaged by incoming fire. Another round of fire caused two VNAF C-123s sitting on the parking ramp to be destroyed.

At a 17 May press conference in Pleiku, Vann said that although 20,000 refugees had been evacuated from Kontum, they kept on coming and 30,000 more were waiting to be evacuated.

On 20 May, the enemy launched three assaults against the ARVN 53rd Regiment and pushed the unit out of its positions. The division reserve was committed and the 53rd Regiment retook its former positions after nine M-41 tanks supported by Cobra gunships slashed at the enemy.

The ARVN counterattack on Route 14 sputtered as the enemy assaulted the city again the next morning. One enemy battalion wedged itself between the ARVN 45th and 53rd battalions. The ARVN 3rd/44th Battalion struck south. A second battalion from the 44th Regiment along with a battalion of the ARVN 45th Regiment moved north trying to catch the enemy in a pincer movement. The two forces linked up and cleared the road after an hour of fighting.

Colonel Bá called for a priority air strike to prevent the enemy from settling in between the two regiments. The enemy launched three more counterattacks before air strikes turned the enemy away on 21 May.

On 24 May enemy bombardment picked late at night and sappers came from the South, sneaked inside the city, and positioned themselves near the airfield, the seminary, an orphanage, and a school. The enemy tried to link up with forces from the north to cut Kontum in half, but they failed.[54]

On 26 May, three or four battalions led by tanks stormed from the north, smashed into the 53rd Regiment. One battalion from the 44th Regiment counterattacked with the support of tanks. The enemy attacked again at night after pouring artillery fire on the regimental command posts. B-52s were called in at 0230 the next morning.

On 27 May one regiment of the PAVN 320th Division led by armor pushed down Route 14 toward Kontum. A second regiment from the PAVN 320th Division thrust in from the northeast. Air strikes were again called in to break the attack. The main ammunition depot got hit by enemy mortars. Exploding rounds flew everywhere. Hundreds of pounds of chemical agent billowed into the air, paralyzing friends and foes alike. Many of the ARVN soldiers had gas masks, but the enemy had nothing. For an hour the fighting stopped as both sides struggled to clear their eyes and throats.

Late afternoon on 27 May Colonel Bá decided to tighten up the city's defenses by ordering all units to disengage and move toward the city center. That would prevent the enemy from getting more footholds inside the defensive lines.

Before dawn on 28 May, the enemy dropped 300 to 400 artillery rounds along the northern defensive line. The U.S. Air Force again flew to the rescue. Parts of the ARVN 44th and 53rd Regiments counterattacked behind tanks on the north side of town. The Ruff-Puffs at the South end of Kontum fought from house to house to dislodge enemy soldiers.

Colonel Bá threw more reinforcements into Kontum. The 3rd battalion of the ARVN 47th Regiment was brought in from Pleiku while the 45th Regiment was ordered back into the defensive parameter. By nightfall the defensive lines were still holding. The countless air strikes had taken a heavy toll on the enemy, withered the number of their troops and dampened their resistance. Resupply had been difficult. They had to either win swiftly or pull back and resupply.

On 29 May, the South Vietnamese began to sense that they were at the end of a long ordeal. Light sniper fire and sporadic mortar rounds were recorded besides a total of 30 rounds of artillery.

On 30 May, after a round of mortars, the enemy attacked along the northeastern perimeter. Another mortar round landed in the ammunition dump, which had exploded days earlier. The ammunition exploded when the attackers walked by, killing scores and breaking the attack. All units of the ARVN 23rd Division counterattacked the northern forces. Fierce fighting occurred between the bunkers. Although air power did much to blunt enemy attack, it took infantry to achieve the victory.

At 1440 on 30 May, President Thiệu dropped by and jumped out of his helicopter. He strode straight up to a sheepish looking Colonel Bá, who thanked him for the visit. Thiệu promoted the colonel to brigadier general, pinning the new rank insignia to Bá's collar as guns rumbled close by. Thiệu then wandered among the troops congratulating them on a job well done.[55] Speaking about the ARVN 23rd Division, General Abrams said: "They have been victorious. They *know* it. And they beat the best."[56]

John Paul Vann died on the night of 9 June 1972 when his OH-58 crashed into a patch of tall trees somewhere between Kontum and Pleiku. He was returning from a farewell dinner in Saigon for Brig. Gen. Hill, his deputy, who was awarded the Legion of Merit. John posthumously received the Medal of Freedom, the highest civilian award the Vietnamese nation could bestow, and the U.S. Army's Distinguished Service Cross, second only to the Medal of Honor.

The Battle for An Lộc

The third leg of the three-pronged attack during the 1972 *Mùa Hè Đỏ Lửa* or Fiery Red Summer fell on An Lộc, a small otherwise insignificant provincial town close to the border with Cambodia. Here again intelligence failed to predict the main site of the attack until three PAVN/VC divisions and T-54 tanks showed up in Lộc Ninh then An Lộc.

The battle for An Lộc was a bitter struggle, and certainly the largest siege of the entire war.[57] It was waged in the III Corps whose provinces surrounded Saigon, South Vietnam's capital. Three ARVN divisions served in the area. The ARVN 25th Division from Củ Chi operated in Tây Ninh, Hậu Nghĩa, and Long An Province. The ARVN 18th Division was responsible for Biên Hòa, Long Khánh, Phước Tuy, and Bình Tuy. The ARVN 5th Division positioned in Lai Khê took care of Phước Long, Bình Long, and Bình Dương.

The III Corps commander, Lieutenant General Đỗ Cao Trí (1929–1971), was an aggressive officer. He took his troops into Cambodia to fight against the communists who had built safe sanctuaries there. On the other hand, U.S. troops were prohibited from crossing the borders to Cambodia and Laos, two so-called "neutral" states. Once Trí was killed in a helicopter crash in early 1971, his replacement, Lieutenant General Nguyễn Văn Minh, pulled his troops out of Cambodia.

General Minh served as an airborne officer under the French in 1950. He participated in an unsuccessful coup against then President Ngô Đình Diệm in 1960 and was banished to An Giang Province where he served as a province chief.[58] Following Diệm's death in 1963, he became deputy commander of the ARVN 21st Division in the delta region and was promoted to brigadier general and commander of the same division in 1965.

However, he was not as successful a III Corps commander as a divisional commander. Although an able and energetic administrator, he could not handle both the military situation in the field and the political games in the capital. In December 1971, his airborne division was able to wipe out the PAVN 271st Regiment in Cambodia. Elated, he pulled his troops out of Cambodia, allowing the PAVN regiment to recover and wage war again in 1972.

Prelude

The ARVN 5th Division, whose headquarters was located at Lai Khê, Bình Long Province, moved its command post to An Lộc in preparation for a potential communist attack. Although U.S. and ARVN intelligence expected a North Vietnamese invasion through the III Corps, they misread the timing and place. They thought the attack would occur during the Tết holidays, but when Tết came, the attack never materialized. TRAC intelligence also failed to predict the thrust of the coming PAVN offensive. In late February 1972, it focused on the Tây Ninh area, while one month earlier it gave equal importance to both Tây Ninh and Bình Long Province.[59] In the past, the PAVN came through Tây Ninh, not Bình Long. As a military target, Bình Long with its 60,000 people was insignificant compared to Tây Ninh's 300,000.

Over the border inside Cambodia, the North Vietnamese maintained three divisions. The 5th VC Division was located less than 20 miles northwest of Lộc Ninh. The PAVN 7th Division waited north of Tây Ninh Province in the Dambe rubber plantation. The VC 9th Division operated to the west of Tây Ninh Province in the Chup rubber plantation.

Still unknown to the ARVN but according to a complex enemy plan dotted with an overly optimistic timetable, An Lộc would be taken in five days, not more than ten days. This would allow the establishment of a new communist government at An Lộc by 20 April 1972. Lộc Ninh would be expected to fall within a day or two. The VC 5th Division and the 24th and 271st Regiments would cut off Tây Ninh from the IV Corps to the South and Saigon to the east. By mid–May, the North Vietnamese would turn their attention toward the capital.[60]

First, two independent enemy regiments, the 24th and the 271st, would attack elements of the 25th ARVN Division in the Tây Ninh area. This diversionary attack would allow the PAVN 7th and the VC 9th Divisions to slip from Base Area 708 in Cambodia into Bình Long Province. The VC 9th Division was given the honor of taking An Lộc. The PAVN 7th was to block Route 13 to the South between An Lộc and Lai Khê, preventing any reinforcements and supplies to reach An Lộc. To the north, the 5th VC Division would destroy the ARVN units in Lộc Ninh, the only obstacle standing between An Lộc and the Cambodian border.

But the ARVN did not concentrate all its efforts in Tây Ninh; they also reinforced Bình Long. The III Corps headquarters created Task Force (TF) 52 and kept it at the junction of Route 13 and Route 17, about five miles southwest of Lộc Ninh. TF 52 was composed of one battalion of the ARVN 52nd Regiment and one from the 48th Regiment along with one artillery battery and a 155 mm artillery platoon. With a force of 1,000 men strong and three U.S. advisers, the goal of TF 52 was to block any enemy invasion from the west. The ARVN 9th Regiment would guard against an attack down Route 13 from the north.

The North Vietnamese struck on 2 April. With a few tanks, the PAVN 24th Regiment attacked Fire Base Lạc Long, 35 kilometers northwest of Tây Ninh City. The base was defended by a battalion of the 49th Regiment, ARVN 25th Division. Orders came down to abandon the firebases and form a perimeter around Tây Ninh City.[61]

The PAVN also struck at the Thiên Ngôn Firebase. The defenders after pulling out of the base were ambushed by elements of the PAVN 271st Regiment and lost many artillery pieces and vehicles. Reinforcements from the ARVN 25th Division arrived at the ambush site the following day but to their surprise, found that the PAVN had withdrawn to Cambodia without attempting to drag off the artillery for later use. Although puzzled, ARVN intelligence finally realized that attacks in the Tây Ninh area were only diversionary ones. The real targets were up north in the Bình Long Province: Lộc Ninh and An Lộc.

Lộc Ninh

Lộc Ninh was a town whose 3,000 ethnic Montagnard[62] inhabitants worked for the nearby rubber plantation estates. It sat at the edge of a valley along the Rừng Cam

River. Half a mile west of route 13 stood a local airfield close by the ARVN 9th Regiment base. The latter consisted of three small compounds parallel to the airstrip. On the northern end was the district pacification and police station compound. The center perimeter housed the regiment's artillery. The ARVN 9th Regiment headquarters sat on the southern end of the airstrip. Had the defensive units been located at the firebase, the regiment could have withstood a sizable enemy force attack. But at that time only three infantry companies and the headquarters staff were inside the wire near the command bunker. The regimental commander was an old and worn out Colonel Nguyễn Công Vinh.

In the early hours of 5 April, the VC 5th Division crossed the Cambodian border to stage an attack on Lộc Ninh. They started with a heavy artillery, rocket, and mortar fire on the headquarters of the ARVN 9th Regiment and the Lộc Ninh district compound. This was followed by a VC infantry attack supported by about 25 tanks coming from the west. They tried to overrun the regimental compound on the southern end of the runway. This was the first time that the huge enemy T-54 tanks were seen in action in the III Corps. The artillery crew aimed a 106 mm recoilless rifle and knocked out a T-54 as it moved out of the tree line. The tank shuddered to a halt. A second T-54 that was hiding behind the tree line required a Spectre gunship to be called in to knock it out. ARVN soldiers held their ground and fought desperately to keep the enemy at bay. ARVN artillery men lowered the muzzles of their 105 mm howitzers and fired directly at enemy formations moving through the rubber trees.[63]

During the heat of the battle, Colonel Vinh ordered Task Force 1–5 and the rangers to evacuate Firebase Alpha and return to Lộc Ninh to reinforce it. One adviser told him it was too late; besides they were safer in the firebase, which had artillery and an anti-tank ditch, than outdoors. As soon as they left the firebase, they were fired upon by a force that outnumbered their own. After a while, the 1st Armored Cavalry had surrendered. The rangers and some ARVN infantry made it to the intersection of Routes 13 and 14 where they found a lone M-41 tank and five armored personnel carriers which had been left earlier by the task force. They clambered on top of the vehicles and headed toward Lộc Ninh.[64]

In the afternoon, the enemy launched another assault that was again stopped in its tracks with the help of U.S. AC-130 and AH-1 Cobra gunships. Enemy tanks were either destroyed or had to be pulled back. Infantry attacks, however, continued into the night.

On 6 April, the enemy launched another tank-and-infantry attack on the southern edge of the compound headquarters. It was again repulsed. But the ARVN 9th Regiment had absorbed a significant number of casualties: it had only 50 soldiers left with 150 wounded soldiers in the hospital bunker. Effective antiaircraft artillery prevented resupply and Medevac flights into the area. Around noon, the North Vietnamese were forcing women and children toward the compound while hiding behind the crowd; one poor soul was even waving an American flag as he walked. One adviser fired a burst in front of the crowd which dispersed back to the village.[65] In an attempt to save Lộc Ninh, General Lê Văn Hưng ordered TF 52 to move north to assist the beleaguered 9th Regiment. The 2nd battalion had barely reached the junction of Highway 13 and Route 17 when it was ambushed by a superior force and had to withdraw to An Lộc.

In the afternoon of 6 April, Lộc Ninh was reinforced by the ARVN 3rd

Battalion/9th Regiment and men from the 1st Cavalry Squadron from firebase Alpha who had refused to surrender. During the night enemy's artillery scored a hit on the hospital bunker killing a large number of wounded patients. It also struck the ammunition bunker, which exploded. On the morning of 7 April, the enemy launched another tank-infantry attack. The 200 men of the 9th ARVN Regiment and a Ranger battalion along with their handful of U.S. advisers, beat back the tanks on five occasions, but in the end they were overwhelmed by enemy forces.[66] By 0800, the southern compound was overrun. By 1000, tactical air support was called off to make way for B-52 strikes against VC formations west of Lộc Ninh. By 1630, the VC were in control of Lộc Ninh District.

The following day, under the communist "liberation" policy, civilian administrators, teachers and former government officials were rounded up. The head of the local militia, a sergeant, and one militiaman were publicly executed in Lộc Ninh town square, shot outright without even the benefit of a "people's court." The rest of those arrested as "enemies of the people" were trucked to a secure base near Snoul, Cambodia. North Vietnamese troops ransacked homes and government offices. The most prized booty were the black and white television sets that were sent over the Cambodian border, where NVA officers and cadres closed out each workday by watching programs broadcast from Saigon.[67]

General Lê Văn Hưng

At 39 years of age, Brigadier General Lê Văn Hưng (1933–1975), one of the most successful graduates of the Thủ Đức Military School, was the commander of the ARVN 5th Division. By chance or fate, he had to face the North Vietnamese invasion of the III Corps in 1972. On his small shoulders rested the fate of the Republic of South Vietnam and the more than one million people living in Saigon, the capital of the Republic at the time. Although he probably did not realize it, An Lộc turned out to be the biggest battle of his life. Had An Lộc, which was located 60 miles northwest of Saigon, been lost in 1972, the war would have ended at that time or soon thereafter.

He was modest and unassuming like most "Mekong Delta" officers. A talented and methodical officer, he was an efficient and clean Phong Định Province chief before being awarded command of the 5th ARVN Division on the advice of his friend and mentor, General Nguyễn Văn Minh. At five-foot six, he was slightly taller than his compatriots. An immaculate dresser, he always had his fatigues pressed and his insignia polished and straightened. Typical of the far south or "Mekong Delta" officers, he did not like socializing or boasting about his achievements, and therefore could be seen by some westerners as being "anti–American" or "dislik[ing] overbearing Americans who wanted the war fought according to American rules."[68]

A man of few words, he could be gruff with others and be seen as aloof or in certain cases arrogant and out of touch. In reality, he was somewhat shy and timid and to compensate for this awkward trait, he was comfortable spending time shoring up offensive posts or improving defensive strategies. However, anyone who got to know General Hưng well would find a simple and caring person.

As division senior adviser, Colonel William Miller could not figure out what to make of Gen. Hưng. When Miller came to the ARVN 5th Division in 1971, he wrote to TRAC that "Hưng displays outstanding leadership, is aggressive, organized, and forceful. He appears extremely knowledgeable, has confidence in himself and is quickly gaining confidence of his subordinates." Miller was either being less than candid with his commander or he had badly misread his counterpart.[69]

As time went by, Miller turned sour on Hưng. While the American was an extrovert, an aggressive officer in words and deeds who liked to boast about wins and losses, the general being an introvert, was a self-taught person, a pensive officer who moved slowly and carefully in action and words and tried to improve himself by enduring and overwhelming challenges. In An Lộc's cramped and martial underground bunker, the two most important officers from the free world had two different views of the military situation and the battle. What started as a conflict of personalities evolved into an open confrontation then a mini-war in the stuffed and cramped bunker in the middle of a bloody and violent communist invasion of the III Corps. The war outside and the war inside almost overshadowed the real An Lộc Battle.

"Although he respected Miller, Hưng rarely sought out his advice and often did not inform him of tactical decisions." That brutally hurt Colonel Miller who would add, "Hưng was no coward, but like many other high-ranking South Vietnamese officers he tried to refrain from making tough decisions. If possible he would wait and watch, hoping a bad situation would just go away."[70]

An Lộc

In the evening of 7 April, the Quần Lợi airstrip located about a mile and a half east of An Lộc was shelled and attacked by the enemy. The two ARVN companies that defended the airstrip had to withdraw after destroying their two 105 mm howitzers. It took them two days to reach An Lộc, which was then isolated by air and land. Task Force 52 located in bases halfway between An Lộc and Lộc Ninh was ordered to pull back to An Lộc. They succeeded but were forced to destroy all their artillery.

The ARVN 21st Division from the IV Corps was ordered to reinforce An Lộc. They moved by air to Chơn Thành, 30 miles south of An Lộc. By 12 April, the division was in place and ready to advance up Highway 13, which by then was unfortunately blocked off by elements of the PAVN 7th Division.

The South Vietnamese perimeter was set for the onslaught. On the north side, along the north-south axis of Highway 13, were two battalions of the ARVN 18th Division. On the west flank, the ARVN 7th Regiment manned its defense. On the east side was the 3rd Ranger group, probably the best unit in An Lộc. In the air, Gen. Hollingsworth was ready. He once declared, "Once the communists decided to take An Lộc, and I could get a handful of soldiers to hold and a lot of American advisers to keep them from running off, that's all I needed. Hold them and I'll kill them with airpower. Give me something to bomb, and I'll win."[71]

On the morning of 13 April, after dumping a heavy artillery and mortar barrage on An Lộc, the PAVN tanks slammed into the defenders' west flank. Because of a lack of coordination between cavalry and infantry, the tanks operated on their own. Armor broke through the ARVN defenses and wandered around narrow roadways and sharp turns of the town. While the ARVN 7th Regiment defended the west side of the town, the local Popular Force militia filled the gaps. A brave militiaman pointed an M72 LAW and launched a round at the T-54 tank down the street. With a flash and roar, the tank stopped, smoke billowing from the turret.[72] Once the word got out that tanks were not invincible, soldiers raced through the streets trying to see who could kill the most tanks.

The bulk of the attack was an armor-tipped thrust from the north straight down Highway 13. The South Vietnamese soldiers fell back through the city streets. Another T-54 tank wandered through town and stopped in front of a Catholic church. It pumped round after round through the front wall. Almost everyone inside the church was killed. The tank's gun then fell silent. Out of ammunition, the crew climbed out of the turret, arms raised in surrender. South Vietnamese in no mood to take prisoners emptied their rifles into the hapless enemy tankers. Above An Lộc, B-52s rained down bombs and tactical air strikes pounded supply vehicles behind North Vietnamese units. Never had the enemy been so open. They had massed and attacked in strength allowing the full weight of U.S. firepower to be brought to bear.

In the morning of 14 April, the enemy fired howitzer rounds and 122 mm rockets into An Lộc. When the shelling slacked, tanks came out. The attackers pushed to within a few hundred yards of the ARVN 5th Division command post. General Hưng had to get out of his bunker and call in strikes against the enemy. He then pulled the 1st Airborne Brigade from the southern edge of the town to reinforce and stabilize the northern perimeter. Elements of the airborne brigade and the 81st Ranger group were moved to positions on Windy Hill and Hill 169, both less than two miles southwest of the town.

After the fall of Lộc Ninh, the 6th Airborne Battalion was deployed to Lai Khê, the ARVN 5th Division headquarters, 20 miles south of Chơn Thành. On 14 April, they were ordered to secure Windy Hill and Hill 169 close to the newly established landing zone south of An Lộc. As the airborne moved up the eastern slope of Hill 169, PAVN troops climbed the western slope and managed to get to the top first. As they dug in, the Cobras raked them. The airborne charged ahead and managed to dislodge them, gaining the most strategic high ground south of An Lộc. But the PAVN troops regrouped and prepared for the next assault.

On 15 April, the PAVN attacked again from the North with 11 tanks and came close to taking the center of the town. A single T-54 fired a round point blank into the bunker and wounded three staff members. At the end of the day, the South Vietnamese had destroyed nine of eleven tanks.[73]

By 16 April, the close-quarters fighting had died down. After three days of terrifying and bloody assaults, the North Vietnamese had lost 23 tanks. The South Vietnamese had held on but lost the northern half of the town to the enemy. Attackers and defenders looked at each other on opposite sides of Nguyễn Trọng Trực Street. Col. Miller wrote to TRAC on 17 April, "The division is tired and worn-out; supplies minimal—casualties continued to mount—medical supplies and coverage is low. Wounded a major problem—mass burial for military and civilian—morale at low ebb."[74]

As the siege dragged on, relations between Colonel Miller and General Hưng worsened. Frustrated by his lack of control, Miller tried hard to coax his counterpart into counterattacking. But Hưng would not hear it. What could he do with one division against three enemy divisions? It would be suicidal to mount any counterattack at that time. A draw was better than a loss. Miller wrote, "The Division CG [commanding general] is tired—unstable—irrational—irritable—inadvisable—and inapproachable. When the chips are down, he looses [sic] all his composure."[75]

Hill 169

On 18 April, a company of the 92nd Border Ranger Defense Battalion in Tây Ninh ambushed and killed an important enemy soldier. On his body was a letter from the political commissar of the VC 9th Division to COSVN confirming that the PAVN would launch another attack on An Lộc on 19 April, the next day. They also announced that An Lộc would be liberated on 20 April and would become the seat of the National Liberation Front. Another letter revealed that the VC 9th Division and its commander had been castigated for failing to take over An Lộc within the first few days of the attack.

On 19 April, the PAVN launched an attack from the North similar to the 13 April attack. The defenders began to break and there were no troops to plug the holes. But the 81st Ranger Battalion materialized and saved the day. On 20 April, the PAVN decided to send the 275th Regiment/ VC 5th Division and the 141st Regiment/ PAVN 7th Division accompanied by six tanks to knock out the lone 105 mm howitzer the 1st Airborne Brigade had inserted on Hill 169. This battery was critical to the South Vietnamese defense. All six tanks were destroyed by ARVN soldiers with LAWs, but the assault took a toll on the airborne brigade. Fewer than 100 soldiers were still in fighting condition and they were ordered off the summit of Hill 169.

The violence, the killing, the trauma of the war so shell-shocked the combatants that it left them speechless and unable to comprehend. Even the most seasoned warriors were not spared. Lieutenant Colonel Định, commander of the 6th Airborne Battalion, was one of those. He ordered some of his men to dig a hole, then climbed in, hunkered down and would not leave it. Airborne soldiers looking for cover were waiting for orders, only to be told there were none. The battalion operations officer told one adviser, "Định has made his peace with dying."[76]

The airborne planned their escape. Under the path made by a B-52 strike, the survivors ran away while an ARVN AC-119 Stinger strafed their front to keep the North Vietnamese at bay. They reached a stream after dawn and were filling their canteens when a squad of North Vietnamese broke out of the woods on the far bank. Both sides were stunned and after the firing was over, the airborne continued their journey south knowing that larger enemy units would be on their heels. It was only at 1745 on 21 April that a few Hueys would come down to a nearby clearing to pick them up.

After capturing Hill 169, the VC 9th Division again attacked the southern perimeter of the town; but the ARVN held on. B-52s and tactical air strikes had made a difference. The 20 April deadline for capturing An Lộc thus came and passed. At TRAC headquarters, Maj. Gen. James Hollingsworth, commander of Third Regional Assistance Command, regarded the inability of the North Vietnamese to take An Lộc on 20 April as a psychological victory. Adviser Miller wrote of General Hưng, "Counterpart ti-ti [a little] cooler but worn out. Like good whiskey, [Hung] will improve with age."[77]

The tactical situation around An Lộc remained unchanged from 22 April to 10 May. Early on 10 May, Colonel Ulmer flew to An Lộc to replace Colonel Miller. Half-an hour past midnight on 11 May, the North Vietnamese rained down on the town a heavy and concentrated barrage of artillery, which by the end of the day totaled up to 8,500 rounds, most of them mortar shells. Intelligence had predicted that a major attack would follow within 24 hours.

Ulmer was a very different officer than his predecessor. While Miller was passionate and intimately wrapped up in the details of his relationship with division commander General Hưng, Ulmer was detached and observant. While Miller was emotional and moody, Ulmer was rational and coldly calculating. Ulmer gave the commander [Gen. Hưng] the benefit of the doubt considering that he had been under siege since early April and alone carried the responsibility for the defense of An Lộc. Hưng seemed weary and cautious, but he was clearly in command.... Hưng never buckled, though he was clearly concerned.

Hưng had survived three major North Vietnamese assaults so far and knew that another, perhaps bigger, attack was coming within a few hours. Ulmer saw the general lose his composure a couple of times as the tension rose. He screamed into the radio at his regimental commanders ... but it was just nerves, an understandable condition given the circumstances.[78]

Suddenly the heavy shelling stopped and enemy troops assaulted from all sides, supported by 40 tanks. Tactical air and gunships that had been standing by for some time thundered overhead and dropped their ordnance. The SA-7 heat-seeking surface to air missiles, or Strela, were also spotted in the sky over An Lộc. All four prongs of the attack pushed toward the center of the city. The attackers sensed that this was their final chance. All the base areas in Cambodia were being depleted to sustain the extended attack. Inside An Lộc, the defenders seemed to sense the enemy's desperation and held their ground. The attackers, however, came close as they punched a wedge in the northeast end of the town. General Hưng ordered the 5th Airborne Battalion from the secure southern perimeter into the fighting in the northeast. Their weight turned the tide.

On the west side, Vietnamese Air Force A-1E Skyraiders and American AC-130 Spectre gunships methodically destroyed the North Vietnamese before they could dig in. The B-52 bombers began arriving by 0900 to execute their Arc Light strikes. By noon on 11 May it was over. The North Vietnamese had failed to take An Lộc.

The Fight for Highway 13

The ARVN 21st Division was brought in from the IV Corps on 12 April to unblock a section of Highway 13 south of An Lộc between Lai Khê and Chơn Thành. In the end, it turned out to be two months of violent fighting on this highway that involved tanks, helicopters, A-37s, and even B-52s as well as mortars, missiles, and bombs. Troops of the NVA 7th Division battled against those of the ARVN 21st Division. The communists fought for a piece of land in this area to establish the capital of the National Liberation Front (NLF). The ARVN soldiers tried to keep An Lộc free and the Highway 13 open. It took the ARVN 21st Division two months to free up about 30 kilometers of highway that the communists were committed to blocking off.

The PAVN 101st Regiment first blocked off an area on the highway about 15 kilometers north of Lai Khê, the headquarters of the ARVN 5th Division. It took two weeks to dislodge them from their positions. The known battle of Blue Bus took place between 24 and 29 April 1972. The communists moved to five kilometers north of Chơn Thành or 30 kilometers north of Lai Khê where they established another blocking position. The battle of Bench Mark 75, as it was known, lasted the first two weeks of May. It required eight B-52 strikes, 142 sorties of tactical air support and over 20,000 rounds of artillery to dislodge the enemy.[79] The PAVN 165th and 209th Regiments participated in the battle.

The 209th Regiment, elements of the 7th PAVN Division, the 94th Sapper Company and the 41st Anti-Tank Company manned the third blocking position about 35 kilometers north of Lai Khê. The battle of Tàu Ô Bridge lasted five weeks (14 May–22 June). The enemy had dug in deep, building bunkers with two feet of overhead cover to shield them from the bombs. Even B-52 strikes, tactical air support, and artillery could barely dislodge the defenders. Colonel Franklin, adviser to the ARVN 21st Division, later said, "Once in a while we would break through and push a mile, but the attack was being fought piecemeal ... all the good leaders had been killed."[80]

Despite being displeased with the slow progress, TRAC headquarters were convinced that the ARVN 21st Division was having a positive progress on battle progress. The enemy was more intent on preventing the ARVN 21st Division from reaching An Lộc than on defeating friendly forces around the provincial capital. The enemy was incapable of putting pressure on both An Lộc and Highway 13 simultaneously.[81] The drive to relieve An Lộc fizzled and died. The ARVN won some and lost some. But by late June, although they did not reach An Lộc, it no longer mattered—An Lộc was out of danger.

On 15 May as the fighting at Tàu Ô Bridge was still going on, General Hollingsworth persuaded General Minh, III Corps commander, to place a fire support base (FSB) at Tân Khai, a deserted hamlet ten kilometers south of An Lộc and five kilometers north of Tàu Ô Bridge. It would be in position to harass the enemy on both fronts. Having set up the FSB at Tân Khai, the two battalions of the ARVN 15th Regiment and the two battalions of the ARVN 33rd Regiment, plus task force 9th Cavalry, struck out north from Tân Khai to relieve An Lộc. It would take them a month to cover the ten kilometers distance. But by diverting part of the PAVN 141st Regiment from around the city, the ARVN at Tân Khai bought An Lộc a much needed respite.

The turning point on Highway 13 came on 4 June when the reconstituted 6th Airborne Battalion was airlifted to FSB Tân Khai. They brought with them 300 replacements for the 15th Regiment. Led by Lieutenant Colonel Nguyễn Văn Định, who had vowed to avenge the destruction of his unit on Hill 169, the paratroopers overcame enemy forces with light casualties. They linked up with TF 15 about 3 kilometers south of An Lộc and released the reinforcements to the task force commander. On 8 June, the fresh troops overwhelmed the enemy at the village of Thanh Bình. Later that afternoon, the paratroopers linked with the 8th Airborne of the 1st Airborne Brigade in the rubber plantation south of An Lộc.

By 12 June, remnants of the North Vietnamese western salient were mopped up by the ARVN 7th Regiment. By noon, the whole city of An Lộc was under friendly control. On 14–15 June, 1,500 fresh troops from the ARVN 18th Division were airlifted into An Lộc to replace the haggard South Vietnamese defenders. On 17 June, the ARVN 48th Regiment seized Hill 169 lost to the enemy two months earlier.

On 7 July, President Thiệu visited An Lộc to honor the troops. He smiled and hugged Brigadier General Hưng, the division commander, and placed the National Order Medal Third Class with Gallantry Cross and Palm around his neck. He walked around the ruined buildings, burned out enemy tanks, and piles of captured weapons. He said, "An Lộc's victory was not only that of the RVNAF over three enemy divisions, but also a victory of the free world's democracy over communist totalitarianism."[82]

On 11 July, the ARVN 18th Division replaced the weary 5th Division inside the city. General Hollingsworth bragged, "I think it [An Lộc] will go down in history as the greatest victory in the history of warfare."[83]

The Battle for Charlie (25 March–15 April 1972)

On 25 March 1972, the ARVN 11th Airborne Battalion with its four companies (111, 112, 113 and 114) was airlifted into the area of operations to build up the Fire Support Base Charlie. The latter was part of the Airborne's defending ring that protected the left side of National Route 14 (QL 14) and blocked the critical mountain passes from Cambodia to the Kontum region.[84] Hill 1015 was the best crossing point. In fact, the battle for Charlie was a bloody sideshow of the battle of Kontum.

Deployment

Firebase Charlie 2 (FSB C2) was a former U.S. Marine and U.S. Army firebase established in 1967 at 12.5 km northwest of Đông Hà. The bunkers were reinforced in 1968. In 1969, its responsibility passed from the Marines to the U.S. Army. Charlie consisted of three hills: C, C1, and C2 stretching from North to South with varying altitudes.

- C or Charlie with an altitude of 960 m was held by company 111 commanded by Lieutenant Thịnh, a young officer from class 25 of the Thủ Đức Reserve Infantry Officer School.[85]
- C1 was held by Captain Hùng's company 113.
- The rest of the battalion and the command post held C2 that has an altitude of 1,062 m with a landing zone for helicopters.
- Captain Phan Cảnh Cho's company 114 was located on a southern hill. Various trees surrounding the barbed wire fences around the fire base may conceal the approach of enemy forces.

Lieutenant Colonel Nguyễn Đình Bảo, the fearless and determined commander of the ARVN 11th Airborne Battalion, was deployed along with his battalion.[86] Major John Duffy was an experienced advisor on his third tour in Vietnam. He was big, tough and combat savvy, although he had no back-up this time. From the beginning, Lt. Col. Bảo and his officers realized that the mission to defend Charlie was not a good one. It was purely defensive and the assigned hills, being much lower in altitude than those of the enemy—which were from 1,274 to 1,773 meters—would be exposed to artillery shelling. The commander told his soldiers to aim all of their bullets because there would be no resupply. They had to dig in deep and prepare for combat.[87]

The Battle

On the first night, they could hear the rumbling generated by PAVN convoys moving along the western and southwestern sides of the Trường Sơn range. The headlights of these convoys could be visible from afar. The following day, on 26 March 1972, Major Lê Văn Mễ, the deputy commander of the battalion, led companies 112 and 114 to relieve a unit of the 2nd Airborne Battalion that was besieged on one of the southern hills. The airborne attack was fierce with artillery and air support. Although the enemy resisted, they were overcome. Elements of the enemy F-320 Division counterattacked using human waves and supported by 75 mm artillery guns firing from the next hill. To avoid unnecessary casualties, Mễ ordered the two companies to withdraw and used artillery along with air support to push back the attack.

The following days were relatively calm: the usual "calm before a storm." Companies launched daily reconnaissances to look for the enemy, who were hiding in mountain hideouts. Fragmentation bombs did not have any effect on their U-shaped tunnels or bunkers. On 27 March, PAVN heavy artillery (105 mm, 122 mm, and 130 mm) began falling around Charlie. As spotters came closer, they gave better coordinates and more precise fire direction. Shells then fell inside Charlie as the enemy's 130 mm guns outranged all ARVN artillery guns (11 km range for 105 mm and 15 km range for 155 mm guns).

Early in the morning of 1 April 1972, after four-hour artillery preparation, troops of PAVN 64th Regiment of the elite 320th Division began assaulting in human waves from the South. There was total chaos: a real inferno of smoke, dust, flame, gunshots, and artillery shells. Friendly bases (FSB 5, FSB 6, FSB Yankee, and FSB Hotel) fired their artillery guns in support. Then came the gunships and Skyraiders of the USAF and VNAF. After many hours of fierce fighting, the enemy assaults were repulsed with heavy losses. Charlie remained under ARVN control.

After one week of continuous attacks against Captain Cho's Company 114, elements of the PAVN 320th Division could not take down Charlie despite leaving heavy losses outside the barbed wire fences. But Lt. Col. Bảo was really concerned. Under heavy attacks from the enemy, his troops also sustained some losses. Numbers of wounded and killed had increased. Ammunitions, food, and water supplied by helicopters were hard to come by because of the presence of heavy antiaircraft artillery.

For the next several days, the enemy continued to shell and bomb Charlie whose positions had been surrounded by PAVN troops. The 320th Division had been reinforced by units of the PAVN 66th Regiment. This time, enemy troops moved out during day time. The clanking sounds of enemy tanks could be heard after each artillery shelling. The Forward Air Controllers (FAC) of the USAF and VNAF had discovered nine new positions of PAVN antiaircraft guns, which ringed Charlie in an attempt to suppress air support.

On 12 April, about 3,000 rounds of 130 mm fell on C2 over a four hour-period. These 130 mm shells, made in the USSR, penetrated the ground before exploding. No bunker on Charlie could protect any soldier against these deadly shells. One shell landed right on Lt. Col. Bảo's bunker killing him instantly.[88] Two more rounds followed immediately to complete the work. He lay alone without bugles or a rifle salute.[89] Major Mễ, the deputy commander, and Major Duffy, the American adviser, were only wounded. Mễ took over as the new battalion commander. Despite the loss of their commander, the airborne fought well and repulsed attack after attack. But Mễ did not feel good because he was overwhelmed by the loss of his commander and friend. At night, they washed the body of one of the most famous battalion commanders of the ARVN's airborne division before laying him to rest. His 12 years of military service led him from battlefield to battlefield, from North to South, from East to West before he succumbed on Hill 1062 on the Trường Son Range.

On 13 April, close air support was called to prevent the enemy from penetrating the perimeter of C2, the main base of FSB Charlie. Two A-1E Skyraiders of the VNAF's 530th Jupiters Fighter Squadron flew by and dropped napalm bombs on the approaching human waves. The assault was broken, but one Skyraider was hit. Lieutenant Dương Huỳnh Kỳ went down with it. He was flying at 200–300 m above ground when he was hit. The plane clipped the trees with its right wing, flipped and crashed into a huge fireball in the jungle. No chute was seen. The pilot was lost and would be honored.

On 14 April, the PAVN launched a major attack on C2 to open a path to attack Tân Cảnh, the headquarters of the ARVN 22nd Infantry Division. The airborne stood in the trenches and fought back. The PAVN were within 5–10 m of the base perimeter. A decision was made to secure an LZ to get out. But they were again assaulted at the LZ and many lost their lives. The remnants of the battalion scattered into the jungle.

The Withdrawal

On 15 April, the FAC led them to the picking zone (PZ) of the 11th Airborne Battalion. Four Hueys went in one by one covered by two Cobra gunships. Number one took fire but got out OK. Numbers two and three had no problem. But when number four came in, the incoming fire was so heavy that the approach had to be aborted.[90]

One thing needs to be recounted on this famous pick-up. The U.S. air crews wanted to evacuate the American advisor Major Duffy first. But Duffy told the airborne soldiers with whom he fought, slept, and ate for the last two weeks, "I cannot leave you behind. You are my brothers-in-arms. If I go in the first flight, there will be no helis coming back to pick you up." He thus voluntarily stayed back to be picked up last. From that moment, Major Duffy went into the military history of the ARVN Airborne Division as a heroic and legendary American advisor. Men like him made the famous MACV's 162nd Advisory Team immortal in the memory of the South Vietnamese Airborne soldiers.[91]

The last four officers (Mễ, Duffy, Hải, and Long) tried to evade their aggressive pursuers. Duffy called the two new Cobras on station to pick them up *now* or *never*. The Huey of Dennis Watson approached the landing zone with Captain Hải as the last man to climb aboard. The NVA shot Hải and hit him in his foot. Duffy jumped out of the helicopter, which was hovering above the ground, to cover his comrade-in-arms. The helicopter landed again while the enemy continued to fire. Duffy dragged Hải into the helicopter, which then lifted off. The Huey was hit nine times. The door gunner, Dallas Nihsen, was struck by an AK-47 round. His blood spurted onto Duffy and Hải. He was pronounced dead at the Kontum Field Hospital. It was supposed to be his last mission before he took the flight back home.

The 11th Airborne Battalion went in with 451 paratroopers. After almost three weeks of fighting, they pulled out with only 37 survivors—bloodied but unbroken. They fought against the PAVN elite 320th Division reinforced with the 66th Regiment of PAVN 3rd Division (Gold Star).

The late Colonel Nguyễn Đình Bảo was later memorialized among friends and family members. He died as a hero of his country and for the freedom he cherished.[92] Major Lê Văn Mễ became one of the best battalion commanders of the airborne. He rose to the rank of colonel and worked as Operations Officer of the Airborne when the war ended in 1975.[93] He was one of Vietnam's most decorated officers: National Order of Vietnam, Knight; Army Distinguished Service Cross; seven Gallantry Crosses with Palm; six Gallantry Crosses with Gold, Silver, or Bronze Stars. His American medals were Silver Star; Bronze Star with Valor Device. Major Duffy was honored with the Distinguished Service Cross for actions with the 11th Airborne Battalion.[94]

The Ones Who Stayed at Charlie

In the aftermath of the battle for Charlie, the celebrated author, lecturer, talk show host and former ARVN Captain Phan Nhật Nam wrote the award winning book *Mùa Hè Đỏ Lửa* or The Fiery Red Summer after interviewing the airborne soldiers admitted to the military Cộng Hòa General Hospital near Saigon for treatment.

A song composed by song writer Trần Thiện Thanh, "*Người ở lại Charlie*" or "The Ones Who Stayed at Charlie," was dedicated to soldiers who died in battles and whose bodies were not recovered, such as at Charlie, Dak To, Snoul, Kre, Laos, and so many elsewhere.

> Forever. We'll love you forever.
> My warrior who will not return,
> I say one more time, one more time
> I say goodbye to you on Charlie.

(The late Colonel Nguyễn Đình Bảo[95] and his soldiers forever rested on the far-away and magic hills of the Trường Sơn range. They had become immortal souls that wandered high in the mountains of Central Vietnam.)

The song forever immortalizes those souls who died on battlefields but whose bodies were never recovered for appropriate burial. This is true especially in Vietnam, where burial is thought to be important to appease those souls, lest they become violent wandering souls. Dead elders are thought to protect their kin who are still alive; therefore, not antagonizing them is essential. Besides, immortalizing them in songs is another way of thanking them for their patriotic service and deep devotion to the country. For their sacrifice, they forever live in the South Vietnamese minds, especially when the Vietnamese sing these songs.

11

1973

Nguyễn Văn Thiệu's Four Wars

President Nguyễn Văn Thiệu loomed large in the Saigon political arena as the ARVN general turned politician who dominated the Second Republic of South Vietnam. In fact, he presided or exerted influence from behind the scenes over 10 of the 12 years of the Republic's existence (1963–1975). To paraphrase Thiệu's Four No's,[1] the best way to understand him and his role is to look at him as fighting the "Four Wars"—one against his comrades-in-arms, two against North Vietnamese troops and the fourth against Henry Kissinger who was instrumental in knocking him off his presidency and sending him into exile.

The Making of a President

Born of humble origin on 24 December 1924 (year of the Rat)[2] in Trí Tuy hamlet near Phan Rang, central Vietnam, he was the youngest of seven children. His father was a part time farmer and drove cattle from one province to another to make a living. As a learned man, he not only taught his son the classic Confucian virtues of loyalty, righteousness, filial piety, courage, sincerity, respect, but also advised him to be cautious and careful in life. The young Thiệu, orphaned at age 11, sold rice cakes made by his mother, at the market early in the morning before starting school. He excelled in high school where he learned French and English.[3] Many decades later in Guam, it was reported that he had held discussions with Nixon in English for many hours without the help of an interpreter.

Before the end of World War II as the French continued to hold some control over Vietnam, especially in the South, he, like thousands of non-communist Nationalists at the time,[4] joined the communists to fight against the French. Like others, he soon realized the ruthlessness of the communists, "They shot people, they overthrew the village committees, they seized the land," said Thiệu in an interview. Having landed on the Việt Minh's assassination list because of his frequent questioning, he decided to flee his village.

Once in Saigon, he enrolled in the first officer class of the Vietnamese Military Academy, which was located in Huế before being moved to Dalat. The academy's instructors were French at the time. In 1954, he led a battalion in expelling the communists from his native village. Two years later, he was promoted head of the Vietnamese National Military Academy (1956–1960) before becoming a colonel and commander of the ARVN 7th division in Biên Hòa. Thiệu earned a reputation as a bright, skilled, ambitious officer who was brave in combat and accepted responsibility.

Although a Buddhist by default like the majority of Vietnamese, he married the Southern Catholic Nguyễn Thị Mai Anh in 1951 and was baptized in 1957. Unlike other Catholic officials, he never became a favorite of the Catholic President Diệm. Nor did he join Diệm's Cần Lao Party, a stepping stone for higher positions; he instead committed himself to the Đại Việt, one of the other nationalist parties fighting the French.[5]

When the November 1963 coup was organized against President Diệm in Saigon, then Colonel Thiệu suddenly found himself again in the thick of the action through one of the quirks of history. In late December 1962, Diệm who did not fully trust Nguyễn Đức Thắng, commander of the 7th Division, which was located in Bien Hòa 20 miles northeast of Saigon, moved him and his division to Mỹ Tho. Diệm then replaced Thắng with Thiệu and his ARVN 5th division. That selection later turned out to be a mistake. Two years earlier in 1960, Thiệu was the commander of the 7th Division when a coup broke out against Diệm. The insurgents moved against the Palace but stopped to negotiate a power sharing with Diệm. Thiệu with his 7th Division came to the rescue of Diệm and quelled the insurrection. As a reward or a demotion depending on how one looked at it, Thiệu was sent to command the ARVN 1st Division in Huế in faraway central Vietnam until he was recalled back to Saigon in December 1962.

And there was Thiệu, a man whose support became critical to any coup plotter because as commander of the 5th Division, he was within a stone's throw of the Presidential Palace. When asked by General Dương Văn Minh, the 1963 coup leader, Thiệu agreed to switch camp, join the plotters,[6] and was given the task of leading the attack against Diệm's Palace. When Thiệu's troops stormed the palace, they found it empty because Diệm had managed to escape through one of the palace's tunnels. Lacking military support, Diệm surrendered to the plotters a day later and was murdered on the way to the military headquarters. As a reward, Thiệu was made general by the junta when the latter took power. Although not directly involved in the plot to kill Diệm, it was not difficult for him to realize how easy it was to unseat an elected President. Having witnessed the murder of Diệm, the nightmare of the assassination would from then on color his relationship with the Americans: on one hand he needed them to stay in power, on the other hand, he was afraid of any American-led coup against him.

After the 1963 coup came a two-year turmoil that was marked by the coming and going of waves of generals who took over the military leadership but proved themselves inept at running a civilian government. Thiệu proved to be a shrewd politician who was able to position himself as the leader of the "Young Turks," a group of young generals who controlled the army and forced the older generals to retire. In 1965, he became the figurehead head of state while his rival, Air Force Marshall Nguyễn Cao Kỳ, led the government as Prime Minister. Outmaneuvering the bumbling General Nguyễn Khánh and the brash, but ineffective Air Marshall, he again positioned himself as the Armed Forces candidate to run for the country's presidency in 1967.[7] He then won the presidency with Kỳ as a rival and running mate.

The 1968 Tết Offensive or First Communist Invasion Attack

Having won the presidential election, Thiệu was inaugurated on 1 November 1967. His victory, however, was short lived. Profiting from all the years of political and military dysfunction in Saigon, the communists had gained control of the countryside and stockpiled armament and troops in the South.

The 1954 Geneva Accords ending the First Indochina War, among other provisions, called for the removal of foreign forces from Laos. The northeastern provinces of Laos and the eastern part of the panhandle were controlled by the Pathet Lao, proxies of the Vietnamese communists. This meant that the communist People's Army of Vietnam (PAVN), which never withdrew from Laos, retained control of a vast strip of territory in eastern Laos bordering both Vietnams, North and South. The strip sheltered an embryonic transportation network, which in 1959 underwent massive reconstruction to become the dreaded Hồ Chí Minh Trail used by the communists to transport troops and materiel southbound into South Vietnam.

War escalated in South Vietnam from 1959 to 1967 as Hanoi managed to build up a real army in South Vietnam. By 1968, time was ripe to move from an insurgency war to a full scale divisional attack against the ARVN. In mid–September 1967, Hanoi's communist Politburo called for an all-out attack against cities in South Vietnam in full violation of the Geneva Accords in combination with a general uprising.

At 0300 hours on 31 January 1968 three months into the Thiệu's presidency and as people were celebrating the first day of the Tết (Vietnamese lunar New Year) and during a truce agreed upon by Saigon and Hanoi, communist units launched coordinated attacks throughout South Vietnam. By the end of the day, 27 of South Vietnam's 44 provincial capitals, five of its six autonomous cities, 58 of its 245 district towns and more than 50 hamlets were attacked. Although most of the assaults failed to breach the defense of most urban centers, the communists fought their way into Saigon, Quảng Trị, Huế, Đà Nẵng, Qui Nhơn, Nha Trang, Kontum, Ban Mê Thuột, Mỹ Tho, Cần Thơ, and Bến Tre. In most cases, they were driven out within two or three days while the battle was protracted in Saigon and Huế.[8]

In Saigon, the communists targeted six objectives: the Joint General Staff headquarters, the Independence Palace, the American Embassy, Tân Sơn Nhứt Air base, Radio Saigon, and Navy headquarters. They were rapidly turned away leaving hundreds of dead, although they remained at the Phú Thọ race track and occupied a northern suburb of Saigon, and part of Chợ Lớn.

In the city of Huế, which they occupied for almost a month, the communists set up their own administration with their own mayor. The latter was tracked down and later found to be a former chief of police of Huế City. The communists ordered inhabitants in their controlled areas to report to the revolutionary committees, to turn in their weapons, ammunitions, and radio receivers; they were then sent home after registering their names. During subsequent days, they were called back and were never heard from again. Later information revealed they had been ordered to dig "shelters." They did not suspect that these shelters were to become their own graves. When the communists were driven out on February 26, mass graves were found on the campuses of the Gia Long and Gia Hội High schools. Other graves were found in outlying areas such as the forests surrounding the tombs of Emperors Tự Đức and Minh Mạng. More than 3,000 skeletons, young and old, were unearthed.⁹ Many had their hands tied behind their backs with skulls showing fractures suggestive of heavy blows to the head. Many Huế victims were members of the anti-colonialist Đại Việt and Vietnamese Nationalist Party, whom the communists viewed as rival nationalists.

Civilian losses were found to be heavy in both human and material terms. More than 75 percent of the houses near the citadel had been destroyed and people suffered from food and water shortage and from the smell of putrefying corpses. The nation's infrastructure was heavily damaged and 1968 became the deadliest year for South Vietnam with 28,000 ARVN soldiers killed and 600,000 civilians displaced on top of the 800,000 from previous years.

From the South Vietnamese point of view, the absence of a general uprising following the attack represented a victory for South Vietnam and a political failure for the communists. People ran away from the communists, trying to avoid being caught in crossfire, but they did not panic. They had seen those young peasant insurgents and were not impressed by them. They strongly believed in the ARVN troops who had fought gallantly against the invaders with the support of Americans. On 1 February, Thiệu declared martial law and in June, the National Assembly approved his request for a general mobilization of the population. The victory brought with it a surge in nationalism. By September, 240,000 young men had flocked to draft centers volunteering their services ahead of schedule. This forced military training to be cut from 12 to eight weeks.¹⁰ Thiệu had just weathered and won his first battle against the communists in his first year in office. But storms were brewing elsewhere.

Anatomy of a Betrayal

Thiệu had supported Nixon and did his best to help him win the presidency in 1968. But he soon realized that Nixon was a smooth lawyer who tried to reassure Thiệu on one side, but let Kissinger plot to dismantle South Vietnam. Although this may have been Kissinger's real intention, the eventual result of Nixon's and Kissinger's combined maneuvering proved deadly for South Vietnam. In a 14 May 1969 speech, Nixon lyrically talked about U.S. commitment, which no doubt pleased and reassured Thiệu:

> A great nation cannot renege on its pledge. A great nation must be worthy of trust. When it comes to maintaining peace, "prestige" is not an empty word. I am not speaking of false pride or bravado—they should have no place in our policies. I speak rather of the respect that one nation has for another's integrity in defending its principles and meeting its obligations. If we simply abandoned our effort in Vietnam, the cause of peace might not survive the damage that would be done to other nations' confidence in our ability.¹¹

Kissinger, on the other hand, had been secretly meeting with Lê Đức Thọ since 30 July 1969 to put an end to the war. However, Nixon did not inform Thiệu of this until the meeting was completed. From then onward, Thiệu grew concerned because Kissinger just gave him sketchy reports of the talks and when asked directly, he provided vague answers, which worsened Thiệu's worries.¹²

Saigon did not know that on August 16, 1971, the U.S. had already promised to withdraw U.S. troops within nine months of an agreement. When General Haig presented Thiệu with another secret plan, which called for his resignation, Thiệu realized that Kissinger was disturbingly weakening the American position by offering one concession after another to the communists.

Thiệu became more worried when Nixon announced he was making a ground-breaking trip to China. He suspected that Kissinger's concessions to the North Vietnamese were linked to Nixon's hopes for success in Beijing. Nixon then revealed that Washington had dropped its demand for mutual withdrawal of forces by both sides. This meant communist forces could remain in South Vietnam long after U.S. forces were gone. Having given his proxy to Kissinger, Thiệu felt betrayed, but still hoped Nixon could help him out.

In private, Nixon told Mao that he wanted to withdraw from Vietnam in return for the release of American prisoners of war and a cease-fire.[13]

On his return from China, Nixon wrote again to reassure Thiệu:

"You may be certain that I will do all in my power to ensure that the enormous sacrifices of the Vietnamese and American people do not come to nothing."

Richard Nixon
28 February 1972[14]

To force Thiệu into accepting the terms of the Paris Accords negotiated by Henry Kissinger and Lê Đức Thọ, Nixon wrote a series of letters assuring Thiệu of U.S. support in case Hanoi violated the terms of the agreements, e.g., escalating the war or invading South Vietnam.

"In the period following the cessation of hostilities you can be completely assured that we will continue to provide your Government with the fullest support, including continued economic aid and whatever military assistance is consistent with the ceasefire provisions of this agreement."

Richard Nixon
16 October 1972

"You have my absolute assurance that if Hanoi fails to abide by the terms of this agreement it is my intention to take swift and severe retaliatory action."

Richard Nixon
14 November 1972[15]

"Should you decide, as I trust you will, to go with us, you have my assurance of continued assistance in the post-settlement period and that we will respond with full force should the settlement be violated by North Vietnam."

Richard Nixon
5 January 1973

Let me state these assurances once again in this letter:
- First, we recognize your Government as the sole legitimate Government of South Vietnam.
- Secondly, we do not recognize the right of foreign troops to remain on South Vietnamese soil.
- Thirdly, the U.S. will react vigorously to violations of the [Paris] Agreement....

Richard Nixon
17 January 1973[16]

The year 1973 saw an Arab oil embargo and a series of revelations about the Watergate scandal. The scandal escalated and on 9 August 1974 Nixon resigned in the face of almost certain impeachment and removal from the office. Within 24 hours of succeeding to the presidency, Gerald Ford wrote to Thiệu affirming that "the existing commitments this nation has made in the past are still valid and will be fully honored in my administration."[17]

When Kissinger met with Thiệu on 27 August 1972 in Saigon, both of them spoke past each other as Thiệu objected to the unilateral U.S. withdrawal with PAVN forces remaining in South Vietnam. Thiệu also argued against the NLF (National Liberation Front: Việt Cộng) participating in the coalition government of the South.[18] Kissinger received Nixon's "far from enthusiastic" approval to proceed without Thiệu's acceptance of the revised American position.[19] As Thiệu continued to object to Kissinger's concessions, Nixon openly "threatened Thiệu with a coup or worse if he did not accept the terms Kissinger had worked out." On 6 October 1972 Nixon warned that Thiệu "faced forcible removal from power unless he cooperated."[20]

> "I would urge you to take every measure to avoid the development of an atmosphere which could lead to events similar to those which we abhorred in 1963 and which I personally opposed so vehemently in 1968."
>
> Richard Nixon
> 6 October 1972.[21]

On 17 October 1972 Thiệu ordered the Joint General Staff to bring to Saigon immediately a ten-page document captured in the underground bunker of a VC district commissar in Quảng Tín Province. Entitled "General Instructions for a Cease-Fire," the document contained the draft text of the agreement being negotiated between Kissinger and Lê Đức Thọ. While Thiệu had not been advised about Kissinger's concessions and the draft agreement, communist cadres had been studying the draft document and preparing for the operations based on them.[22] Thiệu was shocked by the news.

Kissinger handed to Thiệu one single English copy of the draft on 18 October in which the Republic of Vietnam did not exist as a legitimate government. It spoke only about three countries: Laos, Cambodia, and Vietnam being represented by the Democratic Republic of Vietnam (Hanoi). Thiệu said he wanted to punch Kissinger in the mouth.[23] When asked about the PAVN troops in South Vietnam, Kissinger said that because of disagreement, the topic was not included in the draft. The Vietnamese then asked for the Vietnamese version of the agreement and time to study the draft.

Since the Vietnamese version differed sharply from the English text, Saigon asked for 23 points to be clarified by Kissinger. The latter insisted that 16 of them could be manageable, but the remaining seven were not negotiable. The points raised by the Vietnamese were the presence of PAVN troops in South Vietnam and the status of the Council of Reconciliation and Concord. Kissinger then handed Thiệu a letter from Nixon urging Thiệu to sign the agreement; otherwise military aid would be cut off. The next day, Thiệu told Kissinger he could not sign the Accords as they existed. Kissinger became enraged and called Thiệu "an obstacle to peace" who would go on his own. Thiệu charged that Kissinger had "connived" with China and the Soviet Union to sell out South Vietnam. Arguments flew back and forth and Kissinger finally said to Hoàng Đức Nhã who was translating Thiệu's remarks in Vietnamese,

> "Why does your president play the role of a martyr? He does not have the stuff to be a martyr."
> "I'm not trying to be a martyr," Thiệu answered. "I'm a nationalist and I am trying to be a very pragmatic man who is trying to get answers to valid points."[24]

While Kissinger described Thiệu as a "loyal ally," it mattered little whether he showed any loyalty to Thiệu. Saigon at that time needed an advocate who could negotiate in a skilled and knowledgeable manner, not someone who was always looking for a compromise as in a civil jurisdictional dispute. Kissinger's attitude led to his being distrusted and even hated by the South Vietnamese. While his memoirs carry photographs of him smiling and shaking hands with Hanoi leaders, there was no photo with him and President Thiệu.[25]

The negotiations stalled in November when Kissinger suggested to Hanoi that there should be two Vietnams, which live in peace with each other as suggested by Saigon. Hanoi argued that Washington wanted to strengthen the "puppet administration" of Saigon. For every concession he made, Lê Đức Thọ withdrew two. Nixon finally set a deadline of Inauguration Day, 20 January 1973 for signing the agreement with Hanoi.

On 17 December 1972 Nixon ordered Operation Linebacker II for B-52s to raid North Vietnam and to mine Hải Phòng Harbor. At the same time, Nixon continued to threaten Thiệu, who according to Haig, seemed desperate. Thiệu felt that the Paris Accords would leave South Vietnam open to northern infiltration. The B-52 bombing continued until 30 December, except for Christmas Day. The U.S. had lost 30 aircraft including 15 B-52s all downed by SAM missiles. Nixon, however, did not allow the bombing of SAM assembly plants. Reports leaked out that Hanoi was exhausted and was running out of SAM missiles. Had the bombing continued, Hanoi would have been on its knees.

On 14 January 1973 Nixon told Kissinger to get Thiệu on board. "Brutality is nothing. You have never seen it if this son of a bitch doesn't go along, believe me."[26] Nixon promised a cut-off of economic aid if Thiệu refused to sign the agreement; but also a promise not to recognize the right of foreign troops to remain in South Vietnam and to react strongly if the agreement were violated.

Thiệu did not yield, but asked for another round of changes. He wanted to stall until the U.S. Inauguration Day, 20 January. On 21 January, he called in Ambassador Bunker and told him, "I have done my best. I have done all I can for my country." Nixon in his memoirs paid tribute to Thiệu's courage, saying, "even though his conduct had been almost unbearably frustrating, I had to admire his spirit."[27]

On 23 January 1973 Kissinger and Lê Đức Thọ initialed the Paris Agreement in 36 places. "Kissinger's utter contempt for the South Vietnamese government meant that he never fully consulted Saigon about important matters. He was content to negotiate an end to the war on American terms, and then he coerced Saigon into accepting its fate.... He therefore recklessly sought ends beyond his means."[28] To the South Vietnamese, the four years of fighting from 1969 to 1973 accomplished nothing. The cease-fire meant a new phase of warfare and a return to terrorism and subversion. As for the $750 million worth of equipment turned over to Saigon as part of Enhance Plus program, F-5A and C-123 aircraft were old and not operational. Without spare parts and funds to keep the flow of supplies in operation, operation Enhance Plus was little more than an empty gesture.

For General Murray, head of the DAO (Defense Attaché Office), Enhance Plus was a fallacy. "What was turned over was battle damaged, other damaged, worn out—or nearly so—or obsolete.... These were major end-items—not operational or sorely needed spare parts which the war had exhausted." The special tools that went with major items were missing and "requisitions for direct delivery of these shortages to ARVN were later canceled. ARVN were left holding the bag."[29]

The 1972 Fiery Easter Offensive or Second Communist Invasion

While Kissinger was trying to negotiate America's way out of the war throughout 1972, North Vietnam flagrantly ordered the second invasion of South Vietnam in violation of the 1954 Geneva Accords. In 1972 Hanoi launched the Nguyễn Huệ campaign by sending 14 divisions south to try to weaken or topple the South Vietnamese government. A communist B-5 front communiqué stated, "It doesn't matter whether the war is promptly ended or prolonged.... Both are opportunities to sow the seeds; all we have to do is to wait for the time to harvest the crop."[30]

Back in the summer of 1971, Hanoi was also caught off guard by news of Nixon's visit to China. To placate its ally's suspicions, China promised further aid to Hanoi in the beginning of 1972. The Soviet Union sought to widen the rift between China and North Vietnam by sending some more aid without strings attached. Hanoi could not be happier. Thus the Soviets and Chinese between 1970 and 1972 gave to North Vietnam $1.5 billion in military aid, double what the U.S. agencies had estimated. Hanoi got top of the line military hardware: 400 T-34, T-54 and Type 59 (a Chinese version of the T-54) medium and 200 PT-76 light amphibious tanks, hundreds of anti-aircraft missiles, including the shoulder-fired, heat-seeking SA-7 Strela (called the Grail in the West), anti-tank missiles, including the wire-guided AT-3 Sagger and heavy-caliber, long-range artillery. To man the new equipment, 25,000 North Vietnamese troops received specialized training abroad, 80 percent of them in the Soviet Union or Eastern Europe.[31]

On 30 March 1972 the North Vietnamese sent three divisions and roughly 30,000 men and 200 Soviet T-54 tanks across the demilitarized zone (DMZ) to attack the northern part of South Vietnam. Kontum and An Lộc were also attacked with PAVN troops coming from Cambodia and Laos. A total of 14 PAVN divisions and 26 independent regiments totaling 150,000 men were thrown against the ARVN on these three fronts. Allied intelligence failed to predict the scale of the campaign as well as the method of attack giving the communists "the inestimable benefit of shock effect." Bearing the brunt of the attack was the ARVN 3rd division, newly created in October 1971, five months before the attack. On April 1, General Vũ Văn Giai ordered the withdrawal of the ARVN 3rd Division south of the Cửa Việt River for his troops to reorganize. The following day, Colonel Phạm Văn Định, commander of the ARVN 56th Regiment surrendered Camp Carroll and his 1,500 troops, allowing the communists unrestricted access to western Quảng Trị Province north of the Thạch Hãn River. But the PAVN units stopped there for three weeks allowing the ARVN to counterattack. Due to conflicting orders between Generals Lâm, I Corps commander and Giai, ARVN units splintered and collapsed.

Đông Hà and Quảng Trị in I Corps and Kontum in II corps were overwhelmed by NVA advanced weaponry, like 133 mm recoilless artillery and Soviet made T-54 tanks. Since Saigon did not have any sophisticated weaponry to control the attacks, it asked for American M-48 tanks, TOW anti-tank missiles, and 175 mm howitzers. Almost all Americans troops were out of Vietnam except for a small number of advisers. The South Vietnamese were on their own.

Nixon was angered to see the communists widening the war while his envoy Kissinger was negotiating for a disengagement. He ordered the bombing of North

Vietnam within 25 miles north of the DMZ first, then up to the 20th parallel. He considered the mining of Hải Phòng Harbor, where the communists received their sophisticated Soviet war equipment.

Thiệu dismissed the ineffective General Hoàng Xuân Lãm and appointed in his place General Ngô Quang Trưởng, an effective combat leader with a reputation for integrity and honesty. A southerner from the Mekong delta, he was an intense warrior with no political ambition. He rallied his troops and began the slow task of counterattacking. The ARVN 1st Division moved westward toward Laos while the Marine and Airborne divisions moved northward toward Quảng Trị. The defense of the city and its walled citadel was left to communist replacement units and militia. Recalled one participant: "The new recruits came in at dusk. They were dead by dawn.... No one had time to check where they were from, or who was their commander?"[32] The heavily defended citadel was retaken on 16 September. ARVN forces moved to the Thạch Hản River unable to push up to Đông Hà. Lieutenant Colonel Turley later wrote, "Vietnamese Marines, short in stature, rich in courage, and full of determination, stood tall in the eyes of all Marines." The South Vietnamese Marines lost 3,658 men during the seven-week battle to recapture the citadel. Almost one out of every four Marines in the entire division was wounded or killed.[33]

In the III Corps, the PAVN sent three divisions stationed in Cambodia against the town of An Lộc after wiping out the village of Lộc Ninh. This turned out to be World War II–vintage warfare during which General Lê Văn Hưng and his men sustained a two month siege while fighting against infantry and tank attacks under a heavy daily barrage of artillery shelling. Although the PAVN breached the defenses on various occasions, they were never able to dislodge the defensive forces from their positions.[34] Kontum in the II Corps also held its own against three PAVN divisions.

The Fiery Offensive in the end turned out to be a disaster for the North Vietnamese who lost half of its invasion force, some 75,000 men killed or wounded, as well as losing almost all the tanks committed (134 T-54s, 56 PT-76s and 60 T-34s).[35] In return, it had gained control of half of the four northernmost provinces—Quảng Trị, Thừa Thiên, Quảng Nam, and Quảng Tín.

The Third Communist Invasion (1975)

As described in the Military History Institute of Vietnam, the official postwar report of the CPV (communist party of Vietnam),

> the quantity of supplies transported along the strategic transportation corridor from the beginning of 1974 until the end of April 1975 was 823,146 tons, 1.6 times as much as the total transported during the entire thirteen years. [Also] ... during the years 1973–1974, more than 150,000 youths entered the army. Many combat units at full strength, 68,000 replacement troops, 8,000 cadres and technical personnel, and scores of thousands of assault youth members marched off to the battlefields.[36]

On 1 July 1973, U.S. Congress passed legislation prohibiting any direct or indirect U.S. combat activities over or in Laos, Cambodia, and both Vietnams. On 7 November the legislative branch overrode Nixon's veto of the War Powers Act, which prohibits the President from engaging in war without the approval of Congress. During 1972–1973, South Vietnam had received $2.2 billion in U.S. assistance. In 1973–1974, that figure was slashed to $965 million, an almost 60 percent reduction of military aid.[37]

In mid–1974, the ARVN began to feel the pinch of U.S. aid cuts, which resulted in increased casualty rates. "Military hospitals were overcrowded ... they were critically short in medicines, especially dextrose, antibiotics, and also plasma.... In Saigon, the ambulance units were so short in gasoline that in order to evacuate the wounded, they had to tow four ambulances in a row with a 2½ ton truck...."[38]

Besides the misery of continuing warfare, 1974 added the hardships of an economic crisis that was comparable to the U.S. 1930's Great Depression. South Vietnam's depression was related to the worldwide economic dislocation that followed the Arab oil embargo of late 1973 and the consequent quadrupling of oil prices. But Vietnam's economy was skidding downward since 1972 with two contributing factors. One was a rice shortage in 1972 caused by poor harvests throughout Asia, which increased the price of Vietnam's food staple. The U.S. troop withdrawal closed American bases and wiped out about 300,000 jobs; this sent shock waves throughout South Vietnam's economy. In 1971, Saigon earned $400 million a year from the U.S. presence but in 1974 less than $100 million.

With the 500,000 GIs out of the country and the U.S. Congress cutting its aid, South Vietnam sunk into a deep economic depression. Unemployment was estimated at one million, about one-fifth of the civilian work force. Living costs nearly doubled in a year and a half: 65 percent inflation in 1973, 27 percent in the first six months of 1974. Soldiers and low ranking officials earning monthly salaries of VN$20,000 (or US$36 at the official rate in force), could not support their families for more than two weeks per pay check. Soldiers and policemen, even school teachers, drove pedicabs to supplement their incomes. Wives who did not work now sold cigarettes and papers on the sidewalks. In 1973, cash allowances were substituted for soldiers' monthly rice allowances. With inflation, the cash, which bought less rice each month, amounted to a severe pay cut. This affected "tactical performance as well as morale," reported the U.S. Defense Attaché office. Moonlighting, theft or corruption became necessities for survival.[39] The Joint General Staff (JGS) was of no big help.

General Trần Thiện Khiêm was a bespectacled southerner who looked and acted more like a mid-level businessman than an army general, the rank he held as Prime Minister and Minister of Defense during the Second Republic. Khiêm remained in the background, avoided controversy and direct responsibility. He deferred everything to Thiệu while providing him with the necessary political support. He could have been more helpful to Thiệu had he dealt with political warfare, which the ARVN and the country needed during the two-decade war, or taken care of the economic needs of civilians and soldiers who were suffering from the U.S. aid cuts.

General Cao Văn Viên, only one of two South Vietnamese four-star generals during the Vietnam War, was a southerner and a serious Buddhist. He was until the end and for eight years the Chairman of the JGS. Considered one of the "most gifted" military leaders of South Vietnam,[40] he was deemed to be an "admirable man: honest, loyal, reserved, scholarly, diplomatic."[41] But he never acquired the administrative and managerial skills to transform the Joint General Staff into a coherent organization to replace the American Military Assistance Command. "Although he was a brilliant paratrooper in the field, Vien was a mediocre staff officer, without imagination."[42] However, the cuts were so drastic that even an able manager could not handle it. As conditions worsened, he shunned responsibility and often went to meditate on top of a tower in his backyard.[43] General Lâm Quang Thi called him a "colorless" man who preferred practicing yoga over leading troops.[44]

They both could have helped clean the government to set up a new political organization to deal with the communists. They could have served as ballast to Thiệu's ambitions and strategic military misconceptions or offer him critical advice about the war's directions. They could have helped keep South Vietnam afloat by controlling the economic costs of the war although economists made some unrealistic projections: a six-fold increase in South Vietnam's export earnings, which was ludicrous in a time of war; or a nine-fold increase in aid from non–U.S. sources, also unrealistic.

One of Saigon's cheerleaders was the indefatigable U.S. Ambassador Graham Martin who "held his views with dogmatic passion and expressed them with a self-righteousness that sometimes verged on megalomania.... He saw very little of the country whose cause he espoused so fervently or of the huge staff that worked under him. 'He worked brutally long hours. God,'" as one embassy aide called him: "I know he exists, but I haven't seen him."[45] Martin became the truest of the true believers in the South Vietnamese cause. He came to regard himself as the president's word made flesh, the embodiment of Richard Nixon's and later Gerald Ford's promises not to allow South Vietnam's defeat. The charge against him was that his reports to Washington "distorted Vietnamese realities, concealing the Thiệu regime's weaknesses and leaving policy makers with faulty perceptions of their ally's strength and effectiveness."

Worse, General Murray, his defense attaché, believed

> he misled South Vietnam's leaders much more disastrously by dogmatically repeating presidential promises of adequate support long after congressional approval of the administration's aid proposal was clearly in doubt. When President Ford sent to Thiệu a letter the day after he succeeded Nixon as president promising support, Martin told the Vietnamese leader that the letter meant they would eventually get the full amount of aid the administration had proposed. This caused Thiệu to believe more in Martin until Saigon's hopes were crushed by congressional votes to cut off aid.[46]

On 10 March 1975 the communists attacked Ban Mê Thuột, which was not well protected because General Phạm Văn Phú, disregarding intelligence warnings, thought enemy forces were attacking Kontum, the headquarters of the II Division and Corps.[47] He therefore entrusted the town defense to a Ranger group and a few thousand Popular and Regional Forces units. Under communist attack, Ban Mê Thuột fell in ten days, causing the panicked Thiệu to make some strategic mistakes. He ordered Phú who just lost Ban Mê Thuột, to withdraw from the highlands. On hearing rumors of the retreat, the panicked civilians swelled the retreating military convoy impeding its movement through rough mountain roads. The convoy thus became an easy target for the communists who attacked and hit it with artillery shells, mortar rounds, and rockets. The retreat turned into a rout. Of the 60,000 troops that started from Pleiku, only one third reached the coast. Of the 180,000 civilians that joined the convoy only one third got through.

Thiệu then withdrew the airborne brigade from the I Corps, destabilizing it; he ordered General Ngô Quang Trưởng to withdraw his troops to Đà Nẵng then changed his mind and decided to hold Huế. After a series of orders and counter-orders, the troops no longer listened to orders and disbanded. As the PAVN forces drove down

Highway 1 toward Saigon, they encountered ARVN troops at Xuân Lộc, the gateway to the capital. The 18th ARVN division under the General Lê Minh Đảo put up a stiff defense fighting hand-to-hand in many cases. Đảo defiantly proclaimed, "I vow to hold Xuân Lộc. I don't care how many divisions the other side sends against me. I will knock them down." The town soon turned into a pile of rubble, but the ARVN refused to yield. It held out for three weeks against overwhelming odds, destroying 37 NVA tanks and killing over 5,000 attackers.[48] The NVA bypassed the town and put the siege on Saigon.

On 21 April 1975, under intense political pressure, Thiệu resigned as president after losing the confidence of his closest domestic allies. Saigon fell on 30 April 1975. The night fell on that city and South Vietnam leading to the end of the 21-year war. There was not much to rejoice because the Rape of Saigon immediately began. That same day, terror had begun. The communists taking over the Cộng Hòa General Hospital, a tertiary military hospital in Saigon, where all the heavily wounded ARVN soldiers were being treated, ordered them out of the hospital no matter their medical condition. One by one, each helping the other, whether they were convalescing or recovering from an operation, they straggled with tears in their eyes across the Cộng Hòa gate. They limped because they were forbidden to use any hospital motorized vehicle. Many died that day. In the face of this inhumane treatment, people in the area opened their doors to welcome the wounded and let them recover in their own homes before sending them home. Others called taxicabs to transport the sickest ones to public or private hospitals. The communists took over and confiscated institutions, businesses, private properties, bank accounts, lands, and anything they wanted. Soldiers and government officials were sent to reeducation camps and civilians to new economic zones—the civilian equivalent of the reeducation camps. Everything of importance was looted and sent to Hanoi including South Vietnam's gold reserve. There was no liberation after the war, only subservience, for South Vietnam became Hanoi's new colony. Four decades or more of terror, oppression, incarceration, mistreatment followed, during which the South Vietnamese were treated as slaves in their own land.

Conclusion

Being orphaned since age 11, Thiệu was a self-made man who from his humble origin in Phan Rang rose to become the leader of the "Young Turks" and President of the Second Republic. Schooled under the French, he tried to fit himself into the American system and to reorganize the Vietnamese army and society. He claimed no tutor and relied on the ARVN as his lone supporter. Trained in the school of hard knocks, he was no match for the Harvard-educated Kissinger. He never accepted the policy of gradualism, limited bombing to encourage negotiations, as advocated by McNamara and adopted by Lyndon Johnson. He expected that Nixon would keep his word to use "full force" when Hanoi launched its invasion after the cease-fire.[49]

A shrewd and cautious leader, he helped stabilize the Second Republic and brought some degree of respectability and commerce to South Vietnam, although he was neither a good tactician nor a framer of public opinion. "He was neither loved, nor deeply hated.... He used his power less oppressively than Mr. Diệm had...."[50] His biggest failure came from his inability to build a military and political infrastructure to fight against the communists and to reorganize a war-torn society, which was a difficult if not an impossible task in a time of war. Internal divisiveness in the South and the lack of a unifying ideology, more than corruption, weakened South Vietnam. Although Thiệu was able to build a government of men based on self-interest, he was unable to rally his people without continued American support.[51] Under pressure, he initiated two withdrawals, one in the II Corps and the other in the I Corps leading to their collapse and subsequent downfall of South Vietnam.

During his presidency, he waged two types of war: a political one against the Kissinger-led Americans and a military war against the Lê Duẩn led CPV. Having lost his war against Kissinger, he went on to lose the war against Hanoi and in the process his presidency. It was a downhill ride from there, forcing him to lead an exiled life in the West. In England he refused to see anyone or give out any interview and in Boston, he kept quiet and did not ink any autobiography. To some overseas Vietnamese who blamed him for the loss of Vietnam, he told them, "You criticize me, everything. I let you do that. I [sic] like to see you do better than I."[52]

The war as he saw it was a war against evil, against communism. Had the Americans persisted in their zeal to wage war, they might have won it. Hanoi was close to exhaustion and was sending all its reserves, a total of 16 divisions, down south. The brand new recruits were 15- or 16-year-old youngsters who had no war experience, were also tired and afraid of the prolonged bloody war. When America blinked and withdrew, it lost Nguyễn Văn Thiệu and his 18 million South Vietnamese. As a result, Indochina fell under the red blanket with resulting wholesale slaughter in Cambodia, reeducation camps, and the emergence of an oppressive, repressive and corrupt regime all through Vietnam. Although Thiệu was battling against Kissinger and Nixon, the main culprits of the U.S. withdrawal and aid cuts were the Democratic-leaning U.S. Congress and the anti-war movement.

The story of Nguyễn Van Thiệu is one of misunderstanding between two allies who had diametrically opposed visions of the war: one wanting to rebuild his country and the other to disengage and go home. This eventually culminated in the United States' abandonment of its ally. And finally was defeat inevitable? Many including Le Gro thought that Vietnam needed a few more years to mature before a younger generation would take over and institute new leadership and reforms.[53]

12

1974

The Paracel Islands, Thượng Đức, Phước Long

Three events stood out in 1974: (1) the battle of the Paracel Islands in early January 1974, and (2) the two battles of Thượng Đức and Phước Long. They are discussed in this chapter.

The Battle of the Paracel Islands (1974)

On 19 January 1974, the naval forces of the PRC (People's Republic of China) and the Republic of South Vietnam engaged in a battle in the disputed Paracel Islands. The short but intense battle left China in control of the islands and surrounding waters in the South China Sea.

A Contested Region

The Paracel Islands are a group of islands known to the Chinese as Xisha and to the Vietnamese as Hoàng Sa. In 2021, they are claimed by the PRC, Socialist Vietnam (taking over from the Republic of South Vietnam), the Philippines and Taiwan. However, only Vietnam and the PRC had a documented historic past on these islands.[1]

The Vietnamese called these islands Hoàng Sa or Yellow Sands or Yellow Sandbank. Under the reign of Emperor Lê Thánh Tông (1460–1469) they began conducting commercial activities on and around Hoàng Sa, including harvesting abundant sea-products and conducting salvage operations on shipwrecks.[2]

In 1827, a world atlas produced by Belgian geographer Philippe Vandermaelen was published in Belgium. Vietnam was described by four maps in this atlas. One of these maps was titled, "Partie de la Cochinchine" (part of Cochinchina), in which the Paracel Islands were included, indicating that they were part of Cochinchine or Cochinchina (southern Vietnam region).[3]

In 1951, at the International Treaty of San Francisco conference, Vietnam's representative claimed that both the Paracels and Spratlys are territories of Vietnam, and was met with no challenge from all nations at the event. However, neither the PRC nor the ROC participated in the conference.

In 1954, Vietnam was partitioned into communist North Vietnam and the Republic of Vietnam (South) through the 17th parallel. At this time, maps and other official documents of the North Vietnam government asserted that the islands belonged to the PRC, mainly due to the fact that the PRC was the largest supporter of North Vietnam during the Vietnam War.

In 1956, after the French withdrew from Vietnam, South Vietnam replaced France as far as control of the islands was concerned. By February 1956, the South Vietnamese Navy was already stationed on Pattle Island by order of Ngô Đình Diệm.[4] In 14 September 1958, North Vietnamese Prime Minister Phạm Văn Đồng wrote to Zhou Enlai recognizing Chinese sovereignty over the Paracels and the Spratly (Trường Sa).[5] South Vietnamese objected and experts later agreed that the letter represented a diplomatic gesture of goodwill that has no legal relevance to the current territorial dispute.[6]

On January 19, 1974, the Battle of the Paracel Islands occurred between the PRC and South Vietnam. After the battle, the PRC took control over the entire Paracel Islands. In 1982, Vietnam established Hoàng Sa District in Quảng Nam–Đà Nẵng covering these islands. In July 2012 the National Assembly of Vietnam passed a law demarcating Vietnamese sea borders to include the Paracel and Spratly Islands.

The Geostrategic Context

The Paracel Islands are located 300 kilometers south of Yulin, Hainan Island, and 370 kilometers west of Đà Nẵng. They are divided into two island groups. To the northeast, the Amphitrite group is dominated by Woody, the largest island. To the southwest, the Crescent group consists of Pattle, Money and Robert Islands on the western side and Drummond, Duncan and Palm Islands on the eastern side. Eighty kilometers of water separate the Amphitrite and Crescent groups. The Paracels sit astride vital lines of communications between China, Japan in the North and Jakarta, and Singapore in the South. In the 1970s, the promise of offshore oil further intensified the dispute in the South China Sea.

In 1973, a series of provocations and reprisals set China and South Vietnam on a collision course. In August, South Vietnam seized six islands in the Spratlys and a month later four more islands in the same area. In October, two Chinese fishing trawlers, Nos. 402 and 407, appeared in the area and began working near the Crescent Group, which was claimed by South Vietnam. As a result, the South Vietnamese chased them off the islands or brought them to Vietnamese courts.

On 10 January 1974, Chinese crews constructed a seafood processing plant on Robert Island, claimed by South Vietnam. The following day, the Chinese foreign ministry reiterated China's sovereignty over the Paracels, the Spratlys, and Macclesfield Bank. Four days later, the RVN Navy dispatched frigate HQ-16, which ordered trawlers 402 and 407 to leave the area.

The Battle of the Paracels

The South Vietnamese Navy had four frigates: HQ-5, HQ-4, HQ-16, and HQ-10, the last one struggling with a disabled engine. China also had four warships present: the minesweepers *271*, *274*, *389* and *396*. Although four ships were engaged on each side, the total displacements and weapons of the South Vietnamese ships were superior. The RVN Navy clearly outsized and outgunned the PLAN or People's Liberation Army Navy.

In the early morning of 19 January 1974, South Vietnamese soldiers from HQ-5 landed on Duncan and Palm Islands and came under fire from Chinese troops. Three South Vietnamese soldiers were killed and many more were wounded. Finding themselves outnumbered, the South Vietnamese ground forces withdrew by landing craft.

Unable to dislodge their foes at sea and ashore, the RVN warships repositioned themselves into battle formation. HQ-5 and HQ-10 opened fire on the Chinese warships. The PLAN units returned fire and sped forward toward the RVN Navy. The sea battle lasted about 40 minutes, with vessels on both sides taking damage. The tactic was to draw so near that the enemy's main deck guns would overshoot their targets. The smaller Chinese warships managed to maneuver into the blind spots of the main cannons on the South Vietnamese warships to nullify the superior range and lethality of the enemy's firepower. The PLAN commanders chose a knife fight against an adversary expecting a gunfight.[7] They damaged all four South Vietnamese ships, especially HQ-10, which could not retreat because her last working engine was disabled. The crew was ordered to abandon ship, but her captain, Lieutenant Commander Ngụy Văn Thà, remained on board and went down with his ship.

The next day, Chinese aircraft from Hainan bombed the three islands, following which Chinese troops landed. The outnumbered South Vietnamese marine garrison on the islands was forced to surrender, and the damaged navy ships retreated to Đà Nẵng. The Chinese moved quickly to retake Vietnamese-occupied islands fearing a counterattack with reinforcements. They held 40 prisoners including one American observer; they were later released in Hong Kong through the Red Cross.

The RVN Navy sent two destroyers to reinforce Đà Nẵng and directed six warships to head toward the Paracels. President Thiệu, who arrived in Đà Nẵng to oversee his forces personally, allegedly ordered his air force to bomb Chinese positions on the Paracels before rescinding the decision. At the same time, Saigon requested assistance from the U.S. Seventh Fleet, but to no avail.[8]

Battle Assessment

The Chinese had planned ahead with the political leadership to retain a firm grip on all aspects of the campaign. They had drafted a response plan and the PLAN knew what they had to do and were decisive in their approach.

The PLAN's success resulted as much from Vietnamese incompetence and mistakes as it did from Chinese tactical virtuosity. HQ-10 went to war with one disabled engine. The second engine broke down during the battle. HQ-4's main guns malfunctioned during the first critical minutes of the battle. In the confusion of the skirmish, HQ-16 was struck by friendly fire.[9]

In battles, it has been mentioned that the "countless minor incidents ... combine to lower the general level of performance."[10] One has to overcome these adverse incidents to achieve success. Chance also favored the Chinese who were plagued with command-and-control problems that were luckily overcome in time. The operation took place during the northeast monsoon season, when surges—involving gusts of 40 knots or more—can strike without much warning. Had nature turned against the PLAN, the small combatants would have trouble handling the rough seas, spelling trouble for the entire operation. The Chinese militia on the islands had ready access to grenades, high-powered rifles, and machine guns below decks. They also worked closely with the PLAN and shared intelligence about the RVN Navy with them.[11]

The Paracels battle was the first step in China's long effort to establish its presence in the South China Sea. In 1988, it seized six reefs and atolls in the Spratly Island after another battle against communist Vietnam. In 1994, it built structures on Philippines-claimed Mischief Reef. In 2012, it compelled the Philippines to yield control of Scarborough Shoal.

When China placed an oil rig close to the Paracels in May 2014, violent protests targeting Chinese businesses broke out across Vietnam. At sea, Vietnamese maritime law enforcement vessels sought to break the security cordon formed around the rig by Chinese civilian, paramilitary, and naval vessels. The contest is far from over.

Battle of Thượng Đức (August–November 1974)

The five northernmost provinces that formed the I Corps included from north to south: Quảng Trị Province adjacent to the Demilitarized Zone. Next came Thừa Thiên with the old imperial capital city of Huế. The Quảng Nam Province housed the second-largest city in Vietnam, Đà Nẵng. Next were the provinces of Quảng Tín and Quảng Ngãi.

Geographically, the I Corps was limited by the sea on the east side and the mountains on the west, making it difficult to defend the land or to escape from it. The only escape route was through Highway 1 that ran north-south and parallel to the coastline and became easily congested during emergency situations. Any attack on the highway would block people's movement, creating panic and pandemonium among the trapped people.

Battle

The PAVN by that time had perfected the "strategy of indirect approach" by making a frontal attack using a small force while executing a deep envelopment and attacking from the rear.[12] The strategy could take down the CP, which was usually located in the rear, prevent a reorganization in the rear, and potentially disrupt the enemy's communication system.

On 18 July, the PAVN 324th Regiment overran a small district town deep in the mountain before attacking the district town of Thượng Đức that led directly to Đà Nẵng. Gen. Ngô Quang Trưởng moved a Ranger battalion from Quảng Ngãi to guard the town. When the Rangers held out despite persistent attacks, PAVN troops dismantled their 37 mm antiaircraft guns and hauled them through the mountains to the front line to use as direct fire weapons.

In August, the PAVN attacked Thượng Đức again. Antiaircraft guns were used to dismantle the Ranger bunkers causing them to back down. Trưởng sent another Ranger group and a regiment from the ARVN 1st Division to control the situation, but the PAVN poured in another regiment of their own. Gen. Nguyễn Duy Hinh, the 3rd Division commander sent in additional reinforcements that stabilized the situation. PAVN soldiers dug in the nearby hills and stopped Hinh's advance two miles from the town. The fighting was ferocious. Ammunition cuts prevented Gen. Hinh from retaking Thượng Đức. Hinh could only fire fewer than 500 artillery shells each day and his command helicopter was limited to four hours of flight time per week.

With the situation being stable, Trưởng pulled out the 1st Division regiment and the Ranger group back to I Corps Forward. Once the forces were withdrawn, PAVN moved forward and seized a dominant hill known as Hill 1062, three miles east of Thượng Đức. Enemy 130 mm artillery was within range of Đà Nẵng. Gen. Trưởng ordered Airborne commander Brig. Gen. Lê Quang Lưởng to retake Hill 1062.

Vietnamese airborne troops, following French tradition, wore red berets, hence the nickname "Red Berets" attached to them. Methodically they pushed forward and on 18 September, retook Hill 1062, but a counterattack the next day drove them off. PAVN casualties were high, causing the need for a regiment of the 304th Division to replace the 324th Division's regiment. The PAVN dug in waiting for the Red Berets to come back.

On 2 October, the Red Berets launched a surprise attack, killing 400 North Vietnamese and dislodging them from Hill 1062. The PAVN came back with a second regiment of the 304th Division. They were mowed down, but continued to press forward. Gen. Văn Tiến Dũng, the chief of the General Staff, was mad and the PAVN sent the third 304th regiment with two battalions of engineers and 4,000 rounds of artillery and mortars ammunition.

On 1 November the PAVN attacked with the third regiment and drove the airborne off Hill 1062. The PAVN built extensive fortifications to protect their hard won positions. Despite the heavy fortifications, the airborne recaptured the hill two days later. Both sides were tired. In six weeks of fighting, the airborne lost 500 dead and 2,000 wounded while claiming the PAVN lost seven thousand. Thượng Đức remained in enemy hands.[13]

The ARVN, especially the airborne, had fought hard and well. And people in the I Corps knew it. Therefore, when the airborne were recalled back to Saigon in March 1975 to serve as reserve units, the population panicked.

The year 1974 was difficult for South Vietnam. Despite brilliant successes, the cut-off of U.S. military aid had a profound impact on ARVN morale. This was reflected by the "loss of men and weapons at a fearful rate." According to the U.S. Defense Intelligence Agency, the South Vietnamese lost 816 crew-served weapons in 1974 compared to only 384 in 1972, the year of the Easter Offensive. Soldiers lost 19,340 individual weapons in 1974, well above the 1972 figure of 16,897.[14] More than 200,000 soldiers and militiamen deserted during 1974, about one-fifth of South Vietnam's entire strength. As the ARVN awaited the more severe tests that would come in 1975, the ARVN was a "tired, dispirited, and frightened force, lacking confidence in its leaders, its future and itself."[15]

The Battle of Phước Long

The Phước Long Battle was one of the thousands of battles waged between the People's Army of Vietnam (PAVN or NVA) and the Republic of Vietnam Armed Forces (RVNAF) during their 21-year fratricidal war (1954–1975).

If the 1968 Tết Offensive marked the end of the guerrilla war (most of the southern guerrillas were wiped out after Tết) and the beginning of the conventional phase of the war, the Phước Long Battle, however, marked the beginning of the end of the Republic of Vietnam, which was characterized by: (1) violation of Paris Peace Accords by Hanoi, which spearheaded new attacks in South Vietnam[16]; (2) the failure of the U.S. to intervene in the conflict; (3) and the eventual demise of South Vietnam.

Behind the scenes, President Nixon had expressly written on 5 January 1973, to South Vietnamese President Nguyễn Văn Thiệu, that *"if Hanoi fails to abide by the terms of this agreement it is my intention to take swift and severe retaliatory action."*[17] Whether Nixon (and then Ford) would follow through with his promise remained to be seen.

The "Indecent Interval"

Unbeknownst to Thiệu and the South Vietnamese, on August 3, 1972, Nixon had already looked for ways to get out of South Vietnam more or less victoriously (he called it "peace with honor," although there was neither peace nor honor). Kissinger, who had been shuttling back and forth to Paris, had suggested, "We've got to find some formula that holds the thing together for a year or two, after which—after a year, Mr. President [Nixon] Vietnam will be a backwater. If we settle it, say, this October [1972], by January '74, no one will give a damn."[18]

Historians called it "the decent interval"—the period after U.S. withdrawal and the eventual collapse of South Vietnam. Having promised to Saigon that communist troops would not be allowed to remain in South Vietnam after the signature of any treaty, Kissinger negotiated the opposite. Through that maneuver, he "had just deceived both his enemy and his ally and had led the United States into an act of bad faith that can have few parallels in its diplomatic history."[19] The U.S. withdrew in 1973 and Saigon fell in 1975, leaving Washington off the hook. The "indecent interval" was marked by major changes within the parties involved.

1. Thiệu entered this period with no major innovative idea. The RVNAF was a large army with a huge administrative and logistical "tail," a legacy the U.S. army left to South Vietnam. After the cease-fire, it received a lot of military equipment; yet, these were "airplanes they couldn't fly, ships they couldn't man, and tanks and other equipment they couldn't maintain."[20]

Although after the cease-fire, Thiệu issued the four "No's"—which spelled out as (a) no relinquishing territory, (b) no coalition government, (c) no negotiation with the enemy, and (d) no communist or neutralist activity in the country—he did not use the precious time to fix the flaws of his government and armed forces. On the other hand, although he knew what his enemy was planning, he did not have the resources and manpower to fight back.

The South Vietnamese society, although not as free as a Western society, was, in a time of war, a relatively free society: "authoritarian enough to be unpopular, democratic enough to be inefficient."[21] As such, it was pluralistic, divided, and almost anarchic—a legacy of its freedom. The northern regime, on the contrary, looked from the outside to be unified, monolithic, and totalitarian. Hanoi, the Việt Cộng, southern intellectuals, some religious groups using the limited freedom available, competed to tear the southern society apart. It was "internal divisiveness ... the lack of a unifying ideology, more than corruption [that] weakened South Vietnam."[22] It was not surprising to see that some politicians and religious leaders would demand that Saigon stop the war while they never asked the real culprit, Hanoi, to do the same thing. They always asked the weaker side to stop the war. They never dared to tell the stronger side to stop.

2. In the U.S., Congress and the media also tried to end the war in Vietnam. Nixon, caught in the Watergate affair, had no energy or mental concentration to wage another war in Vietnam. Congress passed the Case-Church Amendment, which prevented any direct or indirect activities in Laos, Cambodia and both Vietnams after 15 August 1973. It cut aid to Vietnam from $1.6 to $1.1 billion a year. Eventually $625 million was appropriated for 1975. When shipping costs were subtracted, total aid amounted to only $500 million.[23]

3. Through the Paris Accords, Hanoi not only did not have to pull its troops out of South Vietnam, it also used 1973 and 1974 to build up these forces. On 6 February 1973, a 175-truck convoy crossed through the demilitarized zone (DMZ) and 223 tanks from Laos and Cambodia rolled into South Vietnam. In 1973 alone, Hanoi infiltrated 75,000 troops, increased its tank strength from 100 to 500, and doubled its heavy artillery strength.[24]

Politically, Hanoi went into the offensive. It explained to the "world" that the communists were abiding by the agreements while South Vietnam constantly violated them. The propaganda worked as Nixon testified, "If Saigon had tried to interrupt or interdict Hanoi's build up, the uproar in Congress would have been deafening."[25]

Hanoi further accused Saigon of obstructing political accommodation. This was another falsehood, because neither side wanted "reconciliation and concord." Hanoi in fact was the worst offender. It would not accept any party other than the communist party. Until today, it has remained a one-party communist country. It leveled charges of corruption against Saigon; some were true others were not. Anti-Thiệu pressures on congressmen forced Congress to grant Jane Fonda and Tom Hayden the use of a congressional room to promote a North Vietnamese program designed to shatter American support for the war.[26]

4. Anti-war dissent in Congress and universities became more strident with time.[27] Although demonstrators knew almost nothing about the war, the U.S. government and Saigon failed "to convince them that their knowledge was limited and what they were advocating was surrender to ruthless totalitarians."[28]

By the end of 1974, Thiệu knew that Vietnamization—a misnomer used to characterize the process by which the RVNAF assumed *total* military defense of the country—was not working well. From an advisory position (the U.S. had 23,300 people by January 1, 1965), U.S. forces began ground operations after 6 April 1965 relegating many RVNAF units to care for counter-insurgency and pacification projects.

First, Vietnamization started too late, only in 1969; had it started in 1965, the RVNAF could have taken advantage of the U.S. shield to develop and mature its forces.[29] The U.S. sacrificed quality, experience, leadership of officers and competence of units when it tried to expand the RVNAF size too quickly after 1969. RVNAF officers tended to rely on their advisers' suggestions, presence, and access to technology, thus losing their "character," command capabilities, and leadership.[30] The first group of leaders had started to blossom as evidenced by the victories at Quảng Trị and An Lộc in 1972. Gen. Ngô Quang Trưởng (savior of Quảng Trị), Gen. Lý Tòng Bá (savior of Kontum), Gen. Lê Văn Hưng (the hero of An Lộc who survived in the bunker for three months under the relentless shelling of the Việt Cộng),[31] and Gen. Lê Minh Đảo (hero of Xuân Lộc) were fine examples, to name a few.

Second, Vietnamization might have worked had the Vietnamese received a constant and steady stream of armaments and replaced parts they could rely on. This turned out not to be the case because Congress had sharply cut aid to Vietnam. James Schlesinger, U.S. Defense Secretary, argued against the cut in early 1975:

> The failure to support South Vietnam to the degree we gave them to understand we would, would be a failure of moral commitment of the United States and a failure of American foreign policy.... It would be a serious error on the part of the United States, and I believe, a serious moral lapse for us to contemplate the semi-abandonment of an ally by failure to provide them with the appropriate financial resources.[32]

The RVNAF, trained to fight the war "American style"—high technology devices, air mobility, and profuse expenditures of ammunitions—could not do much without these technologies.[33] In 1974, due to aid cuts, inflation, a 400 percent rise in oil prices, and a 27 percent rise in ammunition costs, it was forced to fight an expensive war on a "pauper's budget." The result was disastrous. Use of helicopters and cargo aircraft was cut in half. A lack of spare parts forced the cannibalization of functioning aircrafts leading to an overall decrease in ready and available planes. Artillery and mortar fires were curtailed. Rifle ammunition was cut in half. A 2½-ton truck was used to pull in a row four to five gasless ambulances to conserve fuel.[34] Patients had to wait for other ambulances to be filled with patients before being transported to medical facilities. Medicines, especially dextrose, antibiotics, and plasma, and other medical supplies were in short supply.

Shortages devastated soldiers' morale and impacted their military effectiveness. They could not even rely on adequate evacuation when wounded. Clothing allowances were cut as well as boot replacement. Unemployment was estimated at one million, about one-fifth of the civilian force. The inflation rate was 67 percent in 1973 and 27 percent in the first six months of 1974.[35] Ninety percent of soldiers polled stated their pay did not meet their family's minimum needs. Wives had to do extra work to put meals on tables. Men started to desert to care for their families. The fact that they did not switch sides proved that freedom was still cherished by these people. A paralysis began to grip the RVNAF—a lethargic acceptance that the war was not going well and would eventually be lost.[36]

Having neither the time element nor the deep pocket of Uncle Sam, Thiệu had to rely on U.S. military support or at least B-52 air support for survival. Until the end, he "clung adamantly to this illusion of American intervention," although there were signs that the U.S. would not reenter the war.[37] One could not blame Thiệu, because (1) Hanoi had also entertained that possibility, otherwise it would have attacked South Vietnam in 1973 or 1974, and (2) Nixon had assured Thiệu of his support on various occasions.[38] Then there were constant reassurances from U.S. Ambassador Martin, who had lulled Thiệu deeper into his illusion.[39] For a man gasping for air, belief was his principal force. But as a leader, Thiệu ought to have been smarter and more careful in his thinking. This turned out to be one of the factors that may have contributed to an early Saigon loss, for without U.S. aid and B-52 cover, Saigon's fate was pretty dim. If his regime had grave defects, he was a capable organizer. He could not have governed South Vietnam for eight difficult years without considerable talents, although they were more manipulative than inspirational.[40] It was certainly hard to be inspirational in the face of aid cuts, threats to his life, a lengthy and bloody war, an economy in shamble, a complex society free enough to voice different opinions, an enemy dedicated to winning the war no matter the cost...

The South Vietnamese, being free thinkers and entrepreneurial people, used to believe in a single opinion leader, although they listened to no one; northerners' strength, on the other hand, came from the unity of the group, the Politburo.[41] While freedom is good for economy, trade and innovation, crowd thinking is good for an insurgency war—a grinding, long-term war that never ends until one of the two parties crumbles. More than crowd thinking, it is adherence to a protocol, blueprint or goal that would lead to success.[42]

While southerners and the U.S. wavered and looked for one solution after another and while Saigon tried to build a nation and wage a destabilizing war at the same time, northerners just focused on winning the war. They carried it on year after year without paying attention to the economy, the well-being and poor economic condition of their people. When they failed (like in the 1968 Tết Offensive and the 1972 Fiery Red Summer Offensive), they kept going back to the basics by building up their networks, sending more troops to the South, and increasing their military capability. In 1973, they just did that and by mid–1974, with new reinforcements of troops and armaments, the tide had switched to their side. Thiệu, abandoned by the U.S. Congress and the White House, could not rearm and reenergize his army, consolidate his weaknesses, and prepare for the future.

Saigon and Hanoi approached the war differently. The war being waged in its backyard, Saigon had to care for its civilians, improve their livelihood, and stabilize the economy while fighting off the invaders. It also had to build a free and democratic society. All these demands placed a lot of burdens on Saigon. Hanoi, being a totalitarian society, did not care about these subtleties: freedom and the economy were nonexistent in the North. But Hanoi covered these deficiencies so well that no one knew or cared about these facts.

Hanoi waged a revolutionary war, which by definition was a protracted and total war designed to gain political control in the South. There was no middle way for there was no substitute for victory. People were "indoctrinated, tightly organized, and grossly exploited to support the revolutionary war effort." This explains why the North took casualties and destruction that would have politically undermined a Western nation.[43] This was the tale of two cities, two countries, two ideologies, and two ways of thinking as Hanoi and Saigon emerged from this lull period after the signing of the Paris Peace Accords.

The Phước Long Battle

Phước Long lay at the southern end of the Trường Sơn range—Vietnam's spine—that goes from South to North. Its sparse population was predominantly tribal. Although ethnically and economically linked to the highlands, it was under the command of the III Corps, the Saigon command. The provincial capital, known as Phước

Long City or Sông Bé, stood close to the Cambodian border, beyond which the PAVN was resting in preparation for the next attack. Although located 80 miles north of Saigon, access to this hilly and isolated region was difficult. The province consisted of four districts: Bồ Đức, Phước Bình, Đôn Luân, and Đức Phong.

The idea of attacking Phước Long was PAVN Gen. Trần Văn Trà's. Born in Quảng Ngãi in 1918, he became a communist in 1940, regrouped to the North in 1954, came South in 1963, and became a lieutenant general and commander of the B2 Theater—the southern half of South Vietnam. He believed in an all-out assault on Saigon, had his chance during the 1968 Tết Offensive, but failed with heavy losses.

In the fall of 1974, he again prepared plans to make an all-out assault on Saigon in 1975 or 1976. His shorter goal was to clear the bases around Tây Ninh (80 miles east of Saigon) and Đôn Luân (Đồng Xoài) and Phước Long (90 miles north of Saigon) so that he could bring in troops and tanks from Cambodia. He thus asked his General Staff for four divisions to prepare for the attack. Hanoi refused and Gen. Văn Tiến Dũng (acting on Lê Duẩn's order) cancelled his plans. Trà directly took his case to Lê Duẩn, who relented.[44]

On December 7, 1974, Trà ordered diversionary attacks on Long Khánh, Bình Tuy province, east of Saigon as well as west of Saigon on Mount Bà Đen (Black Virgin Mountain)—a black symmetrical mountain, dominating the Tây Ninh plain where the RVNAF maintained a relay communication and observation site. Originating from Cambodia, PAVN troops then launched assaults on scattered outposts (Bồ Đức, Đức Phong, and Đôn Luân) around Phước Long on December 13, 1974. Đôn Luân held on while the Regional Force (RF) positions at Bồ Đức and Đức Phong were overrun. RF Fire Support Base Bunard was captured along with four 105 mm howitzers. The enemy then concentrated its attack on the Sông Bé airfield, about two miles southwest of Phước Long City.

These coordinated and almost simultaneous attacks kept the newly promoted III Corps commander, Gen. Dư Quốc Đống busy putting the fires out all over his Corps area. In addition, he did not have enough resources to throw into Phước Long when he realized the enemy's intentions. The strategic reserve, the Marines and the airborne divisions were being tied up in the I Corps in the northern part of the country. Shifting some of the overextended troops to Phước Long would endanger another place, while allowing Phước Long to fall would undermine Saigon's political position. Gen. Đống ordered the 2nd battalion of the 7th Infantry Regiment of the RVNAF 5th Division airlifted into the city. This only regular unit and two good RF battalions became the main resistance units of Phước Long City. There were also 3,000 disorganized and shaken RF and Popular Force (PF) troops, which had been driven from the outposts into the city. Regular RVNAF units launched a successful counterattack and retook Bồ Đức. On 22 December, the NVA recaptured Bồ Đức for good.[45]

The PAVN possessed overwhelming forces: the NVA 7th Division and the newly formed PAVN 3rd division reinforced by two separate infantry regiments, an antiaircraft regiment, an artillery regiment, a tank battalion, and local sapper units. The result of this lopsided battle was foregone.

Đôn Luân (70 miles north of Saigon) was a small village at the junction of several highways 320, 1A, and 14 held by a RF battalion of 350 men. On 26 December 1974, the NVA rained a ruthless 1,000 round artillery barrage on the village, which withstood the first attack. Route 14 was closed by the communists who soon captured the

RF units. Phước Long City, about 20 miles north of Đôn Luân, was now isolated and ripe for the plucking.[46]

On 1 January, the NVA launched another infantry-armor attack and overwhelmed the RF positions on Bà Ra Mountain overlooking Phước Long City. Using the Bà Ra guns, they neutralized eight RVNAF 105 mm howitzers and four 155 mm guns. They set up antiaircraft weapons on the mountain to prevent any fixed wing aircraft or helicopter from landing on the town airstrip.

VNAF pilots did their best to neutralize T-54 tanks and helping defenders to hold off PAVN attacks. Due to its isolation, approach to the area had been difficult even in normal times. Since 13 December, roads leading to the town being held by the communists, supplies and reinforcements could only come by air. The VNAF could not prevent the disaster. First, it had to face the heavy clouds, which obstructed the view of the town. Once the A-37 fighter planes started flying again, they faced fierce antiaircraft fire. Two C-130 transports (out of a total of 32 available for the whole country) and several other planes had been shot down trying to support the beleaguered force. Soon, pilots did not dare come below 12,000 feet to provide air support. This was not a problem of courage. This was an order: to conserve materiel.[47] This in turn made it impossible for government helicopters carrying reinforcements and supplies to land within the city.[48]

The RVNAF fought with courage but did not fare well under the smothering NVA artillery fire followed by tank-supported infantry attacks. By 3 January, about 3,000 rounds fell on the town each day. A decision was made by the JGS (Joint General Staff) on 2 January 1975, to send the 811th and 814th companies of the 81st Airborne Rangers, totaling 300 skilled commandoes equipped with 90 mm recoilless rifles, to save Phước Long. The rest of the group, 2,500 rangers, would rejoin them within ten days.

On 3 January, they were airlifted from Long Bình to Phước Long but could only circle above the town because of heavy enemy artillery and had to return to Long Bình. On 4 January, the airlift was delayed because of poor weather, clouds and rain. The first wave was led by Lt. Col. Vũ Xuân Thông finally landed safely east of Daklung Bridge and connected with Phước Long defenders. The second group led by Major Nguyễn Sơn was not that lucky. They were met with heavy artillery that caused many casualties. The first group at the same time came under heavy attack by tanks and ground troops.

Under heavy attack, a group of rangers pulled back to Daklung Bridge. Civilians followed them for protection. The rangers, however, held on and repulsed two enemy attacks. After pulling back tanks and troops, the enemy shelled the city for many hours. The medical bunker was full of dead bodies, wounded civilians and soldiers. Late in the afternoon of January 4, the communists launched another attack and engaged in hand-to-hand combat with the 81st Airborne Rangers. Lt. Col. Thông fought against them with hand grenades and pushed back a group of infiltrators. All anti-tank rockets and medical supplies had been used up. Patients died because of lack of blood and medical equipment. Reinforcements and supplies were requested. Night fell and a decision to retreat was made. Civilians cried and moaned, asking to come along. They had to be calmed, although no further decision was made that night.

On 5 January, communists launched a new round of shelling although there was no ground or tank attack. Night fell without a word of reinforcement or retreat. The situation was tense as soldiers prepared for a possible night attack. No one dared to sleep. The shelling began again at dawn of 6 January and continued for many hours. Then tanks and ground troops showed up. The PAVN committed more of their precious T-54 tanks and 130 mm field-gun batteries. The top-of-the line Soviet tanks were equipped with shields to neutralize the effects of armor-piercing shells. One survivor quoted, "Our M-72 rockets were unable to knock them out. We hit them; they stopped for a while then moved on." Sometimes, tanks were so close that rocket launchers did not have the time to arm themselves. RVNAF Major Lê Tấn Đại watched as his men, despite the PAVN's four-to-one superiority of forces, climbed on the backs of the tanks in attempts to throw hand grenades into the hatches. The Phước Long defenders destroyed at least 16 T54 tanks in 48 hours, but more appeared on the battlefield.[49]

The order to retreat was given. A specially-trained company accompanied the medical group. Wounded soldiers who could walk followed the team, the others were taken on stretchers. The group took another direction than the 811th and 814th companies. The province chief and his staff also withdrew from the Sông Bé airport.

After pulling out of the city to Daklung River, Lt. Col. Thông tried to regroup and retake the city, but was unsuccessful. The enemy surrounded the 81st, which was forced to escape under a barrage of shelling and gunfire. Another fight ensued at the Daklung River before they could escape into the Phước Long jungle. Phước Long fell around 7 p.m. on 6 January, 24 days after the first attack. It became the first provincial town in South Vietnam captured by the communists during the war.[50] One airborne trooper, a veteran at An Lộc, said: "The enemy troops were not so good and so courageous as we might have thought. There were simply too many of them.... Our air support was not very effective; the planes flew too high. If only we could have had B-52s like we did in An Lộc."[51]

This was where full use of B-52 bombers was needed. Similar to 1954 when President Eisenhower declined to intervene at Điên Biên Phủ, in 1975 President Ford failed to lift his fingers to release his B-52 bombers. The U.S. did move the aircraft carrier *USS Enterprise* out of the Philippines closer to Vietnam. It alerted the Marine Division in Okinawa.[52] These political gestures, having no strategic meaning, helped seal the fate of Phước Long City and ultimately led to the fall of South Vietnam.

Washington later sonorously but emptily warned that North Vietnam "must accept the full consequences of its actions." The editor of the communist party newspaper, *Nhân Dân*, told the visiting American writer Frances Fitzgerald, "There was a theory of a 'decent interval.' According to this theory, Mr. Kissinger's 'honorable solution' to the war meant a two-year interval between the withdrawal of American troops and the fall of Thiệu. Well, the two years are over."[53]

The Aftermath

Phước Long was the Vietnamese Alamo. The RVNAF units stood its ground and fought bravely almost to the last man. Composed mainly of RF and PF, they were no match for and were overwhelmed by larger PAVN forces. Casualties were heavy. Out of the 5,400 men of different units committed, only 850 survived. The two companies of Airborne Rangers lost all but 85 men, the RVNAF infantry regiment all but 200. Of the 30,000 civilians, only 3,000 Montagnards and Vietnamese escaped communist control. To cap matters off, the communists were cruel in their victory. Civilian (province, village, and hamlet) officials who were captured were summarily executed.[54]

Colonel Nguyễn Tấn Thanh, Phước Long province chief and one of Gen. Lâm Quang Thi's best infantry battalion commanders at the 9th Infantry Division was killed with his troops.[55] So was the battalion commander of the 2nd battalion, 7th Infantry division.[56] Dr. Trần Mạnh Phần, physician-in-chief of the Phước Long Hospital, died in the morning of 5 January 1975 when a Việt Cộng mortar hit the command post. Dr. Trần Kim Phần was killed in the late afternoon from another mortar. Dr. Mai Thế Trang died of wounds and hemorrhaging in the early hours of 6 January. Of the five Phước Long physicians, three of them died within a 24-hour span. The fourth physician was able to escape through enemy lines. The wounded Dr. Phạm Hữu Phước was captured and sent to the North for three years of reeducation.[57] On top of the Phước Long mountain was the administrative center, about one mile by half-a-mile area, that had been shelled 3,000 rounds a day for seven days. Dr. Phước still wonders today how he could have remained alive despite this barrage of shells. Miracles do happen.

Fewer than 100 rangers were picked up by Col. Huấn, commander of the 81st Airborne Rangers, who circled for many hours over the jungle to look for his men. Lt. Đàm Hữu Phước, chief medic, and six other officers from the Tactical Operation Headquarters were taken prisoner around midnight. They were savagely interrogated and transferred to the North for seven years of incarceration in concentration camps.[58] Gen. Đống, III Corps commander, tendered his resignation to President Thiệu who accepted it.

The Phước Long battle revealed the true nature of the communists. They showed no respect for anyone, not even civilians or properties. This was not the first time nor the last. They shelled the town until they obliterated it or until defenders surrendered. That is why some South Vietnamese suggested that the Vietnam War was not only a "civil" war, but also a brutal conquest where people, civilians and soldiers, were slaughtered without pity for a senseless "liberation."

The Phước Long battle demonstrated to Hanoi and Saigon that regardless of provocation, the United States would not intervene to save South Vietnam.[59] It, in a sense, gave the green light to the communists to conquer the whole South. "The little-known battle for Phước Long was one of the most decisive battles of the war, for it marked the U.S. abandonment of its erstwhile ally to its fate."[60] Bùi Tín, former editor of *Nhan Dan*, commented,

> [North Vietnamese Prime Minister] Phạm Văn Đồng said of Gerald Ford..., "He's the weakest president in U.S. history; the people did not elect him; even if you gave him candy, he wouldn't dare to intervene in Vietnam again." We tested Ford's resolve by attacking Phước Long in January 1975. When Ford kept American B-52s in their hangars, our leadership decided on a big offensive against South Vietnam."[61]

When Hanoi drew up plans to attack Phước Long, their goals were two-fold: (1) to test the reaction of Washington in the face of a flagrant attack, (2) to use the town as a staging area for an attack on Saigon in 1976 or earlier. Once the town was captured, Hanoi decided to "liberate" South Vietnam through a final offensive. To achieve that goal, the PAVN launched the "Highland Campaign 275," which would pave the way for the construction and completion of the Eastern Trường Sơn Route or Corridor 613.

The Corridor 613 was basically a mirror image of the Western Trường Sơn Route (Hồ Chí Minh Trail) but would be built on the eastern side of the range and completely inside South Vietnam. A fuel pipeline would run alongside and the corridor, once completed, would allow a battalion to reach the vicinity of Saigon from North Vietnam in less than three weeks, riding all the way on trucks.[62] Its southern and northern anchors were respectively Phước Long and Cam Lộ in Quảng Trị province. The corridor would pass close by Khe Sanh, through Ashau Valley, on the western side of Pleiku and Kontum, through Ban Mê Thuột then to Phước Long. The next military target, therefore, was Ban Mê Thuột. Saigon, at that time, either did not know the purpose of the communist campaign or wrongly estimated the intention of Hanoi.[63]

Clouds on the sky were getting thicker and darker over South Vietnam. The conclusion seemed foregone and Saigon was about to lose the 21-year war. Col. William Le Gro from the U.S. Defense Attaché Office, Saigon, declared in his report that the staggering South Vietnamese losses in Phước Long "made him dizzy." His Vietnamese driver murmured, "Even the gods cried over Phước Long."[64]

The South Vietnamese were stunned. Not only had the U.S. cut them off materially, now it had publicly disowned them.[65] Gen. Cao Văn Viên, RVNAF Chief of Staff, wrote, "Almost gone was the hope that the United States would forcibly punish the North Vietnamese for their brazen violations of the cease fire agreement. The people's belief in the power of the armed forces and the government was also deeply shaken."[66]

On the gloomy future of the South Vietnamese, Isaacs wrote, "To the Vietnamese communists, 'liberation' may mean many things—but never the freedom of the individual human consciousness to doubt, question, dissent, argue, or search for a private path to truth…. To their ungentle hands, Vietnam's future was now committed."[67]

13

1975

Ban Mê Thuột, the Fall of I Corps, Phan Rang, Xuân Lộc

This chapter details the last battles of the Vietnam War: the battle of Ban Mê Thuột; the fall of I Corps; the battle of Phan Rang; and the battle of Xuân Lộc.

The Battle of Ban Mê Thuột (March 10–18, 1975)

Having taken Phước Long, the PAVN set sights on their next objective: Ban Mê Thuột, the third largest town in the highlands of central Vietnam and the site of an RVNAF air base. It sat on Highway 14, the main north-south road, and connected Ban Mê Thuột through Highway 21 to the sea at Nha Trang and Phan Rang. The fall of Ban Mê Thuột would set into motion a chain of decisions and military moves that would drastically change the continued resistance of South Vietnam. The area was large, the terrain favorable to the enemy, and the ARVN forces were widely dispersed throughout the area.

Forces Involved

The ARVN had two divisions along with seven ranger groups and one armored brigade to defend the II Corps, a large mountainous area dotted with a small network of roads. The ARVN 22d Division with its four regiments covered the coastal plains of Phú Yên and Bình Định. The ARVN 23d Division had three regiments in Pleiku and one in Ban Mê Thuột. The ranger groups were located west of Kontum City with one ranger group and some regional force units defending Ban Mê Thuột.

The PAVN for this battle had mobilized five divisions: the 3rd, F-10th, 320th, 968th, and 316th. The 3rd was stationed in the coastal area of Bình Định, the 968th opposite to Kontum and the F-10th, 320th, and 316th concentrating around Ban Mê Thuột. They had 15 additional regiments of tanks, artillery, and antiaircraft, and engineers in the area for a total of 75,000 to 80,000 men. This was a huge and well supplied force led by General Văn Tiến Dũng, General Giáp's deputy. The NVA plan of action was simple. They would attack a small outpost to divert attention away from the primary objective. They would then overwhelm Ban Mê Thuột by cutting inroads into the city and capturing the town airport.

ARVN Major General Phạm Văn Phú was the then II Corps commander. Not only did he lack airlift to move troops to threatened areas, he also made the error of ignoring his Corps' military intelligence report, believing that since the PAVN forces were used to either attack Kontum or Pleiku in their previous forays, they would return to the same targets in 1975 despite the fact that intelligence reports mentioned Ban Mê Thuột as the main target. Although this was a small misjudgment, that error would later be compounded by errors made by his own staff and soldiers, by the insufficient size of his force, his lack of airlift mobility, and the poor network of communicating roads which most likely would be blocked by enemy troops. That simple error would become a military disaster.

Gen. Phú was reluctant to reinforce Ban Mê Thuột because doing that would uncover his defenses in Pleiku (II Corps headquarters) and Kontum. He certainly did not want to be a defeated general, if the enemy attacked his command post.[1] Not believing intelligence reports, however, would lead to another disaster.

The Battle

On 4 March, PAVN troops cut Highway 21 at two places between Pleiku and Qui Nhơn. The following day, they cut Highway 19 in three places between Ban Mê Thuột and Nha Trang. On 8 March, the NVA 9th Regiment cut Highway 14 north of Buon Blech totally isolating Ban Mê Thuột.

At 0200 hours on 10 March, following a powerful artillery barrage, the PAVN attacked Ban Mê Thuột and the airfield east of town at Phượng Đức with two PAVN divisions led by armored and infantry units. By 1000 hours, the 320th Division was inside the city. The Advanced Command Post of the ARVN 23rd Division held out until it was mistakenly bombed by VNAF aircraft attempting to provide close air support. That strike cut all the defenders' communications and disrupted any further organized defense.

The PAVN forces surrounded the 53rd Regiment at Phượng Đức, preventing the unit from coming to the relief of Ban Mê Thuột, and by night time on 10 March, the center of the city was occupied although fighting was still going on west, south and east of the city.

On 11 March, the 23rd Ranger group that had been stationed at Buồn Hô about 20 miles north of Ban Mê Thuột was ordered to reinforce the city. While the rangers were advancing into Ban Mê Thuột, the commander of the 23rd Division, Brig. Gen. Lê Văn Tường halted the ranger counterattack and ordered them to secure a landing zone east of the city to evacuate his wife and children by helicopter. By the time the evacuation was completed, the ranger group was unable to enter Ban Mê Thuột because the enemy had tightly secured it. Tường had squandered the chance to reinforce the city.[2]

On 12 March, Phú announced that the city had surrendered. On the same day, President Thiệu ordered General Phú to retake Ban Mê Thuột. For that purpose, the JGS sent its last reserve troops, the 7th Ranger group, to Kontum to replace the 44th and 45th Regiments of the ARVN 23rd Division. The latter two regiments originally from Ban Mê Thuột were to be airlifted back to Phước An, 20 miles east of Ban Mê Thuột to help retake the city. As the rear base of the ARVN 23rd Division, Ban Mê Thuột also contained the dependents of that division.

The relief operation was badly conceived and could not be executed. Helicopter assets were limited in number and could not bring the troops in the allotted time. The first day, there were seven or eight Chinooks, the next day five, the third day three, then two and one. The counterattack was scheduled for 15 March without tank or artillery support because none could be brought up through the already blocked Highway 21. But before the attack began, the family syndrome kicked in. Once the helicopters landed at Phước An, the troops instead of preparing for the attack broke ranks to look for their family members. Once they found them, the ARVN soldiers threw away their uniforms and weapons and headed toward Nha Trang. The attack collapsed before it even began. The 23d Division commander, Tường, the following day received a minor facial wound. Instead of toughing it out, he had himself evacuated by helicopter to a Nha Trang hospital.[3]

The Fatal Decision

On 11 March, Thiệu called Prime Minister Trần Thiện Khiêm, Lt. Gen. Đặng Văn (Fat) Quang, and the chief of the JGS, Gen. Cao Văn Viên to the Independence Palace for a working breakfast. After breakfast was served, he pulled out a small map of Vietnam and began talking.

He argued that the RVNAF could no longer hold all of South Vietnam because of decreasing U.S. aid support. He would try to hold all the territory south of an east-west line slightly north of Tuy Hòa from the coastline to the Cambodian border. The area contained most of South Vietnam's people and resources. The territory north of the line including the highlands had to be given up. However, he would like if possible to hold to enclaves of large coastal cities like Huế, Đà Nẵng, Quảng Ngải, and Qui Nhơn. He also would like to control the Continental Shelf Line, where oil had been discovered.

The guests were stunned to hear Thiệu reverse course and accept losing territory. He was the one who previously advocated "no territorial concession," which was embodied by his policy of the "Four No's": (1) no negotiations with the communists; (2) no communist political activities south of the Demilitarized Zone (DMZ); (3) no coalition government; (4) and no surrender of territory to the North Vietnamese or VC.[4] In reality, Thiệu had thought about redeploying his forces for some time. The attack on Phước Long then Ban Mê Thuột—the proverbial final drop that causes water to overflow—triggered a drastic revision in Thiệu's policy for the defense of South Vietnam. He called his new strategy, "Light at the top, heavy on the bottom."[5] Then Viên spoke up:

> I said something to the effect that this redeployment was indeed necessary, and that I had embraced such an idea for a long time, but so far *I had kept it to myself* and considered it an improper proposal. First of all, it conflicted with prevailing national policy, and second, if I had made such a suggestion, it could well have been interpreted as an indication of defeatism. What I *refrained* from adding though was that I believed it was too late for any successful redeployment of such magnitude.[6]

Viên, instead of stressing the words "too late," did not elaborate further. Any redeployment of even one division, to be successful, would require a lot of planning at the level of the Joint General Staff and the division itself. Redeployment while the division was under attack was even more difficult, if not disastrous. The 1972 redeployment of the ARVN 3rd Division in I Corps led to the loss of Quảng Trị Province, the dismantling of the division, and the firing of I Corps Commander.

On 13 March, Thiệu called the I Corps Commander, Lieutenant General Ngô Quang Trưởng, back to Saigon and informed him that "he had to give up most of the I Corps." The order was explicit—I Corps was to keep only Đà Nẵng, its seaport and the immediate surrounding. Trưởng was "disturbed" by the order and was aware of the problems related to the movement of refugees and dependents in 1972, which turned a redeployment into a rout.

While the idea of redeployment of the I Corps was entertained, Thiệu asked Gen. Phú, the II Corps commander, to meet him at the American-built air and naval base at Cam Ranh Bay the following day. Present at that meeting were Prime Minister Khiêm, Lt. Gen. Quang, JGS Chief Viên, and President Thiệu. After Phú updated the situation in the II Corps, Thiệu asked him if he could retake Ban Mê Thuột. Phú weaseled and asked for reinforcements. Thiệu responded that he had none. Thiệu then told him about the redeployment concept and asked which route he would use in that situation. Because Routes 21 and 19 were blocked by enemy troops, Phú suggested Route 7B, which was a secondary route branching off Highway 14 about 20 miles south of Pleiku. This was a narrow, ruggedly surfaced road with one damaged bridge that needed repair. Its last section had been mined by Korean forces a few years earlier.[7]

The plan as conceived was (1) to withdraw the regular forces only (remaining elements of the 23rd Division, the Rangers, and the Armor Brigade) from Kontum and Pleiku and move them down the coast; (2) to abandon the Regional and Popular forces, dependents and civilians; (3) to keep the movement secret in order to "surprise the enemy"; and (4) to withdraw down route 7B.[8]

The question that later arose was whether Thiệu ordered Phú to abandon Pleiku and Kontum or just to redeploy forces to retake Ban Mê Thuột. The issue was purely academic because any major redeployment of forces from Pleiku and Kontum would result in the eventual loss of these two towns.

The choice of route 7B for the withdrawal had been criticized because the road had been abandoned and was in a general state of disrepair. It had been mined on both sides and was in need of bridge repair. However, 7B was used because it provided the "advantage of surprise."[9] "Gen. Viên must also bear responsibility for what transpired, if only for acquiescing so readily to Thiệu's omissions and misjudgments. It was Viên, moreover, who dealt the final blow to the chances for success by proposing Route 7B as the avenue of escape without bothering to determine which parts of it were usable and which were not."[10]

The Withdrawal

Phú flew back to his headquarters and had a meeting at 1800 hours with his key staff officers: Brig. Gen. Cẩm (Assistant for Operations), Brig. Gen. Sáng (Commander of the 6th Air Division), Brig. Gen. Tất (Ranger commander), and Col. Lý, his Chief of Staff. He told them about Thiệu's order of abandoning Kontum and Pleiku and leaving by route 7B. Everyone was stunned. Lý asked for a few days to do the planning as heavy equipment had to be moved. No was the answer; the redeployment would start the next day.

Colonel Tất, who had just been promoted to Brig. Gen., would command the redeployment. BG Cầm would be the supervisor. Gen. Phú flew the next morning to Nha Trang taking with him the chiefs of G1, G2, and G3. Gen. Cầm, the supervisor, flew to Tuy Hòa. Tất stayed in Pleiku and took care of his Rangers. Col. Lý had to do everything including notifying the unit commanders, the Americans, the CIA, the consulate, the DAO. The RF/PF, realizing they were left behind, rioted and became undisciplined. The Pleiku airfield was in state of panic as personnel and equipment began to be evacuated. The enemy shelled Pleiku and the airfield, causing additional pressure.

Rumors about the withdrawal forced the civilians also to act. They rapidly decided to join the mass withdrawal that would start on 16 March. The mass of refugees from Pleiku and Kontum began moving down 7B, competing with troops, their dependents and all kinds of transportation. Recovering from their initial surprise at II Corps' decision to retreat down 7B, the communists decided to attack the column at Chèo Reo on 17 March.

The road from Pleiku was terrible. People fell on the road and were crushed by tanks or trucks. Nobody could control anything. Troops were mixed with dependents and civilians and took care of children and wives. An armored unit was mistakenly blown up by VNAF pilots "flying too high."

At Chèo Reo, about 200,000 were crammed together at a small place. Some troops were looting while the enemy shelled the town. Battalion commanders and lower officers marched with their units but soon could not control their famished and tired men. They became easy targets for PAVN soldiers.

About 20,000 of the 60,000 troops that began in Pleiku and Kontum finally arrived in Tuy Hòa, but they were no longer fit for combat. Only 700 of the 7,000 Rangers escaped along with a handful of armored vehicles. Of the 400,000 civilians who tried to escape Kontum, only 100,000 got through.

The withdrawal turned out to be one of the "greatest disasters in the history of ARVN." Gen. Phú had been considered to be a "good division commander," but unfit for a Corps command.[11] Critics also blamed the General Staff for not actively supporting the withdrawal. There was no cooperation between the General Staff and the Corps headquarters for this major endeavor. Others, however, believed that the ARVN should have remained in Pleiku and Kontum and fought.[12]

The Fall of I Corps

The ARVN had five divisions including the Marines and Airborne, one armored brigade, four Ranger groups and some 220 Regional Force companies. The communists had seven divisions along with some reserve divisions above the DMZ.

The situation in I Corps was stable until the fall of Ban Mê Thuột. On 11 March, Thiệu ordered Trưởng to release the Airborne Division for immediate redeployment to Saigon. On 13 March, Trưởng flew to Saigon to explain to Thiệu that without the Airborne, one of the linchpins for the I Corps defense, Quảng Trị Province or even Huế might be lost. Thiệu argued that the Airborne was needed for the defense of the capital and that Trưởng had only to hold Đà Nẵng, with the rest of the I Corps expendable.[13]

Trưởng returned to Đà Nẵng disheartened and confused about his mission. He pulled the Marines out of Quảng Trị and sent the 369th Brigade north of Huế, the 285th Brigade south of Huế, and the 147th Marine Brigade to the old airborne positions west of Đà Nẵng. He then moved the 20th Tank Regiment and several batteries of 175 mm from Huế to an area south of Đà Nẵng. These sudden redeployments from Quảng Trị to Huế frightened the civilians, causing them to flee Quảng Trị for Đà Nẵng. Seeing the flow of refugees, the people of Huế became nervous and joined them by heading south. By 18 March Highway 1 was crowded with refugees and on 19 March, the PAVN reoccupied Quảng Trị without a fight.

The same day, Trưởng flew to Saigon to discuss the difficulties of holding both Huế and Đà Nẵng. Trưởng had devised a plan to hold both Huế and Chu Lai and it took him four hours to convince Thiệu. Before departing, Trưởng told Thiệu about the demoralizing rumor that Thiệu had struck a "deal" to cede the northern provinces to the communists. Thiệu did not respond and left the refugee problem to Trưởng. Prime Minister Khiêm took Trưởng aside and hinted that the president might also pull out the Marines from I Corps. Upon hearing this, Trưởng's spirits were "crushed."[14]

By that time, the PAVN had gathered nine divisions in I Corps to deal with the four ARVN divisions (the Airborne had returned to Saigon). Enemy forces put pressure from the north, south and west to force the ARVN to withdraw into Đà Nẵng for a final battle.

On 20 March, Trưởng flew to the Marine Division Command Post to update them on the latest news. At 1330, Thiệu's recorded message went over the airwaves ordering Huế to be held at "all costs," a major departure from his previous order.[15] When Trưởng returned to his headquarters, he received a "flash" (high priority) message from Saigon stating that the JGS had no resources to resupply the three enclaves: Huế, Đà Nẵng, and Chu Lai and that he was free to redeploy as he saw fit.

On 21 March, the PAVN attacked Highway 1 between Huế and Đà Nẵng. Although the ARVN response had been adequate, the enemy brought in reinforcements overnight that caused severe damage to the ARVN forces. Highway 1 was cut between Huế and Đà Nẵng. The plan was to evacuate the ARVN 1st Division and the Marines half by ship at the Thuận An inlet north of Huế. The other half had to walk to Tư Hiền Estuary, which would be bridged by ARVN engineers, travel overland to catch Highway 1 south of Phú Lộc, and then proceed into Đà Nẵng.[16]

The withdrawal turned out to be a costly failure as neither the Marines nor the Navy carried out their missions. The Navy failed to sink the required boats and many 1st Division soldiers were drowned at Tư Hiền estuary in the rising tide. Others were shot down by PAVN elements because the Marines failed to secure the high ground after crossing the estuary. The withdrawal by sea at Thuận An did not go much better. The Navy ships arrived late and strong seas prevented them from taking more than half of the troops. Equipment had to be left behind and enemy shelling disrupted the evacuation.

At the same time, the situation collapsed in the southern sector of I Corps. On 24 March, after crashing through the defense lines of the 5th Regiment, 2nd Division, one NVA armored column in a daring raid took the capital city of Tam Kỳ by surprise. This cut Highway 1 between Chu Lai and Đà Nẵng. The 2nd Division was forced to withdraw to Chu Lai where, surrounded and disorganized, it was ordered to evacuate by ship to Cù Lao Ré, some 20 miles offshore. Only a portion of the 2nd Division could be evacuated.

With the collapse of the northern and southern fronts of I Corps, the defense rested on the 3rd Division, two Marine brigades, and various Regional and Popular units. They were confronted by five enemy divisions. As more and more refugees poured into this city of 300,000 inhabitants, swelling its population to more than two million people, government control broke down. Refugees coming from overrun district towns helped spread panic and disorder. Bands of children, hungry and thirsty, wandered aimlessly on the streets, demolishing everything which happened to fall into their hands. Đà Nẵng was seized by the convulsions of collective hysteria.[17]

General Trưởng called Saigon to request food and vital provisions as well as transportation to evacuate people. An attempt to stage a massive airlift failed when refugees overran the airfield and mobbed the airplanes as they tried to take off. More than 200 operational aircraft were then left on the airfield.[18]

On 28 March, Gen. Trưởng tried a last ditch effort to restore order and defend the city. Unit integrity had completely disintegrated and many units had ceased to exist as cohesive fighting forces. Even at I Corps headquarters, the men deserted. By nightfall, North Vietnamese forces entered the outskirts of the city. As PAVN shelling severed the lines between Đà Nẵng and Saigon, Trưởng decided to withdraw what remained of his forces.

On 29 March, evacuation began at three embarkation points—the end of Hải Vân Pass, the foot of Non Nước (Marble) Mountain, and the edge of Hội An Estuary. The evacuation was not successful. Only 6,000 Marines and 4,000 other assorted troops succeeded in reaching Navy ships and civilian craft. The Marine evacuation was the most successful and the 3rd Division fared the worst. Of its 12,000 men, only 5,000 reached the embarkation area and 1,000 were evacuated.[19]

By 30 March, the PAVN occupied Đà Nẵng and controlled all of Military Region I. "Faced with superior numbers and firepower, and beset by poor leadership, lack of discipline, rumor, conflicting and confusing orders, and concern for family members, the South Vietnamese troops, for the most part quit fighting and began to fend for themselves."[20]

The ARVN 22nd division not only "fought well, but valiantly under Brig. Gen. Phan Đình Niệm against the PAVN 3rd and 968th Divisions."[21] Two regimental commanders of the 22nd pleaded with their division commander to stay and fight. When he refused, the two colonels refused to leave and committed suicide.[22]

The Battle for Phan Rang (1–16 April 1975)

On 1 April 1975 as the PAVN continued to drive south on Highway 1, the VNAF at Nha Trang AFB moved its 2nd Air Division and their families to Thanh Sơn AB outside Phan Rang, about 50 miles southwest of Nha Trang. The PAVN then captured Nha Trang City and Nha Trang AB the following day.

Thanh Sơn was an American airbase that was progressively handed over to the RVNAF in March–May 1972. It was home to the 6th Air Division until 1 April 1975, when it received the 2nd Air Division from Nha Trang AB. The 92nd Tactical Wing had three squadrons of A-37s and three squadrons of UH-1 helicopters (Medevac).

Air Force Brig. Gen. Phạm Ngọc Sáng, commander of the 6th Air Division, was worried about the overall situation in Thanh Sơn AB as crowds of civilians and soldiers stormed the airfield asking for a ride to Saigon. Security was provided by Col. Lê Văn Phát and his 3rd Airborne Brigade that was retreating from its position at the nearby M'Drak Pass.

On 2 April, 2nd Air Division commander BG Nguyễn Văn Lương left Thanh Sơn AB in his C-47 for meeting at Tân Sơn Nhứt AB setting up panic among RVNAF and ARVN forces at the base who feared being left behind. Order was restored by the 3rd Brigade as the refugees were evacuated by two Australian Air Force C-130s.

The following morning, the RVNAF at Thanh Sơn AB launched a heliborne operation to rescue the remaining ARVN 2nd, 5th and 6th Airborne Battalions that had been cut off at M'Drak Pass successfully evacuating over 800 troopers. The fleet consisted of 40 Hueys, 12 helicopter gunships, the six Chinooks sent by Saigon and a command-and-control helicopter. Two flights of A-37 bombers provided air cover.[23] That same day, the USS *Durham* picked up 3,500 refugees in the waters off Phan Rang.

On 4 April, the two remaining provinces of the II Corps were incorporated in the III Corps, and LG Nguyễn Vĩnh Nghi—former IV Corps commander—arrived to take over the Phan Rang front from BG Sáng. One would ask why Gen. Nghi volunteered for this difficult, if not impossible job; he was probably attempting to redeem his reputation, having been sacked for corruption on 30 October 1974. Nghi brought with him Thiệu's personal promise that two divisions would be assigned to defend Phan Rang. In any case the only troops Nghi brought with him were a few staff officers to form a III Corps Forward Headquarters.[24]

Battle

From 7 and 8 April 1975, the 2nd Airborne Brigade flew into Phan Rang to replace the 3rd Airborne Brigade, which moved back to Saigon. The 3rd Airborne Brigade immediately cleared Highway 1 and recaptured the village of Bà Râu and Bà Tháp while the 11th Airborne Battalion recaptured Du Long Town and Du Long Pass from the VC and the 5th Airborne Battalion cleared route 11.

On 10 April, the PAVN 10th Division moved in the direction of Dalat. After air reconnaissance confirmed the movement of the 10th Division, A-37 airplanes attacked the convoy, destroying six river-crossing vehicles on 10 April, five trucks on 11 April, seven trucks on 12 April, and nine trucks on 13 April.

The 5th Airborne Battalion was withdrawn to Saigon on 11 April and the rest of the 2nd Airborne Brigade was withdrawn on 12 April. They were replaced by the 31st Ranger Battalion and the ARVN 4th and 5th Regiments.

The PAVN meanwhile wanted to neutralize Phan Rang and at 0530 on 14 April, the PAVN 3rd Division began an artillery attack on the 31st Ranger at Du Long pass and the 3rd Airborne at Bà Râu. This was followed by infantry and tank attacks which were repulsed. Two A-37s accidentally bombed the Rangers. The PAVN bypassed the Rangers and attacked Du Long Town, rapidly defeating the Regional Forces. Reinforcements failed to connect with the Rangers who were withdrawn at 1600 hours with only 80 Rangers successfully returning to the Thanh Sơn AB.

At the same time, the PAVN 25th Regiment was able to penetrate the Thanh

Sơn AB despite helicopter gunship fire and head toward the hangar where they were met with the 11th Airborne Battalion waiting transport back to Saigon. Four armored personnel carriers and A-37s forced the PAVN back outside the perimeter with 100 PAVN losses versus six ARVN killed and one M-113 destroyed.[25]

On 15 April, the PAVN shelled the 3rd Airborne Battalion at Bà Râu and Kiên and attacked them. Although outnumbered the airborne held the attacks until midday when they blew the highway bridge before escaping into Ca Dau Mountain to the east.

At 0500 on 16 April, the PAVN launched a massive attack against Ca Dau Mountain and the base perimeter. It began with a heavy bombardment followed by an armored attack led by 20 tanks and armored personnel carriers of the 4th battalion, 203rd Tank Brigade supported by trucks mounted infantry of the 101st Regiment and antiaircraft guns. While the lead tank was destroyed by an ARVN rocket, the PAVN force rapidly cut through the 3rd Airborne Platoon holding Kiên.

Multiple airstrikes were conducted by the A-37s on the armored column, destroying tanks and trucks and dispersing the trucks of mounted infantry. Armed gunships from Lê Văn Bút's squadron soon joined in the fray. The armored column fought back hard, blazing away at the A-37s with antiaircraft weapons. Some planes sustained heavy damage and limped back to base.

While the armored column pushed ahead, the trucks carrying the 101st Regiment's infantry slowed down to take cover. The antiaircraft units protecting the infantry, however, had fallen back behind. Profiting from that development, the A-37s mounted a second attack on the column destroying more vehicles and trucks. The PAVN 3rd Division came to the rescue of the 101st Regiment by pinning down the Rangers and attacking the airborne at Ca Du. By 0700 hours, they controlled Phan Rang. Pushing further south, they secured the Ninh Chu port cutting off Route 1.

A PAVN battalion-sized task force supported by tanks headed toward Thanh Sơn AB via route 11. They routed the 5th and 4th newly reconstituted Ranger Regiments and using explosives cut through eleven rows of barbed wire and stormed the airfield. The base was attacked by two other sides. Helicopter gunships that took off were hit by SA-7 missiles fired from a hilltop near the airfield. Defense continued to crumble. Gen. Nghi ordered a retreat toward Ca Na, a rocky peninsula 19 miles south of Phan Rang. Gen. Nghi, Gen. Sáng, Col. Lương along with James Lewis, a CIA officer at the U.S. Embassy, and a large group of military and civilians escaped through a hole in the fence.

About three miles south of Phan Rang, they decided to hide in a ditch waiting for the night to continue their escape. Around midnight, they punched through a line of PAVN guards and while some broke loose others were caught by nearby troops. Nghi was the highest ranking officer ever captured on the battlefields of South Vietnam. Lt. Col. Bút escaped with Sáng's group. He made it back to Saigon by walking along Route 1. Later, he jokingly talked about "being bombed by my own Air Force the entire way home." At the last minute before Thanh Sơn was being overrun, Col. Lê Văn Thảo radioed one of his A-37s which landed and picked him up. They flew to Tân Sơn Nhứt with what remained of Thảo's wing. Of the 72 A-37s he had in early March, only a third were able to escape on 16 April after more than one month of nonstop fighting. No other RVNAF wing had fought with such courage and aggression as Thảo's 92nd Tactical Air Wing.[26]

Nguyễn Văn Tú, commander of the 31st Ranger Battalion escaped by foot with some of his men. BG. Trần Văn Nhứt escaped by helicopter to a Vietnamese Navy ship off shore. Gen. Nghi, Sáng, and James Lewis were taken to Nha Trang, then Đà Nẵng, then flown to North Vietnam. Lewis was released in December 1975 after having suffered terrible torture. Gen. Nghi was released in 1987 after 12 years of captivity.

As for BG Phạm Ngọc Sáng, because of his staunch anti-communist views he was not released until 1992, when he began bleeding from his colon in the hospital. He was denied any family visit during the first 13 years of his captivity. His courage inspired his men to stand up for freedom. One of his men wrote to him years later:

> I sometimes proudly tell my friends that I was fortunate to serve under a commander such as you—someone who did not, as other commanders and their units did, flee before the enemy arrived. I must thank you for giving me that source of pride. If it had not been for you, perhaps I would not have been imprisoned, my life might have been easier, and my children might have been more successful in life, but for my entire life I would have carried with me the feeling that I had not lived up to my responsibilities.[27]

The Battle for Xuân Lộc (9–21 April 1975)

The loss of I and II Corps dealt a terrible blow to the prestige and morale of the RVNAF because it involved the most capable ARVN units. Except for the two Airborne brigades withdrawn from I Corps and the few units that could be reconstituted from the demoralized troops extracted from the northern Corps areas, the defense of South Vietnam now rested with the six divisions and two Armored brigades and the various Ranger groups, Regional and Popular forces of the III and IV Corps.[28]

The three regular divisions deployed in the IV Corps area (the 7th, 9th, and 21st) were pinned down by local communist units and not available to help with the defense of the III Corps or Saigon. Toward the end of April, there were some 13 PAVN divisions ringing around Saigon with another four or so held in reserve. While Xuân Lộc sat on National Route 1, the nearby town of Dầu Giây lay at the intersection of Routes 1 and 20, two of three paved highways linking Saigon to the northeastern section of the country. Thus controlling Xuân Lộc would give access to Saigon, South Vietnam's capital.

The battle of Xuân Lộc was: (1) the only sustained battle of division-sized forces; (2) the one place where tactical air support was employed with significant effect; and (3) the only engagement where major ARVN forces stood their ground and consistently fought well.

Order of Battle

The ARVN 18th Division at Xuân Lộc, 38 miles northeast of Saigon, had three regiments (43rd, 48th and 52nd Infantry Regiments). There were also five armored brigades, four regional force battalions, two artillery units equipped with 42 artillery guns, and two companies of civilian self-defense forces. On 12 April, Xuân Lộc was reinforced with the 1st Airborne Brigade, three armored brigades, the 8th Task Force from the ARVN 5th Division, and the 33rd Ranger Battalion. The ARVN 18th

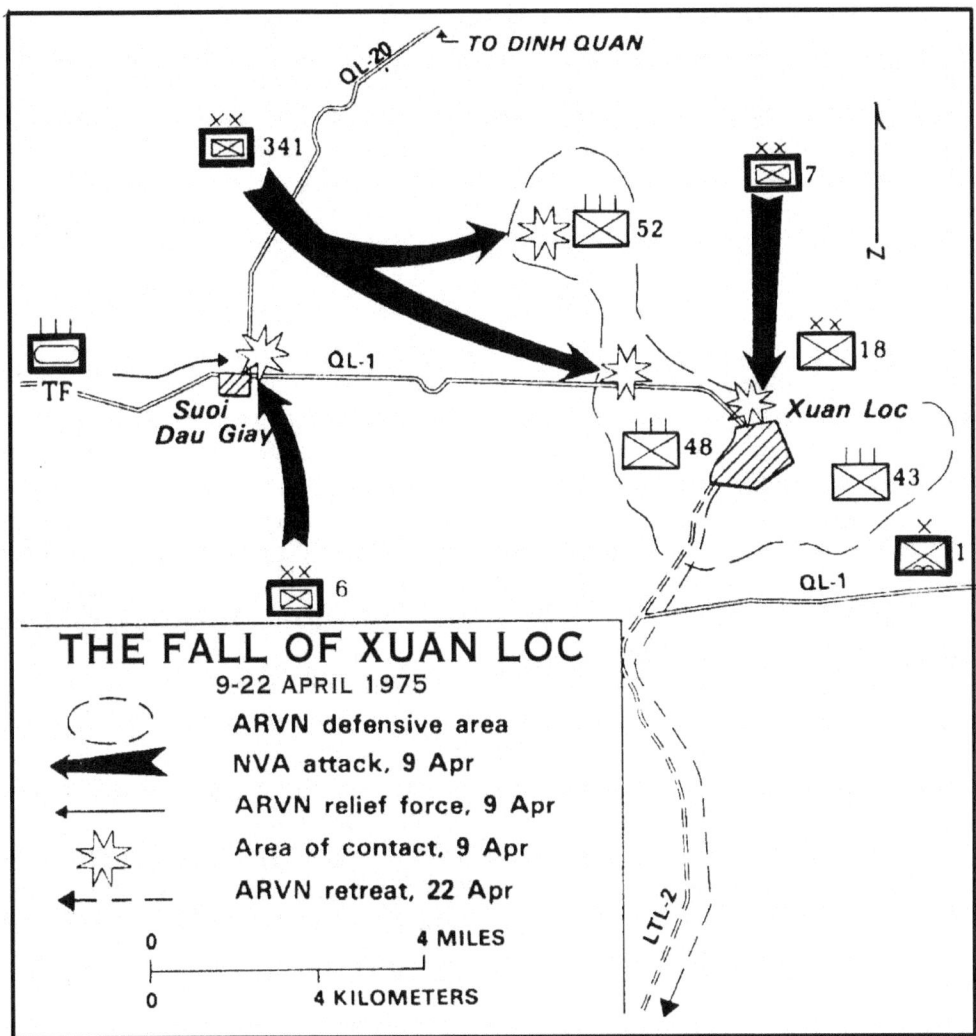

Figure 13-01: Battle of Xuân Lộc (Cao Van Vien, *The Final Collapse*. Washington, D.C.: Department of the Army, 1983, p. 131).

Division was commanded by Brig. Gen. Lê Minh Đảo, who was ready to receive them, although his forces were stretched thin. Lê Minh Đảo proclaimed, "I vow to hold Xuân Lộc. I don't care how many divisions the other side sends against me, I will knock them down."[29]

The PAVN 4th Army Corps, which overran Phước Long several months earlier, approached Xuân Lộc from the north-east after conquering Tây Ninh, Bình Long and Long Khánh. It fielded three combat divisions (6th, 7th and 341st Infantry Divisions). Those divisions had support from the 71st Anti-Aircraft Regiment, two combat engineering regiments, the 26th Communications Regiment, two armored battalions, two artillery battalions. The 3rd Army Corps, on the other hand, came from the north-west after defeating the ARVN in the Central Highlands. NVA Gen. Hoàng Cầm, commander of the PAVN 4th Army Corps, decided on a frontal assault of the ARVN forces at Xuân Lộc.

Battle

On 9 April, after a 4,000-round mortar, artillery, and rocket barrage, the NVA 341st Division attacked Xuân Lộc from the northwest while the NVA 6th and 7th Divisions pounded from the east and north-northeast respectively. They held the police station and the local ranger base although they faced stiff resistance by the defenders. The ARVN soldiers fought hard because their families had been evacuated to Saigon.

Đảo had his "meat grinder" set up by asking his artillery chief to preregister all his 36 guns (24 105 mm and 12 155 mm) onto likely avenues of approach. Revetments were used to protect the guns, which once fired were pulled back into bunkers. This would render counter-battery fire ineffective. "Their artillery could not find us," he later remarked.[30] He also moved his soldiers to the outskirts of the city, thinking the communists would concentrate their opening barrage on the city center. He was correct as the first shot scored a hit on his own house in Xuân Lộc. Luckily, he was not at home.[31]

Hoàng Cầm's main assault forces were pinned down not only by artillery and air strikes, but also by determined infantry. Each ARVN soldier had been assigned his own defensive position. By midmorning Đảo's forces counterattacked encircling enemy's unit. But the 4th Corps had cut off Route 1 at the Dầu Giây intersection isolating the ARVN 52nd Regiment from Xuân Lộc.

On 10 April, the ARVN 43rd Regiment made counterattacks against the PAVN, causing it to yield ground. Although reserve regiments from the PAVN 6th and 7th Divisions were thrown into the battle, ARVN soldiers doggedly held onto their positions. The communists fired another 1,000 rounds into the smoking city. Xuân Lộc was a burning pile of rubble. Virtually every building was in ruins.

RVNAF fighter-bombers from Biên Hòa and Tân Sơn Nhứt Air bases flew more than 200 bombing sorties in support of the ARVN 18th Division. That afternoon, the ARVN counterattacked again. This proved to be too much for the two regiments of the PAVN 341st Division trapped at the edge of the city. By night time, Xuân Lộc was back into ARVN hands.

On 11 April, the PAVN struck again for the third day in a row, but the ARVN 43rd and 52nd Regiments counterattacked on the enemy's flanks. The JGS ordered additional troops from the Củ Chi area and airlifted the 1st Airborne Brigade into an area just south of Xuân Lộc. Encouraged by the RVNAF's determination, General Smith sent a message to the JGS lauding the "valor and aggressiveness of GVN troops."

Gen. Cầm wrote in his *Memoir*, "This was the most ferocious battle I had ever been involved in! My personal assessment was that, after three days of battle, even after committing our reserves, the situation had not improved and we had suffered significant casualties."[32] The *History of the People's Army* reported, "The 341st Division alone lost 1,100 cadres and soldiers killed and wounded during just the first two days—9 and 10 April. Our artillery ammunition became seriously depleted. More than half of our tanks were knocked out."[33]

Gen. Toàn, ARVN III Corps commander, moved the 1st Airborne Brigade, commanded by Colonel Nguyễn Văn Định, to reinforce the 18th Division. Although cut off and under artillery fire, the 52nd Regiment still held at Dầu Giây intersection. On the night of 11 April, Gen. Đảo secretly relocated his headquarters to the military zone of Tân Phong to continue his fight.

On 12 April, Cầm launched two more attacks against the northeastern edge of the city. Both were broken up by VNAF air strikes. PAVN losses climbed to 2,000 dead and wounded in four days of fighting, while ARVN casualties were only several hundred.

Facing stiff ARVN resistance, PAVN Gen. Dũng told Giáp that because of a supply problem, particularly of artillery and tank ammunition, an attack on Saigon had to be delayed. He decided to attack Đảo's two weaknesses: the 52nd Regiment and Biên Hòa Air Base. On 13 April, he moved the armor-supported NVA 95B regiment against the 52nd Regiment and ordered Artillery Group 75 to train its long range 130 mm guns on the airbase in Biên Hòa to keep the VNAF on the ground.

Fighting became fierce, as the PAVN used massive artillery fire and "human sea" infantry tactics to launch one assault after another against the GVN's defensive forces. On 14 April, VNAF C-130 transport aircraft were converted to a bombing mode and were used to drop 15,000-lb. "Daisy Cutter" bombs on enemy concentrations. Cluster bombs (CBU) were also used with great effect at Xuân Lộc. After Saigon had exhausted its supply of CBU, the defense could no longer be sustained.

On 15 April, a sapper squad infiltrated the Biên Hòa airbase and blew up part of its ammunition dump. Four 130 mm guns began shelling the airbase cratering the runway and damaging several planes.

The NVA 95B Regiment and the 33rd Regiment, 6th Division began attacking the ARVN 52nd Regiment respectively at Horseshoe Hill and Dầu Giây. In perhaps the 18th Division's finest moment, in one day of heavy fighting, two ARVN companies supported by artillery had stopped and severely damaged one of the finest PAVN regiments.[34]

The ARVN 18th Division had fought valiantly, but by the evening of 15 April sheer numbers and superior firepower turned the tide. General Đảo was forced to evacuate his forces from inside the city. On 16 April, helicopters extracted the survivors of the 43rd Regiment. That same day, the PAVN overran the 52nd regiment, which by that time had lost 70 percent of its original strength. The ARVN 18th Division had held out for three weeks against all odds, destroying 37 tanks and killing over 5,000 attackers.[35]

The Retreat

Lacking further reinforcement the 18th Division and other defenders were withdrawn on 21 April. Orders had been given to retreat along Route 2, the dirt road leading out of Xuân Lộc. This would be a 25-mile march at night to an assembly area in Phước Tuy. However, to get out of Xuân Lộc safely was a tricky problem. First, Đảo developed a deception plan to distract his opponent. He ordered the Airborne Brigade to mount an attack against the PAVN 7th Division east of Xuân Lộc on 20 April. Đảo would walk with his retreating troops while Colonel Ngô Kỳ Dũng would fly overhead in Đảo's helicopter to provide command and control.

The first unit to leave Tân Phong at 2000 hours was the 48th Regiment, followed by the armor, then the remaining artillery and logistics units. When the artillery reached the Long Giao outpost, it would establish a firebase to support the retreat.

Next would be the RF and any civilians. The two battalions of the 43rd Regiment, the 2nd Battalion/52nd Regiment and the Airborne.[36]

Despite the difficulties, Đảo and the 18th Division conducted a masterly retreat. Đảo's personal leadership made the difference. He walked with the troop column to provide command and take immediate response to any problem encountered. All forces safely reached the assembly area in the morning of 21 April.

14

Self Sacrifice, Reeducation Camps, Postwar Killings

This chapter discusses (1) *tuẫn tiết*, or self-sacrifice, in Vietnamese history in general and the Vietnam War in particular; (2) the re-education camps; and (3) extra-judicial killings during the postwar period.

Tuẫn Tiết in Vietnamese History

To die for one's country is not only an act of bravery, it is also *the* act of bravery. For soldiers, it is just an extension of their military career, a part of their duty. As leaders have asked their soldiers to sacrifice themselves for the good of the society, it is only right for leaders to go through the same motion and practice what they have preached.

As war is seen as a noble act in response to outside aggression, *tuẫn tiết* (self-immolation, or suicide) serves as a redemption in case of defeat. It is also a way to tell the enemy: "You might have won the battle/war, but you don't deserve it because you don't have *chính nghĩa* (just cause)." It is not only just cause, it is also the belief that the cause one fought for, deserves one's total sacrifice.

Although *tuẫn tiết* involves a suicide, there is no good corresponding word in English because the act itself is not practiced in the Western world. Secondly, the word suicide does not convey the moral and courageous implication of the act itself. It is a closer equivalent of hara-kiri or seppuku.[1] Although hara-kiri is practically a disembowelment, its practice varies from person to person. If the blade is inserted deeply enough, it could cause immediate death through intra-abdominal bleeding. If inserted superficially, the still alive victim would be beheaded by the assistant. While *tuẫn tiết* and hara-kiri can be technically different, the end result is the same: the death of the person through his own hand or the hands of his assistant.

Vietnam is one of the rare countries in the world where leaders killed themselves when they lost a war. We will review these cases of *tuẫn tiết* during the pre- and anti-colonial wars and the anti-communist war.

I. Past Self-Immolation

At least seven Vietnamese leaders are known to have killed themselves for their country during the anti-colonial war: Võ Tánh, Ngô Tùng Châu, Võ Duy Ninh, Trương

Công Định, Phan Thanh Giản, Nguyễn Hữu Huấn, and Hoàng Diệu. Many more officials could have committed suicide throughout history although their deeds may not have been recorded.

1. Võ Tánh and Ngô Tùng Châu

Võ Tánh was one of the military warlords from Gò Công in the Mekong Delta who had defeated the Tây Sơn around Gia Định-Saigon in 1783.[2] Nguyễn Ánh, the scion of the Nguyễn dynasty, realized he needed this valiant free spirit's assistance if he wanted to defeat the Tây Sơn. It was only in 1787 that he was able to lure and recruit him into his army by giving him his sister as concubine. From that time onward, Võ Tánh participated in most of Nguyễn Ánh's battles against the Tây Sơn and proved to be one of his best generals.

In March 1799, Võ Tánh's troops besieged Qui Nhơn—a port city in central Vietnam—which surrendered after four months of resistance. Nguyễn Ánh changed the city's name to Bình Định (Pacified). He left Võ Tánh and Ngô Tùng Châu in charge of the city that remained in a rebel controlled area and returned to his base in Saigon.

Nguyễn Ánh at that time was waging a seasonal or "monsoon" war against the Tây Sơn by attempting to retake rebel-controlled regions one by one from south to north. In the spring, when the winds blew away from the Indochinese peninsula, he loaded his crack troops onto his sailboats and headed toward a military target in the Vietnamese central coastal area. He dropped them off close to the target area where he met the rest of his troops that had arrived by land. The combined army then attacked the target, which was decisively taken. In the fall, he left troops to guard the newly conquered region and headed home to Saigon with the monsoon winds, which in November blew back toward the peninsula. Each year, he had about a six to eight-month window to wage war as the winds shifted biannually.[3]

Realizing the strategic loss of Bình Định, which controlled access to Phú Xuân (Huế)—the Tây Sơn headquarters—Tây Sơn General Trần Quang Diệu decided to retake the city and its surroundings. In early 1800, Diệu had his troops guard all land exits of Bình Định while a Tây Sơn naval fleet blocked the sea approach. Nguyễn Ánh in early April came to the rescue of Võ Tánh who had been holed up inside the besieged Bình Định. It was a tough battle, which lasted until February 1801 (ten months) before the Tây Sơn fleet was destroyed after a bloody 28-hour sea battle. With the sea approach cleared, Nguyễn Ánh ordered Võ Tánh to get out of town: the latter refused to leave without his soldiers.

Nguyễn Ánh at that time realized that the bulk of the Tây Sơn troops were encamped in front of Bình Định leaving the capital Phú Xuân almost defenseless. Leaving Võ Tánh to hold the Tây Sơn army in place, he moved with his fleet to Phú Xuân and up the Hương River where as expected he found minimal resistance. His troops took over the city on 15 June 1801—26 years after the day he was forced to leave that city.

Bình Định in the meantime was still besieged by the Tây Sơn. For the last 17 months, the defenders had put up a valiant resistance. Running out of food supplies, they finally decided to kill their animals (horses and elephants) for their meat. Võ Tánh knowing the end had arrived, discussed the surrender with General Diệu: his only request was that his soldiers would be spared. He then had a scaffolding built on which he stacked the remaining gunpowder. Dressed in full military regalia, he got up on the scaffolding and lit the powder, which blew him into pieces. That was the signal for his men to open the garrison's gates for the Tây Sơn to take over. Ngô Tùng Châu had preceded him in death by taking poison. When General Diệu entered the citadel, he realized the bravery of his adversaries and had their remains buried with honors.[4]

2. Võ Duy Ninh

A combined Franco-Spanish force (2,500 French troops aboard 13 warships and 450 Spanish troops on a warship) attacked Đà Nẵng on 1 September 1858. It was met with severe resistance from the Huế imperial troops, led by General Nguyễn Tri Phương. After five months of fierce combat, the invaders could only control an inhabited stretch of shore. Frustrated, the French commander Rigault de Genouilly took two-thirds of his troops and ships and sailed on 10 February 1859 toward Vũng Tàu where he thought he would face lesser resistance. He blasted his way along the Saigon River before taking the Gia Định citadel on 17 February 1859.[5]

Aware of the Đà Nẵng attack by the French, General Võ Duy Ninh, the military commander of Gia Định-Saigon citadel, thought his troops would need some retraining to keep abreast of new tactical maneuvers. The Vietnamese used breech loading muskets and each soldier was able to practice shooting one single round each year. He unfortunately picked the wrong time for the exercise: he did it when the French came to town. The remaining troops that guarded the citadel were unable to hold the French in place. Frightened by the massive shelling, they ran away. General Ninh, when made aware of the defeat, committed suicide rather than surrender the Gia Định citadel to the French.[6]

3. Trương Công Định (1820–1863)

Định, born in 1820 in central Vietnam, moved with his father—a colonel—to Saigon. He later married a wealthy Định Tường landowner's daughter and used his wife's financial resources to build a đồn điền (plantation). He began enrolling impoverished workers and soldiers to assist him in his agricultural business. After Võ Duy Ninh committed suicide in February 1859, Định rallied around him imperial troops that had fled in disarray. With about 1,000 troops, he began a guerrilla warfare against the French. His initial military successes led the king to grant him the title of deputy commander of the southern forces.

By 1861, his army of 6,000 men gave him many battle successes. The following year, he was promoted to commander of all the southern nghĩa quân (volunteer soldiers for a cause). The French were frustrated at not being able to crush the rebels as they "were everywhere and nowhere." He then moved his troops to Gò Công where he continued his guerrilla movement.

When the 1862 Saigon treaty was signed,[7] the Huế court cut off its support to Định and his nghĩa quân for fear that the French would use the insurrection as an excuse to expand their conquest in the South. The court even ordered Phan Thanh Giản to pressure Định to lay down his arms. Định not only lost the logistical support of the imperial court, but the French were also free to focus their effort on fighting the rebels. Local people who collaborated with the French gave the rebels new problems. Định, however, refused to comply with the court's pressure, arguing that his mandate came not from Huế but from the will of the people in the occupied territories. He gave himself the title of Great General for the Pacification of the Westerners and asked for the financial and moral support of the local people now that he had lost the court's support.

In February 1863, Admiral Bonard encircled Định in his stronghold of Gò Công from which he escaped after sustaining heavy casualties. On 19 August 1863 betrayed by a former rebel, he was ambushed and wounded. Facing imminent capture, he took his own life.[8]

Years later, Định's wife returned to her hometown much impoverished. King Tự Đức felt that Định was a righteous man who deserved praise. He felt a need to support his widow who was alone, poor, sick and miserable. He granted her a monthly allowance of 20 *quan* of cash and two phường of rice. This was more than a mandarin could expect for his pay.[9]

4. Phan Thanh Giản (1796–1867)

Giản was the first southerner to pass the mandarinate exam—which would qualify him for an administrative or military position in the king's government—with honors at the very young age of 30. Many qualified candidates could not pass the exam until their mid-forties. In 1831, he was appointed province chief of Quảng Nam. The troops he sent to quell a Cham rebellion were defeated and caused him to be removed from his post. Although he was given another position, he learned to accept failures and successes in a dignified and stoic, if not fatalistic way.

The Huế court at the time of the French invasion was divided between the chủ chiến (hawks led by Nguyễn Tri Phương, Hoàng Diệu, Tôn Thất Thuyết, and Hoàng Tả Viêm) and the chủ hòa (doves led by Phan Thanh Giản, Lâm Duy Hiệp, Nguyễn Bá Nghi, and Trương Đăng Quế). Despite being hawkish, the chủ chiến were unable to think of any strategy to oppose the French invasion. They did not contemplate mass resistance probably because the court had in the past so antagonized the South that any thought in that direction would prove futile. They had taken down the Lê Văn Khôi rebellion, sentenced the leaders to death, and massacred about 2,000 people. They had desecrated Lê Văn Duyệt's tomb and put three generations of his family to death. They had placed the South under direct court control and sent all southern generals and lettered men away from the South, the upper leadership of which was no longer native. Southerners no longer felt like trusting the government. The chủ hòa, on the other hand, felt that they could no longer resist the overwhelming firepower and military force of the foreigners.

The court sent Phan Thanh Giản and Lâm Duy Hiệp to negotiate the Saigon treaty, which was signed on 5 June 1862. Besides the loss of three eastern provinces, freedom for Catholic priests to proselytize was granted throughout Vietnam. King Tự Đức flew into a rage when he heard the news. By performing a necessary but unpleasant duty, Giản and his colleagues were not only vilified by the court, but also rebuked by Tự Đức, who called them "criminals."[10]

Tự Đức, however, did not take any sanctions against them; on the contrary, he elevated Giản to Viceroy of the Southern Region and Resident Grand Dignitary and Plenipotentiary (Chánh Sứ Toàn Quyền Đại Thần). Giản, being 67 at that time, requested permission to retire, but his request was denied. He was sent to France to negotiate the return of the three eastern provinces, although he was not successful. He became aware of France's technical and military advances. He saw trains running faster than horses, ports crowded with ships armed with powerful guns, and gas lamps burning brighter than oil lamps. When he told Tự Đức about his assessments, the latter brushed away Giản's apprehensions by stating that "if people were faithful and sincere, tigers would pass by without hurting them, crocodiles would swim away and everyone would listen to them."

Tự Đức—as the top Confucian man in the country—implied that foreigners, French included, would respect a man of a high level of rectitude like Phan Thanh Giản if the latter fully believed in the Confucian doctrine. Having seen power slipping away from him—through loss of territorial integrity to the French, civilian unrest in northern and central Vietnam, internal division between the chủ chiến and chủ hoa, powerlessness against the French—Tự Đức could not help but ask himself why everything was falling apart from under him. He probably wanted to reassure himself first. Akin to Montezuma, who tried to stop the advance of the Spanish conquistadors with arrows and human sacrifices, akin to Nguyễn Văn Thiệu, who in 1975 tried to stop the advancing communists with the magic words of the Paris Accords, Tự Đức attempted to repel the French with sharpened staves, swords, and righteousness. He lived in an ancient Confucian world and belatedly realized that the French did not believe in righteousness, but only in guns and cannons.

There were, however, heroism and self-righteousness in abundance in the Mekong delta. Nguyễn Đình Chiểu (1822–1888), who was legally blind at that time, heaped scorn on those who collaborated with the French. He would not touch anything that was Western in origin like soap, powder, or perfume.

The Vietnamese at the time, however, did not have the economic and technological means to build up a strong military response. The Huế government, as a Confucian state, did not have a foreign ministry and was not able to keep up with news and advances of the Western world. The ministers at the court, locked in their gilded ivory tower and their thousand-year-old Confucian culture, did not care about what was happening in the modern world. The few who had traveled abroad, like Nguyễn Trường Tộ and Phan Thanh Giản, and talked about Western technological advances were simply laughed at.

Using another pretext, the French conquered three southwestern provinces and forced Giản to sign the 1867 treaty granting France the control over the whole of South Vietnam or Cochinchina. He returned home dejected and declared that the French flag would not be allowed to fly above the fortress as long as he was alive. He returned to the king all badges of office and the 23 royal awards he had acquired during a lifetime of distinguished service, and intended to fast until he died. In contrast to other officials, he did not have a big estate or retinue to serve him. Being still alive two weeks later, he took additional poison that finally killed him.[11]

The chủ chiến sprang into action. They declared him guilty of the loss of the six southern provinces. Having killed himself, they thought he should be spared posthumous decapitation. Tự Đức, however, revoked all his titles, positions and grades, had his name removed from the stele of the tiến sĩ degree-holders, and ordered his body exhumed and decapitated (trâm hầu).[12] "We leave for a thousand generations the sentence of trâm hầu. Thus we execute those who are already dead in order to warn those who are still living."[13]

Thus died in infamy one of Vietnam's greatest civil servants and patriots. As an abiding Confucian and a victim of the Nguyễn's failed policies of neo-Confucianism and self isolation,[14] he took the blame for the loss of the six provinces with equanimity.

The "thousand generations" sentence did not last even one generation. King Đồng Khánh rehabilitated him 19 years later (1886) and returned to his family his titles and medals.

5. Nguyễn Hữu Huân (?–1875)

Also known as Thủ Khoa Huấn,[15] he was one of the leaders of the resistance movement in the South. Caught by the French, he was forced to wear a cangue—a wooden framework—around his neck as a portable pillory. It was a sign of infamy. He bit his tongue and died before being executed by the French. He left a few verses that forever immortalized him. Forced to wear a cangue, although stooping under the weight of the device, like a hero he held his head high and straight.[16]

6. Hoàng Diệu (1829–1882)

Peasant unrest, tribal rebellions, Catholics, pirates, and the Lê restoration movements contributed to the chaos in North Vietnam, which remained an unsettled region under the Nguyễn regime. When the southern Nguyễn conquered North Vietnam, which had been under the Lê for more than four centuries, and after reunifying the country following a complete North South division for two centuries (1600–1802), northerners were, as expected, not happy to submit to the Nguyễn and demonstrated for the restoration of the northern Lê.

A French merchant trying to find a way to get to China using the Red River fought verbally with officials in Hanoi. In 1873, French officials in Saigon dispatched Captain Francis Garnier to solve the problem. The 200-men French force backed by powerful artillery, using this excuse, overran the Hanoi citadel, which was defended by 7,000 men. The French suffered only one killed and two wounded. They soon controlled four provinces in the Red River delta. Garnier was ambushed by the Black Flag river bandits and killed. A treaty was signed the following year with the Huế court allowing the French to trade and proselyte Catholicism all over Vietnam.[17]

Chaos resulted as the nghĩa quân joined the battle against the French. Tự Đức had to call on China for help. In 1882, French troops led by Captain Henri Rivière attacked the Hanoi citadel for the second time. Although the defense had improved this time, Vietnamese soldiers could not withstand the shelling of the naval artillery. The ammunition depot was hit and blew up. Soldiers scrambled for their lives. The commanding officer, General Hoàng Diệu calmly wrote the report and hung himself from a tree amidst the burning city. His body was brought back to his home town of Quảng Nam for burial. Rivière went further but again was ambushed and killed by the Black Flags.

It is interesting to note that while Tự Đức could not do anything against the French, the river brigands were able to kill two French officers and hold off their offense.

II. Modern Self-Immolation

In 1975 as the fall of Saigon was taking place, many high level officers and Saigon officials who refused to surrender to the communists took their own lives.

1. General Nguyễn Khoa Nam (1927–1975) graduated from the Thủ Đức Military Academy in 1953 and chose to serve in the airborne unit. He fought against the Bình

14. Self Sacrifice, Reeducation Camps, Postwar Killings

Xuyên in Saigon in 1955 and the Việt Cộng around Saigon during the 1968 Tết Offensive. He molded the ARVN 7th Division into one of the most efficient South Vietnamese units. As a major general and commander of the IV Corps and Military Region, he used to drop by to see and support his soldiers during their military operations. A vegetarian, he led a simple life and followed Buddhist rules closely.

Until the end, he requested every officer and soldier to remain at their posts. When designated President Minh announced his surrender to the communists, he reluctantly went along with the decision. He and General Hưng gathered their staff and saluted the South Vietnamese flag one last time at the IV Corps headquarters court. They then bid farewell to the staff and to each other. He went to the Phan Thanh Giản Military Hospital in downtown Cần Thơ to comfort and bid farewell to the hospitalized soldiers.

When he returned to his headquarters, he was told that General Hưng had taken his own life. At 2300 hours on 30 April 1975, he called Mrs. Hưng to offer his condolences. As a man of war, he did not believe in surrendering to people he thought he could defeat. Alone in his desk, he put on his white uniform along with his medals, sat on his desk and shot himself in the head in the early hours of 1 May 1975. His body was taken to the morgue and he was later buried at the Cần Thơ Military Cemetery among his peers. In 1994, his remains were exhumed and cremated. His ashes were stored at the Gia Lâm Pagoda in Gia Định, South Vietnam.

2. Two-star General Lê Văn Hưng (1933–1975) graduated from the class 5 Thủ Đức Reserve Officers School and was known as one of the five "Tiger Officers" of the ARVN. He was made general and commander of the ARVN 5th Division in 1972 when North Vietnamese General Giáp unleashed a three-pronged attack on Quảng Trị (I Corps), Kontum (II Corps) and An Lộc (III Corps) during the summer of 1972. General Hưng and his soldiers defended An Lộc during a two-month-siege and defeated an overwhelming enemy force. He was later promoted to the post of deputy commander to General Nam. In late April 1975, these two generals were offered evacuation thrice, but they flatly declined the offer.

By 1600 hours on 30 April 1975, General Hưng was still proclaiming he would not surrender to the Việt Cộng. He later met with his wife and son and told her to be brave and to raise his son as a man. He gathered his staff and told them: "I will not abandon you in order to evacuate my family. I cannot surrender in this shameful situation. If I had yelled at you on occasions, when mistakes were made, please forgive me." He shook their hands and drove them out of his office, after which he locked himself in. Not even his wife was allowed to remain in his office. A gunshot was later heard. His family and staff broke into the room and found the general, his arms outstretched, still convulsing with blood all over his uniform. He had shot himself in the head at 2045 hours on 30 April 1975.[18]

3. General Lê Nguyên Vỹ (1933–1975) graduated from the Officers Candidate Course at the MRII Regional Military School, class of 1951, at Phú Bài near Huế. He was a colonel at the An Lộc battle in 1972. As the attack raged on and as the enemy got closer, he singlehandedly took an M-72 antitank gun and shot a communist T-54 tank. He became deputy commander of the 21st ARVN division before going to the U.S. in 1974 for military training. On his return, he was named commander of the

ARVN 5th Division. When Saigon surrendered, he gathered his staff and bid them farewell. He locked himself in his office and shot himself with a Beretta 6.35 mm. When the VC officer came to take over the military office, he calmly saluted the general and said: "This is how a general should behave."[19]

4. General Trần Văn Hai (1925–1975), then a colonel, parachuted himself at the famous battle of Khe Sanh in 1968. He became commander of the ARVN 7th Division in 1974 and was known as a brave and clean officer who also cared for his soldiers. In April 1975, President Thiệu offered to take him out of the country, but he refused. He remained at his post and was notified of a heavy concentration of enemy troops across the border in Cambodia. He called the CIA representative to request air support, "We have them on the open. Now it's the time to get them…. I need help. Help me, CIA man." But the agent could not do anything and the general watched hopelessly as the enemy crossed the border and overran his troops. General Hai committed suicide instead of surrendering to the enemy.[20]

5. General Phạm Văn Phú graduated from the Dalat Military Academy, class 8. He ordered the withdrawal from the II Corps under Thiệu's insistence. The Việt Minh held him prisoner after the fall of Điện Biên Phủ, although they later released him. He had vowed never to become prisoner of the communists. He committed suicide on 30 April 1975.

6. Many more officers had committed suicide during the last days of the war, although most of these cases had not been fully reported. This should not come as a surprise. Many of them had spent their youths fighting the communists and the end result was heart- and dream-shattering. Colonel Nguyễn Hữu Thông, commander of the 42nd regiment of the 22nd division, also took his own life instead of surrendering.[21] Colonel Hồ Ngọc Cẩn, commander of the 15th Regiment 9th Infantry Division refused to surrender to the enemy. He and his men fought until the end and he was captured before he could kill himself. He asked to salute his flag a last time before being executed by firing squad. Lieutenant Colonel Nguyễn Văn Thông saluted the Soldier Statue in central downtown Saigon before pulling the trigger on himself. Around 1400 hours on 30 April, after a decent meal, Major Đặng Sĩ Vinh had his wife and seven children drink some medicine before killing them and himself. His last note read like this, "Forgive us. We do not want to live under a communist regime."[22] Former Prime Minister Trần Chánh Thành, fearing a fall into the hands of the communists he had deserted before 1954, ended his life by taking a poison. There were many more undocumented and unreported cases.

This was a mass suicide never seen before in Vietnamese history. At least five generals, three colonels, a major and a politician took their own lives in various places throughout Vietnam.

III. Discussion

Southerners have always put up resistance against invaders and foreigners: they fought against the Chams, the Khmers, the French, and then the communists. This is not to say that they are xenophobic. Far from that, they had always welcome

14. Self Sacrifice, Reeducation Camps, Postwar Killings

The National Gratitude Shrine at the Sid Goldstein Memorial Park in Westminster, California, displays the names of ARVN officers who killed themselves instead of surrendering to the communists at the end of the Vietnam War in 1975. It includes the names of 5 generals (courtesy David Hanna).

Left: Brigadier General Trần Văn Hai, 1925–1975 (courtesy David Hanna). *Right:* Brigadier General Lê Văn Hưng, 1933–1975 (courtesy David Hanna).

Brigadier General Lê Nguyên Vỹ, 1933–1975 (courtesy David Hanna).

Major General Nguyễn Khoa Nam, 1927–1975 (courtesy David Hanna).

Major General Phạm Văn Phú, 1927–1975 (courtesy David Hanna).

foreigners and were open to commerce, trade, and industry. They have a long history of mingling with the Chams, Khmers, and Chinese, especially during the period of southern migration.[23] However, the French by landing in Saigon in 1859 forced the southerners to bear arms against them.[24] In the 20th century, they fought against the communists who took over the power in North Vietnam in 1945.

Võ Tánh and Ngô Tùng Châu fought for the South. They sacrificed themselves to preserve their honor and not to fall into the hands of their enemies, the Tây Sơn. They at the same time tried to preserve their moral purity.

All these heroes lived for their *nghĩa* (righteousness): duty to the king and country. As Phan Thanh Giản was 67, he no longer wanted to work and had asked the king for the chance to simply retire; however, under the insistence of the king, he took on the position of Viceroy of the South. This was a losing proposition because there was no way anyone could defend the South against the French who were mighty militarily as well as eager to conquer Vietnam. Giản had asked Tự Đức on various occasions to reorganize the army, buy new guns and artillery pieces, but to no avail. The end result was almost foreordained. Despite these facts, he tried to deflect the blame away from the king by assuming all the blame by himself.

Trương Định wanted to fight on, but the king ordered him to lay down his arms. He decided to carry on the insurgency warfare anyway making sure to deflect the blame away from the king.

During the anti-communist war, more than 300,000 South Vietnamese soldiers lost their lives to defend South Vietnam against the Hanoi government. They were great, courageous men who had dedicated their lives to their country. When the latter sank, some killed themselves rather than surrender. Instead of flying out, they preferred to die in their own country. Despite being offered to be flown away, Generals Nam and Hưng refused and killed themselves. General Lê Minh Đảo, commander of the Xuân Lộc region—the last bastion of resistance against the North Vietnamese during the Vietnam War—also declined to be airlifted by the U.S.; he ended up being confined to concentration camps for the next 18 years during which he almost lost his life. There was no greater dedication and self-sacrifice like this.

These people had a high sense of responsibility and morality. They were ashamed of handing over troops under their command to the enemy or to turn themselves in. They felt they were betraying "not their emperor, but a sovereign state that had ceased to exist long before, whose ideals, they as military officers, still respected."[25] Although South Vietnam had lost the war, the fact that five generals, scores of colonels and officers of various ranks, and even civilians took their own lives at the end of the war showed that there was something bigger than defeat or victory. There was pride and belief that what they were fighting for—freedom and dignity of human life—was worth more than life itself. By sacrificing themselves, they implied that life without freedom was not worth living. By dying, they made a mockery of communism, a political theory they fought against and died to resist it.

Westerners do not believe in taking their own lives when they lose the ultimate battle, although it is known that ship captains have gone down with their sinking ships. South Vietnamese Captain Ngụy Văn Thà did go down with his disabled destroyer HQ10 during the Paracels battle against the Chinese in 1974.[26] Easterners, on the other hand, were willing to die following crucial battle losses to preserve their honor. They did not want to surrender, to be caught and have to go through the shame of being held prisoner. By taking their own lives, they still felt they had control of their lives or had redeemed their honor. This is an expression of extreme courage and nationalism.

One soldier prefers to die with his glory intact. The other was willing to suffer from the humiliation of defeat. There is no intention to belittle those who had surrendered. They did it in order to save their troops or the civilian population; they did it because the commander-in-chief, President Dương Văn Minh, had ordered them to surrender.

Each man chose his version of glory, each man his pain and suffering. There is no right or wrong solution to the problem. Each person is the master of his own life. What is unique about the Vietnamese (at least the South Vietnamese) culture is that over the centuries, *tuấn tiết* has been a part of the tradition. The Japanese shared that same tradition. Great numbers of officers, soldiers, and even civilians killed themselves when faced with defeat and the prospect of being captured. They felt that a man of honor should not allow himself to be captured by his enemy. Only hara-kiri could erase shame, express ultimate devotion, or register a protest.

It should be noted that South Vietnam has been in existence since 1600 while communism has been present only for the last seven decades or so. While southern nationalists believe in *tuấn tiết*, northern leaders who demanded that soldiers sacrificed themselves for the Party, did not. Although General Giáp—who had sacrificed (in Vietnamese, the word is *nướng*, or roasted) tens of thousands of North Vietnamese soldiers during the Tết Offensive and lost many more during the 1972 Easter Offensive—had been demoted from his position of Commander of the People's Army, he still held on to power and did not believe in killing himself.

Vietnamese Reeducation Camps

Reeducation camps were nothing new to the communists who built them to control their adversaries and keep themselves in power: the system was thus imbedded in their repressive regime. When the communists officially took power in North Vietnam in 1954, they used many such camps to keep northern nationalists, Catholic natives of Quỳnh Lưu district in Nghệ An Province, and adversaries away. Twenty-one years later, when the north-south war ended on 30 April 1975, they sent South Vietnamese high ranking officials and officers to the same northern camps, allowing the 1975 losers to meet the 1954 losers for the first time.[27]

It was an ironic meeting indeed as the older detainees had hoped the newcomers would win the war against the communists and come to liberate them. Unfortunately, both wound up in the same jails. For both, the future was bleak. While the old-timers would spend more time in the camps, the newcomers began to realize for the first time that their stay in these camps could last two decades or longer. One of the prisoners told Nguyễn Công Luận, "For twenty years since 1954, we have been waiting for you to march north to liberate us. But you come here at last as prisoners. You are shameful! You have betrayed us."[28]

I. Goals of the Reeducation Camps

The purpose of the reeducation camps was to introduce a real *hell* to "punish people and to frighten others with a special police force made up of beings devoid of conscience and entirely devoted to the government in power."[29] The techniques used were many, including locking up, beating, torturing, starving, demeaning, dehumanizing, and killing if necessary. All these activities were necessary for the communists to enforce their rules in order to take over, annihilate, and assimilate another society. Behind the call for cooperation, equality, patriotism, lay the ruthless and hideous face of revenge, killing, and extermination displayed in the communist reeducation camps.

A. INCARCERATION

The first goal required an elaborate scheme designed to catch all the southern military personnel and government officials into a huge, nationwide net. This crucial first step was essential for the neutralization and assimilation of the southern state because, they thought, the diverse, free thinking southern society would not surrender itself easily. As proof, 130,000 southern people took to the seas and escaped abroad right after the fall of Saigon. This was the first of the many waves of free thinkers who opted to abandon everything, including their properties, ancestors' graves, and beloved homeland, in order to preserve their freedom and to bypass the communist reeducation camps.

On 3 May 1975, three days after the fall of Saigon, all South Vietnamese officials and military personnel were ordered to report to local authorities: generals from 8 to 9 May, colonels from 8 to 11 May, and the remaining officers from 8 to 14 May with their badges, uniforms, and guns. Most of them, except for high ranking officials, were sent home after filling out a questionnaire detailing their personal history and past activities from 1954 until 1975.

On 10 June, enlisted soldiers and low-ranking officials were ordered to report to certain areas along with clothing and a three-day food supply. They were sequestered at schools, gymnasiums, theaters and sent home after a three-day reeducation course.

High-ranking officials, majors and above, were ordered to report on 15 June with a 30-day food supply and were either shipped or flown to northern camps. Officers from captains and below had to report on 23–24 June with a 10-day food supply. Despite being warned by northerners who had migrated to the South in 1954 and knew of the communists' dark intentions, that detainees might be imprisoned a long time, southerners had no choice but to submit to the new authorities. The latter painted the scheme as a clemency policy to allow southerners to clear out their capitalistic thoughts.[30] When the mid-level officers reported to the authorities, they were held in schools and fed with brown rice, fried pickled cabbage, fat meat cooked with brine and thin cabbage soup by one of the best restaurants in Cholon. The waitresses told them the communists brought rice and some money and told them to cook for the detainees. Despite the money, the restaurant still lost money but had to comply for fear of consequences.[31]

From Saigon, they were then transported aboard Soviet-made Molotova trucks to a previous South Vietnamese military installation (Trạng Lớn and Long Khánh for the III Corps, Chi Lăng for the IV Corps) like a "consignment of pigs to the market."[32] They were left pretty much to themselves, ordered to do menial work, cook for themselves, and listen to communist propaganda while their paperwork was being processed. In some camps, they were told to write their biographies and to criticize themselves at the end of each day.

By the end of three to four weeks, as they ran out of money and food and became restless, discipline got tighter. They finally realized that the first camps they were locked in were just triage camps and they would be incarcerated for a long time. The 10- or 30-day session would become a three- to 20-year imprisonment in hard labor camps where the real work began.

Overall, more than a million men and women—the cream of the southern society—were sent to the camps.[33] With all active males locked up, the communists had a free hand to reform the southern society. They took over all government buildings, private businesses, banks, houses, properties, lands, gold, monies, cars, all the way down to the prostitutes.[34] Rapacious, they then hauled the bounties back to the North. This period could be called the ransacking or more appropriately the "rape" of South Vietnam, the extermination of the southern society.

Incarceration gave the communists the "legal" right to mistreat or dispose of any detainee they wanted, whether through torture, confinement, starvation, lack of medical care, or hard labor. It basically legalized the killings, mistreatments, and unusually harsh punishments. It condoned and looked away at the mistreatments imposed on the inmates by asserting that the latter were jailed because they were *a priori* guilty even without trial or conviction. That was the difference between democracy and communism.

Hanoi's Prime Minister Nguyễn Cơ Thạch once accused the South Vietnamese of being criminals for having fought against the revolution. According to him, they all needed to be incarcerated and reeducated. On the other hand by using that same reasoning, Hanoi and the communists were guilty of two things: (1) of invading South Vietnam and violating the 1954 Geneva Accords and the 1973 Paris Accords; (2) of killing and torturing detainees under their care. By doing that, they had committed crimes against humanity in general and against the Vietnamese people in particular.

B. Starvation

Food rations in the beginning consisted of gruel twice a day, causing prisoners to begin to starve and lose weight. They soon lost their hair, their bones became brittle, their teeth decayed. As conditions stabilized, their rations went from 16 kilos (32 pounds) of rice per month in certain areas especially in the South, to 12 kilos (24 pounds) a month of a combination of flour, corn, cassava or manioc, sweet potato, and *bo bo*.[35] The latter was imported grain used to feed horses. Therefore, these grains were coarse, hard, and almost impossible for detainees to chew. Once ingested, they caused flatulence, abdominal cramps, constipation and then diarrhea, and inflicted grave discomfort and pain upon the detainees.

Hunger, which had become pervasive because of the lack of food and meat, caused them to dream about food all the time. At night, the rumbling of empty stomachs prevented them from sleeping, which adversely affected their health status.[36] In their hunt for food, they turned to consuming rats, lizards, centipedes, birds, grasshoppers, and snakes, any animal that moved, as substitutes.

In northern camps, the only way to get food was to forage in the fields for cassava roots, grains, berries, and even grass. They tried to eat any kind of wild plants and fruit they judged edible. And many got poisoned as a result. They developed constipation and then dysentery for eating wild bananas that contained a lot of tannin. As northern camps did not even carry medication to control dysentery, they had to drag themselves to the toilets 10 or 20 times a day and finally died as result. Twelve men in a camp of 500 died from eating wild fruit and vegetables.[37]

Hunger caused inmates to do strange things. They fought for and positioned themselves to get the last drop of soup or rare morsels of meat. They watched the food handlers carefully to make sure that all the portions were equally divided among them. One spoon more or less could cause fights to break out. On many occasions, rice that spilled on the ground was rapidly scooped up and consumed by inmates. In their fight for survival, many lost their manners and reverted to their basic instincts. Those who were not fast enough or did not fight lost out.

A few would do anything to secure an extra bowl of rice. Some became the much feared, yet despised "antennas" of the communists by reporting any illegal activity or unwise comments against the jailers. The unwise targeted victim got shackled and punished whether the report was correct or falsified, while the antenna received his reward. Others would volunteer to clean the pigsties in order to steal some rice reserved for the pigs. The *bộ đội* (communist soldiers) valued their pigs so much that they fed them "white" rice while inmates received only "red" or coarse rice or even mildewed rice. One inmate volunteered to dig a well for another for a few sugar cubes: one cube for the first meter of well and two cubes for the second meter and so on.

The *bộ đội* used food as a weapon to their advantage. To punish detainees, besides isolation, they simply withheld their rations causing them to toe the line. There was no bigger deterrent to opposition than starvation.

C. Executions, tortures

In a Nghệ An camp, detainees were ordered to carry fresh human wastes with their bare hands to fertilize the fields. They were not allowed to bathe in the pond or wash their hands. On their way back to the camp, they were forced to eat with their dirty hands.[38] Random beatings were so common as to be the norm. Detainees were beaten whenever the "guard felt like it" and wherever he had the urge to do it, often without rhyme or reason. Many were brutally beaten because they had stopped to rest during work or on the way back to the camp. "Guards use bamboo canes and rods to beat prisoners who fall asleep or refuse to answer questions. They tie up men and women, corner them against a wall, shove them to the ground, trample their bodies, and kick their heads. The students call the camp the 'Blood University.'"[39]

There were cruel forms of torture known only to the communists who devised them. Detainees, especially those who had never faced the communists before, were able to witness for the first time the wickedness of their jailers. Detainees were confined to isolation holes, wells, rooms, or tiger cages depending on their availability. Any cramped space could be used to detain or torture the detainees. Holes were dug out in the ground; they were about four feet deep and small enough to prevent the detainee from squatting or standing fully upright. A wooden board was used to cover the opening. A few hours in the hole would render anyone miserable, let alone a day or two.

In the north, detainees were shackled by their ankles to a railing. The punishment called for a nine-day shackling session at a time. Once released from the shackles and after suffering in that position for nine consecutive days, the detainee could no longer walk in an upright position; he could only crawl. At the Hà Giang Camp, the detainee was spread-eagled on a board with four limbs tied to the four corners of the board. A hole was cut in the middle to allow the detainee to void. In that position, he could not defend himself against rats that would gnaw at his buttocks all the way up to his bones. He would die in pain in a week. At K20 Camp in Bến Tre Province, the detainee would be tied in a spread-eagle position on the clay ground with a log placed under his back. During daytime, he was burned by the sun and at night, the mosquitoes would take care of him. After one day of such treatment, the detainee would either cry for forgiveness or just pass out.

Cadres and *bộ đội* were free to distort the truth and sow innuendos and suspicions that resulted in widespread confusion, resentment, distrust, and fear among detainees.

Many executions were made on the spot without due process while others were just bureaucratic formalities. As one detainee fought back when he was caught escaping from a camp, the *bộ đội* simply "[bayonetted] him right through the mouth to the back of his neck."[40] On another occasion, when prisoners became rowdy during a meeting in a camp, the "feared and fawned upon chief of the labor camp, a clever and cruel person" had no qualms about pulling out his gun, "pointing it at the middle of the prisoner's head and pulling the trigger."[41] The sudden execution of a random prisoner immediately reestablished order in the camp.

Executions were part of the deal at other camps as well. At the Minh Lương camp, 44 prisoners were waiting for the execution call at one time. Twice a week, loudspeakers blared the names of the convicted (without any trial) followed by an "account of offenses against the country, a conviction, and a death sentence— never a defense or last rite." All the crimes were the same for all prisoners who were led to the forest. Eleven pistol shots. Then it was over. This was typical of communist expediency. One prisoner in the camp murmured, "No law, no reason, no mercy."[42]

Women Army Corps (WAC) Second Lieutenant Nguyễn Thị Kim Lang was sentenced to death and executed at the Gò Công City soccer field on 15 July 1975, while she was pregnant, after she voiced vehement protest against the communist policies.[43] During a failed escape attempt at camp Tân Hiệp, Quách Hồng Quang was wounded in the middle of the barbed wire fence. An NVA lieutenant executed him by shooting him three more times with his K-54 pistol.[44] Major Trần Văn Bé and Major Nguyễn Văn Thịnh were also caught while escaping and executed in April 1976 at camp Tân Hiệp.[45]

Many more random executions have been reported elsewhere.[46] Desbarats found that "two-thirds of the executions occurred in 1975 and 1976 mostly in Saigon and the Mekong Delta and involved high ranking officials. A Berkeley group of human rights researchers had estimated the number of political killings to be '65,000 after Hanoi took over Saigon.'"[47] This was based on statistical analyses and computations of one million people going through reeducation camps. Aurora foundation later raised the number to more than 160,000 detainees dying in the camps.[48] Metzner, on the other hand, suggested a 250,000 number.[49]

D. HARD LABOR AND POOR MEDICAL CARE

A ten-hour daily work period was followed by three-hour political indoctrination and an hour of self-criticism. A typical schedule was as follows:

0530 hours: communist national anthem
0700–1200 hours: work
1200–1300 hours: lunch
1300–1700 hours: work
1700–1800 hours: dinner
1800–2100 hours: political indoctrination
2100–2200 hours: self-criticism
2200 hours: bedtime

At the Da Bàn camp, inmates had to move big tree trunks from the forest to the camp after cutting them down. All the work was done by hand, without chain saw or forklift. Each trunk was about three feet in diameter and 15 feet long. It had to be carried by hand from the work site to the river and then rafted back to the camp. The water was cold and full of leeches; the mountain river could be 60 feet wide and the current swift and dangerous in certain areas. If they were not careful, they could be crushed by the trunks, stabbed by branches, or impelled by the currents against the big rocks lining the course of the river.[50]

In the malaria-infested forests of the highlands, they were ordered to build their own camps (Bù Gia Mập, Bù Lợi, Da Bàn) where none had existed before. By building the dwellings, they basically dug their own graves. If they did not die from exhaustion and malnutrition, they would eventually die from malaria. Under these working conditions, they could catch any tropical disease—especially tuberculosis, which was endemic in Vietnam and many detainees had died of advanced tuberculosis as no drugs were available at the local dispensaries or hospitals.

Although physical labor was hard, the combination of beating, torture, indoctrination, humiliation and starvation made life in the camp much harder to tolerate. The real purpose of the reeducation process was to diminish, to debase, to starve and to annihilate the individual,[51] who no longer felt himself as an individual but a cornered beast. From there to a downhill course and death, the path was not long for the weak and those who did not believe in themselves.

In Trạng Lớn, Hiệp Tâm, and Phú Quốc camps,[52] the most cruel work assignment was to clear out land mines. Without any training, mine detector, or special equipment, inmates were down on their knees, huffing, puffing, and sweating profusely due to a combination of anxiety and fear, trying to uncover and defuse mines one by one. The order from the cadre was to lift up the mine and carry it to the jungle. By following the cadre's method, one of the inmates was blown up and a few got injured. At the Minh Lương camp, inmates were told to clear two separate parallel paths 15 yards apart in a minefield. Ropes were tied to opposite ends of a log. A team of three men on each side pulled on the ropes while walking on the cleared paths. They detonated the mines by dragging the log on the ground between them. One inmate blew off his hand while another suffered a wound on the lower leg. The wardens replaced the log and the two injured prisoners and work continued as if nothing had happened.[53]

There was no first aid kit in most camps. Bandages and antiseptics were nowhere to be found and medical personnel were nonexistent. The treatment of abdominal colic was "young buds of guavas," for tooth aches kitchen salt, and for colds "crushed garlic to be injected in the nostrils."[54] A lieutenant colonel died a horrible death. In the last three days of his life he had diarrhea 20 to 30 times a day until he was completely exhausted and dehydrated. When he could not walk, he crawled; when he could no longer crawl, he dirtied his own platform-bed.[55]

Amputations were done without anesthetics by a nurse. Three or four inmates simply held the patient down while the nurse—not even a doctor—performed the operation with a handsaw sterilized in hot water. The patient cried and struggled and fainted as the procedure went on as if nothing had happened. Of course the stump got infected and the patient eventually died because of lack of antibiotics. Six men in a camp died in a similar fashion.[56]

E. *Cải tạo* or Thought reform

The culmination of the reeducation process was the attempt to change the mind of the inmates and to break their spirits in order to make them into new "socialist" people or render them obedient[57] so that they could no longer resist the system. The indoctrination began the day they were sent to the labor camps, with constant reminders that since they owed "blood debts," they had to pay for them. It was followed by daily self-criticism and punishment by food withdrawal and confinement to dark rooms where they were shackled for many days or weeks in a row. In the South, they were confined to conex—metallic cargo containers—that were hot like ovens during the day and cold at night. A light was left on all night long to prevent the detainee from sleeping. Through intimidation, beating, isolation, starvation, and deprivation of sleep, the communists intended to break the will of the detainees. In the North, detainees who were not given blankets and warm clothing, shivered from the cold weather—there was no heating system—and could not sleep with temperatures hovering at 30 degrees Fahrenheit at high elevations at night.

Detainees were terrorized, subjected to ruthless rounds of punishment, taunting, and tortures, and even threatened with execution.[58] As "the power of their masters was total and totally arbitrary,"[59] *cải tạo* broke many detainees spiritually and mentally. As a result, tens of thousands of detainees died of mistreatment, despair, starvation, malnutrition and disease. Others bore permanent physical and psychological scars the rest of their lives. These scars widened the chasm between oppressors and oppressed, northerners and southerners and left minimal room for reconciliation. Whatever faint admiration a few might have for the steeliness of the socialist army that had defeated them would soon give way to a loathing of the communists.

Many were so upset by the communists and their oppressive system that as soon as they were released from the camps, they tried to escape from Vietnam if they had the resources or later through the Orderly Departure Program (ODP) that allowed them to emigrate abroad. The reeducation treatment was so arbitrary, unjust, and irresponsible that it rendered their captives "utterly cynical, concerned only with getting out of Vietnam or with the survival of themselves and their families in a society from which they were completely alienated."[60]

F. Corruption

Discipline broke down among the wardens. Prisoners, while still in Saigon, were allocated food at average rations in the first weeks and then the rations decreased in the following months. Corruption ran wild as PAVN supply officers stole from the food allowance by sharing illegal profits with civilian food providers.[61]

The prisoners reported all their pills to the camp wardens on their arrival to the Hoàng Liên Sơn 4 camp. The wardens confiscated all the medications and sold them to villagers, collecting in the process a large sum of money for themselves. When the prisoners suffered from illnesses, they did not have any medications to care for themselves. Twenty prisoners in five camps thus died of dysentery.[62]

II. Northern Reeducation Camps

The reeducation camps were scattered throughout Vietnam, North and South, and estimated to range from a few hundred in number to more than a thousand, because of the way they were set up. One camp could have five to six sub-camps. Some were old prison camps left over by the French and used by the communists to detain northern nationalists when they took over North Vietnam in 1954. Many were brand new constructions built by the detainees themselves in the middle of the forests, in deserted areas or in the highlands.

"There were more reeducation camps than schools. There were over 600 district reeducation camps, more than 100 provincial camps and more than 20 national camps."[63] Some camps did not have a name: one camp was known as 3721 (later called Bù Gia Mập). Camps set up in the jungles or mountains carried an alphabet letter followed by a number. Camps in the Phú Yên-Cung Sơn districts in central Vietnam were labeled as T-50, T-51, T-52, T-53, and T-54.[64] The Thủ Đức camp (close to Saigon) had a sub-camp located in Hàm Tân close to Phan Thiết, some 90 miles away. The frightening camp Cổng Trời (Gate to Heaven), from which only a few inmates would walk out alive, therefore its sadistic name, was not listed in any camp directory.

Northern camps were notoriously worse than southern camps because they were established decades earlier, their wardens had been trained in the Soviet Union and communist China in the role of torturing inmates, and because of their close proximity to Hanoi leadership. This was why high level South Vietnamese officials and officers were shipped there first. Being older than detainees in southern camps, they harbored various medical problems (high blood pressure, diabetes, heart disease, cancer...) which required close medical attention. Yet northern, like southern, camps lacked everything from medical personnel to basic medications. The harsher weather, stricter rules, location of the camps in remote northern highlands, and the lack of food, medications, and family visitations compounded the problem and made life tougher for detainees sequestered in the North.[65]

At the northern Thanh Phong camp that lay close to the Chinese border, detainee mortality was so high that Hanoi had to close the camp. "When you got sick, you died. There was no medical treatment. We ate only rice and some vegetables we picked from the jungles." said one inmate.[66] If the southern *bộ đội* were cruel but unsophisticated, the northern wardens were cunning and knowledgeable. They knew how to break the inmates, play with their morale, and bend them to their will without even beating them. They, however, could be ruthless and cruel because they "considered themselves exiled too. For them, it was the end of the world. They were desperate. Their food was little better than ours."

Appendix I lists a series of reeducation camps in Vietnam. Although it contains many camps not seen in previous lists, no list can be called complete until Hanoi opens its files to the public.

III. The Detainees

A description of the reeducation camps would be incomplete without detailing some of the detainees who lived, toiled, and suffered in these camps, year in and year out until their captors decided to release them. They were called "prisoners of conscience" because they fought for their freedom despite losing the war. They were never tried before a jury nor convicted of any war crime, just thrown into jails like criminals and tortured.

Many high-ranking officers and officials were detained up to 17 years without trial or charges. They were left to rot in jails right in Hỏa Lò Jail, in the heart of Hanoi.[67] Among them were General Bùi Văn Nhu of the Saigon police and Colonel Trần Văn Thắng, former director of the ARVN military security, and many other South Vietnamese officials.

General Lê Minh Đảo, commander of the 18th ARVN division and General Lý Tòng Bá, commander of the 25th ARVN division were jailed in northern camps for 17 and 13 years respectively.

General Trần Bá Di, commander of the 9th ARVN Division, a clean and honest officer who later became the deputy commander of the IV Corps,[68] spent 17 years in reeducation camps. He immigrated to the U.S. in 1993 where he did not mind taking menial jobs for another 15 years before taking retirement.

Lieutenant Colonel Trần Ngọc Huệ was a POW during the 1971 Lâm Sơn Operation in southern Laos. Wounded, he was forced to walk back to Hanoi on the Hồ Chí Minh Trail to seek medical treatment. But he was so sick that his soldiers had to carry him on a man-made stretcher. He was interned at Hỏa Lò Jail and spent 13 years in various northern reeducation camps. He immigrated to the U.S. under the Humanitarian Operation program.

Phan Nhật Nam, Airborne major, wartime journalist, and author served in the ARVN for 14 years before spending another 14 years in communist reeducation camps, eight of which in total isolation. He immigrated to the U.S. in 1993 and once said, "I survived the war; I survived prison. Now I must survive my freedom and it is very hard. We are old men now. We have lost the ability to adapt and renew." He wrote about post-traumatic stress disorder (PTSD), which he and many other ARVN suffered.

Tâm Minh Phạm, a West Point graduate, class of 1974, returned to Vietnam to serve in the ARVN. After the war, he spent six years in reeducation camps before his release in 1981. It took his West Point classmates ten more years to get him out of Vietnam.[69]

Lý Tống, a South Vietnamese Air Force veteran who served in its elite Black Eagle fighter squadron, was shot down as the war neared its end and sent to reeducation camps. He escaped from the camps in 1980 and after a 17-month trek to freedom through five countries was accepted as a refugee in the U.S. He earned a degree in political science from the University of New Orleans. In 1992, a man who never accepted defeat, he hijacked a commercial plane from Bangkok to dump leaflets over Saigon calling for a popular uprising. He then parachuted himself down to certain capture. He was released after spending six years in jail. In 2000, he dropped anti-communist leaflets over Havana and the Cuban-Americans gave him a victory parade in Florida. The following year, he dropped leaflets for the second time over

Saigon following which he was jailed in Bangkok for another six years before returning to the U.S. He died in San Diego in early 2019. "Mr. Tống offered an alternate reality—a vision of courage and action, a tragic hero in the tradition of Vietnamese history."[70]

Hoàng Xuân Tựu, Senator (1967–1973) and vice-president of the South Vietnamese Senate, died at Nam Hà camp in 1980 after five years of incarceration. Senator Trần Thế Minh (1967–1973) died at Nam Hà Camp in 1977 of poisoning. His family had to bribe camp officials to have his body exhumed and brought back to Saigon for burial. The cemeteries of Nam Hà Camp were littered with the graves of thousands of "puppet soldiers and civil servants."

Trần Văn Tuyên, an attorney and former president of the Saigon Bar Association, was interned in various camps in the north. A former Saigon congressman, he was the leader of one of Saigon's opposition groups. When he was sent to northern camps, he was treated so poorly that he committed suicide in 1976.

Father Hoàng Quỳnh, former leader of the anti-communist forces at the northern Bùi Chu-Phát Diệm dioceses before 1954, was tortured to death at Chí Hòa Jail in early 1977. Dr. Phan Huy Quát, a physician and former South Vietnamese minister, was left to die at Chí Hòa Jail.

The venerable Thích Thiện Minh, who was one of the Buddhist leaders calling for the cessation of the bombing of North Vietnam, died at the Hàm Tân Z-30D reeducation camp after a long period of torture and mistreatment.

Catholic Cardinal Nguyễn Văn Thuận, who was a civilian, was held incommunicado for 10 years at Camp 6, Thanh Chương District, Nghệ An Province. Each cell measured seven by ten feet and was worse than the so-called "tiger cages" of Poulo Condor Island in the South, which had been criticized by the Western press during the war.[71]

And the list goes on and on.[72] Of the more than 80,000 officers jailed in various camps, half of them in northern camps and half in the South, it was estimated that 32 of the total 112 imprisoned were generals, 350 of the 600 full colonels, 1,700 of the 2,500 lieutenant colonels, 5,500 of the 6,500 majors, and 72,000 of the 80,000 captains and lieutenants.[73]

An additional 200,000 non-military prisoners (writers, poets, artists, songwriters, members of nationalist parties, etc.) were also incarcerated.[74]

IV. Orderly Departure Program (ODP)

In the face of the huge number of people rushing out to the high seas—who came to be known as "boat people"—trying to escape an oppressive communist regime in an attempt to reach other southeastern Asian shores, on 30 May 1979, UNHCR (United Nations High Commissioner for Refugees) and the Socialist Republic of Vietnam signed a Memorandum of Understanding establishing a program for legal emigration from Vietnam, known as the Orderly Departure Program, or ODP. The ODP was intended to make it possible for persons wishing to leave Vietnam to do so in a safe and orderly manner, rather than having to join the ranks of the Vietnamese boat people. This pertains only to family reunion and other humanitarian cases.

Questions were soon raised about Vietnamese motives since communist Vietnam was at the root of the boat people phenomenon. Was it a ploy for Vietnam to enhance its sinking international standing? Was it trying to dump unwanted elements, like the ethnic Chinese, many of whom—having made payment to the government in order to get out—were still stuck inside Vietnam because no third-country would accept them? While discussions were ongoing, the boat flow continued unabated and by the end of June 1979, only 6,700 people had departed legally from Vietnam, most of them going to France.[75]

Facing lukewarm reaction from ASEAN countries, Vietnam promised to crack down on "illegal" boat departures. Overnight, boat arrivals plunged drastically from 56,941 in June to 9,734 in August, causing ASEAN countries to reopen their shores. Sea escapes, however, were not joy rides; they were filled with horror stories: "…wanton killings, rape, abductions. We had people with gold fillings torn out of their mouths; infants thrown in the water in front of their mothers; people dipped in fishing nets into the sea until they drowned; people attacked with harpoons and ice picks. The tales of rapes—they passed the girls around like bees finding a field full of flowers."[76]

In late 1979, under the ODP, the U.S. and Vietnam exchanged the first lists. Those listed on both lists would be eligible for resettlement. The U.S., which had no consular relations with Vietnam, had to rely on UNHCR as an intermediary to bring the list to Bangkok. The U.S. list had 4,000 names of people with family links or who were pre–1975 employees of the U.S. government it wanted out of Vietnam. The Vietnamese list had 21,000 names of people it wanted to get rid of—most of them ethnic Chinese living in the Chinese suburb of Saigon who had paid their way out of the country. Since the match turned out to be only a dozen names, it took 18 months to clear 1,700 people for departure.

As clandestine departures dropped, orderly departures rose, although they were mostly Chinese for a long time. By 1982, boat arrivals slipped to 43,800 while ODP departures rose to 10,000 for the first time. In 1984, there were 24,865 boat arrivals compared to 29,100 ODP departures. Despite the program's success, problems remained. The U.S. by 1982 wanted specific groups of people of particular priority to the program: American citizens, current and former reeducation prisoners, Amerasian children and others it could admit as immigrants instead of simply dealing with family reunion cases, which were counted as refugees.

By 1985, as the U.S. considered the issues of priority and reciprocity, it deferred final decisions on many ODP people who had been interviewed. This resulted in a backlog that rose to 22,000 cases. Vietnam imposed a moratorium on new interviewing until the caseload was cleared. In January 1986, the last two U.S. interviewers were asked to leave the country. While the U.S. and other countries worked on their backlog, by 1987 Southeast Asian countries began to see a new rise in Vietnamese boat arrivals.[77]

The ODP departures resumed in 1988 following the passing in December 1987 of the Amerasian Homecoming Act—which set a numerical target for admission and funding for the special resettlement of Amerasians and their families. There was still no agreement on resettlement of the reeducation prisoners. That would come almost two years later on 30 July 1989, when the U.S. and Hanoi finally allowed the released reeducation center detainees closely associated with the U.S. along with their close relatives to leave for the U.S.

The first group of 190 former reeducation detainees arrived at San Francisco airport on January 1990. The flow of detainees then just kept pouring out and by 1991, the ODP departures totaled 86,451 worldwide including 21,500 detainees and their families and nearly 18,000 Amerasians. From 1991 to 1995, orderly departures averaged more than 66,000 people per year before tailing off in 1996.

In all, the U.S. accepted 140,000 former reeducation prisoners and family members and 40,000 Amerasians. The breakdown includes 34,641 former prisoners and 128,068 of their relatives who fled to America, according to the State Department.[78]

In sum, the violence and cruelty committed by the communists against South Vietnam and its people did not stop after 30 April 1975. One in three South Vietnamese families had a relative in a reeducation camp. Not happy with defeating their enemies, the communists went on to destroy the southerners, their society, and their way of living. They sent more than one million of them to reeducation camps, where 160,000 died of starvation, torture, and diseases.[79] The terror unleashed on the southern population forced them to escape as boat people, of which more than 100,000 died at sea and many more inside South Vietnam.

Overall, half a million additional people (see below) died after the war ended in order for Hanoi to complete the assimilation of the southern society after the war ended. This was the price of conquest. In the hands of Hồ Chí Minh-Lê Duẩn and the communist party, who had engineered and pursued the conquest of South Vietnam, lay the blood of these people.

When the Southern General Robert E. Lee surrendered to the northern General Ulysses S. Grant at Appomattox Court House on 9 April 1865, signaling the beginning of the end of the U.S. Civil War, Grant allowed southern soldiers to return home without being held prisoner or prosecuted for treason. Officers were allowed to keep their sidearms and horses. He also gave food rations to Lee's starving army, which did a lot toward healing the country. For this reason the U.S. remains today, more than 150 years after the Civil War, one of the strongest and most powerful nations on earth. On the other hand when the communists took over Saigon, all men and government officials were sent to reeducation camps and their properties confiscated; the remaining people, if they could afford it, were driven out of the country by boats by persecution and discrimination. The unlucky ones and those too poor to buy their way out remained, poor and persecuted, as second-class citizens in their own country. In 2019, Vietnam ranks 128th out of 180 countries in term of economic freedom, well below neighboring Laos and Cambodia.[80] The inhumane treatment of the South Vietnamese in the hands of the communists will only keep the nation forever divided.

Extrajudicial Killings After the Vietnam War

"The Vietnamese communists are experts in mass murder: they have had nearly 40 years of practice at it" (when they entered Saigon in 1975), Nguyễn Văn Cảnh, professor at the Law School of Saigon University warned us. They are good at killing military personnel on the battlefields as well as civilians in towns and cities. After wiping out the members of the various nationalist parties in northern Vietnam in 1945–46 and killing 50 to 70 thousand northern landowners in 1953–56, they proceeded with suppressing government representatives in South Vietnam in 1954–60 and outright killing more than 3,000 civilians during the Tết Offensive in 1968.[81]

The communist road to total control of Vietnam was littered with the blood of Vietnamese people. The present work deals only with the killings committed by the Vietnamese communists after 1975. They systematically proceeded with eliminating people they did not like. Extrajudicial killings and deaths can be grouped into four categories: wanton killings, reeducation camps, new economic zones (NEZ), and boat escapes. While some were local and fairly unorganized, others were widespread and sophisticated in scheme and organization.

1. Wanton Killings

The first thing the communists did when they entered Saigon on 30 April 1975 was to take control of all South Vietnamese institutions, including hospitals. By 1400 that day, they began kicking out all the hospitalized patients of the 2,000-bed Cộng Hòa Military Hospital including patients on the operating tables. "Seriously wounded soldiers whose limbs were torn and bleeding, some with stomachs cut open and intestines exposed were pulled out to the terrace in front of the hospital gate. Many died in a short time. I had never imagined that such barbarism would happen."[82] Hundreds of cyclo drivers having heard about the story came by to offer their services for free. To sympathize with the patients' ordeal, they either transported them to local private hospitals or bus stations because many lived outside the city or bought them food. Other people gave patients money to buy tickets to return home.

According to Nguyễn Công Hoàn, a legislator under Thiệu and then under the Socialist Republic of Vietnam until he escaped by boat in 1977, "over five hundred people in the villages of Hoa Thắng, Hoa Tri, Hoa Quang, and Hoa Kiên (all in Tuy Hòa district) were murdered during the first days of the [communist] occupation."[83]

Reprisals by the Việt Cộng can be grouped into secret liquidations or so called people's trials followed by official executions. The extreme cruelty and barbarity of these killings were part of the communist plan to terrorize the population. Beheading, stabbing, and denial of burial served to outrage and humiliate the victims' families.[84]

The whole country was under seclusion. Internment camps were set up or built anew, often by the prisoners themselves. The highest ranking officials, civilians and officers, were said to have "committed serious crimes against the people" and sent to northern camps. Included were members of the Airborne, Marines, and Rangers; members of nationalist parties; police and intelligence officers. The southern camps tended to be more specialized.

The purpose of the camps was to lock up and "exact revenge against whole classes of people, with scarcely a pretense of legality and with total disregard for human rights." Nguyễn Mạnh Côn, a writer, was shot at Xuyên Mộc Camp in Đồng Nai Province because he had begun a hunger strike in an attempt to gain his release. Venerable Thích Thiện Minh, vice president of the United Buddhist Church, died in Hàm Tân Z-30D Camp on 17 October 1978 after imprisonment and torture.[85]

2. New Economic Zones (NEZ)

Civilians were sent to the NEZ that functioned as "reeducation camps without fences." People were forced to move to the NEZ under the threat of being sent to reeducation camps, having their food ration cards withdrawn, or not allowing their children to go to schools.

Most NEZ were disastrous failures. Such was the case of the Lê Minh Xuân NEZ, about 30 km northwest of Saigon. The party cadres in charge of the projects failed to take a soil sample before ordering the land plowed and diked. About a foot below the surface was a layer of acid soil. When mixed with water, the soil poisoned the entire planting area. The land, freshly plowed, irrigated and worked on had turned to wilderness again. Huts were deserted and villages abandoned. People tried to return to the city, where since their homes had been confiscated, they joined the thousands already sleeping in the streets. In Minh Hải Province, people were dumped in a NEZ where land was inundated with salt water. The only way to live was to dig clams, but there were not enough of these to go around.[86] The unschooled and ignorant communists created one disaster after another.

3. Boat Escapes

Unable to live under the erratic and repressive communist regime, people looked for ways to escape. It had been said that had lamp posts known how to run, they too would run out of Vietnam. The massive refugee exodus was not merely a result of the harshness of life there, but was part of Vietnamese strategy in Southeast Asia. The risks were terrible: death by inanition because of lack of food, water, or fuel, or encounters with pirates, government officials, or inclement weather like storms; probably half of those who left had been drowned. The choice was tragic and unhuman: it was either death under a repressive and cruel government or from drowning at sea.

The four ways of becoming a refugee were: (1) **Escape** (*đi chui*): people bought a fishing boat, worked temporarily as fishermen, sold fish to the government and officially bought gas, which they saved for a planned escape. If caught, they got arrested. (2) **Escape with the permission of local authorities** (*mua bãi*): they offered bribes to local authorities in an attempted escape during nighttime. They sometimes got caught by higher echelon officials or the Naval Patrol Forces who were not involved in the bribery scheme. This could mean more bribes or imprisonment: a hellish circle of loss and suffering. The usual bribe was six to twelve taels of gold per person.[87] (3) **The semi-official way** (*đi bán chánh thức*): the provincial party committee was in charge of the matter. Each refugee paid 12 taels of gold to the organizer, who bought the boat and gas and handed over half of the bribe to the party committee. The refugees offered their possessions: houses, cars, and so on to the party committee before leaving. (4) **official registration** (*đăng ký chánh thức*). This was handled by the central government for ethnic Chinese. Each refugee paid 12 taels and handed over the family book and personal possessions. Steel-hulled refugee ships were used to carry 3,000 to 4,000 refugees.

Over half a million people were released under Hanoi's human trafficking scheme. Boats were sunk and a great number of refugees drowned.[88] Millions of others escaped unofficially. It was surprising to witness a bloody and idealistic "liberation" movement degenerate into a corrupt human trafficking scheme.[89] The irony of the situation was that if attempted escapees had bribed local officials, they could be caught by higher government officials.

4. Continuing Repression

The southerners who either did not have the means or were unlucky in their escape attempts were forced to remain in their country where they were treated as third-class citizens subjected to the whims of the rulers. The cost of the occupation of South Vietnam after 1975 was high. Some authors have tried to estimate it and came back with almost half a million casualties (see below).

Table 14-1. Extrajudicial Killings After the Vietnam War

Rummel RJ: https://www.hawaii.edu/powerkills/SOD.CHAP6.HTM

Events	Estimated Number of Casualties	Authors
Killings	60,000 (low)	Desbarats (90)
	100,000 (high)	Rummel (91)
Reeducation camps	95,000	Rummel (91)
New economic zones	100,000	Rummel (91)
Boat people	250,000	Rummel (91)
Total	485,000	Rummel (91)

In conclusion, although there was no "visible" blood bath immediately after the war (1975) like the one in Cambodia—how many people have to die, to call it a bloodbath?—60 to 100 thousand South Vietnamese were killed, most of them during the first two years after the war.[90] There was and is a continuing repression as well as killing of southerners under the present regime: a low-key, insidious blood bath that continues today. Overall, the Socialist Republic of Vietnam (SRV) and its followers had killed close to half a million South Vietnamese since 1975 (table 14–1). They are the real murderers.

"Crimes against humanity" have been defined as "Murder, extermination, enslavement, deportation, and other inhumane acts committed against any civilian population before and during the war; or persecutions on political, racial, or religious grounds in execution of or in connection with any crime within the jurisdiction of the Tribunal, whether or not in violation of the domestic law of the country where perpetrated."[91]

"War crime" was defined as "The deportation, enslavement, or mass scale and systematic practice of summary executions, abduction of persons following their disappearance, torture, or inhuman acts inspired by political, philosophical, racial, or religious motives, or organized for the purpose of implementing a concerted effort against a civilian population group."[92]

The SRV had committed both war crimes and crimes against humanity in its conquest and occupation of South Vietnam. History will someday judge Hồ Chí Minh, Lê Duẩn and the Communist Party of Indochina members as flawed, rogue, and corrupt leaders in their quest to conquer South Vietnam. They had erred into spreading communism instead of bringing freedom and independence to the people of Vietnam. Their regime is one of "mendacity"[93] and they in a twisted irony had managed to become a puppet of communist China.

Under the communist regime, Vietnam is stuck on the lower rung of the world community: a 20 out of 100 freedom index and ranking 135th globally in GDP per capita.[94] Vietnam as a proud nation claiming a 4,000 year history deserves better leaders.

15

Identity

Where do the South Vietnamese stand now, as (1) they no longer have a country to call a homeland and (2) as they differ so much from the North Vietnamese in political, military, and social aspects? This chapter is devoted to the new identity of the South Vietnamese.

The Two Vietnams

As I stand on the southern bank of the Potomac River and look toward Washington, DC, I imagine myself standing 44 years ago on the bank of the Saigon River looking back at my beloved downtown Saigon. When April 30, 1975, came, northern communist soldiers with their tanks broke through the gates of the Independence Palace and took over the country. The first wave of 130,000 Vietnamese fled the country to look for freedom elsewhere.[1] The consequences—psychological, social, political, economic, and moral—were tragic and painful.

To fully understand these consequences and their impact on the South Vietnamese, one has to understand the loss in general, the Little Saigons, and the two Vietnams.

The Loss

With the fall of Saigon, the world as the South Vietnamese knew it ended abruptly. The new era was marked by hardships:

1. *Punishment.* Trương Như Tảng acknowledged that "in the first year of liberation, some 300,000 people were arrested."[2] Overall, more than a million government officials and military personnel were hauled into reeducation camps where they were starved and forced to do hard labor.[3] This was a wholesale enslavement of the country not heard of in human history, except under communist regimes. Prisoners were treated harshly without any rights. "We were less than animals and not really human."[4] Even the communist Bùi Tín wondered after visiting various reeducation camps in the South as well as in the North, "why pursue a policy of such harshness towards hundreds of thousands of people?"[5]

2. *Suppression of basic freedoms.*[6] One could not even visit one's friend a few miles away without approval from government officials. Basic freedoms were

abolished and replaced by communist rules—those of the invaders. "In the eye of our communist leaders, an enemy 'puppet' whether alive or dead, was always a puppet—a second class citizen who had no citizen's rights at all."[7] Even today, Father Lý, who has fought for human rights in Vietnam for decades, was gagged in front of the court by a Công An (secret police) to prevent him from speaking up. This was a far cry from the so-called "liberation" of Saigon.

3. *Impoverishment.* Private properties, bank accounts, houses, and businesses were confiscated and turned over to communist officials. The latter "fought each other over houses, cars, prostitutes, and bribes. Soldiers and officials ... were suddenly confronted with what seemed to them an almost fairy tale richness, theirs for the taking."[8]

4. *Escape and adjustment.* Unable to tolerate an illegitimate and cruel regime, more than two million people braved the seas, storms, and pirates to look for freedom elsewhere.[9] This was a massive exodus by sea and land of epic proportions.

5. *Nightmares.* They have been the constant followers of many Vietnamese for the last 45+ years, especially those who had gone through re-education camps. The inhumane treatment[10] of the prisoners by sadistic jailers—"they did not kill you outright in the camp by shooting you. Instead they slowly tortured and terrified you"[11]— left an indelible and painful mark on many. And today, a scratching at the door would wake up a former camp inmate sweating all over.[12]

San Juan wrote about a refugee who had relocated to the United States[13]: "It is hard to say that the war was over... The past like a nightmare endlessly haunts... It is like a dream he cannot forget... The past that [he] enjoyed in South Vietnam is meaningless in the United States... [His] dream torments and has no satisfactory resolution in the present."

Memories have become a prominent feature of those who escaped from Vietnam—the overseas Vietnamese. They led to community-building and place-making. "Periodically these festering wounds bleed again ... [resulting] in vigorous protests. What the Vietnamese-American community wants to do with these protests is to remind themselves, and others too, not to forget the old South Vietnam that they know and love."[14]

In life, one could define three levels of loss: First, there is the trivial loss—money, wallet, keys—that could be replaced. The second type of loss is that of a friendship. One day, he/she left us: that person who had been so dear to us in many ways is no longer around. We become heartbroken. And until we recover, we feel that something in us is missing. We are no longer wholesome. Our mind wanders around making it difficult for us to concentrate and work. The third type is the loss of a country: the biggest of all losses, for "There is no greater loss than that of losing one's country," claimed Phan Bội Châu, one of Vietnam's greatest non-communist revolutionaries in 1906.[15] What he meant was losing independence to France was akin to losing one's country, although it physically was still there.

But in 1975, the South Vietnamese lost it completely. It was a complete loss with no chance of regaining it back. It left them disoriented in time and space. By escaping to America, they now experience the feeling of belonging to two worlds—"Vietnam and Vietnamese America—and to neither and of responsibility for the communities to which [they] are not always sure to belong."[16]

The Little Saigons

With time, Vietnamese immigrants became Vietnamese-Americans—people who walk around with hyphens between their names. They may no longer be Vietnamese, but not yet or never Americans. They are in limbo between the two worlds, one that had rejected them and one they have not become familiar with. This is not a new phenomenon, as the sociologist Georg Simmel once confronted in the 1900s. He wrote about the immigrant, "The stranger intends to stay, although he cannot even become native." Born of Jewish parents in Berlin, Germany—his father later became a Roman Catholic and his mother a Lutheran—he never felt accepted by German academia despite his talents. He was turned down for many vacant chairmanship positions before being elevated to "full professor without chair" in 1901.[17] He, therefore, knew what it meant to be a "stranger" in a new land.

Along that same vein, a successful Vietnamese business-lady, despite having married an American military lawyer and having children with him, declared: "As for me and the Vietnamese of my generation, there will always be memories of another time and place, another life. I will forever remain an immigrant here. And even when I am happiest, I will remember my beloved Vietnam and the fate of my people. I am the child of war, I am a Vietnamese."[18]

The Vietnamese-Americans, therefore, have to define themselves and their identity before being able to sell it to the American public. They have to submerge into or feel confident about their native culture before feeling comfortable with the American culture. Vietnam for the community is an "era, an epoch, and of course the war, but not a people or a nation. Vietnamese-Americans put forth their own social memories as a way to assert their presence in this country."[19] In order to preserve their identity, their wholesomeness, to validate themselves, and to some degree to boost up or restore their pride and strength, they congregate in ethnic enclaves that are called "Little Saigons," where they could express their Vietnam-ness within the boundaries of the American society.

This may apply to the older generation—the Saigon government officials and military personnel who wielded power in the past, were sent to re-education camps for a long time and had lost everything including their ranks, properties, belongings, and prestige. This may not apply to Vietnamese who came later to make a new life or to second generation Vietnamese-Americans. The latter, born and raised in the U.S., feel at ease within the American society. At home, however, some feel pressure from their parents who push them to follow Vietnamese traditions and remain Vietnamese instead of Vietnamese-Americans. Those who do not want to disrespect their parents, therefore, could be torn apart by the different Vietnamese and American traditions.

The Vietnam War was a war of conquest—an invasion by superior northern military forces against the Republic of (South) Vietnam. By April 1975, Hanoi had sent all of its 16 military divisions—minus one left to protect North Vietnam—racing down National Highway 1 toward Saigon. The arrival of northern communist tanks through the gates of the Independence Palace was a flagrant violation of the 1954 Geneva Accords and the 1972 Paris Accords, two of a long series of violations of human rights against the South Vietnamese. Hanoi had finally thrown down its mask and proved to the world that it had waged for more than two decades a war of conquest against South Vietnam.

When the South Vietnamese Trương Như Tảng, a national Liberation Front (NLF) official and Minister of Justice of the Provisional Revolutionary Government (PRG), returned from the jungle to Saigon on the bandwagon of the northern communists, his mother told him, "My son. You have abandoned everything ... to follow the communists. They will never return to you a particle of the things you have left. You will see. They will betray you, and you will suffer your entire life."[20]

On May 15, 1975, in Saigon, Tảng witnessed on the review stand with northern officials a parade celebrating the conquest. One military organization after another paraded in front of the officials, followed by representatives of all northern military units. At last came a few unkempt NLF troops under Hanoi's flag. Befuddled, Tảng turned to General Văn Tiến Dũng to enquire about the NLF 1st, 3rd, 7th and 9th divisions. Dũng told him: "The army has been reunified."[21] Tảng soon realized that the PRG was only subordinate to the Hanoi government and all the orders came from Hanoi. Realizing a little bit too late that he had been betrayed by Hanoi, Tảng retired from the PRG and escaped from Vietnam as a boat refugee in 1978.

Hanoi has thus committed crimes against humanity by invading South Vietnam, waging a 21-year war, killing millions of people, incarcerating hundreds of thousands and shoving millions of others to the sea. By reaction, it has caused tens of thousands of angry overseas Vietnamese to become more vocal and anti-communist than before. Anti-communism has become the rallying point against the new Vietnamese rulers and the Vietnamese-Americans' new identity. The old divide between expatriates and present Vietnamese rulers, capitalism against communism, has become more visible than in the past as the former try to affirm their identity.

The Two Vietnams

The Two Vietnams was the title of a book published by Bernard Fall in 1963 in which he compared the two Vietnamese states—northern communist and southern democratic—following the partition of the country in 1954. What Westerners did not realize or want to acknowledge was that Vietnam had been psychologically, socially, geographically, and politically divided into two or more entities on various occasions since its formation some 4,000 years ago.

According to mythology, the Vietnamese are the offspring of King Lạc Long Quân (Dragon King) and the fairy Âu Cơ. The latter gave birth to a sac containing 100 eggs that developed into 100 children. The idyllic dragon-fairy union, however, did not last long because Lạc Long Quân one day asked for a divorce. As the couple split up, Âu Cơ took 50 children to the mountains and Lạc Long Quân guided the remaining 50 to the seaside.[22]

This was probably the first recorded divorce by any country in the world. The legend has been so engrained into Vietnamese psyche that it has almost become a reality. Descendants of the highlanders (Mường or Thượng) and lowlanders (Kinh) presently account for 15 and 85 percent of Vietnam's population respectively. That ancient rivalry or split between Thượng and Kinh gave way to a northern-southern rivalry by the end of the 16th century. Either by design or fate, the Vietnamese have long been divided into two different entities. That design eventually became a "curse" for the Vietnamese people.

Between 1627 and 1802 and for almost 200 years, Việt Nam was divided into two states: đàng ngoài (North) and đàng trong (South), the boundaries of which roughly correspond to the 1960s North and South Vietnam. The North was ruled by the Lê kings with the support of the Trịnh lords while the South was controlled by the Nguyễn lords. Without political connection and commerce between the two states, northerners and southerners evolved apart. The short period of reunification (1802–1859) under the southern Lê Kings could not erase the two-century cultural and economic differences between North and South.

When the French moved into and controlled Việt Nam (1859–1945), they separated central Việt Nam from the South and attached it to the North to reshape the country according to administrative and political realms of the times. Since the Vietnamese king ruled from Huế, central Vietnam, the French could not leave it connected to the South without destroying the unity of his kingdom. Cochinchina (South), which was first occupied in 1859, became a French colony that was directly ruled from Paris. The bloc Annam (center) and Tonkin (north) in 1884 became a French protectorate that was nominally administered by a Nguyễn king. Cochinchinese subjects therefore enjoyed rare political perks unknown to those living in Annam or Tonkin: they could become French citizens and had the rights to own a newspaper (freedom of press).

During the Việt Nam War (1954–1975), Việt Nam was divided into two regions described earlier by Bernard Fall through the 1954 Geneva Accords: a communist North Việt Nam and a democratically-oriented South Việt Nam. Therefore, throughout this nearly 400 year history (1600–1975), North and South had evolved separately for 290 years or 70 percent of the time.[23] That separation no doubt has left deep marks on both sides of the country, marks manifested by major cultural, social, economic, and political differences that will not be easily erased by a short reunification period and lingering suspicions between northerners and southerners.

Table 15-1. Political Anatomy of Vietnam During the Last Four Centuries

Period	North	South
1600–1802	đàng ngoài Lê-Trịnh	đàng trong Nguyễn
1802–1859 (Unification)	Đại Việt	Đại Việt
1859–1945	Annam-Tonkin Protectorate	Cochinchina Colony
1954–1975	North Vietnam Communist	South Vietnam Democracy
1975–present	Socialist Vietnam Totalitarian	Little Saigons Democracy

South Việt Nam has existed as a viable state with its own particularities and flavors for the last four centuries, while communist North Vietnam has existed only since 1945. The fall of Saigon, the capital of the South, was due to the barbaric aggression of communist Hanoi against the southern state. Its remnants moved to America and the rest of the free world to establish the Little Saigons.

The history of the fall of Saigon is that of a country divided by two ideologies, totalitarian communism against democratic capitalism,[24]

> One party state against democracy,
> Repression enslavement against freedom[25]
> Red flag against yellow flag,
> Hanoi against Little Saigons
> Injustice against Justice
> Enslavement against Freedom.

As long as there are injustice, corruption, one-party state, and communism, there will always be *two Việt Nams*: before the mid–1970s, a democratic South Vietnam vs. a totalitarian communist North Vietnam[26] and after the 1970s: democratic Little Saigon enclaves vs. a communist Vietnam.

A New Way of Being Vietnamese

How does one define the South Vietnamese, their war, and their patriotism? Is there such a thing as southern patriotism? During the war, Westerners raised questions about the South Vietnamese nationalism, which was thought to be at best soft or nonexistent based on the simple fact that they did not fight as hard as they should have to protect their identity. To link battle losses to a lack of mental vigor or even patriotism is to make a superficial and erroneous assumption about the Vietnamese or worse, to know very little about the lengthy and convoluted Vietnamese history.

The Vietnamese have a long history of fighting against outsiders as well as insiders from 939 CE until today to preserve their freedom. They fought wars, but also built a new nation out of nothing because South Vietnam did not exist prior to 1600 CE. The land that people called South Vietnam once belonged to the Chams and Khmers, Hinduized cultures that once flourished on the Indochinese peninsula.[27] And the year 1600 marked the date when the Vietnamese—mature enough—began splitting up into two nations, North and South, that would rise and compete with each other. This is not to deny its ancient and rich root that took place in its legendary history some four millennia ago.

The Vietnamese came from a noble and supernatural union—that could not expect to last—of a man, a mortal and a *tiên*, a fairy. After laying off 100 "eggs"—from which developed 50 boys and 50 girls—the couple split up. This union became the earliest documented marital divorce in the world.[28] Not acknowledging this Vietnamese duality—there are at least two groups of people in Vietnam[29]—has led to mountains of historical errors and misinterpretations until Bernard Fall wrote *The Two Vietnams* in 1963.

The South Vietnamese are reserved who like to keep their feelings and views private and rarely share intimate feelings, except with trusted friends. This does not mean they are heartless or secretive. Schooled under strict Confucian teachings for the last two millennia, they perceive the self as egocentric that needs to be suppressed in favor of the common interest of society. As in any other Asian society, individualism—and by extension, self-promotion—is rarely viewed as a virtue, although the degree of individualism rises as one goes from North to South Vietnam.

Vietnam is a country built by wars so much that wars are in the blood of the Vietnamese. They live in wars, with wars, and by wars. It seems that no Vietnamese generation has been immune to wars. If there is no major warfare, there would be some type of revolt or uprising somewhere that required to be dealt with.

During the four centuries 1600–2000, Vietnam was embroiled in four major wars that lasted a total of 105 years. The internecine First Vietnamese War (1627–1675) pitted the North (*đàng ngoài*) against the South (*đàng trong*). Without external help, the war dragged on for 48 years until both sides could no longer afford to fight. They finally settled for a truce that kept *đàng ngoài* and *đàng trong* separated and divided for almost 200 years (1627–1800). The Second Vietnamese War (1773–1800), which lasted almost 30 years, began as a civil war in the South pitting the southern Tây Sơn against the Nguyễn before involving the northern Lê/Trịnh regime. It became an Asian regional war as the Siamese (Thai) and Chinese jumped in to fight on one side or another, and finally ended with a definitive victory of the southern Nguyễn over the Tây Sơn and northern Lê/Trịnh. Then came the Third (1945–1954) and Fourth (1954–1975) Vietnam Wars, wars between the Vietnamese communists and nationalists (they were not allied) against the French, then the communists against the Americans and Vietnamese nationalists respectively. Besides these major wars, there were innumerable other battles that pitted one region against another, one sect against another, one minority against the other. All these wars destroyed properties, harvests, countryside, and economy, leaving people destitute. Not acknowledging these Vietnamese wars would also lead to major historical errors.

Without wars, Vietnam would not have been enslaved by foreigners or insiders. Without wars, it would not have been a free country. Defeat and humiliation are followed by victories and triumphs. And the link between these events is war and death. Safer commented that the fabric of Vietnam is "soaked in humiliation and triumph and the blood of millions."[30]

Wars create their own heroes. And people love to recount the heroic tales that make them proud of their heritage. There is nothing like a war victory to boost people's emotions and hormones and to make them feel like enrolling in the army to wage more wars. Victory is intoxicating. There is nothing like a victory to pull people together.

Wars, however, are destructive and its people usually lose when they get involved in them, winners included. Carnage and destruction ravage each party's countryside. If wars enslave people, they also destroy society, justice and properties, impoverish everyone, and tear families apart, especially with the way Hồ, Giáp and Lê Duẩn prosecuted the war. Safer writes that Giáp is "utterly brainwashed by ambition. Sending so many young men to die is never a matter of moral hesitation.... Brave men are the tools for carving one's initials in the pantheon."[31]

Wars are a tragedy, especially in Vietnam where they are so common. This has to do with Vietnam's being a nation or coalition of polarized people. The civil war between communist North and nationalist South Vietnam represented a fight over the *nature* of the Vietnamese society. They fought over whether the country should become a Western democratic society or a totalitarian communist country. The fact that the South Vietnamese lost does not mean that their cause—freedom and independence from the communists—was wrong. It simply means that they have been outmaneuvered.[32] Their cause will stand and be picked up by other people for democracy to prevail.

Four decades after the fall of Saigon, Americans still talk about "The Unending Debate"[33] and the "War that Never Ends."[34] They argue back and forth about the orthodox, revisionist, and anti-revisionist theories and wonder why the ghost of the Vietnam War is still around 50 years later. They simply forget that it was a three-way war: North and South Vietnamese and Americans, or a five-way war if we include the Chinese and the Russians, not two like some authors have written in the past. Take one party out of the equation and the war does not make sense. Second, the Americans just packed their bags in 1973 and decided that the "Mission was accomplished and we are heading home" while the war was still raging on. Third, it was not a usual type of war because its end has been negotiated on the backs of the South Vietnamese. It was a war that ended unjustly, suddenly, and in such an incoherent manner that it has left many South Vietnamese short for words. It was that injustice that has caused the war to be debated again and again. What if the Americans had remained until the end? We will never know the answer.

The war ended as a violent and bloody military conquest of South Vietnam by the communists. If the South Vietnamese could not withstand the communist invasion, they still continue to fight today for the freedom and human rights of the Vietnamese people living under the communist regime. In sum, the South Vietnamese have been at the forefront of Vietnamese culture and civilization:

- It was their forebears who promoted the *nam tiến* (southern expansion), vastly expanding the nation from north to south while carving out under Lord Nguyễn Hoàng and his successors a frontier region named "South Vietnam." They were in Huế in 1400, Qui Nhơn (1471), Nha Trang (1653), Saigon (1698), and Hà Tiên (1780). Without them, there would be no South Vietnam.
- A southerner, Lord Nguyễn Ánh (King Gia Long), reunified the northern and southern parts of the country in 1800, doubling its original size and renaming it Đại Việt.
- Southerners fought against communism from 1954 to 1975 and paid dearly as a result. They not only lost their country and identities, but were also sent to reeducation camps only to escape later from communist enslavement as refugees.
- From 1975 onward, those who could escape abroad (three million people) built diasporic communities worldwide that stand in opposition to the Hanoi communist regime. Today, more than four decades after the fall of Saigon, they stand under the yellow South Vietnamese flag, which is better known overseas than the red communist flag. No other exiled community has been able to fly its flag overseas as freely and proudly in the U.S. as the South Vietnamese do. Second, the Vietnamese are rather insular people. Despite having a long coastline, they have never ventured very far from their shores. But in 1975, they spearheaded a massive sea escape from Vietnam that transformed 3,000,000 insular people into modern seafarers. This was the

Nam tiến (southern advance) (author's map).

largest diaspora in world history of a people in search of freedom and away from Marxism-Leninism. They settled worldwide in Australia, Africa, Asia, Europe, and America.

It is time to acknowledge the existence of two Vietnams: a communist Vietnam as well as a democratic Vietnam, as there are two Koreas and two Chinas. It was the pioneering spirit of the South Vietnamese that brought them to South Vietnam from the 16th to the 18th centuries where they flourished and prospered into an independent and vibrant *đàng trong* (South Vietnam). Through sheer military power, they reunited Vietnam in 1800 and fought in the late 1970s to preserve its independence from communist attack and oppression. By escaping overseas following the fall of Saigon, they reaffirmed their rights and freedom to live in a land free of communism.

The fighting spirit and the pioneering zeal of the South Vietnamese characterize their *New Way* of being Vietnamese. What defines the South Vietnamese are the *nam tiến* and the diaspora. By leaving Hanoi in 1600 CE, they founded South Vietnam, and through the diaspora, by abandoning Saigon to the invading communists in 1975, they found *True Freedom* elsewhere in the world.

Epilogue

One could not look at the Vietnam War without recognizing it as a major tragedy in Vietnamese history that cost the lives of more than 4,000,000 people, civilians as well as soldiers from both sides, North and South. Millions of others were injured or traumatized physically, emotionally and psychologically during the postwar period. The economy underwent a downward spiral for more than a decade after 1975. In the 45+ years since the war, Vietnam has remained stuck at the bottom third of the world. With a GDP per capita of $2,342, it ranks 135th over 192 countries,[1] roughly at the same level as Cambodia and Laos, two neighboring countries it "controls." The revolution not only was a huge failure in terms of financial and human costs, it also kept dividing the Vietnamese: communists inside Vietnam and non-communists overseas.

To understand the Vietnam War, one has to live in it, breathe it and feel it. And no one has lived and suffered in it as much as former Captain Phan Nhật Nam, as a representative of the first generation Vietnamese-American. No one has understood it better than Ms. Thu Anh Nguyễn, a teacher at Sidwell Friends School in Washington, DC, as a representative of the second generation Vietnamese Americans.

Phan Nhật Nam and Thu Anh Nguyễn

Phan Nhật Nam was born on 9 September 1943 in Phú Cát, Thừa Thiên Province, although his ID card recorded the date as 28 December 1942 at Nại Cửu, Quảng Trị Province just below the DMZ.

He enrolled into the Airborne unit following his 1963 graduation from the Dalat Military School until the end of the war. Overall, he spent 14 years in the ARVN and another 14 years in reeducation camps, of which eight were spent in isolation in northern communist camps. In the camps, he had the chance to meet another well-known dissident and prisoner of conscience, Father Thadeus Nguyễn Văn Lý, who counseled him to pray. Father Lý on his part had spent a total of 15 years in reeducation camps.[2] Phan Nhật Nam finally emigrated to the U.S. in 1993 under the ODP program. In the U.S., he continued to write and work as a commentator for the Vietnamese-American television network SBTN.

During the war, as a paratrooper he participated in many battles against the communists and witnessed the many victories as well as the horrors of the war. He was in Quảng Trị in 1972, in An Lộc in 1972, and in the II Corps during the retreat from the highlands in 1975. He was at the exchange of war prisoners when 31,961 communist prisoners were exchanged against 5,000 ARVN soldiers in 1973.³

His vast experience of the Vietnam War led him to write essays and books about the war during and after the event, for which he received many awards. Although he was not a professional writer or a correspondent, he felt the need to detail the war because he had seen a lot of pain, misery, and suffering in that country in turmoil. He wrote about the loss of humanity, the horrors of the war and the pain and misery suffered by civilians and soldiers.⁴ "Writing is like praying in the depth of one's isolation. Writing helps to see the invisible tears rolling down the cheeks after periods of impassibility; writing is like letting a deep sigh out of clenched teeth. I write to let out a long sigh in the night," he once confided to another author and friend. To this day, he suffered from PTSD, which he called a "non-bleeding trauma."⁵

The painful and troubling realities that Phan Nhật Nam saw in his 14 years of war against the communists were far more sinister than those seen by any American GI who had spent at most 12 months of his career in Vietnam, unless he volunteered for another tour of duty. But one year in Vietnam was probably enough for anyone not interested in war.

On the other hand, extrapolating one year of war-experience into the whole 21-year history of the war would not be correct, but would only create many more myths, because each war-year was different from the one that preceded or followed it. Some years were more violent than others and battles did not always occur at the same place twice, except maybe in Quảng Trị.

Ms. Thu Anh Nguyễn, a second-generation Vietnamese-American who had not seen much of the war herself but may have read a lot about it in the American literature, was offered after graduation from college a position teaching English literature to ninth and eleventh graders at a school in Washington, D.C. Among the books she was asked to teach was Tim O'Brien's *The Things They Carried*. During the first year, she did her best teaching the book although she did not like it. Even after taking copious notes of the way her colleagues taught the material and trying to mimic their way of teaching, she was still not happy with the results.

As a Vietnamese immigrant—the daughter of a man who fought the war alongside an American—she wondered how she could teach a book about the Vietnam War when there are no Vietnamese in it. The main scene describes Vietnamese people who are symbolized by a buffalo. Like the water buffalo, Vietnamese people were shot and killed. They have no personalities. No families. They only serve as a backdrop for American bravery and grief.

Since she had the option to choose another book, she opted to teach *The Gangster We Are All Looking For* by Lê Thị Diễm Thúy. It is a novel written by a Vietnamese refugee about the harrowing journey and resettlement of six Vietnamese refugees in late 1970s San Diego. Its broken narrative is a much more realistic reflection of post-traumatic stress disorder than O'Brien's perfectly crafted allegories. As she was able to teach the Vietnam War through the perspective of a Vietnamese family, she found her voice. As she found her voice, her students found her. They said they liked the book. It felt real because it *was* real— because it i*s* real to tell the story of the Vietnam War through a Vietnamese perspective.⁶

The 'Nam War

The ARVN had waged war against the communists since the end of World War II, first alongside the French then with the Americans, and every day since the 1950s from the level of platoons to that of divisions. They would have continued the fight had the U.S. granted them continuing military support. The ARVN and the PAVN knew each other well since they are from the same Kinh stock.[7] The 'Nam War was a war of aggression by northerners against southerners, not a war for independence or of liberation like the communists had claimed. And the VC was just a creation of northerners for as soon as the war was over in May 1975, the VC was pushed aside and discarded like dead wood. It was felt that we [Hanoi] "were not obliged to unveil our cards" during the war, the big Hanoi generals told the VC Trương Như Tảng[8] during the victory parade in Saigon after the war.

For more than four decades after the war, the communists had ruled over Vietnam and wrecked it politically and economically. As a result, Vietnam is no better than its poor neighbors, Cambodia and Laos. "While Hồ Chí Minh and his comrades won the battle to control Vietnam, they lost the war to establish Communism there.... Communism, it turned out, was not a viable way of life, but, to borrow the words that have been used to describe and dismiss South Vietnam, rather a pseudo, counterfeited system," wrote Michael Kort in his analysis of the war.[9]

It was wrong to assume that South Vietnam did not contribute anything to the war effort. By accepting to fight communism, it put its economy on hold and used all its economic and manpower resources to build up its war machinery. The more than 350,000 ARVN war deaths from a population of 16 million would be equal to 4 million deaths from a country the size of the U.S. One just has to figure how the Americans—especially those who had violently opposed the war when the death toll rose to 30,000 people—would have reacted had they faced even 100,000 or half-a-million war deaths.

Over the years, the ARVN had markedly grown in size and displayed a remarkable fighting power from an almost nonexistent army in the 1950s to a million-man army ten years later. That rapid expansion had led to a decline in leadership that could not be addressed right away. Had the ARVN been strengthened by U.S. forces, like the Korean forces were in the 1950s, its fighting power would have been markedly increased. By relegating the ARVN to a "pacification duty," Westmoreland significantly curtailed the growth of the ARVN for many crucial years. New military schools, which were planned back in the late 1950s when the Americans took over from the French, were only established in 1967; and new armaments (M-16 rifle, M-79 grenade launchers) were only provided to the fighting ARVN in late 1968, four long years after the VC and PAVN forces received theirs.

This resulted in ARVN having a lower "kill ratio"—the number of enemy killed proportional to losses—than U.S. forces. Abrams was quick to point out the reason why. "The ARVN doesn't have the firepower; it doesn't have the mobility; it doesn't have the communications. It also doesn't get the allocation of air support."[10]

Despite these drawbacks, the ARVN fought well from 1965 onward. And they fought better during the Tết Offensive when the VC and PAVN troops decided to attack the cities and provincial capitals, even though ARVN units were at half-strength because of the Tết truce. They even fought better during the 1972

Easter Offensive when they defeated the enemy at An Lộc, Kontum, and Quảng Trị. "The improvements that took place in those four years [1968–72] were fantastic—in the quality and fighting abilities of the Vietnamese, the arms that they had, and the improvement of the Regional and Popular Forces," suggested Berger.[11] Veith also mentioned that

> The South Vietnamese were far from the incompetent bunglers so often depicted. Many of them demonstrated incredible courage, even in hopeless situations such as the battles of Tan Son Nhut, Ho Nai and many others. By 1973, the South Vietnamese military, despite numerous internal and economic issues, had developed into a fighting force quite capable of defeating the North Vietnamese. If it had been adequately supplied, and with steady American post-ceasefire support, the outcome of the war might have been vastly different.[12]

The best acknowledgment came from Colonel William Le Gro, a senior staff officer with the U.S. MACV and its successor, the U.S. DAO, who wrote the following dedication to the ARVN in his book *Vietnam from Cease-Fire to Capitulation*: "… with enduring respect to all the fighting men of South Vietnam, especially the infantry, rangers, airborne troops, and marines. May this book preserve at least a partial record of those who fought long, bravely, and under great handicaps and hardships to preserve individual freedom in their country."[13]

"Unit for unit and man for man, the combat forces of South Vietnam repeatedly proved themselves superior to their adversaries," wrote Le Gro.[14] South Vietnam and the ARVN, however, suffered from a lack of political-military leadership, which was normal for a country that just emerged from 87 years of colonialism. It used to be said that "South Vietnam was a country with half of everything. It was half-democracy and half-dictatorship and the measures taken by the government were most of the time half-measures. The result of this was that nothing worked as it should." Also "there was no sense of purpose or direction among the high officials of the government, and strangely enough, [no] sense of urgency about the situation."[15]

Some ARVN officers also argued that "President Thiệu was a good officer but a mediocre general. His combat record was unimpressive."[16] He was prone to "inaction" and was

> very slow to change his mind … and clung stubbornly to ideas and policies once he had developed them. … Being an Army general, the President actually enjoyed the idea of personally exercising his authority as the Commander-in-Chief of the Armed Forces. And he could not resist the temptation to direct military operations from his office…. Meanwhile the Ministry of Defense had no real authority over the JGS (which itself had little authority…).[17]

The ARVN also suffered from a lack of planning. "Knowing the Americans were leaving, the GVN did not have any plan to hold onto the territory, no spoiling attack against enemy infiltration, pipeline, highway built by the NVA."[18] And "The JGS was very weak in concepts and in personnel. Its Chief, described as very passive, remained in place…. General Viên did nothing and it was hard to reach him. That was because he did not want the job. He wanted to quit for a long time and no one would let him go."[19]

Saigon planners lacked options. They did not have the mobility or firepower or strategic reserves for an effective defense against strong attacks, let alone for large spoiling operations against the enemy's massive inroads. They could not surrender territories as that meant surrendering populations to the enemy. The only thing the ARVN could have done was to cause damage to the enemy as much as they could for their own honor and the maintenance of their own morale, and partly to put up a good show, slow up the enemy.[20]

General Abrams wrote in May 1972, "Enemy staying power is his most effective battlefield characteristic. It is based first on his complete disregard for the expenditure of resources, both men and materiel, and second on discipline through fear, intimidation, and brutality. An enemy decision to attack carries an inherent acceptance that the forces involved may be expended totally."[21]

The Americans really wanted to help South Vietnam but did so very poorly, whereas the French meant to exploit them and did quite well at that.[22]

Hastily and poorly conceived, the [Enhance] program[23] had no military value. In fact, a lot of this equipment could not be effectively used because they needed men and money just to care for and service them. Each of them had its special nuts, bolts, parts, batteries, oils, and so on, without which they could not function. Even General Davidson noted, "Enhance and Enhance Plus had loaded the RVNAF with equipment, but it soon became apparent that the United States had given South Vietnam airplanes they couldn't fly, ships they couldn't man, and tanks and other equipment they couldn't maintain."[24]

The decrease in economic/military aid in turn affected the economic and social stability of the country. Signs of political instability began to appear and support of the government became somewhat diminished. The ARVN's fighting spirit was reduced in the final months of 1974, at a time when the enemy began its attack on Phước Long. One bit of bad news after another dampened the mood of the population.

The effect of reduced aid adversely impacted on ARVN's operations. It caused an increase in the rate of casualties. Military hospitals were overcrowded; they were short in blood, plasma, dextrose, medicines, and antibiotics. Combat units saw their ranks decrease. Recruiting operations became difficult. These factors, added to the economic difficulties, decreased the morale of the army and the country.

The War Could Have Been Won

There were also missed opportunities from the American side. General Lâm Quang Thi suggested that the war could have been won had the U.S. generals had more "imagination and charisma."[25] With its powerful military strength, the U.S. could have defeated the enemy in 1968 or soon thereafter. The basic flaw of U.S. policy in Vietnam was the "lack of clarity of mission."[26]

Had a U.S. division taken the ARVN under its tutelage from the beginning, as the U.S. did with the South Koreans in Korea, or had the Vietnamization started in 1964 or earlier, the ARVN would have been in a much stronger position and taken over the defense of the country by 1968 or soon after. And U.S. forces would have gone home earlier with a lot fewer casualties.

The United States policy in Vietnam, although well-intentioned, was at best erratic in execution. At a time when things were getting better, the U.S. decided to fold and get out. "American support for an indefinite period would have made a difference. Given more time, a new generation of younger South Vietnam leaders probably could have produced the leadership to institute the internal reforms so badly needed," remarked former Colonel LeGro.[27] It was also not good for the U.S. to take over the war in 1964 and drop the ball in 1968. "Better they do it imperfectly than you do it perfectly, for it is their country, their war, and your time is limited," T.E. Lawrence once advised in his *Seven Pillars of Wisdom*.[28]

One good thing is that the population trusted and had faith in the ARVN; they kept coming back to seek out protection from the communists. In Quảng Trị in 1972 and 1975, they voted with their feet and ran toward the ARVN forces. In the highlands, they ran with the ARVN to the point of preventing the troops from retreating in good order. John Vann said not long before the 1972 Easter Offensive, "The basic fact of life is that the overwhelming majority of the population—somewhere around 95 percent—prefer the government of Vietnam to a communist government or the government that's being offered by the other side."[29]

The ARVN is dead. It did not save South Vietnam and the South Vietnamese, but it helped a younger generation to mature and emerge in order to survive a diaspora and thrive in the free world; and also, it helped the Yellow Flag[30] to unite them in the fight for the freedom of all Vietnamese. By 2020, the ARVN could be seen as ushering the South Vietnamese to the new lands of Freedom, a Freedom that they fought for so long but could not find it under a communist Vietnam. Like their forefathers who in 1600 moved to the southern lands to build and create a new South Vietnam that did not exist before, the South Vietnamese of 1975 had to move to western foreign lands to find their freedom and peace.

This book is about the ARVN, an above average army that had shown persistence and great courage before adversity in war as well as peace; that had suffered through deprivation, pain, blood, tears, life and death, battles, inadequate manpower and materiel, reeducation camps, and even diaspora. This was an army that had gone through reeducation camps and whose five generals, along with scores of other officers and soldiers, killed themselves instead of surrendering.

Although many people do not believe it, the Vietnam War was a war of ideologies fighting for the freedom and independence of the Vietnamese people. That a small country of 16 million people was willing to sacrifice more than 350,000 soldiers and untold numbers of wounded to defend unto death its freedom against the invading northern communists vividly proved the persistent gallantry of the ARVN men and the just cause they were fighting for. They will never bow to communism. Long live freedom. Long live the ARVN.

Glossary

AB—air base
ABD—airborne division
ACR—armored cavalry regiment
AID—Agency for International Development
AK-47—standard communist 7.62 mm automatic rifle
Annam—Central Vietnam (during the French colonization period)
APC—armored personnel carrier
ARVN—Army of the Republic of Vietnam
ATF—Armored Task Force
CBU—Cluster bomb Fuel Air Explosive
CIDG—Civilian Irregular Defense Group
CINCPAC—Commander in Chief Pacific Fleet Headquarters
CIP—Commercial Import Program
CO—commanding officer
Cochinchina—South Vietnam (during the French colonization period)
COMUSMACV—commander, U.S. Military Assistance Command Vietnam
CP—command post
CORDS—Civilian Operations and Rural Development Support
COSVN—Central Office for South Vietnam (communist)
Đại Việt—Nationalist Party of Greater Vietnam
DAO—Defense Attaché Office
DMZ—demilitarized zone
DTOC—Division Tactical Operations Center

FAC—forward air controller
FO—forward observer
FEC—French Expeditionary Corps
FSB—fire support base
GP—general purpose
GVN—Government of Vietnam (Saigon)
HQ—headquarters
ICP—Indochinese Communist Party
IDP—Industrial Development Project
IIFFV—II Field Force Vietnam
JDOC—Joint Defense Operations Center
JCS—Joint Chiefs of Staff (U.S.)
JGS—Joint General Staff (Vietnamese)
LAW—66 mm light antitank weapon
LZ—Landing zone
M-14—non-standard U.S. 7.62 mm automatic rifle
M-16—standard U.S. 5.56 mm automatic rifle
M-60—standard U.S. 7.62 mm machine gun
M-79—standard U.S. 40 mm grenade launcher
MAAGV—Military Assistance Advisory Group, Vietnam
MACV—Military Assistance Command Vietnam
MAP—Military Assistance Program
MI—military intelligence
MPC—military payment certificates
MP—military police

MSG—military security guard
NCO—noncommissioned officer
NLF—National Liberation Front (communist)
NVA—North Vietnamese Army
PAVN—People's Army of Vietnam (or NVA)
PLAF—People's Liberation Armed Force (or VC)
PLAN—People's Liberation Army Navy (communist)
PF—popular forces
PRC—People's Republic of China (communist)
RF—regional forces
ROC—Republic of China (nationalist, non-communist)
RPG—rocket-propelled grenade
RVN—Republic of Vietnam (South Vietnam)
RVNAF—Republic of Vietnam Armed Forces
S1—personnel officer at battalion or brigade level
S2—intelligence officer at battalion or brigade level
S3—operations officer at battalion or brigade level
S4—logistics officer at battalion or brigade level
SOG—Studies and Observation Group
SP—security police
SPS—security police squadron
SRAG—Second Regional Assistance Group

TCK–TKN—Tổng Công Kích-Tổng Khởi Nghĩa (General Offensive–General Uprising)
TF—task force
TOC—tactical operations center
Tonkin—North Vietnam (during the French colonization period)
TOW—Tube-launched, Optically tracked, Wire-guided antitank missile
TRAC—Third Regional Assistance Command
TRIM—Training Relations and Instructions Mission
TSNSA—Tân Sơn Nhứt Sensitive Area
USA—United States Army
USAF—United States Air Force
USMACV—U.S. Military Assistance Command, Vietnam
USMC—United Marine Corps
VC—Việt Cộng
VCP—Vietnamese Communist Party
Việt Minh—Việt Nam Độc Lập Đồng Minh Hội (League for the Independence of Vietnam)
VNQDD—Việt Nam Quốc Dân Đảng or Vietnamese Nationalistic Party
VNA—Vietnamese National Army
VNAF—Vietnamese Air Force
VNMC—Vietnamese Marine Corps

Appendix I

List of Vietnamese Reeducation Camps

Saigon-Thủ Đức Region

An Dương
Bạch Đằng
Chí Hòa
Đại Lợi Hotel
Đại Nam Hotel
Hóc Môn Thắng Lợi
Cảnh Sát Quốc Gia
Phạm Đăng Lưu
Tô Hiến Thành
Thủ Đức
Cảnh Sát Saigon

Sông Bé Region

Bù Đốp
Bù Gia Mập
Bồ Lá
Long Nguyên
Phước Long
Phước Bình
Phú Lợi

Đồng Nai Region

Xuyên Mộc
Xuân Lộc
Biên Hòa
Long Thành
Long Giao
Long Khánh
Bà Rịa
Hố Nai
Gia Rây (Z-30)
Trảng Bờm
Suối Máu
Trang Tao

Tây Ninh Region

Trạng Lớn
Bầu Cơ
Đồng Ban
Cây Cay (A and B)
Katum
Tây Ninh
Suối Nước

Cữu Long Region

Gò Nhum
Vĩnh Long
Châu Thanh
Cần Thơ
Vĩnh Châu

Hậu Giang Region

Bạc Liêu
Bầu An
Can Bình
Chương Thiện (D18)
Sốc Trăng
Trà Chốt
Cồn Cát

Tiền Giang Region

Cái Bè
Mỹ Tho
Vường Đào

Bến Tre Region

Bến Tre
Ba Tri
Bầu Sen
Bến Giá
Con Ông

Minh Hải Region

Kinh Ngang
Quản Long
Cây Gùa
Rạch Ruộng

An Giang Region

Long Xuyên
Chi Lăng
Châu Đốc
Cái Lăng

Kiên Giang Region

Rạch Giá
Kinh Một
Hà Tiên
Phú Quốc
U Minh

Thuận Hải Region

Hàm Tân (Z-30D)
Bình Tuy
Chân Chùa
Đá Mài
Phan Rang
Phan Thiết

Darlac Region

Ban Mê Thuột
Đức Lập

Quảng Nam- Đà Nẵng Region

Tiến Lành
An Điềm
Quảng Nam
Đà Nẵng

Nghĩa Bình Region

An Khê
Ba To
K18
Qui Nhơn
Quảng Ngãi
Trà Bồng
Tam Quang

Phú Khánh Region

Ngân Điền (T51, 52, 53, 54)
Nghĩa Phú
Lạc Chi (A 30)
Lu Ba

Lâm Đồng Region

Di Linh
Đại Bình
Madagui

Gia Lai-Kontum Region

Kontum
Gia Trung
Pleiku

Thừa Thiên Region

Huế

Vịnh Region

Tam Đảo
Vịnh

Thanh Hóa Region

Thanh Lam

Thiếu Yên (Lý Ba So)
Thanh Phong

Hà Nam Ninh Region

Ba Sao (Đầm Đùn)
Ninh Bình
Nam Định
Nam Hà
Song Me

Hà Sơn Bình Region

Ba Vì
Hòa Bình

Nghệ Thanh Region

Con Cuôn
Thanh Chương
Hà Tĩnh
Nghệ Tĩnh

Hà Tây Region

Hà Tây

Hải Hưng Region

Hải Dương

Hà Tuyên Region

Hà Giang
Nghĩa Lộ
Quyết Tiến (Cổng Trời)
Tuyên Quang

Yên Bái Region

Liên Trại 1

Hoàng Liên Sơn Region

Phố Lử
Lao Kai
Phong Quang

Vĩnh Phú Region

Vinh Quang (A, B)
Phú Sơn
Vĩnh Phú (Tân Lập)

Hà Bắc Region

Yên Thế

Lại Châu Region

Lại Châu

Sơn La Region

Điện Biên Phủ

Cao Lạng Region

Cao Bằng
Lạng Sơn

Quảng Ninh Region

Quảng Ninh

Bình Trị Thiên Region

Đồng Hới
Khe Sanh
Lao Bao
Quảng Trị

Chapter Notes

Introduction

1. William Waddell, *In the Year of the Tiger. The War for Cochinchina, 1945–1951* (Norman: University of Oklahoma Press, 2018), pp. 5–6. While Europeans hunted the boars to show their martial prowess, Asians preferred the tigers. The latter are furtive and silent, their ranges are immense and it is difficult to track them down. To hunt the tiger requires a different mindset.
2. Belote is a card game similar to bridge. It is popular in France and other European countries.
3. Jean Larteguy, *The Centurions* (New York: Penguin Classic, 2015), pp. 181–182.
4. Even after leaving North Vietnam, the French lingered in Saigon and South Vietnam for two more years during which they prevented Prime Minister, then President, Ngô Đình Diệm to build a new non-communist nation as well as a new army.
5. Lewis Sorley, *Westmoreland. The General Who Lost Vietnam* (Boston: Houghton Mifflin Harcourt, 2011), pp. 77–79.
6. https://en.wikipedia.org/wiki/William_Westmoreland, accessed November 30, 2019.
7. The Americanization of the war began in March 1965 when 3,500 Marines landed ashore in Đà Nẵng and the drawdown began in 1969 (4 years) and completed in 1972 (7 years). The active participation at most was 7 out of the 21-year war duration or 33 percent.
8. Quoted in Robert K. Brigham, *ARVN: Life and Death in the South Vietnamese Army* (Lawrence: University Press of Kansas, 2006), p. x.
9. "Memorandum from Secretary of Defense McNamara to President Johnson, March 26, 1964," *Foreign Relations of the United States* (hereafter *FRUS*), *Vietnam 1964–1968*, Vol. 4 (Washington, D.C.: Government Printing Office, 1994), p. 732.
10. "Memorandum from George Carver of the Vietnamese Affairs Staff, Central Intelligence Agency to Director of Central Intelligence Helms, July 7, 1966," *FRUS, Vietnam 1964–1968*, Vol. 4, p. 486.
11. Frances Fitzgerald, *Fire in the Lake: The Vietnamese and Americans in Vietnam* (New York: Vintage Books, 1972), pp. 263–266.
12. Mark Bowden, *Hue 1968. A Turning Point of the American War in Vietnam* (New York: Atlantic Monthly Press, 2017), p. 14.
13. Max Hastings, *Vietnam: An Epic Tragedy: 1945–1975* (New York: Harper, 2018), p. 279.
14. Stephen Hosmer, Konrad Kellen, and Brian Jenkins, *The Fall of South Vietnam* (New York: Crane Russak, 1980). Hosmer's detailed book describes the perceptions of 27 former high ranking South Vietnamese officers and civilians about the fall of Saigon; Robert Brigham, *ARVN. Life and Death in the South Vietnamese Army* (Lawrence: University of Kansas Press, 2006). Brigham's book is a "social history" book; Nathalie Nguyen, *South Vietnamese Soldiers. Memories of the Vietnam War and After* (Santa Barbara, CA: Praeger, 2016); Julie Pham, *Their War. The Perspectives of the South Vietnamese Military in the Words of Veterans—Émigrés* (Amazon, 2019). Pham's 85-page long book was an interesting undergraduate thesis that was written in 2001 and republished in 2019.
15. Pham, *Their War*, p. 13; Hosmer, Kellen, and Jenkins, *The Fall of South Vietnam*, pp. 72–76.
16. *Ibid.*, pp. 40–41.
17. Brigham, *ARVN*, p. 47.
18. Pham, *Their War*, p. 47.
19. *Ibid.*, pp. 53–54.
20. Clarke, *Advice and Support*, p. 503.
21. Pham, *Their War*, pp. 53–55.
22. Hosmer, Kellen, and Jenkins, *The Fall of South Vietnam*, pp. 180–181, 240.
23. Nguyen Cong Luan, *Nationalist in the Vietnam War: Memoir of a Victim Turned Soldier* (Bloomington: Indiana University Press, 2012), p. 556.
24. Hastings, *Vietnam: An Epic Tragedy*, p. 192.
25. Nghia M. Vo, *The Bamboo Gulag: Political Imprisonment in Communist Vietnam* (Jefferson, NC: McFarland. 2004), pp. 209–214. Situated in the outskirts of Saigon, built in 1960, modeled after Arlington National Cemetery and dedicated in 1966, the Biên Hòa National Cemetery was designed to be the final resting place of thousands of soldiers who had served and given their lives to their country.
26. David Lamb, *Vietnam Now: A Reporter Returns* (New York: Public Affairs, 2003), p. 100.
27. During the years in concentration camps, they did not earn any money, leaving their families poor and destitute. Their wives had to sell

household belongings or do menial work to survive and once released from the camps, they did not have any savings account to either buy their way out of the country or file the necessary paperwork to immigrate to the U.S.

28. Luan, *Nationalist in the Vietnam War*, p. 557.

29. Nguyen Dinh Sai, "The National Flag of Viet Nam: Its Origin and Legitimacy," (The Yellow Flag), https://web.archive.org/web/20050512031344/http://www.vpac-usa.org/flag/The%20National%20Flag%20of%20VN.pdf. It has been in existence since the end of the nineteenth century (1802) and represented the flag of the Nguyen dynasty.

30. Anh Do, "Nearly 40 Years After War's End, Flag of South Vietnam Endures," *Los Angeles Times*, December 27, 2014, https://www.latimes.com/local/california/la-me-ff-south-vietnamese-flag-20141228-story.html; Shawn Crispin, "South Vietnam Flag Still Flies High," *ATI News*, July 23, 2017, https://cms.ati.ms/2017/07/south-vietnam-flag-still-flies-high/.

Chapter 1

1. The Vietnamese had been fighting against each other since the birth of their nation in the tenth century C.E. There had been two other Vietnam Wars—as defined by involvement of North and South Vietnam—prior to the 1945–1954 Vietnam War; the latter should then be labeled as the Third Vietnam War to be correct (see chapter 15). This is the chronology of these wars:
   - 1627–1675: First Vietnam War between *đàng trong* (South Vietnam) and *đàng ngoài* (North Vietnam)
   - 1773–1800: Second Vietnam War, which began between two southern factions: the Nguyễn and the Tây Sơn. It then involved these two factions against the northerners (the Lê/Trịnh)
   - 1945–1954: Third Vietnam War involving the French and South Vietnamese against the North Vietnamese
   - 1954–1975: Fourth Vietnam War involving the Americans and South Vietnamese against the North Vietnamese communists

2. Waddell, *In the Year of the Tiger*, pp. 6–7.

3. Arthur Dommen, *The Indochinese Experience of the French and the Americans, Nationalism and Communism in Cambodia, Laos and Vietnam* (Bloomington: Indiana University Press, 2001), pp. 39–40; Neil Jamieson, *Understanding Vietnam* (Berkeley: University of California Press, 1993), pp. 178–180.

4. Dommen, *The Indochinese Experience*, pp. 45–46, 53–54; Robert Turner, *Vietnamese Communism. Its Origin and Development* (Stanford, CA: Stanford University, 1975), pp. 58–59, 177.

5. Người Việt, người *Kinh* designated a Southeast Asian ethnic group that lived in or close to the cities. They are to be distinguished from the other 54 non–*Kinh* ethnic groups called highlanders or *Mường*.

6. Hinduized or Indianized.

7. Nguyễn Hoàng quoted in George Dutton, Jayne Werner, and John Whitmore, *Sources of Vietnamese Traditions* (New York: Colombia University Press, 2012), p. 155.

8. K.W. Taylor, *A History of the Vietnamese* (New York: Cambridge University Press, 2013), p. 252.

9. Confucianism is a system of philosophical and ethical teachings founded by the Chinese Confucius and developed by Mencius.

10. The French subdivided Vietnam into three regions: 1. North Vietnam (Tonkin); 2. Central Vietnam (Annam); and 3. South Vietnam (Cochinchina). The North Vietnamese call these regions: Bắc Bộ, Trung Bộ, and Nam Bộ. The South Vietnamese use the names: Bắc Kỳ, Trung Kỳ, Nam Kỳ. The 1954 Geneva Accords divided Vietnam into two states: the northern communist Democratic Republic of Vietnam or DRV (Tonkin) and the Republic of South Vietnam (RVN) or Government of Vietnam (GVN), which comprises Annam and Cochinchina.

11. Hue Tam Ho Tai, *Millenarianism and Peasant Politics in Vietnam* (Cambridge, MA: Harvard University Press, 1983), pp. 11–12.

12. Bernard Fall, "The Political Religious Sects in Vietnam," *Pacific Affairs* 28, no. 3 (1955): pp. 235–253.

13. Waddell, *In the Year of the Tiger*, pp. 47–53.

14. Dommen, *The Indochinese Experience*, p. 255.

15. *Ibid.*, pp. 176–177.

16. Bao Dai, *Le Dragon d' Annam* (Paris: Plon, 1980), p. 177. All non-communist nationalist parties and their members were gradually eliminated by the communists until only the communist party was left.

17. Dommen, *The Indochinese Experience*, pp. 185–189.

18. Saigon Consulate General to State, telegram 193, June 14, 1949, *FRUS 1949*, vol. VIII, pt. 1, pp. 47–48. Caodaism is a syncretic, monotheistic religion established in the city of Tây Ninh, South Vietnam in 1926. It combines Buddhism, Christianity, Taoism, Confucianism, and Islam. Hòa Hảo is a lay peasant Buddhism founded by the reformer Huỳnh Phú Sổ in 1939 in the Mekong River Delta. Bình Xuyên was a criminal organization that traded support for legal protection of their rackets: gambling casinos, opium dens.

19. Paris Embassy to State, telegram 3037, July 24, 1949, *FRUS 1949*, vol. VII, pt 1, pp. 69–70.

20. Yves Gras, *Histoire de la Guerre d' Indochine* (Paris: Plon, 1979), pp. 357.

21. Bảo Dai, *Le Dragon d' Annam*, pp. 250–253.

22. James Collins, *The Development and Training of the South Vietnamese Army* (Washington D.C.: Department of the Army, 1975), p. 1.

23. Gras, *Histoire de la Guerre d' Indochine*, pp. 578–579.

24. See table 8-4, chapter Eight. The ARVN lost 58,877 soldiers under the French during the First Vietnam War and close to 300,000 during the Second Vietnam War.
25. Collins, *The Development and Training of the South Vietnamese Army*, p. 4.
26. *Ibid.*, pp. 1–2.
27. Memorandum from Young to Hoover, Washington, December 14, 1954. *FRUS 1952–1954*, vol. XIII, pt. 2, pp. 2369–2375.
28. Dommen, *The Indochinese Experience*, p. 282.
29. Saigon Embassy to State, telegram 4194, March 30, 1955. *FRUS 1955–1957*, vol. I, pp. 159–163.
30. Dommen, *The Indochinese Experience*, p. 283.
31. Seth Jacobs, *America's Miracle Man in Vietnam* (Durham: Duke University Press, 2004), p. 195.
32. Memorandum of conversation, Mansfield and Young, Washington, April 8, 1955, *FRUS 1955–1957*, vol. I, pp. 221–222.
33. Dommen, *The Indochinese Experience*, p. 289.
34. Joseph Buttinger, *Vietnam: A Dragon Embattled* (Santa Barbara: Praeger, 1967), pp. 881–883.
35. Dommen, *The Indochinese Experience*, p. 291. Many officers of the Vietnamese National Army were either French citizens by birth through their naturalized landowner-parents or became naturalized after getting promoted as officers in the VNA.
36. Lam Quang Thi, *The Twenty Five Year Century* (Denton: The University of North Texas Press, 2001), p. 87.
37. Philip Catton, *Diem's Final Failure: Prelude to America's War in Vietnam* (Lawrence: University Press of Kansas, 2003), pp. 2–3.
38. *Ibid.*, p. 19.
39. Tran Van Don, *Our Endless War Inside Vietnam* (Novato, CA: Presidio, 1978), pp. 148–149.
40. Robert McNamara, James Blight and Robert Brigham, *Argument Without End: In Search of Answers to the Vietnam Tragedy* (New York: Public Affairs, 1999), p. 321.
41. Brigham, *ARVN*, p. 5.
42. Don, *Our Endless War*, p. 149.
43. Don, *Our Endless War*, p. 150; Brigham, *ARVN*, p. 6.
44. Don, *Our Endless War*, p. 150.
45. Dong Van Khuyen, *The RVNAF* (Washington, D.C.: U.S. Army Center of Military History, 1984), pp. 34–50.
46. Brigham, *ARVN*, p. 18.
47. Catton, *Diem's Final Failure*, p. 23. Diệm, Ngô Đình Diệm, and the Ngos are used interchangeably.
48. Collins, *The Development and Training of the South Vietnamese Army*, pp. 5–6.
49. *Ibid.*, pp. 8–9, 16.
50. *Ibid.*, pp. 17–18.
51. Catton, *Diem's Final Failure*, pp. 40–41.
52. Brigham, *ARVN*, p. x.
53. Catton, *Diem's Final Failure*, pp. 33–36.
54. John M. Shaw, *The Cambodian Campaign. The 1970 Offensive and America's Vietnam War* (Lawrence: University of Kansas, 2005), p. 2.
55. Shaw, *The Cambodian Campaign*, p. 3.
56. Interview of Nguyễn Hữu Lâm, Virginia, USA, April 2019.
57. Shaw, *The Cambodian Campaign*, p. 3.
58. Nathalie Chau Nguyen, *South Vietnamese Soldiers* (Santa Barbara: Praeger, 2016), p. 217, note 36. This is one of the books dealing with the ARVN by Australian researcher Nathalie Chau Nguyen. She set out to interview a series of ARVN veterans living in Australia.
59. Shaw, *The Cambodian Campaign*, p. 5.
60. Bao Ninh, *The Sorrow of War* (New York, Riverhead Books, 1995), p. 18.
61. *Ibid.*, p. 12.
62. The ARVN, *Vietnam Bulletin* (Washington D.C.: Vietnam Embassy, 1969). This is a 30-page newsletter issued by the Republic of Vietnam Embassy in Washington DC in 1969.
63. Brigham, *ARVN*, pp. 119–120.
64. *Ibid.*, p. 121.
65. Andrew Wiest, *Vietnam's Forgotten Army. Heroism and Betrayal in the ARVN* (New York: New York University Press, 2008), p. 121.
66. James Willbanks, *Abandoning Vietnam. How America Left and South Vietnam Lost its War* (Lawrence: University Press of Kansas, 2004), p. 267.
67. Văn Tiến Dũng. *Đại Thắng Mùa Xuân* (Our great spring victory) (Hanoi: Nhà Xuất Bản Quân Đội Nhân Dân, 1977), p. 167.
68. Mark McLeod, *The Vietnamese Response to French Intervention 1862–1874* (New York: Praeger, 1991), p. 62–65.
69. Nghia M. Vo, *Saigon. A History* (Jefferson, NC: McFarland, 2011), pp. 92–93.
70. *Ibid.*, pp. 94–95.
71. David Marr, *Vietnamese Tradition on Trial, 1920–1940* (Berkeley: University of California Press, 1981), pp. 188–193.
72. Van Nguyen Duong. *The Tragedy of the Vietnam War* (Jefferson, NC: McFarland, 2008), p. 39.
73. Catton, *Diem's Final Failure*, p. 41, 46.
74. *Ibid.*, p. 49.
75. Tuong Vu, *Vietnam's Communist Revolution* (New York: Cambridge University Press, 2017), p. 1.
76. *Ibid.*, p. 7.
77. *Ibid.*, pp. 18–19.
78. *Ibid.*, pp. 20–21.
79. See tables 8-3 and 8-4, chapter Eight. The ARVN lost 58,877 soldiers under the French during the First Vietnam War and close to 300,000 during the Second Vietnam War.
80. http://www.soft-vision.com/ranger/index2.html?http%3A//www.soft-vision.com/ranger/home/htm.

81. Cầu Lê quoted in Gil Dorland, *Legacy of Discord: Voicers of the Vietnam War Era* (Sterling, VA: Potomac Books, 2001), p. 143.
82. Collins, *The Development and Training of the South Vietnamese Army*, p. 151.

Chapter 2

1. COSVN or Central Office for South Vietnam: imagined headquarters of the communist forces in South Vietnam. Its existence, physical location, and importance are contentious subjects.
2. Ha Mai Viet, *Steel and Blood. South Vietnamese Armor and the War for Southeast Asia* (Annapolis, MD: Naval Institute Press, 2008), p. 362, note 19.
3. Hastings, *Vietnam: An Epic Tragedy*, p. 160.
4. Ha Mai Viet, *Steel and Blood*, p. 10.
5. Mark Moyar, *Triumph Forsaken. The Vietnam War, 1954–1965* (New York: Cambridge University Press, 2006), p. 187. That was the way the communists worked: luring a small number of government forces into a trap where they held advantage to ambush them.
6. Larry Berman, *Perfect Spy. The Incredible Double Life of Pham Xuan An* (New York: Harper Perennial, 2007), pp. 134–143.
7. The Bảo An or Civil Guards were para-military organizations that were coalesced together and converted into Regional Forces in 1964.
8. Ha Mai Viet, *Steel and Blood*, p. 11.
9. More than sixty U.S. and VNAF planes participated in the battle of Tây Ninh in War Zone C.
10. Moyar, *Triumph Forsaken*, p. 188.
11. Vinh Truong, *Vietnam War. The New Legion*, Vol. 1 (Victoria, Canada: Trafford, 2010), p. 361.
12. Moyar, *Triumph Forsaken*, p. 189.
13. Ly Tong Ba, "The Battle of Ap Bac. Myth and Reality," http://baovecovang2012.wordpress.com/2013/01/15/tran-ap-bac-thuc-te-va-huyen-thoai-chuan-tuong-ly-tong-ba/.
14. Ha Mai Viet, *Steel and Blood*, p. 13.
15. Moyar, *Triumph Forsaken*, p. 190.
16. Ha Mai Viet, *Steel and Blood*, p. 15.
17. Truong, *Vietnam War*, p. 377.
18. Moyar, *Triumph Forsaken*, p. 191.
19. Truong, *Vietnam War*, p. 407.
20. Ly Tong Ba. *Hoi Ky 25 Nam Khoi Lua* (Memoir of 25 Years of Warfare) (Westminster, CA: Self-Published, 2001), 5th Edition, pp. 65, 75. In Bá's drawing, Tan Thoi was placed south of Ap Bac, which is not correct.
21. Moyar, *Triumph Forsaken*, p. 193.
22. Ibid., p. 194.
23. David Halberstam, *The Making of a Quagmire* (New York: Random House, 1965), p. 154; Neil Sheehan, *A Bright Shining Light: John Paul Vann and America in Vietnam* (New York: Random House, 1988), p. 277.
24. *The New York Times*, January 11, 1963.
25. Ha Mai Viet, *Steel and Blood*, p. 16.
26. Moyar, *Triumph Forsaken*, pp. 194–196.
27. Kevin Kilbride, *Military Assistance Advisory Group-Vietnam (1954–1963): The Battle of Ap Bac* (Thesis presentation: Fort Leavenworth, KS, 2012), pp. 91–92. https://apps.dtic.mil/dtic/tr/fulltext/u2/a563005.pdf; Halberstam, *The Making of a Quagmire*, pp. 163–165.
28. Ha Mai Viet, *Steel and Blood*, p. 17.
29. Huynh Van Cao, "One Life," in Ha Ma Viet, *Steel and Blood*, p. 18.
30. Bruce Palmer, *The 25 Year-War. America's Military Role in Vietnam* (Lexington: University Press of Kentucky, 1984), p. 11.
31. John A. Nagl, *Learning to Eat Soup with a Knife. Counterinsurgency Lessons from Malaya and Vietnam* (Chicago: University of Chicago Press, 2002), pp. 132–133.
32. Ibid., p. 130.
33. Ibid., pp. 134–135.
34. Palmer, *The 25 Year-War*, p. 12.
35. Cao Van Vien, *U.S. Adviser*, Indochina Monographs (Washington, D.C.: U.S. Army Center of Military History, 1980), p. 33. According to the memorandum (1) the adviser assists and advises ARVN commanders on "strictly technical aspects"; (2) the adviser has no command nor supervisory capacity; (3) the ARVN commanders should exercise their own judgments in making use of the advice offered.
36. Ha Mai Viet, *Steel and Blood*, pp. 363–364, note 18.
37. Kilbride, *Military Assistance Advisory Group-Vietnam*, p. 88; David Toczek, *The Battle of Ap Bac Vietnam. They Did Everything but Learn from It* (Annapolis, MD: Naval Institute Press, 2001), p. 71.
38. Halberstam, *The Making of a Quagmire*, p. 146.
39. Sheehan, *A Bright Shining Light*, p. 209.
40. *The New York Times*, January 11, 1963.
41. Moyar, *Triumph Forsaken*, p. 176.
42. Kilbride, *Military Assistance Advisory Group-Vietnam*, p. 113.
43. Toczek, *The Battle of Ap Bac Vietnam*, p. 156.
44. Moyar, *Triumph Forsaken*, p. 205.

Chapter 3

1. Moyar, *Triumph Forsaken*, p. 337.
2. Tran Ngoc Toan, "The Bình Giã Front," http://www.k16vbqgvn.org/tranbinhgia.htm.
3. United Press International, "6-Day Battle at Binh Gia Ends in Defeat for Saigon," *The New York Times*, January 3, 1964.
4. Collins, *The Development and Training of the South Vietnamese Army*, p. 47.
5. Dommen, *The Indochinese Experience*, p. 636; Collins, *The Development and Training of the South Vietnamese Army*, p. 101. The VC received AK-47 rifles and RPG launchers in 1964 while the

ARVN troops were still armed with WWII weapons. The ARVN captured AK-47 rifles during 1964.

6. *Ibid.*, p. 127.
7. William Colby, *Lost Victory. A Firsthand Account of America's Involvement in Vietnam* (New York: Contemporary Books, 1989), pp. 161–174.
8. J. P. Harris, *Vietnam's High Ground: Armed Struggle in the Central Highlands, 1954–1965* (Lawrence: University Press of Kansas, 2016), p. 217.
9. Merle Pribbenow, *Victory in Vietnam. The Official History of the People's Army* (Lawrence: University Press of Kansas, 2002), pp. 137–138.

Chapter 4

1. In *grab them by the belt technique*, the VC and PAVN try to stay as close as possible to the ARVN and U.S. forces, so that they do not get shelled by the ARVN or U.S's artillery due to the ARVN and U.S. fear of injuring friendly forces.
2. Gregory Daddis, *Westmoreland's War. Reassessing American Strategy in Vietnam* (New York: Oxford, 2014), p. 156. The ARVN received their M-16 rifles only four years later after the 1968 Tết Offensive.
3. Brigham, *ARVN*, p. 86.
4. Jack Langguth, "U.S. Planes Drive VietCong Raiders from a Key Town," *The New York Times*, May 12, 1965.
5. Moyar, *Triumph Forsaken*, p. 398.
6. "Battalion History: Battle of Đồng Xoài," http://www.145cab.com/History/NL16HIST.htm.
7. *Ibid.*
8. Moyar, *Triumph Forsaken*, p. 401; "Battalion History: Battle of Đồng Xoài."
9. Moyar, *Triumph Forsaken*, p. 402.
10. Moyar, *Triumph Forsaken*, p. 403.
11. Shelby Stanton, *The Rise and Fall of an American Army* (Navato, CA: Presidio Press, 1985), p. 6.
12. Brigham, *ARVN*, p. 87.
13. Neil Sheehan, Hedrick Smith, E. W. Kenworthy, *The Pentagon Papers: The Secret History of the Vietnam War* (New York: Racehorse, 2017), pp. 419–420.
14. Harris, *Vietnam's High Ground*, p 284.
15. Harris, *Vietnam's High Ground*, p. 305.
16. John Laurence, *The Cat from Hue: A Vietnam War Story* (New York: Public Affairs, 2002), pp. 260–261.
17. Harris, *Vietnam's High Ground*, pp. 319–321.
18. Charles Beckwith, and Donald Knox, *Delta Force: The U.S. Counter-Terrorist Unit and the Iranian Hostage Rescue Mission* (London: Arms and Armour, 1984), p. 68.
19. Harris, *Vietnam's High Ground*, p. 322.
20. Beckwith and Knox, *Delta Force*, p. 71.
21. Harris, *Vietnam's High Ground*, p. 324.
22. Laurence, *The Cat from Hue*, pp. 255–257.
23. Harris, *Vietnam's High Ground*, p. 334.
24. Dommen, *The Indochinese Experience*, p. 637.
25. Memorandum of conversation, Thieu, Rusk, Lodge, and others. Saigon, January 15, 1966. *FRUS 1964–1968*, vol. IV, pp. 65–69.
26. Philip Davidson, *Vietnam at War: 1946–1975* (Novato, CA: Presidio, 1988), p. 357.

Chapter 5

1. Dommen, *The Indochinese Experience*, pp. 555–557.
2. Strategy used to isolate the rural population in fortified hamlets from contact with and influence by the Viet Cong.
3. One has to differentiate between the 1963 Buddhist crisis (May–November 1963) and the 1966 Buddhist Struggle movement (March 26–June 8, 1966). The 1963 crisis was a period of political and religious confrontations between the Catholic-led government of South Vietnam and the Buddhist groups, which eventually led to the downfall of the Diệm government in November 1963. The 1966 Buddhist Struggle movement was another period of confrontations between the Kỳ-led military government and the Buddhist youth headquarters. The young Buddhist demonstrators (mostly students) demanded that the military-led government be replaced by a civilian government formed by religious groups. The movement was not only anti-regime, it was also anti-American and anti-war.
4. Dommen, *The Indochinese Experience*, p. 642.
5. Timothy Hallinan, "Economic Prospects of the Republic of Vietnam," November 1969, www.rand.org/pubs/papers/2008/P4225.pdf.
6. Nguyen Anh Tuan, *South Vietnam Trial and Experience. A Challenge for Development* (Athens: Ohio University Press, 1987), p. 95.
7. *Ibid.*, p. 99. Hallinan, "Economic Prospects of the Republic of Vietnam," p. 21.
8. Edward Doyle, and Stephen Weiss, *The Vietnam Experience. A Collision of Culture* (Boston: Boston Publishing, 1984), p. 18.
9. *Ibid.*, p. 19.
10. *Ibid.*, p. 21.
11. *Ibid.*, p. 74.
12. *Ibid.*, pp. 76–78.
13. *Ibid.*, pp. 86–87.
14. *Ibid.*, p. 157.
15. Nguyen Anh Tuan, *South Vietnam Trial and Experience*, p. 100.
16. *Ibid.*, p. 104.
17. *Ibid.*, pp. 105–106.
18. *Ibid.*, pp. 108–109.
19. *Ibid.*, pp. 109–110.
20. *Ibid.*, p. 118.

Chapter 6

1. The First Republic was led by President Ngô Đình Diệm from 1955 to 1963. Following Diệm's ouster and assassination, the military junta took over the government but was challenged by monk Thích Trí Quang. It took four years for the military junta to assert its control over the government.
2. Keesing's Research Report, *South Vietnam. A Political History, 1954–1970* (New York: Charles Scribner's Sons, 1970), pp. 118–129.
3. Sorley, *Westmoreland*, p. 131.
4. Davidson, *Vietnam at War*, p. 426.
5. Harry Summers, *Historical Atlas of the Vietnam War* (New York: Houghton Mifflin, 1995), p. 116.
6. Davidson, *Vietnam at War*, p. 428.
7. The Central Office for South Vietnam (COSVN) designated the supreme politico-military headquarters of the VC and PAVN forces in South Vietnam during the war. It was thought to be a strong and sturdy physical structure that the Americans looked for but never found. They downgraded it to a "Bamboo Pentagon," but still could not locate it. It turned out that the leadership lived in simple thatched huts like the guerrillas and moved around to avoid bombing and search and destroy missions. COSVN was finally located around the Cambodian Mimot plantation. The area was bombed then searched, but the leadership safely escaped to Kratie. COSVN was actually "a staff of 2,400 people who are widely dispersed and highly mobile" traveling between bunkers and meeting places on bicycles and motorcycle (*Times*, June 1, 1970.)
8. Summers, *Historical Atlas of the Vietnam War*, p. 118.
9. Davidson, *Vietnam at War*, pp. 430–432.
10. Summers, *Historical Atlas of the Vietnam War*, p. 124. Of the 6,500 members, 1,000 were U.S. civilians and the rest were military personnel. The civilians held most of the top jobs.
11. Davidson, *Vietnam at War*, pp. 459–460.
12. James McAllister, "What Can one Man Do? Nguyễn Đức Thắng and the Limits of Reform in South Vietnam," *Journal of Vietnamese Studies* 4, no. 2 (2009), pp. 117–153.
13. Summers, *Historical Atlas of the Vietnam War*, p. 124.
14. Davidson, *Vietnam at War*, p. 435.
15. *Ibid.*, pp. 431, 437–438.
16. *Ibid.*, pp. 462–64.
17. *Ibid.*, pp. 451–455.
18. Westmoreland, "Vietnam Blunders," *Honolulu Advertiser*, March 26, 1978.
19. Quoted in Sorley, *Westmoreland*, p. 150.
20. Lien Hang Nguyen, *Hanoi's War. An International History of the War for Peace in Vietnam* (Chapel Hill: University of North Carolina Press, 2012), pp. 90–94.
21. Davidson, *Vietnam at War*, pp. 442–446.
22. *Ibid.*, p. 447.
23. Summers, *Historical Atlas of the Vietnam War*, p. 126.
24. *Ibid.*, p. 128.
25. Westmoreland, "Vietnam Perspective," *Military Review* (January 1979), pp. 34–35.

Chapter 7

1. Ngoc Lung Hoang, *The General Offensives of 1968–69* (Washington, D.C.: U.S. Army Center of Military History, 1981), p. 147.
2. Leonard Scott, "The Battle of Hill 875, Dak To, Vietnam, 1967," Army War College, 1988, https://apps.dtic.mil/dtic/tr/fulltext/u2/a195360.pdf.
3. Andrew Rawson, *The Tet Offensive 1968* (Stroud, UK: The History Press, 2013), p. 52.
4. James Willbanks, *The Tet Offensive: A Concise History* (New York: Columbia University Press, 2008), p. 25.
5. Rawson, *The Tet Offensive 1968*, p. 57.
6. *Ibid.*, p. 48.
7. *Ibid.*, pp. 72–73.
8. Michael Sullivan, "Recalling the Fear and Surprise of the Tet Offensive," *NPR*, January 31, 2008, https://www.npr.org/templates/story/story.php?storyId=18551391.
9. Peter Arnett, "What Happened in the Tet Offensive's 36 First Hours?" *Military Times*, January 13, 2018, https://www.militarytimes.com/news/2018/01/31/what-happened-in-the-tet-offensives-first-36-hours/.
10. Keith Nolan, *The Battle for Saigon: Tet 1968* (Novato, CA: Presidio, 2002), p. 15.
11. Don North, "Assault on the Embassy. The Tet Offensive Fifty Years Later," January 30, 2018. https://consortiumnews.com/2018/01/30/assault-on-the-embassy-the-tet-offensive-fifty-years-later/. Other authors reported 19 sappers squeezing into a Peugeot truck and a taxicab, while Nolan (Nolan, *The Battle for Saigon*, p. 100) wrote about 16 sappers.
12. The local metropolitan police like the U.S. MSG—military security guards—had neither standard infantry weapons nor helmets and flak jackets.
13. South Vietnamese use Thống Nhứt and Tân Sơn Nhứt while North Vietnamese use Thống Nhất and Tân Sơn Nhất.
14. Nolan, *The Battle for Saigon*, p. 110.
15. Robert O'Brien, "The Attack on the American Embassy During Tet: 1968. Factors That Turned a Tactical Victory into A Political Defeat," (Master's thesis, U.S. Army Command and General Staff College, 2009), p. 2, http://www.dtic.mil/dtic/tr/fulltext/u2/a502004.pdf.
16. David T. Zabecki, "Tet 40th Anniversary: The Battle for Saigon," *Vietnam Magazine* (February 2008), p. 28.
17. Nolan, *The Battle for Saigon*, pp. 11, 21.
18. *Ibid.*, p. 14.
19. *Ibid.*, p. 22.
20. *Ibid.*, p. 33.
21. Battle for Saigon, http://www.historynet.com/battle-for-saigon.htm.
22. Nolan, *The Battle for Saigon*, p. 92.

23. *Ibid.*, p. 93.
24. Battle for Saigon, http://www.historynet.com/battle-for-saigon.htm.
25. Nolan, *The Battle for Saigon*, p. 149.
26. Dan Sutherland, "The Tet Offensive: A Reporter Looks Back." *Radio Free Asia*, January 30, 2018, https://www.rfa.org/english/commentaries/tet-offensive-01302018181908.html.
27. *The 1968 Tet Offensive. Battles of Quang Tri City and Hue* (Washington, D.C.: U.S. Army Center of Military History, 2008), pp. 7–8, 25.
28. Bowden, *Hue 1968*, pp. 90–91.
29. Robert Annenberg, "Intelligence Team Under Siege," *Vietnam* (Feb 2001): pp. 34–42.
30. Bowden, *Hue 1968*, p. 98.
31. Palmer, *The 25 Year-War*, p. 120.
32. William Westmoreland, *A Soldier Reports* (New York: Doubleday, 1976), pp. 303, 488.
33. Dale Andrade, *Trial by Fire: The 1972 Eastern Offensive, America's Last Vietnam Battle* (New York: Hippocrene Books, 1994), p. 171.
34. *Ibid.*, p. 172.
35. Palmer, *The 25 Year-War*, p. 145.
36. Bowden, *Hue 1968*, p. 89.
37. *Ibid.*, p. 102–103.
38. *Ibid.*, p. 106 mentioned 6 sappers while the Center of Military History only quoted four.
39. Referred in many maps as Thôn Quê Chủ. In Vietnamese, thôn means hamlet, which is simply called Quê Chủ Hamlet.
40. Thôn La Chủ: hamlet of La Chủ.
41. Bowden, *Hue 1968*, p. 107.
42. *Ibid.*, p. 104.
43. *Ibid.*, p. 109.
44. *Ibid.*, pp. 110–112.
45. *Ibid.*, pp. 146–149.
46. *Ibid.*, pp. 239–240.
47. *Ibid.*, pp. 493–494.
48. U.S. Army Center of Military History, *The 1968 Tet Offensive*, p. 54.
49. *Ibid.*: p. 57.
50. *Ibid.*, p. 58.
51. Alje Vennema, *The Viet Cong Massacre at Hue* (New York: Vantage Press, 1976), pp. 129–139. The book, no longer in print, can be downloaded at: https://www.dropbox.com/s/djqzeu6kxe8wc7s/MassacreAtHue-searchable.pdf?dl=0
52. Stephen Hosmer, *Viet Cong Repression and Its Implications for the Future* (Santa Monica, CA: Rand, 1970), pp. 72–76 https://www.rand.org/content/dam/rand/pubs/reports/2008/R475.1.pdf; Geoffrey Ward, and Ken Burns, *The Vietnam War. An Intimate History* (New York: Alfred Knopf, 2017), pp. 289–289.
53. Ben Kiernan, *Vietnam. A History from Earliest Times to the Present* (New York: Oxford University Press, 2017), p. 444.
54. Oberdorfer, Don. *Tet! The Turning Point in the Vietnam War* (New York: Da Capo Press, 1971), pp. 213–214.
55. *Ibid.*, p. 214.
56. *Ibid.*, pp. 224–225.
57. *Ibid.*, p. 229.
58. *Ibid.*, p. 215; https://www.historynet.com/tet-what-really-happened-at-hue.htm.
59. https://msuweb.montclair.edu/~furrg/porterhue1.html.
60. Keith Richburg, "Twenty Years After Hue, Vietnamese admit 'mistakes.'" *Washington Post*, February 3, 1988, https://www.washingtonpost.com/archive/politics/1988/02/03/20-years-after-hue-vietnamese-admit-mistakes/263c2b5b-2942-46d7-8d17-17fe35682f83/.
61. Olga Dror, "Learning from the Hue Massacre," *The New York* Times, February 20, 2018. https://www.nytimes.com/2018/02/20/opinion/hue-massacre-vietnam-war.html
62. Quoted in Ward and Burns, *The Vietnam War*, pp. 289–289.

Chapter 8

1. Summers, *Historical Atlas of the Vietnam War*, p. 160.
2. Lung Ngoc Hoang, *General Offensive of 1968–69* (Ann Arbor: University of Michigan, 1981), p. 118.
3. Summers, *Historical Atlas of the Vietnam War*, p. 162. This is again another defeatist idea that the U.S. and South Vietnam should get rid of. Although the theory may be correct, they should have fought till the end just because any advantage they had gained or accumulated on the battlefields could put them in a better position at the negotiation table.
4. Summers, *Historical Atlas of the Vietnam War*, p. 165; Davidson, *Vietnam at War*, p. 601.
5. Cao Van Vien, and Dong Van Khuyen, *Reflections on the Vietnam War* (Washington, D.C.: U.S. Army Center for Military History, Indochina Monograph, 1980), p. 91.
6. Davidson, *Vietnam at War*, pp. 605–607.
7. *Ibid.*, p. 611.
8. Lung, *General Offensive*, p. 142.
9. *Ibid.*, pp. 135–136.
10. *Ibid.*, pp. 137–138.
11. Summers, *Historical Atlas of the Vietnam War*, p. 163.
12. Quoted in Summers, *Historical Atlas of the Vietnam War*, pp. 162–164.
13. Lung, *General Offensive*, p. 143. Colonel Hoàng Ngọc Lưng was former JGS intelligence chief.
14. Quoted in Summers, *Historical Atlas of the Vietnam War*, p. 165.
15. Sorley, *Westmoreland*, p. 33.
16. Quoted in Sorley, *Westmoreland*, p. 212.
17. Russel F. Weigley, "Review of *Supreme Command: Soldiers, Statesmen, and Leadership in Wartime* by Eliot A. Cohen," *Journal of Military History*, October 2002, pp. 1275–1276, quotation from p. 1276.
18. Quotation is from Alan Levy, "Two Stars on the Fly," *Courier-Journal Magazine*, February 28, 1960, USMA Archives.

19. Mark Thompson, "The General Who Lost Vietnam," *Times*, September 30, 2011.
20. Hastings, *Vietnam. An Epic Tragedy*, p. 398.
21. *Ibid.*, pp. 408–9.
22. *Ibid.*, pp. 410–11.
23. Sorley, *Westmoreland*, p. 131.
24. Khuyen Dong. *RVNAF Logistics* (Washington, D.C.: U.S. Army Center for Military History, 1980), p. 57.
25. Daddis, *Westmoreland's War*, p. 156.
26. Sorley, *Westmoreland*, p. 140.
27. Daddis, *Westmoreland's War*, p. 158.
28. "We never really paid attention to the ARVN army. We didn't give a damn about them." As quoted in Sorley, *Westmoreland*, p. 140.
29. Schandler in McNamara et al., *Argument Without End* (New York: Public Affairs, 1999), p. 351.
30. As quoted in Sorley, *Westmoreland*, p. 138.
31. Norman Schwarzkopf, *It Does Not Take a Hero. The Autobiography of General H. Norman Schwarzkopf* (New York: Bantam, 1993), p. 126.
32. Daddis, *Westmoreland's War*, p. 183.
33. Cao Van Vien and Van Khuyen Dong, *Reflections* (Washington, D.C.: U.S. Army Center for Military History, 1980), p. 80.
34. Westmoreland, "Vietnam in Perspective," *Military Review*, January 1979, pp. 34–35.
35. Nguyen Duy Hinh, *Vietnamization and the Cease Fire* (Washington, D.C.: U.S. Army Center of Military History, 1980), p. 45.
36. *Ibid.*, p. 39.
37. Jeffrey J. Clarke. *Advice and Support: The Final Years* (Washington, D.C.: Center of Military History, 1988), p. 275.
38. Gras, *Histoire de la Guerre d' Indochine*, pp. 578–579.
39. Willbanks, *Abandoning Vietnam*, p. 55.
40. Dong Van Khuyen, *The RVNAF* (Washington, D.C: U.S. Army Center of Military History, 1979), p. 151.
41. Lung, *The General Offensives of 1968–69*, pp. 153–155.
42. Wiest, *Vietnam's Forgotten Army*, p. 175.
43. "Battle of Hamburger Hill," accessed April 16, 2017, https://en.wikipedia.org/wiki/Battle_of_Hamburger_Hill.
44. Wiest, *Vietnam's Forgotten Army*, p. 166.
45. *Ibid.*, 170.
46. *Ibid.*, 171.
47. Harper, Memorandum for the Record quoted in Wiest, *Vietnam's Forgotten Army*, p. 174.
48. Lewis Sorley, ed., *Vietnam Chronicles: The Abrams Tapes, 1968–1972* (Lubbock: Texas Tech University Press, 2004), p. 194.
49. Wiest, *Vietnam's Forgotten Army*, p. 176.

Chapter 9

1. Shaw, *The Cambodian Campaign*, pp. 9–10.
2. Tran Dinh Tho, *The Cambodian Incursion* (Washington D.C.: U.S. Army Center of Military History, 1979), p. 21.
3. Shaw, *The Cambodian Campaign*, p. 8.
4. Dave Richard Palmer, *Summons of the Trumpet* (Novato, CA: Presidio Press, 1978), p. 229.
5. Palmer, *The 25 Year-War*, p. 184.
6. Shaw, *The Cambodian Campaign*, p. 11.
7. Nixon, *Memoirs*, p. 450.
8. Shaw, *The Cambodian Campaign*, pp. 3–4.
9. Tran Dinh Tho, *The Cambodian Incursion*, pp. 76–77.
10. *Ibid.*, pp. 79–80.
11. Bunker to Nixon telegram, eighty-fifth message, March 27, 1970, p. 18. Virtual Vietnam Archive.
12. Clarke, *Advice and Support*, p. 417.
13. Tran Dinh Tho, *Cambodian Incursion*, p. 114.
14. Shaw, *Cambodian Campaign*, p. 53.
15. Tran Dinh Tho, *Cambodian Incursion*, pp. 59–60.
16. Willbanks, *Abandoning Vietnam*, p. 84.
17. Clarke, *Advice and Support*, p. 418.
18. Willbanks, *Abandoning Vietnam*, p. 85–86.
19. *Time*, June 8, 1970; https://www.facebook.com/notes/captain-james-văn-thạch/the-patton-of-the-parrots-beak/1003293579716860/.
20. Tran Dinh Tho, *Cambodian Incursion*, p. 170.
21. Palmer. *Summons of the Trumpet*, p. 236.
22. J.D. Coleman, *Incursion: From America's Chokehold on the NVA Lifelines to the Sacking of the Cambodian Sanctuaries* (New York: Saint Martin's, 1992), p. 263.
23. Tran Dinh Tho. *Cambodian Incursion*, p. 180.
24. David Fulghum, and Terrence Maitland, *The Vietnam Experience. South Vietnam on Trial* (Boston: Boston Publishing, 1984), p. 65.
25. Davidson, *Vietnam at War*, p. 658.
26. Palmer, *The 25 Year-War*, p. 111.
27. Robert Sander, *Invasion of Laos 1971. Lam Son 719* (Norman: University of Oklahoma Press, 2014), p. 193–194.
28. Willbanks, *Abandoning Vietnam*, 96–99.
29. Davidson, *Vietnam at War*, p. 660.
30. Nguyen Tien Hung, and Jerrold Schecter, *The Palace File* (New York: Harper, 1986), p. 44. Hung insisted Thieu never gave the order for the ARVN to hold its advance.
31. Fulghum and Maitland, *South Vietnam on Trial*, p. 129.
32. *Ibid.*, 79–80.
33. Wiest, *Vietnam's Forgotten Army*, pp. 208–209.
34. Fulghum and Maitland, *South Vietnam on Trial*, p. 85.
35. U.S. XXIV Corps, *After Action Report, Lam Son 719*, April 1, 1971, p. 90.
36. Keith Nolan, *Into Laos: The Story of Dewey Canyon/Lam Son 719* (Novato, CA: Presidio, 1986), p. 360.
37. *Ibid.* 361.

38. Fulghum and Maitland, *South Vietnam on Trial*, p. 87.
39. Wiest, *Vietnam's Forgotten Army*, pp. 220–222.
40. *Ibid.*, pp. 273–276, 290, 292–293.
41. Duy Hinh Nguyen, *Lam Son 719* (Washington, D.C.: Center of Military History, United States Army, 1979), p. 231.
42. Palmer, *The 25 Year-War*, p. 109.
43. Davidson, *Vietnam at War*, pp. 652–654.
44. Nguyen, *Lam Son 719*, p. 244.
45. James H. Willbanks, *A Raid Too Far. Operation Lam Son 719 and Vietnamization in Laos* (College Station: Texas A&M University Press, 2014), p. 168.
46. Sander, *Invasion of Laos*, p. 209.
47. Davidson, *Vietnam at War*, pp. 658–659.
48. *Ibid.*, p. 660.

Chapter 10

1. Davidson, *Vietnam at War*, pp. 673–675.
2. Ngo Quang Truong, *The Easter Offensive of 1972* (Washington, D.C.: U.S. Army Center of Military History, 1979), pp. 8–9.
3. *Ibid.*, p. 13.
4. Andrade, *Trial by Fire*, p. 46.
5. Craig Whitney, "Saigon's Commander in Laos Drive Hoang Xuan Lam," *New York Times*, March 10, 1971, https://www.nytimes.com/1971/03/10/archives/saigons-commander-in-laos-drive-hoang-xuan-lam.html.
6. Charles Melson and Curtis G. Arnold, *U.S. Marines in Vietnam: The War That Would Not End: 1971–1973* (Washington, D.C.: U.S. Government Printing Office, 1991), p. 32.
7. Andrade, *Trial by Fire*, pp. 50–51.
8. Hoang Ngoc Lung, *Intelligence* (Washington D.C.: U.S. Army Center of Military History, 1982), p. 155; G.H. Turley, *The Easter Offensive: The Last American Advisors, 1972* (Navato, CA: Presidio Press, 1985), p. 31.
9. This intelligence disagreement was reported in *U.S. News & World Report*, May 15, 1972.
10. Andrade, *Trial by Fire*, pp. 64–55.
11. *Ibid.*, pp. 84–88; Turley, *The Easter Offensive*, p. 100.
12. Melson and Arnold, *U.S. Marines in Vietnam*, p. 56.
13. Andrade, *Trial by Fire*, p. 91.
14. *Ibid.*, p. 556, note 26.
15. Wiest, *Vietnam's Forgotten Army*, p. 50.
16. *Ibid.*, pp. 117–122.
17. *Ibid.*, p. 120.
18. George Smith, *The Siege at Hue* (New York: Ballantine, 2000), p. 167.
19. *Ibid.*, p. 169.
20. The books include: Keith Nolan, *Battle for Hue* (Novato, CA: Presidio, 1996).
21. Nolan, *Battle for Hue*, p. 185.
22. Wiest, *Vietnam's Forgotten Army*, p. 121.
23. Department of the Army. *The Battle of Hue*, p. 14.
24. Wiest, *Vietnam's Forgotten Army*, p. 166.
25. *Ibid.*, p. 171.
26. *Ibid.*, pp. 253–254.
27. *Ibid.*, p. 259.
28. Andrade, *Trial by Fire*, pp. 108–109.
29. Truong, *The Eastern Offensive*, 37.
30. Andrade, *Trial by Fire*, p. 128.
31. Davidson, *Vietnam at War*, p. 684.
32. Westmoreland, *A Soldier Reports*, pp. 303, 488.
33. Truong, *The Easter Offensive*, p. 62.
34. Andrade, *Trial by Fire*, p. 197.
35. *Ibid.*, p. 202.
36. Melson and Arnold, *U.S. Marines in Vietnam*, p. 105.
37. "Vietnamese Begin to Question If War Was Worth Sacrifices," *Washington Post*, November 12, 1991.
38. Melson and Arnold, *U.S. Marines in Vietnam*, p. 117.
39. G. H. Turley and M. R. Wells, "Easter Invasion, 1972," *Marine Corps Gazette*, March 1973, p. 29.
40. Melson and Arnold, *U.S. Marines in Vietnam*, p. 126.
41. "America's Civilian Warrior in an Era of Vietnamization," *Washington Post,* June 8. 1972; Thomas P. McKenna, *Kontum. The Battle to Save South Vietnam* (Lexington: University Press of Kentucky, 2011), p. 14.
42. McKenna, *Kontum*, p. 27.
43. *Ibid.*, pp. 15–16. The II Corps Headquarters and the First Field Force, Vietnam Headquarters were located in Nha Trang.
44. *Ibid.*, p. xv.
45. Sorley, *Abrams Tapes*, pp. 844–845.
46. McKenna, *Kontum*, p. 97.
47. Sorley, *The Abrams Tapes*, p. 844.
48. McKenna, *Kontum*, pp. 123–124.
49. Andrade, *Trial by Fire*, pp. 286–287.
50. McKenna, *Kontum*, p. 48.
51. Truong, *The Eastern Offensive*, p. 95.
52. Andrade, *Trial by Fire*, p. 317; McKenna, *Kontum*, p. 173.
53. Andrade, *Trial by Fire*, pp. 320–322; McKenna, *Kontum*, pp. 179–180.
54. McKenna, *Kontum*, pp. 213–214.
55. Andrade, *Trial by Fire*, p. 355.
56. Sorley, *The Abrams Tapes*, pp. 867–868. Emphasis in original.
57. Andrade, *Trial by Fire*, p 371.
58. *Ibid.*, pp. 374–377.
59. Project CHECKO Report, "Kontum: Battle for the Central Highlands, 30 March-10 June 1972," October 27, 1972, pp. 88–89.
60. Andrade, *Trial by Fire*, pp. 385–386.
61. Truong, *The Eastern Offensive*, p 113.
62. Native highlander.
63. James H. Willbanks, *The Battle of An Lộc* (Bloomington: Indiana University Press, 2005), p. 44.

64. Andrade, *Trial by Fire*, p 399.
65. *Ibid.*, p. 405.
66. Fulghum and Maitland, *South Vietnam on Trial*, p. 150.
67. Andrade, *Trial by Fire*, pp. 418–419.
68. *Ibid.*, p. 389.
69. *Ibid.*, p 390.
70. *Ibid.*, p 390.
71. Quoted in Fulghum and Maitland, *South Vietnam on Trial*, pp. 151–153.
72. Andrade, *Trial by Fire*, p. 428.
73. Truong, *The Eastern Offensive*, p. 122.
74. Quoted in 5th ARVN Division AAR, p. D12.
75. Msg: Miller to Hollingsworth, subj: For Information, 17 April, 72.
76. Andrade, *Trial by Fire*, pp. 442–443.
77. *Ibid.*, p. 446.
78. *Ibid.*, pp. 473–474.
79. Headquarters, 21st Infantry Division (ARVN) After Action Report, Binh Long Campaign, 1972, p. 4.
80. Fulghum and Maitland, *South Vietnam on Trial*, p. 162.
81. Andrade, *Trial by Fire*, p. 485.
82. *Ibid.*, pp. 494–495.
83. "A Record of Sheer Endurance," *Time*, June 26, 1972.
84. John J. Duffy, *The Battle for Charlie* (Scotts Valley, CA: Create Space, 2014), p. 1.
85. Phan Nhật Nam, *Mùa Hè Đỏ Lửa* (*The Fiery Red Summer*) (Westminster, CA: Sống Publishing, 2015), p. 55.
86. Duffy, *The Battle for Charlie*, p. 5.
87. *Ibid.*, p. 12.
88. *Ibid.*, p. 17.
89. *Ibid.*, p. 18.
90. *Ibid.*, pp. 41–42.
91. The Battle of Charlie, https://forums.armchairgeneral.com/forum/historical-events-eras/vietnam-war/97890-the-battle-of-charlie-1972.
92. Duffy, *The Battle for Charlie*, p. 52.
93. *Ibid.*, p. 48.
94. *Ibid.*, pp. 53–55.
95. He was posthumously awarded a grade higher than when alive: from lieutenant colonel to colonel.

Chapter 11

1. The four No's consist of: "1. No concession of territory to the communists; 2. No coalition; 3. No political activity with the communists; 4. No 'communist-style' neutrality." "The Nation," *New York Times*, October 22, 1972, https://www.nytimes.com/1972/10/22/archives/his-answer-is-still-four-nos-thieu.html.
2. Thiệu was born either in November or December 1924, then changed his birthdate to April 5, 1923 (or the other way around) when he enrolled into a rural school in central Vietnam. According to Butterfield, he changed it in accordance with local customs, on grounds that it was better luck (*New York Times*, October 1, 2001). A rat person possesses a two-sided nature. Outwardly, he is generous and cheery; fair and honest and calm. On the inside, he can be greedy and acquisitive. Rat standards are high. They are not easily seduced by small talk and chitchat. If someone tries to dupe him, he is capable of both vengeance and unreasonable demands for retribution.
3. Dommen, *The Indochinese Experience*, p. 658.
4. The Việt Minh (communist) was the strongest party around, the best organized, but also the most ruthless one to attract eager nationalists. Many like Thiệu quit after learning the truth about the communists while others remained stuck with the communists.
5. Dommen, *The Indochinese Experience*, p. 658; Hung and Schecter, *The Palace File*, p. 39. It has been said that Thiệu was introduced to Nguyễn Thi Mai Anh by her uncle Đặng Văn Quang, a general who later became Thiệu's Minister of Defense.
6. Hung and Schecter, *The Palace File*, p. 74.
7. *Ibid.*, pp. 38–39.
8. Dommen, *The Indochinese Experience*, p. 664.
9. Hoàng Ngọc Lung. *The General Offensives 1968–1969* (Washington, D.C.: U.S. Army Center of Military History, 1981), pp. 81–84.
10. Dommen, *The Indochinese Experience*, p. 670.
11. Hung and Schecter, *The Palace File*, p. 40.
12. *Ibid.*, pp. 16–17.
13. *Ibid.*, p. 49.
14. *Ibid.*, p. 51.
15. *Ibid.*, p. 124.
16. *Ibid.*, pp. 148, 150.
17. *Ibid.*, p. 2.
18. *Ibid.*, pp. 66–67.
19. Henry Kissinger, *White House Years* (New York: Simon & Schuster, 2011), p. 1330.
20. Hung and Schecter, *The Palace File*, p. 73.
21. *Ibid.*, p. 74.
22. *Ibid.*, p. 83.
23. *Ibid.*, p. 88.
24. *Ibid.*, pp. 103–105.
25. Dommen, *The Indochinese Experience*, pp. 754–755.
26. Richard Nixon, *Memoirs of Richard Nixon* (New York: Grosset & Dunlap, 1978), p. 1469.
27. *Ibid.*, p. 751.
28. Robert Brigham, *Reckless. Henri Kissinger and the Tragedy of Vietnam* (New York: Public Affairs, 2018), p. 244.
29. General John E. Murray, *Vietnam Report*. December 12, 1972 to August 21, 1974, pp. 61–62.
30. Fulghum and Maitland, *South Vietnam on Trial*, p. 122.
31. *Ibid.*, 120.
32. Andrade, *Trial by Fire*, p. 213.

33. *Ibid.*, p. 226.
34. Van Nguyen Duong. *Inside An Loc,* pp. 141, 169–170.
35. Hung and Schecter, *The Palace File*, pp. 57, 66; Andrade, *Trial by Fire*, p. 536. Andrade put the number at 100,000.
36. Military History Institute of Vietnam, 2002, pp. 473–475.
37. Anthony Joes, *The War for South Vietnam* (New York: Praeger, 1989), p. 125.
38. Hosmer, Kellen, and Jenkins, *The Fall of South Vietnam*, pp. 34–35.
39. Arnold Isaacs, *Without Honor* (Baltimore: Johns Hopkins University Press, 1983), pp. 300–301.
40. Moyar, *Triumph Forsaken*, p. 267.
41. Westmoreland, *A Soldier Reports,* p. 242.
42. Hung and Schecter, *The Palace File*, p. 79.
43. *Ibid.*, p. 176.
44. Lam Quang Thi, *The Twenty-Five Year Century: A South Vietnamese General Remembers the Indochina War to the Fall of Saigon* (Denton: University of North Texas Press, 2002), pp. 143–148.
45. Arnold Isaacs, *Without Honor* (Baltimore: Johns Hopkins University Press, Revised edition, 1999), pp. 304–306.
46. *Ibid.*, pp. 306–309.
47. William Le Gro, *Vietnam from Cease-Fire to Capitulation* (Honolulu: University Press of Hawaii, 1985), p. 149.
48. Hung and Schecter, *The Palace File*, p. 336.
49. *Ibid.*, 358.
50. Fox Butterfield "Nguyễn Van Thiệu Is Dead at 76; Last President of South Vietnam," *New York Times*, October 1, 2001.
51. Hung and Schecter, *The Palace File*, p. 359.
52. David Lamb, "Nguyễn Văn Thiệu, 78: S. Vietnam's President," *Los Angeles Times*, October 1, 2001.
53. Le Gro, *Vietnam from Cease-Fire to Capitulation*, pp. 179–180.

Chapter 12

1. "Paracel Islands," https://en.wikipedia.org/wiki/Paracel_Islands.
2. Tập San Sử Địa, "Đặc Khảo Hoàng Sa và Trường Sa—A Special Research on Paracel and Spratly Islands" (PDF). *Geographical Digest* 29, Saigon, 1974.
3. Vietnam submitted an 1827 map showing the Paracels as part of Vietnam: http://www.thanhniennews.com/politics/vietnam-submits-atlas-as-proof-of-island-ownership-26288.html.
4. South Vietnam took control of the islands after French withdrawal in 1956: https://www.scribd.com/document/56468/The-South-China-Sea-in-the-Age-of-European-Decline.
5. South Vietnamese critique of Phạm Văn Đồng's diplomatic note—It was a betrayal of the South Vietnamese sovereignty on the islands: https://www.rfa.org/vietnamese/in_depth/Solution-for-Pham-Van-Dong-Diplomatic-Note-09172008164518.html.
6. Discussion about the letter of PM Phạm Văn Đồng: http://www.thanhniennews.com/politics/late-vietnam-pms-letter-gives-no-legal-basis-to-chinas-island-claim-26821.html.
7. Toshi Yoshihara, "The 1974 Paracels Sea Battle," *Naval War College Review* 69, no. 2 (Spring 2016), p. 49.
8. *Ibid.*, p. 50.
9. Do Kiem, Julie Kane, *Counterpart. A South Vietnamese Naval Officer's War* (Annapolis: Naval Institute Press, 1998), pp. 59, 76.
10. Carl von Clausewitz, *On War* (Princeton, NJ: Princeton University Press, 1984), p. 119.
11. Yoshihara, "The 1974 Paracels Sea Battle," p. 55–56.
12. Thi, *The Twenty-Five Year Century*, pp. 328–329.
13. George Veith, *Black April* (New York: Encounter Books, 2012), pp. 94–99.
14. Isaacs, *Without Honor*, p. 328.
15. *Ibid.*, p. 329.
16. Summers, *Historical Atlas of the Vietnam War*, p. 182; Davidson, *Vietnam at War*, p. 730.
17. Hung and Schechter, *The Palace File*, p. 1. Four of Nixon's letters dated October 16, 1972, November 14, 1972, January 5, 1973 and January 17, 1973 conveyed the same message.
18. Rick Perlstein, "Henry Kissinger and the 'Decent Interval,'" http://delong.typepad.com/sdj/2006/11/henry_kissinger.html.
19. Isaacs, *Without Honor*, 1983 edition, p. 47.
20. Davidson, *Vietnam at War*, p. 731.
21. Isaacs, *Without Honor*, 1983 edition, p. 119.
22. Hung and Schecter, *The Palace File*, p. 359.
23. *Ibid.*, p. 233; Davidson, *Vietnam at War*, pp. 740–741, 746. If aid dropped to 1.1 billion, then Military Region I would have been written off. If aid dropped to 600 million, the RVNAF would be hard pressed to hold onto Saigon and the Mekong delta.
24. Davidson, *Vietnam at War*, p. 738.
25. Richard Nixon, *No More Vietnams* (New York: Arbor House Publishing, 1985), p. 184.
26. Davidson, *Vietnam at War*, pp. 746, 808.
27. R. Canfield, personal communication.
28. Chanoff D. Bui Diem, *In the Jaws of History* (Bloomington: University of Indiana Press, 1999), p. 286 (reprinted).
29. Kinnard, *War Managers* quoted in Willbanks, *Abandoning Vietnam*, p. 278. According to Kinnard, 58% of the 175 surveyed U.S. generals who had served in Vietnam agreed that Vietnamization was "soundly conceived," but 73% said it should have been implemented before 1969; Hung and Schecter, *The Palace File*, p. 224; Willbanks, *Abandoning Vietnam*, p. 286.
30. Willbanks, *Abandoning Vietnam*, pp. 279–281.
31. Gen. Lê Văn Hưng was an exemplary officer who had not been well "acknowledged" by the Americans because of his differences in opinion

with his American advisor. Future work will highlight beyond doubt the value of this fine officer who killed himself rather than surrendering to the communists on April 30, 1975.

32. Quoted in Summers, *Historical Atlas of the Vietnam War*, p 190.

33. Dommen, *The Indochinese Experience*, p. 896.

34. Davidson, *Vietnam at War*, pp. 747–748; Hung and Schecter, *The Palace File*, p. 225: The RVNAF had 127,000 different line items that were supplied by the U.S., the Air Force 192,000 items, and the Navy 62,000. Getting hold of these items was very difficult.

35. Isaacs, *Without Honor*, 1983 edition, p. 300.

36. S.A. Herrington, *Peace with Honor*. (Navato, CA: Presidio Press, 1983), pp. 46, 104; Davidson, *Vietnam at War*, pp. 748–749.

37. Davidson, *Vietnam at War*, p. 749.

38. Hung and Schecter, *The Palace File*, pp. 1–2.

39. Isaacs, *Without Honor*, 1983 edition, p. 308. Martin was accused of misleading not only Washington, but also Saigon.

40. *Ibid.*, pp. 101, 114.

41. James Surowiecki, *The Wisdom of Crowds* (New York: Anchor, 2005 [reprint]). Surowiecki argues that "under the right circumstances, groups are remarkably intelligent, and are often smarter than the smartest people in them." Diversity brings in different opinions; people's errors balance each other; independence keeps people from being swayed by a single opinion-leader. However, crowds are not always correct: they tend to panic and often err because of lack of control, such as in cases of stampede or rampage.

42. Medicine has a lot of similarities with insurgency war. Improvements in health care come at a price and depend on adhering to a protocol. Health care in the U.S. is practiced by free spirited, although well-intentioned practitioners. When there is no consensus about a certain treatment, for example prostate cancer, physicians are free to treat their patients differently. The end result is a disorganized treatment that often leads to mistreatment. The group at Intermountain, on the other hand, followed the evidence-based medicine by asking physicians to follow a strict protocol for certain medical conditions. The result is an overall increase in survival rate and decrease in health care cost. See D. Leonhardt, "Making Health Care Better," *New York Times*, November 3, 2009.

43. Davidson, *Vietnam at War*, p. 801.

44. *Ibid.*, pp. 757–761.

45. Willbanks, *Abandoning Vietnam*, p. 225.

46. Davidson, *Vietnam at War*, p. 762.

47. O. Todd, *Cruel April* (Paris: Robert Laffont, 1987), p. 42.

48. "South Vietnam: The Fall of Phuoc Binh," *Times*, January 20, 1975.

49. C. Dougan and D. Fulghum, *The Fall of the South* (Boston: Boston Publishing, 1985), pp. 18–20; Todd, *Cruel April*, p. 43.

50. Summers, *Historical Atlas of the Vietnam War*, p. 192.

51. Quoted in Willbanks, *Abandoning Vietnam*, p. 227.

52. Willbanks, *Abandoning Vietnam*, pp. 325–326.

53. Isaacs, *Without Honor*, 1983 edition, pp. 332–333.

54. Davidson, *Vietnam at War*, p. 763.

55. Thi, *The Twenty-five Year Century*, p. 334.

56. Willbanks, *Abandoning Vietnam*, p. 226.

57. Phước Phạm, *A Yam in Yên Bái*, personal communication.

58. http://www.bcdlldb.com/phuoclong/81st_airborne_ranger_at_battle_Phưốclong.htm. The 81st Airborne Ranger was still defending Saigon on April 30, 1975. Its commander, Col. Huấn was jailed in northern reeducation camps for 13 years.

59. Davidson, *Vietnam at War*, p. 764.

60. H.G. Summers, "The Fall of Saigon: A Bitter End," *Vietnam Magazine*, April 1995, pp. 42–43; Văn Nguyên Dưỡng. *The Tragedy of the Vietnam War* (Jefferson, NC: McFarland, 2008), pp. 184–185.

61. Quoted in Summers, *Historical Atlas of the Vietnam War*, p. 192.

62. Isaacs, *Without Honor*, 1983 edition, p. 334.

63. Văn Nguyên Dưỡng, *The Tragedy of the Vietnam War*, pp.78, pp. 185–186.

64. Todd, *Cruel April*, p. 44.

65. Willbanks, *Abandoning Vietnam*, p. 227.

66. Cao Văn Viên. *Final Collapse* (Washington, D.C.: U.S. Army Center for Military History, 1983), p. 227.

67. Isaacs, *Without Honor*, 1983 edition, p 487.

Chapter 13

1. Hosmer, Kellen, and Jenkins, *The Fall of South Vietnam*, p. 169.

2. *Ibid.*, pp. 170–171.

3. Davidson, *Vietnam at War*, pp. 773–774.

4. Willbanks, *Abandoning Vietnam*, p. 193.

5. Willbanks, *Abandoning Vietnam*, p. 235; Hosmer, *The Fall of South Vietnam*, p. 181. For the country, Saigon was the bottom and for I Corps, the bottom was Đà Nẵng. So what Saigon was for the country, Đà Nẵng was for I Corps.

6. Cao Van Vien, *Final Collapse*, p. 78: Emphasis added.

7. *Ibid.*, p. 86.

8. Davidson, *Vietnam at War*, p. 777.

9. Hosmer, *The Fall of South Vietnam*, pp. 183–184.

10. Frank Snepp, *Decent Interval* (New York: Random House, 1977), p. 194.

11. Hosmer, Kellen, and Jenkins, *The Fall of South Vietnam*, pp. 190–194.

12. *Ibid.*, p. 195.

13. Thi, *The Twenty-five Year Century*, pp. 347–348.

14. Hosmer, *The Fall of South Vietnam*, p. 216.

15. Hung and Schecter, *The Palace File*, p. 273.
16. Hosmer, *The Fall of South Vietnam*, pp. 218–219.
17. *Ibid.*, p. 222.
18. Willbanks, *Abandoning Vietnam*, p. 252.
19. Hosmer, *The Fall of South Vietnam*, p. 223.
20. Willbanks, *Abandoning Vietnam*, p. 253.
21. Le Gro, *Vietnam from Cease-Fire to Capitulation*, pp. 161–162.
22. Vien, *The Final Collapse*, p. 118.
23. Veith, *Black April*, pp. 391–392.
24. *Ibid.*, p. 390.
25. *Ibid.*, pp. 412–413.
26. *Ibid.*, pp. 424–425.
27. Chris Coulthard-Clark, *The RAAF in Vietnam: Australian Air Involvement in the Vietnam War 1962–1975* (Canberra: Paul & Co Publishing Consortium, 1995), pp. 323–324.
28. Hosmer, Kellen, and Jenkins, *The Fall of South Vietnam*, p. 231.
29. Hung and Schecter, *The Palace File*, p. 336.
30. Veith, *Black April*, p. 441.
31. *Ibid.*, p. 443.
32. Quoted in Veith, *Black April*, p. 447.
33. Pribbenow, *Victory in Vietnam*, p. 407.
34. Veith, *Black April*, pp. 454–455.
35. Hosmer, *The Fall of South Vietnam*, p. 242.
36. Veith, *Black April*, pp. 456–457.

Chapter 14

1. Seppuku is the correct term while hara kiri is the commonly used term. The person disemboweled himself with his own sword and was beheaded by his assistant who in a sense completed the victim's work.
2. The South (đàng trong) seceded from the North (đàng ngoài) in 1602; this was followed by a first full scale north-south war from 1627 to 1672. During the revolutionary period (1771–1802), there was no central government in the South because the southern Nguyen had been toppled by the Tây Sơn rebels. The latter had expanded their control over the present-day central Vietnam while the Nguyen scion—Nguyen Anh—barely had control of the Mekong delta. In the North, the Trinh lords controlled the House of Le. Warlords roamed freely. They raised their own armies and fought for whomever they liked.
3. Vo, *Saigon*, pp. 38–39, 43–44; Taylor, *A History of the Vietnamese*, pp. 300–302. Nguyễn Ánh took 26 years to recover his ancestors' throne. He was a methodical, conscientious, and careful fighter. Part of this had to do with the fact that he had to rebuild his government infrastructure to raise funds to continue the war. Secondly, he wanted his army to have sufficient supplies and food they could use without having to steal from peasants and villagers. Everywhere his army went, he had new granaries built for their needs. Third, having lost many battles to the Tây Sơn in the beginning made him more cautious than usual.
4. Le Thanh Khoi, *Le Vietnam* (Paris: Editions de Minuit, 1955), pp. 318–321.
5. McLeod, *The Vietnamese Response to French Intervention*, pp. 43–44.
6. *Ibid.*, 52.
7. The three provinces of Biên Hòa, Gia Định, Định Tường were ceded to the French with a few commercial ports. The Catholic religion could be practiced freely throughout Vietnam.
8. McLeod, *The Vietnamese Response to French Intervention*, pp. 63–65.
9. *Ibid.*, 74.
10. *Ibid.*, 50–54.
11. See chapter I.
12. The names and birthplaces of the graduates of the triennial examination are chiseled in stone steles that sat on stone tortoises housed at the Văn Miếu (Temple of Literature). How one could decapitate a skeleton is anyone's guess. But the king's ruling had to be carried out and decapitation had to be done.
13. McLeod, *The Vietnamese Response to French Intervention*, pp. 55–56.
14. Vo, *Saigon*, pp. 43–45. When Gia Long recovered his throne in 1802, his biggest mistake was to return to the old Confucian system to prop up his regime. Locked in this mentality, he and his descendants completely sealed off their country to modernization and trade. This process weakened their regime so much that it could not put up any resistance against westerners. A few thousand soldiers armed with guns and artillery were able to take over the whole country in a few years.
15. A cử nhân (licentiate) graduate of the regional examinations of 1852.
16. Huynh Sanh Thong, *An Anthology of Vietnamese Poems* (New Haven, CT: Yale University Press, 2001), p. 84.
17. Jamieson, *Understanding Vietnam*, pp. 47–48.
18. Dommen, *The Indochinese Experience*, pp. 921–924. Generals Nguyen Khoa Nam and Le Van Hung had thrice been offered evacuation by their American adviser before he departed and each time refused.
19. Vo, *The Bamboo Gulag*, pp. 18–21.
20. Dommen, *Indochinese Experience*, p. 923.
21. *Ibid.*, pp. 921–922.
22. Nguyễn Công Luận. *Nationalist in the Vietnam Wars. Memoirs of a Victim Turned Soldier* (Bloomington: Indiana University Press, 2012), p. 458.
23. Vo, *Saigon*, pp. 16–19, 54–55. By immersing and melting into the culture of the local Chams, Khmers, by interbreeding with them and the Chinese, the southerners have created a new way of being Vietnamese. They adopted Mahayana Buddhism, culture, food, clothing of the Chams, Khmers, etc.
24. See Truong Cong Dinh above in the text.

25. S. E. French, *Code of the Warrior* (Lanham, MD: Rowman & Littlefield, 2003), pp. 220–223.
26. "Battle of the Paracel Islands," http://en.wikipedia.org/wiki/Battle_of_the_Paracel_Islands.
27. James Freeman, *Hearts of Sorrow. Vietnamese-American Lives.* (Stanford, CA: Stanford University Press, 1989), p. 239.
28. Nguyễn Công Luận. *Nationalist in the Vietnam Wars*, p. 512.
29. Stephane Courtois, et al., *The Black Book of Communism. Crimes. Terror. Repression* (Cambridge, MA: Harvard University Press, 1999), p. 755. This is an excellent book about the terrors and crimes committed by the communist regimes worldwide.
30. Vo, *The Bamboo Gulag*, pp. 53–62. This is a concise depiction about the communist reeducation camps in Vietnam, which are called concentration camps.
31. Tran Tri Vu, *Lost Years* (Berkeley: University of California Press, 1988), p. 3. Brown rice is cheaper than white rice.
32. Desbarat in J. N. Moore, *The Vietnam Debate. A Fresh Look at the Argument* (Lanham, MD: University Press of America, 1990), p. 195.
33. Courtland Robinson, *Terms of Refuge* (London: Zed Books, 1998), p. 195.
34. Truong Nhu Tang, *A Viet Cong Memoir: An Inside Account of the Vietnam War and Its Aftermath* (New York: Vintage Books, 1985), p. 289.
35. Vo, *Bamboo Gulag*, pp. 116–125.
36. Tran Tri Vu in Albert Santoli, *To Bear Any Burden: The Vietnam War and Its Aftermath in the Words of Americans and Southeast Asians* (Bloomington: Indiana University Press, 1999), p. 167.
37. Freeman, *Hearts of Sorrow*, pp. 89, 231.
38. *Ibid.*, p. 246.
39. Anh Do, Tran Phan, Eugene Garcia, "Camp Z30-D: The Survivors," *Dart Center for Journalism and Trauma*, March 1, 2002, http://dartcenter.org/content/camp-z30-d-survivors?section=2.
40. Robert S. McKelvey, *A Gift of Barbed Wire* (Seattle: University of Washington Press, 2002), p. 85.
41. Jade Huynh, *South Wind Changing* (St. Paul, MN: Graywolf Press, 1994), pp. 119–111.
42. X. A. Pham, *Catfish and Mandala* (New York: Picador, 1999), pp. 14–15.
43. Luận, *Nationalist in the Vietnam Wars*, p. 471.
44. *Ibid.*, pp. 472–73.
45. *Ibid.*, pp. 474–75.
46. Vo, *Bamboo Gulag*, pp. 139–142.
47. Desbarats in Moore, *The Vietnam Debate*, p. 196.
48. https://www.youtube.com/watch?v=FiR5sCwFpeA#t=178.
49. E. P. Metzner, *Reeducation in Postwar Vietnam* (College Station: Texas A&M University Press, 2001), p. xiii.
50. Lu Van Thanh, *The Inviting Call of Wandering Souls* (Jefferson, NC: McFarland, 1997), pp. 74–77, 97.
51. G. Sagan in Santoli, *To Bear Any Burden*, p. 34.
52. Huynh, *South Wind Changing*, p. 58; Le Huu Tri, *Prisoner of the Word* (Seattle: Black Heron, 2001), p. 54.
53. X. A. Pham, *Catfish and Mandala*, p. 20.
54. Freeman, *Hearts of Sorrow*, p. 218.
55. *Ibid.*, p. 231.
56. *Ibid.*, p. 261.
57. Vo, *Bamboo Gulag*, pp. 143–150.
58. Huynh, *South Wind Changing*, p. 57.
59. Metzner, *Reeducation in Postwar Vietnam*, p. xiii.
60. Jamieson, *Understanding Vietnam*, p. 365.
61. Luận, *Nationalist in the Vietnam Wars*, p. 472.
62. *Ibid.*, p. 482.
63. Tran Tri Vu, *Lost Years*, p. 23.
64. David Chanoff and Doan Van Toai, *Portrait of the Enemy* (New York: Random House, 1986), p. 193.
65. Vo, *Bamboo Gulag*, pp. 114–116.
66. Courtland Robinson, *Terms of Refuge*, p. 196.
67. Also known as Hanoi Hilton; prison in Indochina first used by the French to incarcerate Vietnamese political prisoners, then by the communists to incarcerate American and South Vietnamese officers.
68. A. J. Langouth, "The Vietnamization of General Di," *New York Times*, September 6, 1970, https://www.nytimes.com/1970/09/06/archives/the-vietnamization-of-general-di-the-vietnamization-of-general-di.html.
69. Christopher Scanlan, "The Liberation of Tan Minh Pham," *Washington Post*, July 5, 1992. https://www.washingtonpost.com/archive/lifestyle/magazine/1992/07/05/the-liberation-of-tam-minh-pham/3ae52e2d-c468-47cf-ab79-9ea01052bed3/?utm_term=.2e46717eb295.
70. Seth Mydans, "Ly Tong, Vietnamese Pilot Who Hijacked Planes to Fight Communism, Dies at 74," *New York Times*, April 6, 2019, https://www.nytimes.com/2019/04/06/obituaries/ly-tong-dead.html?action=click&module=News&pgtype=Homepage.
71. Luận, *Nationalist in the Vietnam Wars*, p. 491.
72. Vo, *Bamboo Gulag*, pp. 169–175.
73. Luận, *Nationalist in the Vietnam Wars*, pp. 506–507.
74. *Ibid.*, p. 508.
75. Robinson, *Terms of Refuge*, p. 57.
76. *Ibid.*, p. 170; Nghia Vo, *The Vietnamese Boat People, 1954 and 1975–1992* (Jefferson, NC: McFarland, 2006), pp. 142–151.
77. Robinson, *Terms of Refuge*, pp. 172–175.
78. *Ibid.*, p. 198; Do, Phan, and Garcia, "Camp Z30-D: The Survivors."
79. Do, Phan, and Garcia, "Camp Z30-D: The

Survivors." The number of deaths in the camps seems to be high. A total of 3 million Vietnamese (civilians and soldiers) died during the 1954–1975 North-South Vietnamese War or approximately 1.5 million each for North and South Vietnam. This may be a low number.

80. "Vietnam," https://www.heritage.org/index/country/vietnam.

81. Nguyen Van Canh, *Vietnam Under Communism 1975–1982* (Stanford: Stanford University, 1981), pp. 120–122; Turner, *Vietnamese Communism*, pp. 53–59, 142–146.

82. Luan, *Nationalist in the Vietnam War*, p. 459–60.

83. Canh, *Vietnam Under Communism*, p. 124. The communists were trustful enough to nominate Hoàn as a legislator in their system. But Hoàn could not trust them therefore had to escape as a boat refugee after serving a few years under the communist system.

84. *Ibid.*, p. 128.

85. *Ibid.*, pp. 210–216.

86. Vo, *The Bamboo Gulag*, pp. 188–197; Canh, *Vietnam Under Communism*, pp. 219–221.

87. Vo, *The Vietnamese Boat People*, pp. 115–129. A tael equals 37 grams or 1.3 ounce.

88. Canh, *Vietnam Under Communism*, pp. 129–130.

89. Vo, *The Vietnamese Boat People*, pp. 193–198.

90. Jacqueline Desbarats, "Repression in the Socialist Republic of Vietnam: Executions and Population Relocation," *The Vietnam Debate: A Fresh Look at the Arguments*, John Norton Moore, ed. (Lanham, MD: University Press of America, 1990), pp. 193–201.

91. R. J. Rummel, "Statistics of Vietnamese Genocide Estimates, Calculations and Sources," from *Statistics of Democide*, https://www.hawaii.edu/powerkills/SOD.CHAP6.HTM.

92. Courtois, et al., *The Black Book of Communism*, p. 6.

93. *Ibid.*, p. 7.

94. In 2019 Vietnam had a freedom index of 20 (with 0 being the worst and 100 the best). https://freedomhouse.org/report/freedom-world/freedom-world-2019/democracy-in-retreat.

With a GDP per capita of $2,715 in 2019, Vietnam ranked 134 over 193 countries in the world. https://en.wikipedia.org/wiki/List_of_countries_by_GDP_(nominal)_per_capita.

Chapter 15

1. Larry C. Thompson, *Refugee Workers in the Indochina Exodus, 1975–1982* (Jefferson, NC: McFarland, 2010), p. 29.

2. Tang, *A Viet Cong Memoir*, p. 282.

3. Vo, *The Bamboo Gulag*, pp. 117–132, 151–156; Freeman, *Hearts of Sorrow*, pp. 244–247; McKelvey, *A Gift of Barbed Wire*, pp. 41–43.

4. McKelvey, *A Gift of Barbed Wire*, p. 155.

5. Bui Tin, *Following Ho Chi Minh: The Memoir of a North Vietnamese Colonel* (Honolulu: University of Hawaii Press, 1995), p. 90.

6. Mary Cargill and Jade Huynh, *Voices of Vietnamese Boat People* (Jefferson, NC: McFarland, 2000), pp. 10–12; McKelvey, *A Gift of Barbed Wire*, p. 199.

7. Bui Tin, *Following Ho Chi Minh*, p. 95.

8. Tang, *A Viet Cong Memoir*, p. 289.

9. Vo, *The Vietnamese Boat People*, pp. 115–129.

10. "Inhumane" was the word used by Bui Tin to characterize the communist leadership: "lack of moral values, the inhumanity and blindness of a communist leadership which had become arrogant and lost touch with the people." Bui Tin, *Following Ho Chi Minh*, p. 95.

11. McKelvey, *A Gift of Barbed Wire*, p. 187.

12. *Ibid.*, p. 67.

13. Karin San Juan, *Little Saigons. Staying Vietnamese in America* (Minneapolis: University of Minnesota Press, 2009), p. 68.

14. Viet Thanh Nguyen quoted in San Juan, *Little Saigons*, p. 84.

15. After failing to mobilize the gentry to get rid of the French, Phan Boi Chau (1867–1940) decided that modernizing the country would reach the same goal. He, therefore, promoted the Dong Du (Eastern Travel) Movement to send students to study abroad, especially to Japan. The movement died down when the French forced Japan to deport Phan in 1909. He then organized open rebellions against the French. Caught in 1925, he was sentenced to life in prison; the sentence was commuted to life under house arrest.

16. San Juan, *Little Saigons*, p. 86.

17. "Georg Simmel," http://en.wikipedia.org/wiki/Georg_Simmel.

18. Nguyen Thi Thu Lam, *Fallen Leaves: Memoirs of a Vietnamese Woman from 1940–1975* (New Haven, CT: Yale Southeast Asia Studies, 1989), p. 206.

19. San Juan, *Little Saigons*, p. 88.

20. Tang, *A Viet Cong Memoir*, p. 260. What his mother had predicted became a reality a year later (1976) when Tang realized that the North Vietnamese ran South Vietnam like a fiefdom. "Communists fought over houses, cars, prostitutes, and bribes." Tang, a communist, escaped from Vietnam as a boat people and landed in France as a refugee. See Tang, *A Viet Cong Memoir*, pp. 289, 304–309.

21. Tang, *A Viet Cong Memoir*, p. 265.

22. David Leeming, *The Oxford Illustrated Companion to World Mythology* (New York: Tess Press, 2005), p. 310.

23. Nghia Vo, "Vietnam and the Vietnamese," in *The Men of Vietnam*, N. M. Vo, et al. (Denver: Outskirt Press, 2009), pp. 7–22.

24. Nghia Vo, "Confucianism and Communism," in *The Men of Vietnam*, N. M. Vo, et al. (Denver: Outskirts Press, 2009), pp. 111–137.

25. Nghia Vo, "The Duality of the Vietnamese Mind," in Vo et al. *The Sorrows of War and Peace*, Vo, et al. (Denver: Outskirts Press, 2008), pp. 111–122.

26. Of course everything was relative in Vietnam because of the war. But before the mid-1970's, South Vietnam was much freer than North Vietnam and life was more tolerable in the South than in the North. There was television in Saigon, twenty-five to thirty daily newspapers, French and American books, music that the VC later called decadent "yellow music," cars and lots of mopeds and motorcycles that clogged the streets, and freedom to vote and to move around; there were more than 20 candidates vying for the post of President of South Vietnam.

27. The Chams and Khmers lived in central and south Vietnam, respectively.

28. Nghia M. Vo, *Legends of Vietnam. An Analysis and Retelling of 88 Tales* (Jefferson, NC: McFarland, 2012), pp. 59–60.

29. Nghia M. Vo, *Reflections About the Vietnam War* (Create Space, 2015), pp. 59–67.

30. Morley Safer, *Flashbacks* (New York: St Martin, 1990), p. 20.

31. *Ibid.*, p. 19.

32. Bernard Fall, *Last Reflections on a War* (Mechanicsburg, PA: Stackpole Books, 2000), p. 220. Fall wrote, "*When a country is being subverted, it is not outfought; it is being out-administered.*" Italics are in the text.

33. Gary R. Hess, "The Unending Debate," *Diplomatic History* (Spring 1994).

34. David L. Anderson, *The War That Never Ends* (Lexington: Kentucky University Press, 2007).

Epilogue

1. https://en.wikipedia.org/wiki/List_of_countries_by_GDP_(nominal)_per_capita.

2. Nguyen Van Tranh, "Catholic Priest, Fr. Nguyen Van Ly, Condemned to Eight Years in Prison," *AsiaNews.it*, March 30, 2007. http://www.asianews.it/index.php?l=en&art=8872&size=. During a televised court appearance in front of foreign reporters, a policeman gagged Father Lý with his hand to prevent him from speaking.

3. David Shipler, "Vietnamese Complete POW Exchange," *New York Times*, March 9, 1974, https://www.nytimes.com/1974/03/09/archives/vietnamese-complete-pow-exchange-special-to-the-new-york-times.html. Of the 31,961 communist prisoners released by Saigon, 26,880 were soldiers and 5,081 were civilians. Of the 5,942 prisoners released by the communists, 5,336 were soldiers.

4. "Phan Nhật Nam Oral History," *Viet Diaspora Stories* (YouTube), October 18, 2017, https://www.youtube.com/watch?v=ylNew2iIydI.

5. Ngo The Vinh, "Phan Nhật Nam và những chấn thương không chảy máu" (Phan Nhật Nam and the non-bleeding trauma), *VOA*, July 30, 2018, https://www.voatiengviet.com/a/phan-nhat-nam-mua-he-do-lua-ngo-the-vinh/4505848.html.

6. Thu Anh Nguyễn, "The Things They Made Me Carry: Inheriting a White Curriculum," *Teaching While White*, February 1, 2018, https://teachingwhilewhite.org/blog/2018/2/1/the-things-they-made-me-carry-inheriting-a-white-curriculum.

7. The Vietnamese are divided into *Kinh* and non-*Kinh* people. The *Kinh* or *người Việt* are a Southeast Asian ethnic group native to present-day North Vietnam. They speak Vietnamese, the most widely spoken Austro-Asiatic language. They comprise 86% of the population of the country while the non-*Kinh* people include more than 50 other ethnic groups. Originally, the *Kinh* designated the people living in the cities in opposition to the non-*Kinh* or *Mường* or highlanders.

8. Tang, *A Viet Cong Memoir*, p. 268.

9. Michael G. Kort, *The Vietnam War Reexamined* (New York: Cambridge University Press, 2018), p. 223.

10. Quoted in Lewis Sorley, *A Better War: The Unexamined Victories and Final Tragedy of America's Last Years in Vietnam* (Boston: Mariner Books, 2007), p. 165.

11. *Ibid.*, p. 383.

12. Veith, *Black April*, p. 499.

13. Le Gro, *Vietnam from Cease-Fire to Capitulation*, Dedication.

14. *Ibid.*, p. 179.

15. Hosmer, *The Fall of South Vietnam*, p. 61.

16. *Ibid.*, pp. 62–63. There were not too many battles going on during the French Vietnam War, especially in Cochinchina (South Vietnam). During the Diệm years, especially between 1954 and 1962, the country was rather pacific. The Vietnamese generals from the old generation faced very few battles throughout their careers.

17. *Ibid.*, p. 66.

18. *Ibid.*, pp. 99–100.

19. *Ibid.*, pp. 102–103.

20. *Ibid.*, p. 113.

21. Quoted in McKenna, *Kontum*, p. 146.

22. Hosmer, *The Fall of South Vietnam*, pp. 93–94.

23. Enhance and Enhance Plus programs were designed to transfer U.S. military equipment and bases to the government of South Vietnam ahead of the Paris Peace Accords. They occurred between May and December 1972.

24. Davidson, *Vietnam at War*, p. 731.

25. Thi, *The Twenty-five Year Century*, p. 157.

26. *Ibid.*, p. 156.

27. Le Gro, *Vietnam from Cease-Fire to Capitulation*, p. 180.

28. Quotation of T.E. Lawrence, by Col. E. F. Pelosky, USA Chief Army Division in Defense Attaché Office, U.S. Embassy Saigon, "Army Division Final Report," executive summary, June 18, 1975, USACMH.

29. John Paul Vann, Remarks, Lexington, KY, January 8, 1972, Vann Papers.

30. The yellow flag—three horizontal red stripes over a yellow background—was the former flag of the Republic of South Vietnam.

Bibliography

Indochina Documents

Clarke, Jeffrey J. *Advice and Support: The Final Years.* Washington, D.C.: Center of Military History, 1988.

Collins, James Lawton. *The Development and Training of the South Vietnamese Army.* 1950–1972. Washington, D.C.: Department of the Army, 1975.

Hinh, Nguyen Duy. *Lam Son 719.* Washington, D.C.: Center of Military History, United States Army, 1979.

———. *Vietnamization and the Cease Fire.* Washington, D.C.: Center of Military History U.S. Army, 1980.

Khuyen, Dong Van. *The RVNAF.* Washington, D.C.: U.S. Army Center of Military History, 1984.

———. *RVNAF Logistics,* U.S. Washington, D.C.: Army Center for Military History

Lung, Hoang Ngoc. *The General Offensives of 1968–69.* Washington, D.C.: Center of Military History U.S. Army, 1981.

———. *Intelligence.* Washington, D.C.: Center of Military History U.S. Army, 1982.

The 1968 Tet Offensive. Battles of Quang Tri City and Hue. Washington, D.C.: Center of Military History U.S. Army, 2008.

Tho, Tran Dinh. *The Cambodian Incursion.* Washington, D.C.: Center of Military History U.S. Army, 1979.

Truong, Ngo Quang. *The Easter Offensive of 1972.* Washington, D.C.: Center of Military History U.S. Army, 1979.

Vien, Cao Van. *Final Collapse.* Washington, D.C.: Center of Military History U.S. Army, 1983.

———. *U.S. Adviser.* Washington, D.C.: Center of Military History U.S. Army, 1980.

——— and Dong Van Khuyen. *Reflections on the Vietnam War.* Washington, D.C.: Center for Military History U.S. Army, 1980.

Books

Anderson, David L. *The War That Never Ends.* Lexington: Kentucky University Press, 2007.

Andrade, Dale. *Trial by Fire: The 1972 Easter Offensive, America's Last Vietnam Battle.* New York: Hippocrene Books, 1995.

Ba, Ly Tong. *Hoi Ky 25 Nam Khoi Lua* (Memoir of 25 Years of Warfare). Westminster, CA, 2001.

Bao Dai. *Le Dragon d'Annam.* Paris: Plon, 1980.

Beckwith, Charles, and Donald Knox. *Delta Force: The U.S. Counter-Terrorist Unit and the Iranian Hostage Rescue Mission.* London: Arms and Armour, 1984.

Berman, Larry. *Perfect Spy: The Incredible Double Life of Pham Xuan An.* New York: Harper Perennial, 2007.

Bowden, Mark. *Hue 1968: A Turning Point of the American War in Vietnam.* New York: Atlantic Monthly Press, 2017.

Brigham, Robert K. *Reckless: Henry Kissinger and the Tragedy of Vietnam.* New York: Public Affairs, 2018.

———. *Life and Death in the South Vietnamese Army.* Lawrence: University Press of Kansas, 2006.

Bui Diem; Chanoff D. *In the Jaws of History.* Bloomington: Indiana University Press, 1999.

Bui Tin. *Following Ho ChiMinh.* Honolulu: University of Hawaii Press, 1995.

Buttinger, Joseph. *Vietnam: A Dragon Embattled.* Santa Barbara, CA: Praeger, 1967.

Canh, Nguyen Van. *Vietnam Under Communism: 1975–1982.* Berkeley, CA: Hoover Institution Press, 1983.

Cargill, Mary, Huynh Jade. *Voices of Vietnamese Boat People.* Jefferson, NC: McFarland, 2000.

Catton, Philip. *Diem's Final Failure: Prelude to America's War in Vietnam.* Lawrence: University Press of Kansas, 2003.

Chanoff, David, and Van Toai Doan. *Portrait of the Enemy.* New York: Random House, 1986.

Clausewitz, Carl von. *On War.* Princeton, N.J.: Princeton University Press, 1984.

Colby, William. *Lost Victory: A Firsthand Account of America's Involvement in Vietnam.* New York: Contemporary Books, 1989.

Coleman, J.D. *Incursion: From America's Chokehold on the NVA lifelines to the Sacking of the Cambodian Sanctuaries.* New York: St. Martin's, 1992.

Courtois, Stephane, et al. *The Black Book of Communism.* Cambridge, MA: Harvard University Press, 1999.

Daddis, Gregory. *Westmoreland's War: Reassessing American Strategy in Vietnam.* New York: Oxford University Press, 2014.

Davidson, Philip. *Vietnam at War: The History 1946–1975.* Novato, CA: Presidio, 1988.
Do, Kiem, and Julie Kane. *Counterpart: A South Vietnamese Naval Officer's War.* Annapolis, MD: Naval Institute Press, 1998.
Dommen, Arthur. *The Indochinese Experience of the French and the Americans.* Bloomington: Indiana University Press, 2001.
Don, Tran Van. *Our Endless War Inside Vietnam.* Novato, CA: Presidio, 1978.
Dorland, Gil. *Legacy of Discord: Voices of the Vietnam War Era.* Dulles, VA: Brassey's, 2001.
Dougan, C., and D. Fulghum. *The Fall of the South.* Boston: Boston Publishing Company, 1985.
Doyle, Edward, and Stephen Weiss. *The Vietnam Experience: A Collision of Culture.* Boston: Boston Publishing Company, 1984.
Duffy, John J. *The Battle for Charlie.* Scotts Valley, CA: Create Space, 2014.
Duong, Van Nguyen. *The Tragedy of the Vietnam War.* Jefferson, N.C.: McFarland, 2008.
Dutton, George, Jayne Werner, and John Whitmore. *Sources of Vietnamese Traditions.* New York: Columbia University Press, 2012.
Fall, Bernard. *Last Reflections on a War.* Mechanicsburg, PA: Stackpole Books, 2000.
FitzGerald, Frances. *Fire in the Lake: The Vietnamese and Americans in Vietnam.* New York: Vintage Books, 1972.
Freeman, James. *Hearts of Sorrow. Vietnamese-American Lives.* Stanford, CA: Stanford University Press, 1989.
French, S.E. *Code of the Warrior.* Lanham, MD: Rowman & Littlefield, 2003.
Fulghum, David, and Terrence Maitland. *The Vietnam Experience: South Vietnam on Trial.* Boston: Boston Publishing Co., 1984.
Gras, Yves. *Histoire de la Guerre d'Indochine.* Paris: Plon, 1979.
Halberstam, David. *The Making of a Quagmire.* New York: Random House, 1965.
Harris, J.P. *Vietnam's High Ground: Armed Struggle in the Central Highlands, 1954–1965.* Lawrence: University Press of Kansas, 2016.
Hastings, Max. *Vietnam: An Epic Tragedy, 1945–1975.* New York: HarperCollins, 2018.
Herrington, SA. *Peace with Honor.* Novato, CA: Presidio Press, 1983.
Ho Tai, Hue Tam. *Millenarianism and Peasant Politics in Vietnam.* Cambridge, MA: Harvard University Press, 1983.
Hosmer, Stephen, Konrad Kellen, and Brian Jenkins. *The Fall of South Vietnam,* New York: Crane & Russack, 1980.
Hung, Nguyen Tien, and Jerrold Schecter. *Palace File,* New York: Harper, 1986.
Huynh, Jade. *South Wind Changing.* St. Paul, MN: Graywolf Press, 1994.
Isaacs, Arnold. *Without Honor.* Baltimore: Johns Hopkins University Press, 1983.
Jacobs, Seth. *America's Miracle Man in Vietnam.* Durham, NC: Duke University Press, 2004.

Jamieson, Neil. *Understanding Vietnam.* Berkeley: University of California Press, 1993.
Joes, Anthony. *The War for South Vietnam.* New York: Praeger, 1989.
Keesing's Research Report. *South Vietnam: A Political History, 1954–1970.* New York: Scribner's, 1970.
Khoi, Le Thanh. *Le Vietnam.* Paris: Éditions de Minuit, 1955.
Kiernan, Ben. *Vietnam: A History from Earliest Times to the Present.* New York: Oxford University Press, 2017.
Kilbride, Kevin. "Military Assistance Advisory Group-Vietnam (1954–1963): The Battle of Ap Bac." Thesis, Fort Leavenworth, KS.
Kissinger, Henry. *The White House Years.* New York: Simon & Schuster, 2011.
Kort, Michael G. *The Vietnam War Reexamined.* New York: Cambridge University Press, 2018.
Lam, Nguyen Thi Thu. *Fallen Leaves.* New Haven, CT: Yale Southeast Asia Studies, 1989.
Lamb, David. *Vietnam Now: A Reporter Returns.* New York: Public Affairs, 2003.
Laurence, John. *The Cat from Hue: A Vietnam War Story.* New York: Public Affairs, 2002.
Leeming, David. *The Oxford Illustrated Companion to World Mythology.* New York: Tess Press, 2005.
Le Gro, William. *Vietnam from Cease-Fire to Capitulation.* Honolulu: University Press of Hawaii, 1985.
Luan, Nguyen Cong. *Nationalist in the Vietnam War: Memoir of a Victim Turned Soldier.* Bloomington: Indiana University Press, 2012.
Marr, David. *Vietnamese Tradition on Trial, 1920–1940.* Berkeley: University of California Press, 1981.
McKelvey R.S. *A Gift of Barbed Wire.* Pullman: University of Washington Press, 1999.
McKenna, Thomas P. *Kontum: The Battle to Save South Vietnam.* Lexington: University Press of Kentucky, 2011.
McLeod, Mark. *The Vietnamese Response to French Intervention 1862–1874.* New York: Praeger, 1991.
McNamara, Robert, James Blight and Robert Brigham. *Argument Without End: In Search of Answers to the Vietnam Tragedy.* New York: Public Affairs, 1999.
Melson, Charles. *U.S. Marines in Vietnam: The War That Would Not End: 1971–1973.* Washington, D.C.: U.S. Government Printing Office, 1991.
Metzner, E.P. *Reeducation in Postwar Vietnam.* College Station: Texas A&M University Press, 2001.
Moore, J.N. *The Vietnam Debate: A Fresh Look at the Argument.* Lanham, MD: University Press of America, 1990.
Moyar, Mark. *Triumph Forsaken: The Vietnam War, 1954–1965.* New York: Cambridge University Press, 2006.
Nagl, John A. *Learning to Eat Soup with a Knife:*

Counterinsurgency Lessons from Malaya and Vietnam. Chicago: University of Chicago Press, 2002.

Nam, Phan Nhật. *Mùa Hè Đỏ Lửa (The Fiery Red Summer).* Westminster, CA: Sống Publishing, 2015.

Nguyen, Lien Hang. *Hanoi's War: An International History of the War for Peace in Vietnam.* Chapel Hill: University of North Carolina Press, 2012.

Nguyen, Nathalie Chau. *South Vietnamese Soldiers.* Santa Barbara, CA: Praeger, 2016.

Ninh, Bao. *The Sorrow of War.* New York: Riverhead Books, 1995.

Nixon, Richard. *The Memoirs of Richard Nixon.* New York: Grosset & Dunlap, 1978.

_____. *No More Vietnams.* New York: Arbor House, 1985.

Nolan, Keith W. *The Battle for Saigon: Tet 1968.* Novato, CA: Presidio Press, 2002 (Reprint).

_____. *Into Laos: The Story of Dewey Canyon/Lam Son 719.* Novato, CA: Presidio Press, 1986.

Oberdorfer, Don. *The Turning Point in the Vietnam War: Tet!* New York: Da Capo Press, 1984.

O'Brien, Robert. *The Attack on the American Embassy During Tet: 1968. Factors That Turned a Tactical Victory into a Political Defeat.* Fort Leavenworth, KS: U.S. Army Command and General Staff College, 2009.

Palmer, Bruce. *The 25 Year-War: America's Military Role in Vietnam.* Lexington: University Press of Kentucky, 1984.

Palmer, Dave Richard. *Summons of the Trumpet.* Novato, CA: Presidio Press, 1978.

Pham, Julie. *Their War: The Perspective of the South Vietnamese Military in the Words of Veteran-Émigrés.* Amazon, 2019. (self-published)

Pham X, Andrew. *Catfish and Mandala.* New York: Picador, 1999.

Pribbenow, Merle. *Victory in Vietnam: The Official History of the People's Army.* Lawrence: University Press of Kansas, 2002.

Rawson, Andrew. *Tet Offensive 1968.* Stroud, UK: The History Press, 2013.

Robinson, Courtland. *Terms of Refuge: The Indochinese Exodus and International Response.* London: Zed Books, 1998.

Safer, Morley. *Flashbacks.* New York: St. Martin's, 1990.

San Juan, Karin. *Little Saigons: Staying Vietnamese in America.* Minneapolis: University of Minnesota Press, 2009.

Sander, Robert. *Invasion of Laos 1971: Lam Son 719.* Norman: University of Oklahoma Press, 2014.

Santoli, Al. *To Bear Any Burden: The Vietnam War and Its Aftermath in the Words of Americans and Southeast Asians.* Bloomington: Indiana University Press, 1999.

Schwarzkopf, Norman. *It Does Not Take a Hero: The Autobiography of General H. Norman Schwarzkopf.* New York: Bantam, 1993.

Shaw, John M. *The Cambodian Campaign: The 1970 Offensive and America's Vietnam War.* Lawrence: University of Kansas Press, 2005.

Sheehan, Neil. *A Bright Shining Light: John Paul Vann and America in Vietnam.* New York: Random House, 1988.

Sheehan, Neil, Hedrick Smith, and E.W. Kenworthy. *The Pentagon Papers: The Secret History of the Vietnam War.* New York: Racehorse, 2017.

Smith, George. *The Siege at Hue.* New York: Ballantine, 2000.

Snepp, Frank. *Decent Interval.* New York: Random House, 1977.

Sorley, Lewis. *A Better War: The Unexamined Victories and Final Tragedy of America's Last Years in Vietnam.* New York: Harcourt Brace, 1999.

Sorley, Lewis. *The General Who Lost Vietnam.* Boston: Mariner Books, 2011.

Sorley, Lewis. *Vietnam Chronicles: The Abrams Tapes, 1968–1972.* Lubbock: Texas Tech Press, 2004.

Stanton, Shelby. *The Rise and Fall of an American Army.* Novato, CA: Presidio Press, 1985.

Summers, Harry. *Historical Atlas of the Vietnam War.* New York: Houghton Mifflin, 1995.

Tang, Truong Nhu. *A Viet Cong Memoir.* New York: Vintage Books, 1985.

Taylor, KW. *A History of the Vietnamese.* New York: Cambridge University Press, 2013.

Thanh, Lu Van. *The Inviting Call of Wandering Souls.* Jefferson, N.C.: McFarland, 1997.

Thi, Lam Quang. *The Twenty-Five Year Century.* Denton: University of North Texas Press, 2001.

Thompson, Larry C. *Refugee Workers in the Indochina Exodus, 1975–1982.* Jefferson, NC: McFarland, 2010.

Toczek, David. *The Battle of Ap Bac Vietnam. They Did Everything but Learn from It.* Annapolis, MD: Naval Institute Press, 2001.

Todd, O. *Cruel April.* Paris: Robert Laffont, 1987.

Tri, Le Huu. *Prisoner of the Word.* Seattle: Black Heron, 2001.

Truong, Vinh. *Vietnam War: The New Legion,* Vol. 1. Victoria, Canada: Trafford, 2010.

Tuan, Nguyen Anh. *South Vietnam Trial and Experience: A Challenge for Development.* Athens: Ohio University Press, 1987.

Turley, G.H. *The Easter Offensive: The Last American Advisors, 1972.* Novato, CA: Presidio Press, 1985.

Turner, Robert. *Vietnamese Communism. Its Origin and Development.* Stanford, CA: Hõver Institution Press, 1975.

Van Nguyen Duong. *Inside An Loc: The Battle to Save Saigon, April–May 1972.* Jefferson, NC: McFarland, 2016.

Veith, George J. *Black April. The Fall of South Vietnam: 1973–1975.* New York: Encounter Books, 2012.

Vennema, Alje. *The Viet Cong Massacre at Hue.* New York: Vantage Press, 1976.

Viet, Ha Mai. *Steel and Blood: South Vietnamese Armor and the War for Southeast Asia.* Annapolis, MD: Naval Institute Press, 2008.

Vo, Nghia M. *The Bamboo Gulag: Political Imprisonment in Communist Vietnam.* Jefferson, NC: McFarland, 2004.

_____. *Legends of Vietnam: An Analysis and Retelling of 88 Tales.* Jefferson, NC: McFarland, 2012.

_____. *Saigon: A History.* Jefferson, NC: McFarland, 2011.

_____. *The Vietnamese Boat People.* Jefferson, NC: McFarland, 2006.

Vu, Tran Tri. *Lost Years.* Berkeley: University of California Press, 1988.

Vu, Tuong. *Vietnam's Communist Revolution: The Power and Limits of Ideology.* New York: Cambridge University Press, 2017.

Waddell, William. *In the Year of the Tiger: The War for Cochinchina, 1945–1951.* Norman: University of Oklahoma Press, 2018.

Ward, Geoffrey, and Ken Burns. *The Vietnam War: An Intimate History.* New York: Alfred Knopf, 2017.

Westmoreland, William C. *A Soldier Reports.* New York: Doubleday, 1976.

Wiest, Andrew. *Vietnam's Forgotten Army: Heroism and Betrayal in the ARVN.* New York: New York University Press, 2008.

Willbanks, James H. *Abandoning Vietnam: How America Left and South Vietnam Lost Its War.* Lawrence: University of Kansas Press, 2004.

_____. *The Battle of An Lôc.* Bloomington: Indiana University Press, 2005.

_____. *A Raid Too Far: Operation Lam Son 719 and Vietnamization in Laos.* College Station: Texas A&M University Press, 2014.

_____. *The Tet Offensive: A Concise History.* New York: Columbia University Press, 2008.

Index

A Shau Valley 101–102
Abrams, Creighton 1, 61, 66, 86, 101, 104, 121, 134, 231
Airborne 25, 77, 165
AK-47 61, 94, 97–98
Altekoester, Alois 91
Americanized 1
Amphitrite 162
An Lộc 135–143, 195
Annam 9, 220
Annenberg, Robert 76
Ấp Bắc 28–35
Army of the Republic of Vietnam (ARVN) 2, 4, 5, 18–20, 28
AT-3 Sagger 131
attrition 1
Âu Cơ 219

Bà Giã 45
Ban Mê Thuột 24, 50, 175–80
Bảo Đại 10, 12
Baraka 110
Beckwith, Charles 47
Belotte 1
Bến Hét 130
Biên Hòa 38, 186
Bình Định 190
Bình Giã 36–39
Bình trạms 113
Bình Xuyên 11, 14
bộ đội 203, 207
border war 50
Bù Đốp 205
Bù Gia Mập 205, 207
Buddhism 10
Bùi Đình Đạm 34
Bùi Thế Lân 127
Bùi Tín 173, 216
Bùi Văn Nhu 208
Burns, Ken 92

cải tạo 206
Cambodia 3
Cambodian Incursion 105–109
Camp Carroll 123–124
Cao Đài 11
Cao Văn Viên 15, 26, 71, 77, 94, 111, 131, 157, 174, 177
Carver, George 2
Cham 10
Chánh Tây Gate 79–80
Charlie 144–45
Chèo Reo 46, 179

Chợ Lớn 73
Chơn Thành 142–43
chromium plating 97
chủ chiến 193
chủ hòa 192
Chu Huy Mẫn 47
Citadel 75, 84–86
civil guard 17
Civil Operations and Rural Development Support (CORDS) 63
Civilian Irregular Defense Group (CIDG) 17–18, 42, 47
Cochinchina 9, 10
Colby, William 63
Collins, General 13
Commercial Import Program 55
Communism 4, 22, 229
Côn Đảo 72
Cồn Thiên 66
concentration camp 5
Confucianism 10
Cộng Hòa Hospital 159
Consolidated RVNAF Improvement and Modernization Plan (CRIMP) 98
Coolican, Jim 76
Cooper-Church Amendment 111
corps, military 23–25
corruption 4, 207
Cửa Việt 122, 127–28
Cushman, Robert 77, 83

Da Ban camp 205
Đá Mài 92
Đà Nẵng 164, 180
Daddis, Gregory 98
Đại Việt 11
Dak To 66, 130
Đàm Hữu Phước 173
đàng ngoài 220, 222
đàng trong 220, 222
Đặng Văn Quang 177
Davison, Mike 109
de Genouilly, Rigault 191
DePuy, William 96
Desbarat 204
Dewey-Canyon 112
Diệm see Ngô Đình Diệm
Điện Biên Phủ 1, 9
Discher, Raimund 91
Đỗ Cao Trí 14, 26, 108, 110, 135
Đỗ Kế Giai 26

Đoàn Văn Bá 83
đồn điền 191
Đôn Luận 170
Đông Ấp Bia 102–103
Đông Hà 121–123
Đồng Văn Khuyên 97
Đồng Xoài 41
Dror, Olga 92
Dư Quốc Đống 117, 170, 173
Duffy, John 146–47
Dương Văn Minh 14, 149

Ely, General 13
embargo 112, 152; US embassy 71–72
émigrés 4
Enhance Plus 154
executions 173, 203
extrajudicial killing 214–15

Fall, Bernard 217
Fishhook 106
Fitzgerald, Frances 2
Ford, Gerald 172–73
Four Nos 166
freedom 144, 166, 168
French Expeditionary Corps 13
frontier land 10

Galvin, John 98
Garand 94
General Offensive-General Uprising 65
Geneva Accords 11
Gia Hội 91
gold 59
guerrilla warfare 15, 17, 191

Hắc Báo 75, 80–81
Hamburger Hill 102–103
Hanoi 65
Harkins, Paul 33
Hastings Max 2, 4
Highway 9 111–115
Highway 13 137, 139, 142–43
Hill 169 140–43
Hồ Chí Minh 4, 21, 229; trail 105, 110–111, 174
Hồ Ngọc Cẩn 196
Hòa Hảo 11
Hoàng Cầm 185
Hoàng Diệu 194
Hoàng Quỳnh 209

259

Hoàng Sa *see* Paracel Islands
Hoàng Xuân Lãm 78, 112, 114, 117, 120–121
Hoàng Xuân Tựu 209
Hollingsworth, James 139, 141
Huế 3, 23, 74–90
Huế Massacre 90–92
hunger 203
Hùynh Phú Sổ 11
Hùynh Văn Cao 25, 32, 33, 35
Hùynh Văn Lương 122

Ia Drang Valley 47
identity 7
ideology 16, 22, 166, 169
incarceration 201–202
Independence Palace 70–71
Indochina 9
inflation 59–60
insurgency 17
intelligence 119, 135, 176
interval, indecent 166–69
Iron Triangle 62
Isaacs, Arnold 174

Johnson, Harold K. 96
Johnson, Lyndon 18, 63–64

Kalashnikov, Mikhail 97
Katum 5
Khe Sanh 68–69
Khmer 10
Kinh 10
Kissinger, Henry 151–53, 160, 166, 172
Komer, Robert 63
Kontum 23, 50, 128–135
Koreanization 95
Kort, Michael 228
Krainick, Horst Gunther 90–91
Kỳ *see* Nguyễn Cao Kỳ

Lạc Long Quân 219
Lai Khê 142–43
Laird, Melvin 93
Lâm Quang Thi 158, 173, 231
Lâm Quang Thơ 29
Lâm Sơn 719 111–117
Làng Vei 68
Lao Kai 5
Laos 6, 9, 12, 17, 25
Larteguy 1
Lê Cầu 22
Lê Duẩn 66, 119
Le Gro, William 174, 230
Lê Minh Đảo 3, 26, 27, 184–88, 208
Lê Nguyên Khang 117
Lê Nguyên Vỹ 24, 26, 195
Lê Tấn Đại 172
Lê Thánh Tông 161
Lê Thị Diễm Thúy 228
Lê Văn Hưng 3, 24, 26, 138–139, 195
Lê Văn Khôi 192
Lê Văn Mề 146–47
Lê Văn Thân 27

Lê Văn Thảo 183
Lê Văn Tường 176
Lê Văn Ty 14, 30
Lê Văn Viễn 13
leadership 4
liberation 174
Little Saigon 218–19
Lộc Ninh 136–38
Lon Nol 106
Lưu Kim Cương 72
Lý Tổng 208
Lý Tòng Bá 3, 24, 26, 30, 131–133, 208

M-1 rifle 61
M-16 rifle 61, 94, 97–98
M-41 tank 81
M-48 tank 118
M-60 machine gun 82, 94, 97
M-72 LAW 84, 122
M-79 grenade launcher 94, 97
Mai Thế Trang 173
Mang Cá 75
Marine 25, 122, 125–7, 156
Marshall, S.L.A. 74
Martin, Graham 158
McNamara, Robert 2, 64
military assistance program 13
Miller, William 138–39
Momyer, William 72
Moore, Harold 47
Mùa Hè Đỏ Lửa 119

Nam tiến 10
National Liberation Front (NLF) 219
Nationalist 148, 151
new economic zones 4, 212–13
nghĩa quân 191
Ngô Đình Diệm 11, 13–16, 21–22, 33, 52
Ngô Dzu 129, 132
Ngô Môn 89
Ngô Quang Trưởng 3, 23, 26, 77–79, 125, 162, 164, 178, 180
Ngô Tùng Châu 190
Ngụy Văn Thà 163, 199
Nguyễn An Ninh 9
Nguyễn Ánh 190
Nguyễn Cao Kỳ 44, 61
Nguyễn Chánh Thi 27, 45
Nguyễn Chí Thanh 65
Nguyễn Cơ Thạch 202
Nguyễn Công Hoàn 212
Nguyễn Công Luận 200
Nguyễn Đình Bảo 144–45
Nguyễn Đình Chiểu 193
Nguyễn Đức Thắng 26, 63
Nguyễn Duy Hinh 23, 125, 164
Nguyễn Hoàng 10, 223
Nguyễn Hữu Huấn 194
Nguyễn Khánh 26, 39
Nguyễn Khoa Nam 24, 26, 194–95
Nguyễn Mạnh Cồn 212
Nguyễn Ngọc 92
Nguyễn Ngọc Loan 26
Nguyễn Sơn 171

Nguyễn Tấn Thanh 173
Nguyễn Thị Kim Lang 204
Nguyễn Trọng Luật 49
Nguyễn Tường Tâm 10
Nguyễn Trường Tộ 193
Nguyễn Văn Cảnh 211
Nguyễn Văn Định 142–43, 186
Nguyễn Văn Lương 182
Nguyễn Văn Lý 217
Nguyễn Văn Minh 135, 138
Nguyễn Văn Nho 36
Nguyễn Văn Sâm 12
Nguyễn Văn Thiệu 3, 24, 44, 61, 76, 94, 98, 134, 143, 148–58, 177, 230
Nguyễn Văn Thịnh 204
Nguyễn Văn Thông 196
Nguyễn Văn Thuận 209
Nguyễn Văn Toàn 132
Nguyễn Văn Tú 184
Nguyễn Văn Vỹ 14
Nguyễn Viết Thanh 27, 108
Nguyễn Vĩnh Nghi 182
Nhã Ca 81, 92
Nixon, Richard 106, 112, 152–54, 166

O'Brien, Tim 228
Orderly Departure Program (ODP) 209–210
Otis, Glen 73

pacification 1
Palmer, Bruce 106, 111
Palmer, Dave 110
Paracel Islands 161–164
Paris Peace Accords 167, 219
Parrott's beak 107
Pathet Lao 113
Pentagon East 72
People's Army of North Vietnam (PAVN) 18–19, 39, 47, 106
personalism 21–22
Phạm Duy Tất 27
Phạm Hữu Phước 173
Phạm Ngọc Sáng 27, 182, 184
Phạm Văn Định 103, 123–124
Phạm Văn Đồng 27, 162
Phạm Văn Phú 27, 176, 196
Phạm Văn Tường 91
Phạm Xuân Ấn 32
Phan Bội Châu 20–22, 217
Phan Châu Trinh 20–22
Phan Đình Niệm 181
Phan Huy Quát 44, 209
Phan Khắc Sửu 44
Phan Nhật Nam 208, 227–28
Phan Thanh Giản 191–93, 199
Phan Trọng Chinh 27
Phnom Penh 105, 106
Phủ Cam 92
Phũ Thư Salt Flats 92
Phước Long 165–74
piaster 59
Plei Mei 47–50
Pleiku 47, 50
Pribbenow, Merle 19

Index

Quảng Trị 75, 120–128
Qui Nhơn 190
Quỳnh Lưu 200

Ranger 17, 25
reeducation camp 200–209
Republic of Vietnam 11, 62, 148–52
Republic of Vietnam Armed Forces (RVNAF) *see* Army of the Republic of Vietnam (ARVN)
Ripley, Captain 122
Rivière, Henri 194
Rock Island East 108
Rocket Ridge 129

Saigon 69–74, 106, 169
San Juan 217
Sapper 71, 79
Schandler, Herbert 98
Schlesinger, James 168
Schwarzkopf, Norman 78, 98
self-defense corps 17
self-immolation *see* Tuần tiết
Sihanouk, Norodom 3, 105–6
Sihanoukville 105, 110
Simmel, Georg 218
Simmons, Charles 96
Sông Bé 40–41, 66
South Vietnam 10, 106
Spratlys 161–62
starvation 202–203
strategy 3, 95, 177
struggle movement 52
summary justice 52
Summers, Harry 93
Sutherland, James W. 112

T-54 tank 130, 137
Tâm Minh Phạm 208
Tân Cảnh 130–131
Tân Khai 143
Tân Sơn Nhứt 72–73, 186
Tân Việt 9
Tàu Ô Bridge 143

Tây Lộc airfield 76
Tây Sơn 190, 222
Taylor, Maxwell 98
Tchepone 112, 115
technical competence 101
Tết 69
Tết Offensive 3, 97
Thanh Hóa 10
Thanh Niên Cao Vọng 9
Thanh Sơn 181–82
Theravada 10
Thích Thiện Minh 209
Thích Trí Quang 44
Thiệu *see* Nguyễn Văn Thiệu
Thompson, Robert 33
Thu Anh Nguyễn 228
Thủ Đức 194
Thuận Man 45–46
Thượng Đức 164–65
Thụt, Major 47
Tiger 1
Toàn Thắng 107
Tonkin 9
torture 203
Trainor, Bertrand 96
Trần Bá Di 27, 208
Trần Chánh Thành 196
Trần Dạ Từ 92
Trần Đình Thọ 110
Trần Kim Phấn 173
Trần Mạnh Phấn 173
Trần Ngọc "Harry" Huệ 79, 81, 115, 208
Trần Quang Diệu 190
Trần Quang Khôi 27
Trần Quốc Lịch 126
Trần Thế Minh 209
Trần Thị Thu Vân *see* Nhã Ca
Trần Thiện Kiêm 157, 177
Trần Thiện Thanh 147
Trần Văn Bé 204
Trần Văn Đôn 14–15
Trần Văn Hai 25, 27, 196
Trần Văn Minh 27
Trần Văn Thắng 208

Trần Văn Trà 170
Trần Văn Tuyên 209
Trạng Lớn 201
Triangle 75, 81–82, 84–86
Truman, Harry S 12
Trương Công Định 191
Trương Đăng Quế 192
Trương Như Tảng 216, 219
Trường Sơn 50
Tự Đức 192–94
Tuần tiết 190–94, 200
tube-launched, optically tracked, wire-guided antitank missile (TOW) 132

Ulmer, Colonel 141–42

Văn Tiến Dũng 65, 175, 219
Vann, JP 29, 33, 129, 231
Việt Cộng 28, 43; terror 56, 148
Việt Minh 9, 148
Việt Nam Quốc Dân Đảng 9, 11
Vietnam War 1, 9–11, 222
Vietnamese National Army 9, 12
Vietnamese people 221–22, 225
Vietnamization 1, 92–96, 167
Vĩnh Lộc 46
Võ Bầm 50
Võ Duy Ninh 191
Võ Nguyên Giáp 74
Võ Tánh 190
Vũ Văn Giai 121
Vũ Xuân Thông 171

wanton killing 212
war crime 214, 219
War Zone C 62
Weigley, Russell 96
Westmoreland, William 1, 18, 45, 62–63, 64–65, 67, 72, 95–96, 97, 98
Weyand, Frederik 69

Xuân Lộc 184–88

Zimmerly, Major 103

www.ingramcontent.com/pod-product-compliance
Lightning Source LLC
Chambersburg PA
CBHW060338010526
44117CB00017B/2878